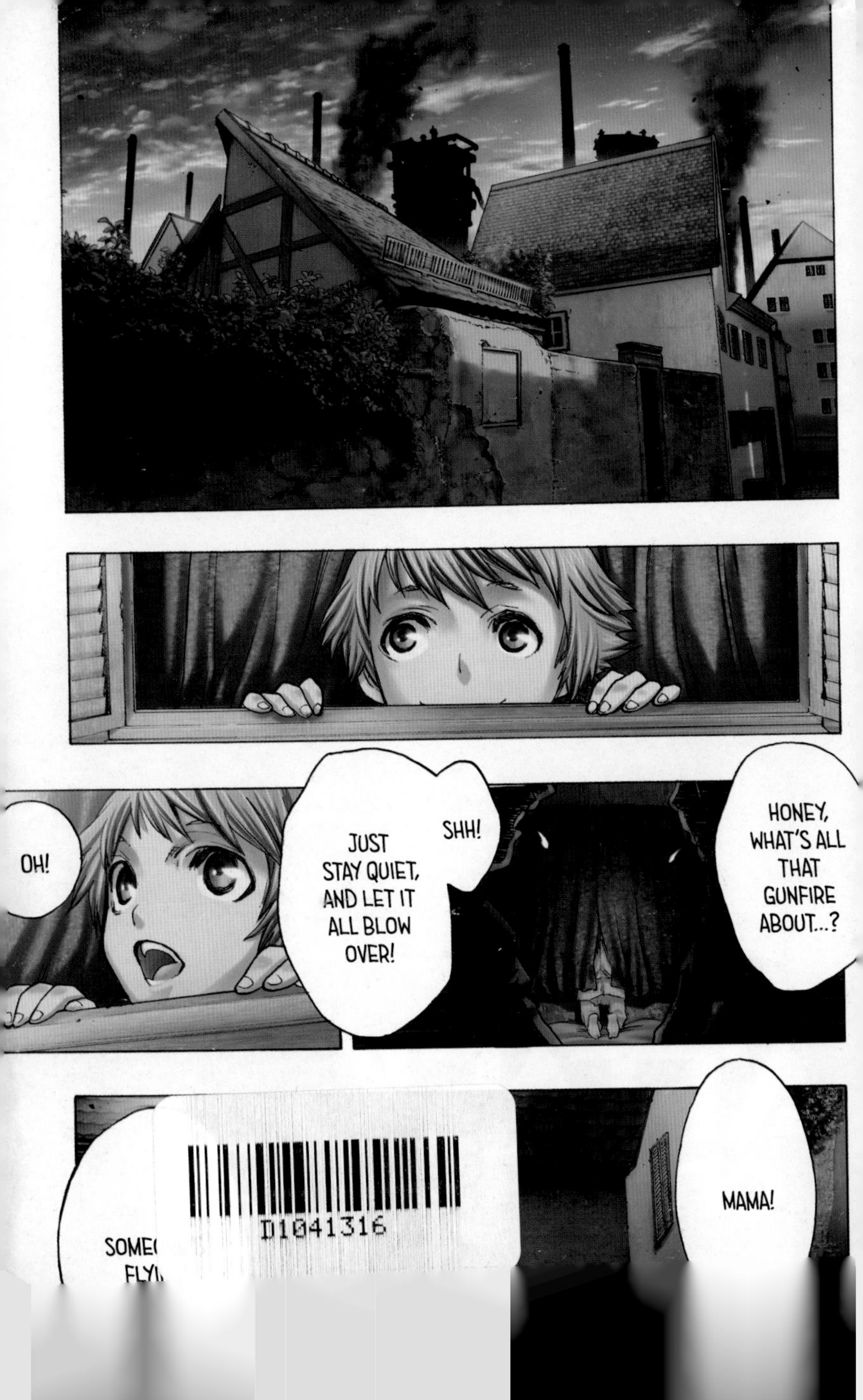
HONEY, WHAT'S ALL THAT GUNFIRE ABOUT...?
SHH!
JUST STAY QUIET, AND LET IT ALL BLOW OVER!
OH!
MAMA!

Contents:

Based on "Attack on Titan"
created by Hajime Isayama
Story by: Ryo Suzukaze
Art by: Satoshi Shiki
Character Designs by: Thores Shibamoto

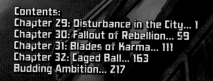

ATTACK ON TITAN 9
BEFORE THE FALL

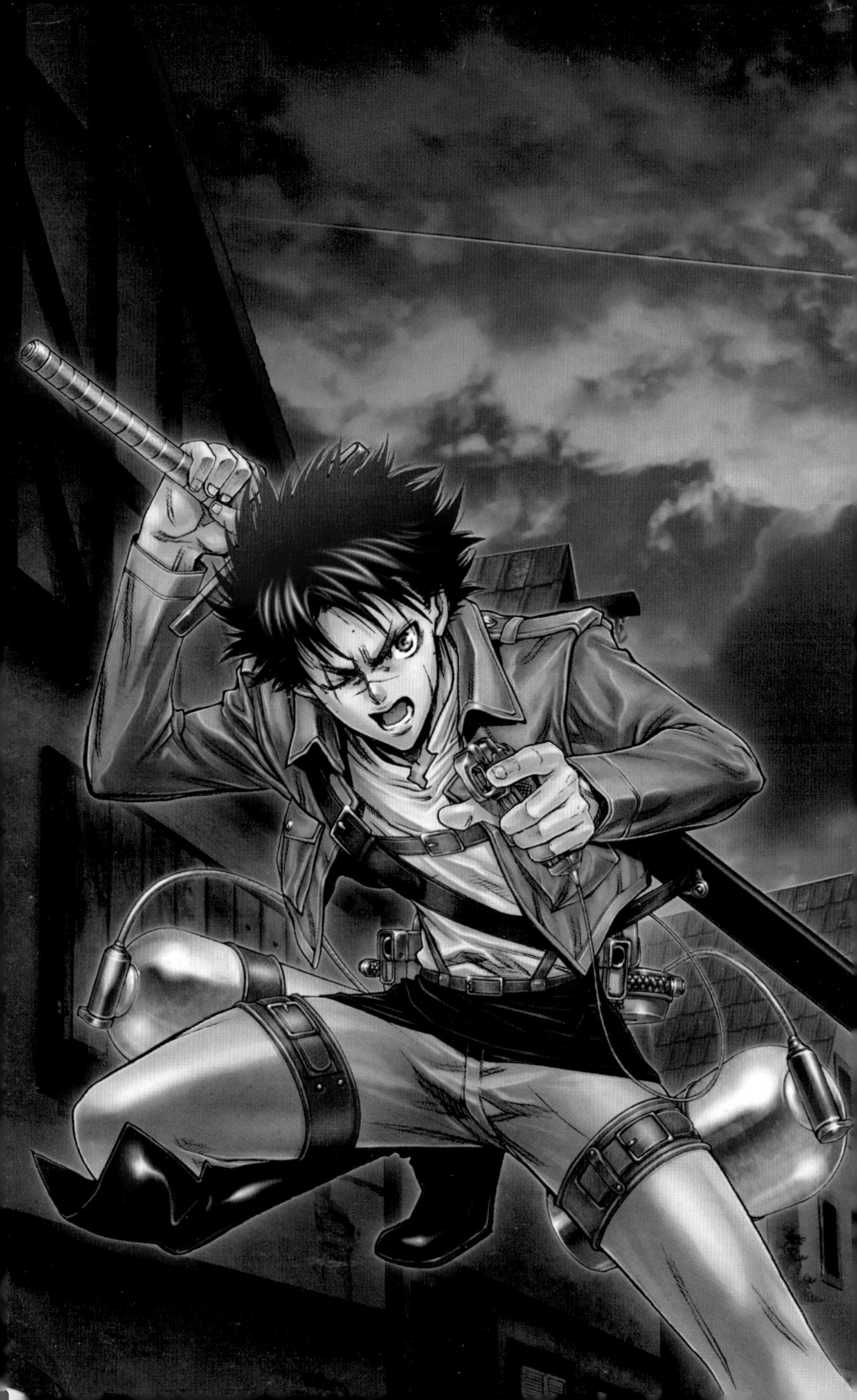

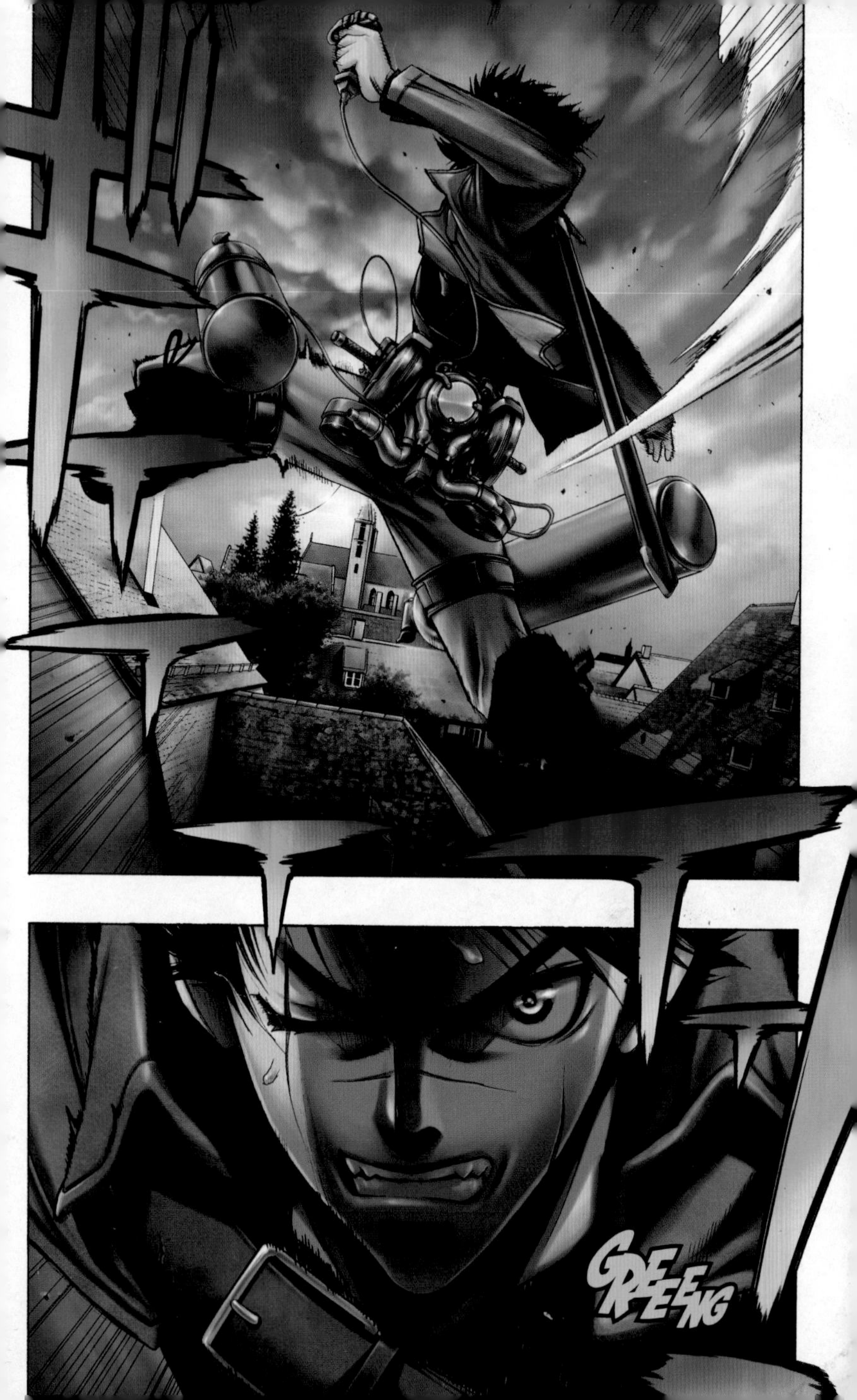
GREEENG

Before the Fall — Character Profiles

Kuklo

A 15-year-old boy born from a dead body packed into the vomit of a Titan, which earned him the moniker, "Titan's Son." He is fascinated with the Device as a means to defeat the Titans. The protagonist of this story.

Sharle Inocencio

First daughter of the Inocencios, a rich merchant family within Wall Sheena. When she realized that Kuklo was a human, she taught him to speak and learn. Currently an apprentice craftsman under Xenophon in the Industrial City.

Xavi Inocencio

Head of the Inocencio family and Sharle's brother. Member of the Military Police in Shiganshina District.

Cardina Baumeister

Kuklo's first friend in the outside world, and his companion in developing the Device.

Jorge Pikale

Training Corps instructor. A former Survey Corps captain who was hailed as a hero for defeating a Titan.

Carlo Pikale

Jorge's son and current captain of the Survey Corps. After they battled Titans together, he has great respect for Kuklo.

Xenophon Harkimo

Foreman at the Industrial City. He took over development of the Device from its inventor, Angel.

Gloria Bernhart

Captain of the Military Police in Shiganshina District. A powerful MP officer with a cold, tactical mind.

The Story So Far

When a Titan terrorized Shiganshina District and left behind a pile of vomit, a baby boy was miraculously born of a pregnant corpse. This boy was named Kuklo, the "Titan's Son," and was treated as a sideshow freak. Eventually the wealthy merchant Dario Inocencio bought Kuklo to serve as a punching bag for his son, Xavi. On the other hand, when she learned he was human and not the son of a Titan, Xavi's sister Sharle decided to teach him the words and knowledge of humanity instead. Two years later, Kuklo escaped from the mansion along with Sharle, who was being forced into a marriage she did not desire.

In Shiganshina District, the Survey Corps was preparing for its first expedition outside of the wall in 15 years. Kuklo wanted to see a Titan to confirm that he was indeed a human being. He left Sharle behind and snuck into the expedition's cargo wagon. As he hoped, the Survey Corps ran across a Titan, but it was far worse of a monster than he expected. The group suffered grievous losses, but thanks to Captain Carlo and Kuklo's idea, they eventually retreated safely behind Wall Maria. Kuklo helped the Survey Corps survive, but inside the walls he was greeted by the Military Police, who wanted the "Titan's Son" on charges of murdering Dario. In prison, he met Cardina, a young man jailed over political squabbles. They hoped to escape to safety when exiled beyond the Wall, but found themselves surrounded by a pack of Titans. It was through the help of Jorge, former Survey Corps Captain and first human to defeat a Titan, that the two boys escaped with their lives. The equipment that Jorge used was the very "Device" that was the key to defeating the Titan those 15 years ago.

Kuklo and Cardina escaped the notice of the MPs by hiding in the Industrial city, where they found Sharle. It is there that the three youngsters learned the truth of the ill-fated Titan-capturing expedition 15 years earlier, and swore to uphold the will of Angel, the inventor of the Device. Next, Kuklo and Cardina headed back to Shiganshina to test out a new model of the Device developed by Xenophon, Angel's friend and rival, but they failed to defeat a Titan with it. As he recovered from his injuries, Kuklo heard ominous rumors about MP activity, and rushed to the Industrial City to protect Sharle. When he got to the gate of the city, he came across the stunning sight of battle between anti-establishment dissidents and the Military Police.

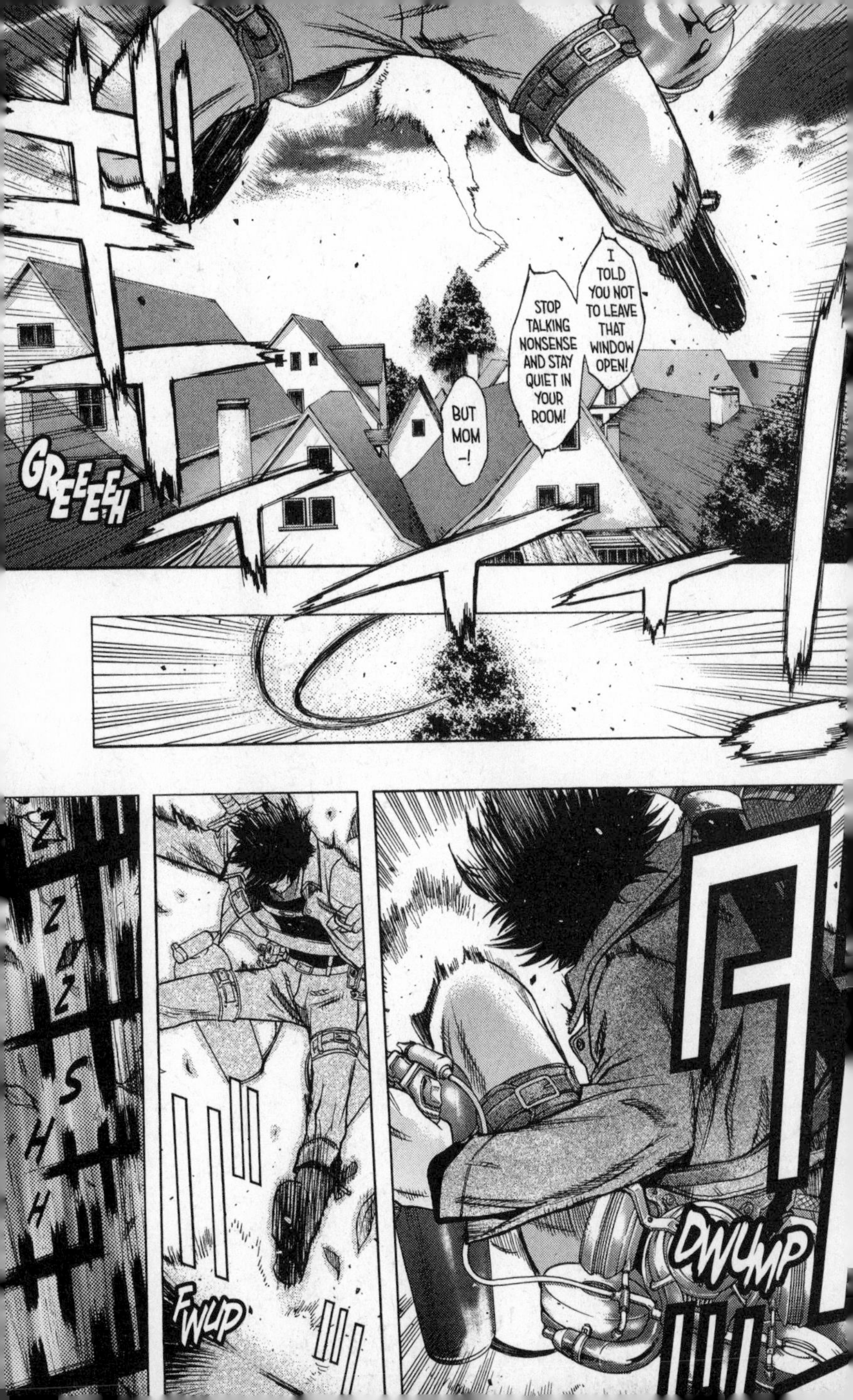
I TOLD YOU NOT TO LEAVE THAT WINDOW OPEN!
STOP TALKING NONSENSE AND STAY QUIET IN YOUR ROOM!
BUT MOM—!
GREEEEH
DWUMP
FWUP

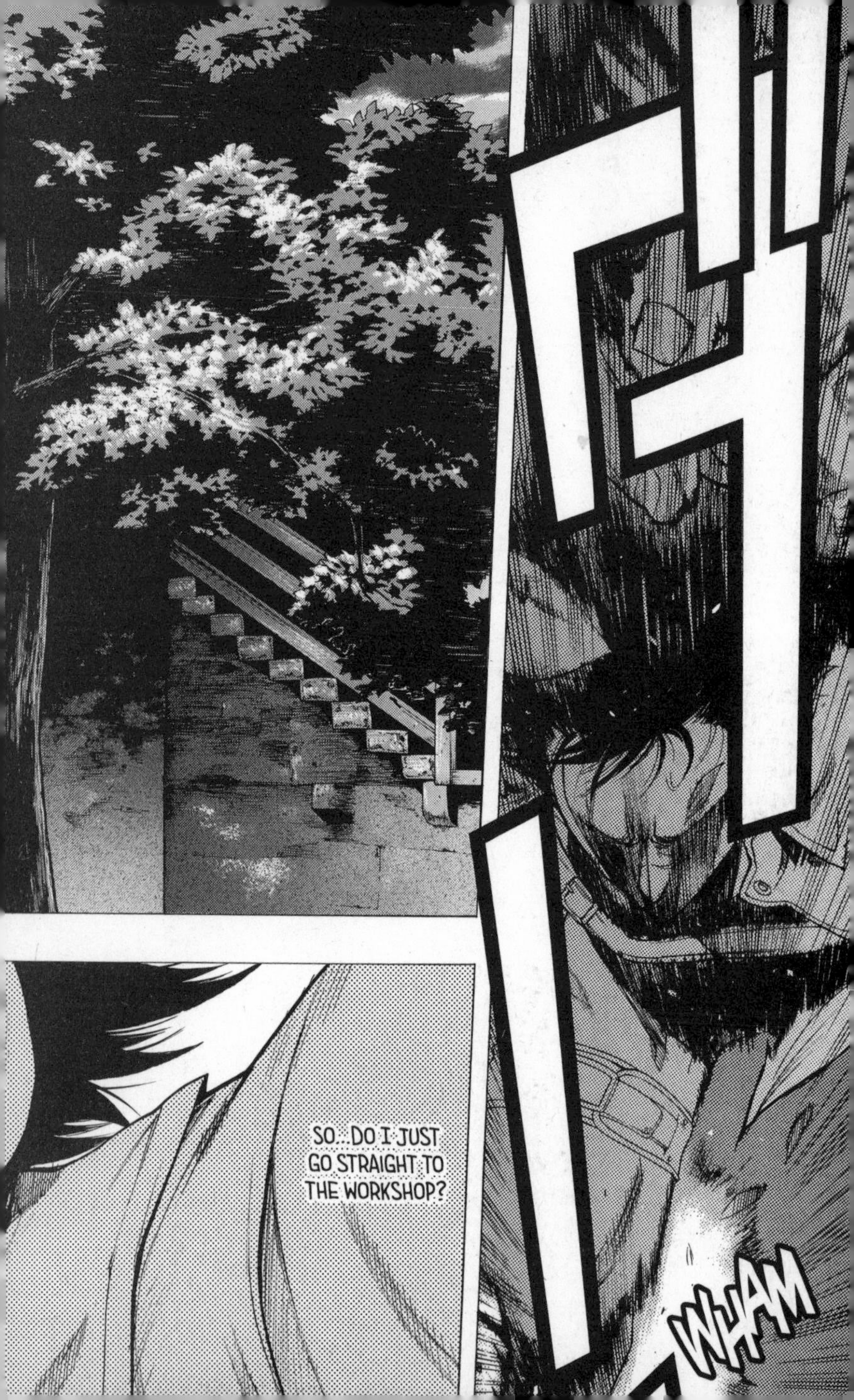
SO...DO I JUST GO STRAIGHT TO THE WORKSHOP?
WHAM

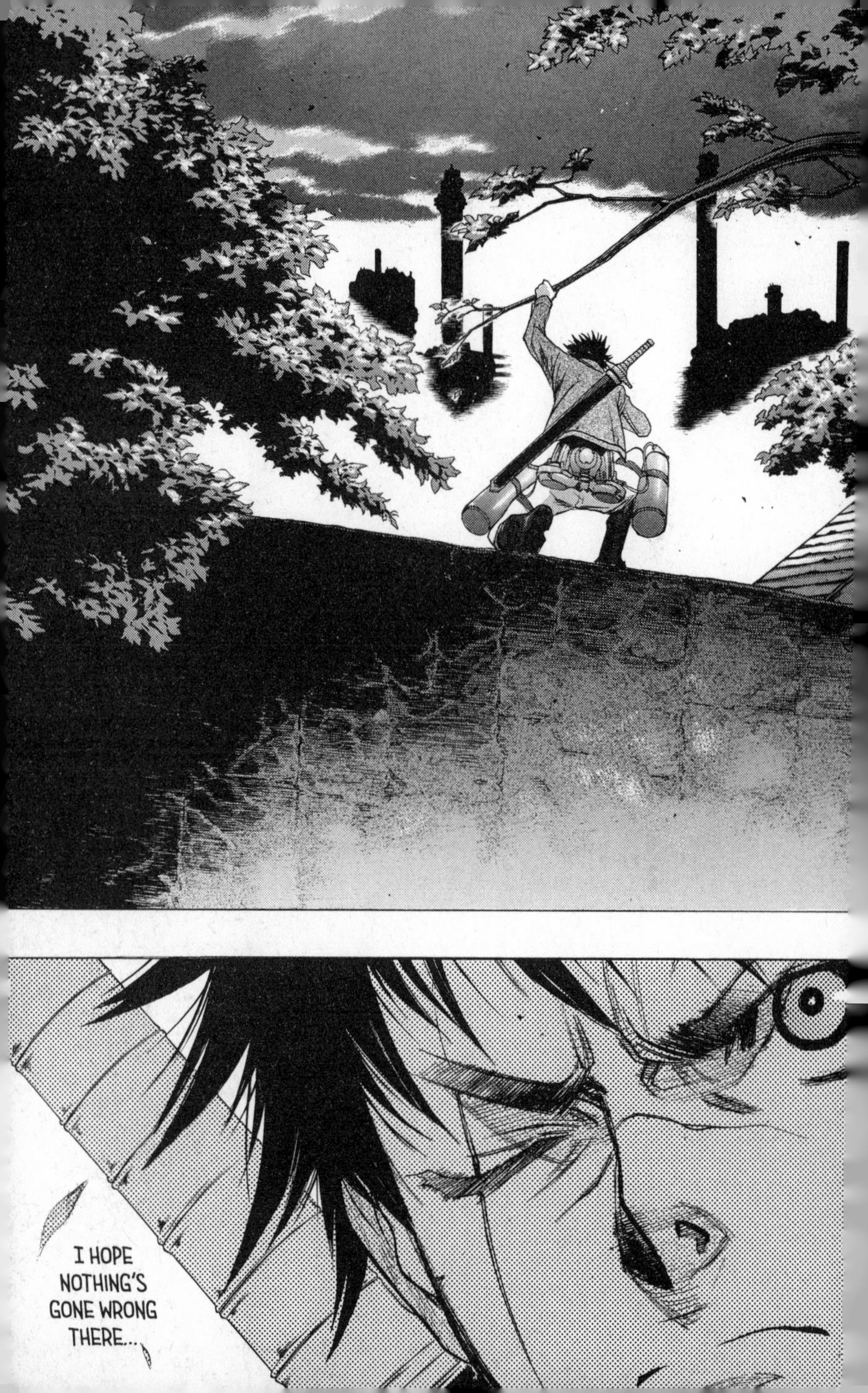
I HOPE NOTHING'S GONE WRONG THERE...

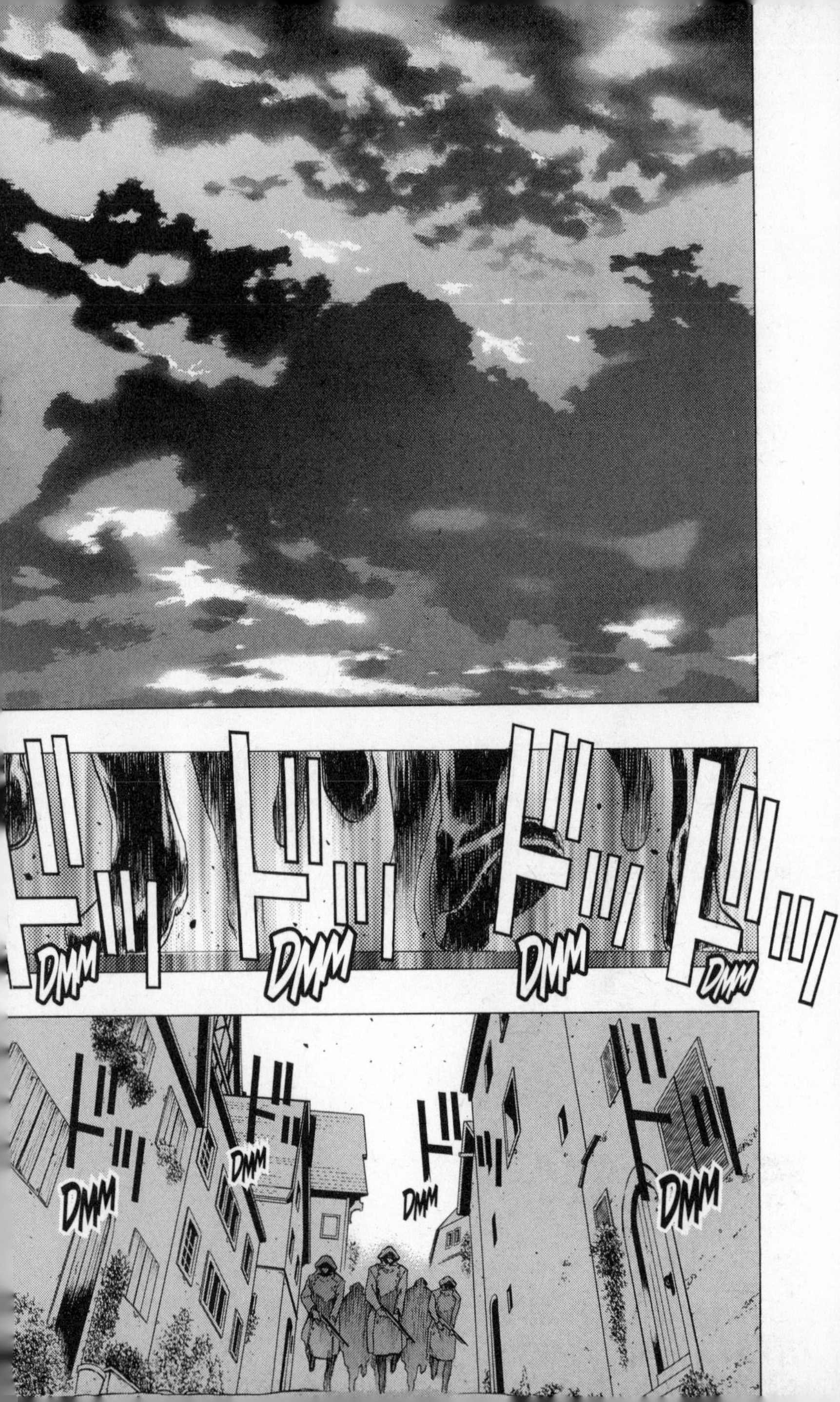
DMM
DMM
DMM
DMM
DMM
DMM
DMM
DMM

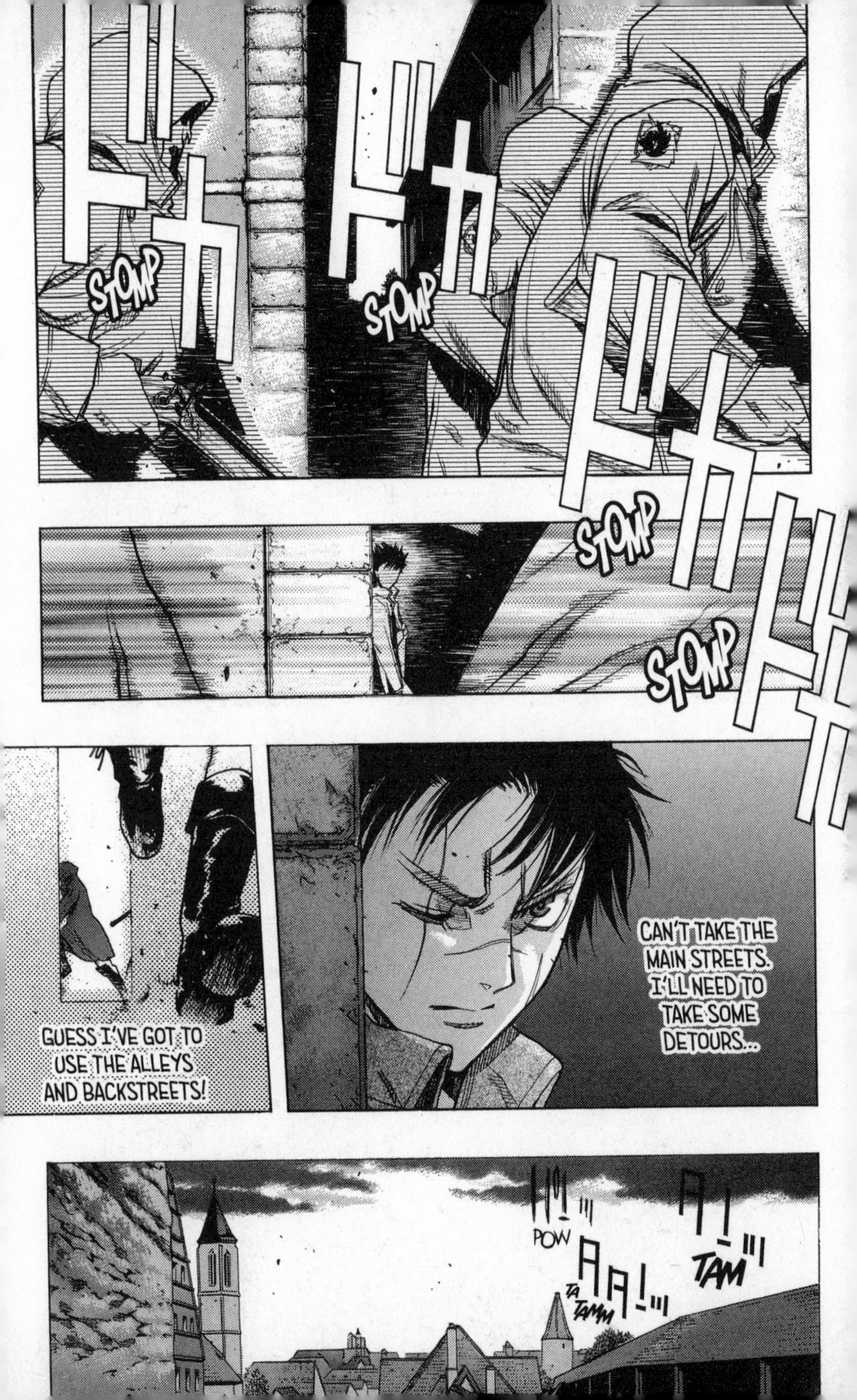
STOMP
STOMP
STOMP
STOMP
CAN'T TAKE THE MAIN STREETS. I'LL NEED TO TAKE SOME DETOURS...
GUESS I'VE GOT TO USE THE ALLEYS AND BACKSTREETS!
TAM
POW
TA TAMM

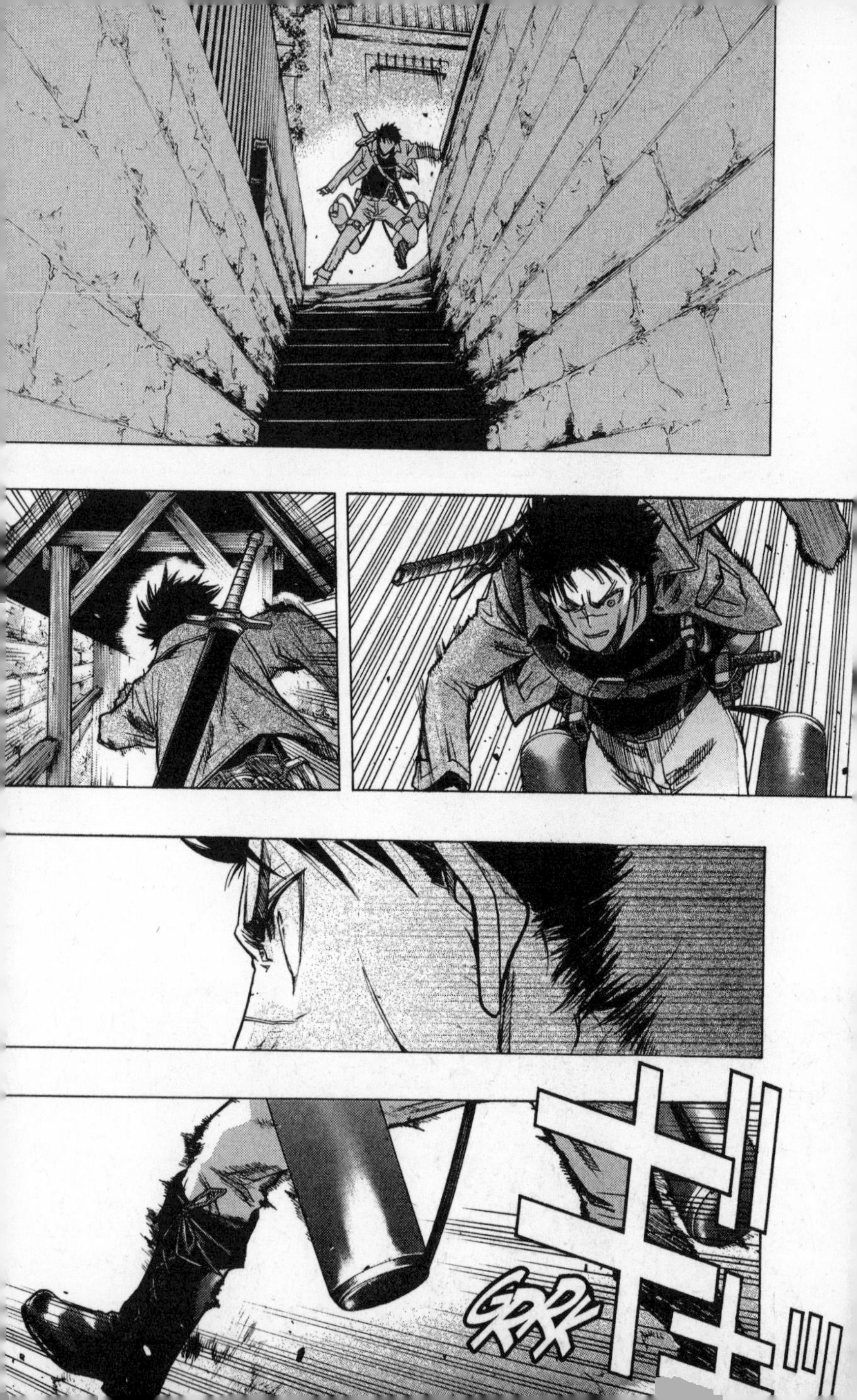
GRRK

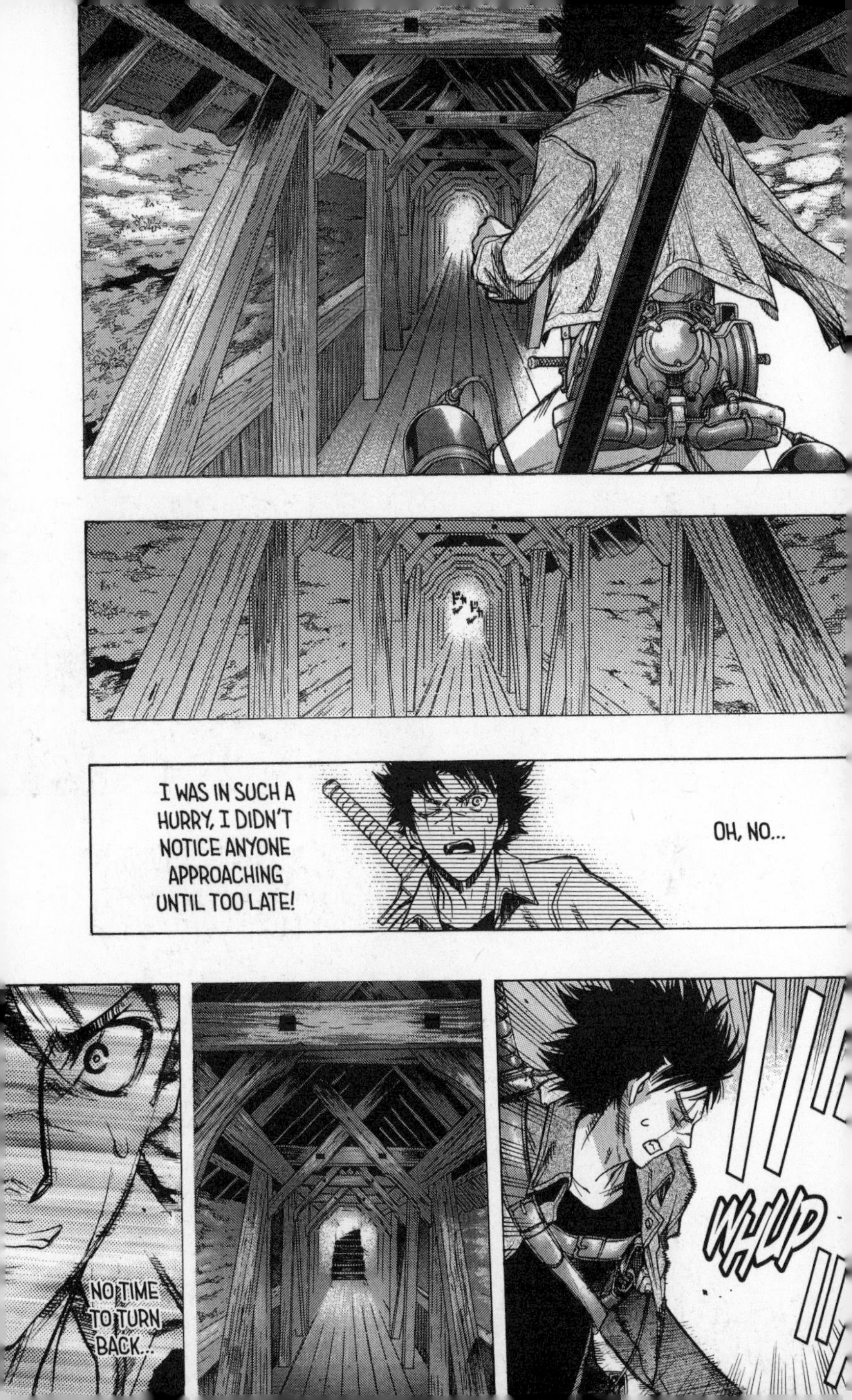
OH, NO...
I WAS IN SUCH A HURRY, I DIDN'T NOTICE ANYONE APPROACHING UNTIL TOO LATE!
WHUP
NO TIME TO TURN BACK...

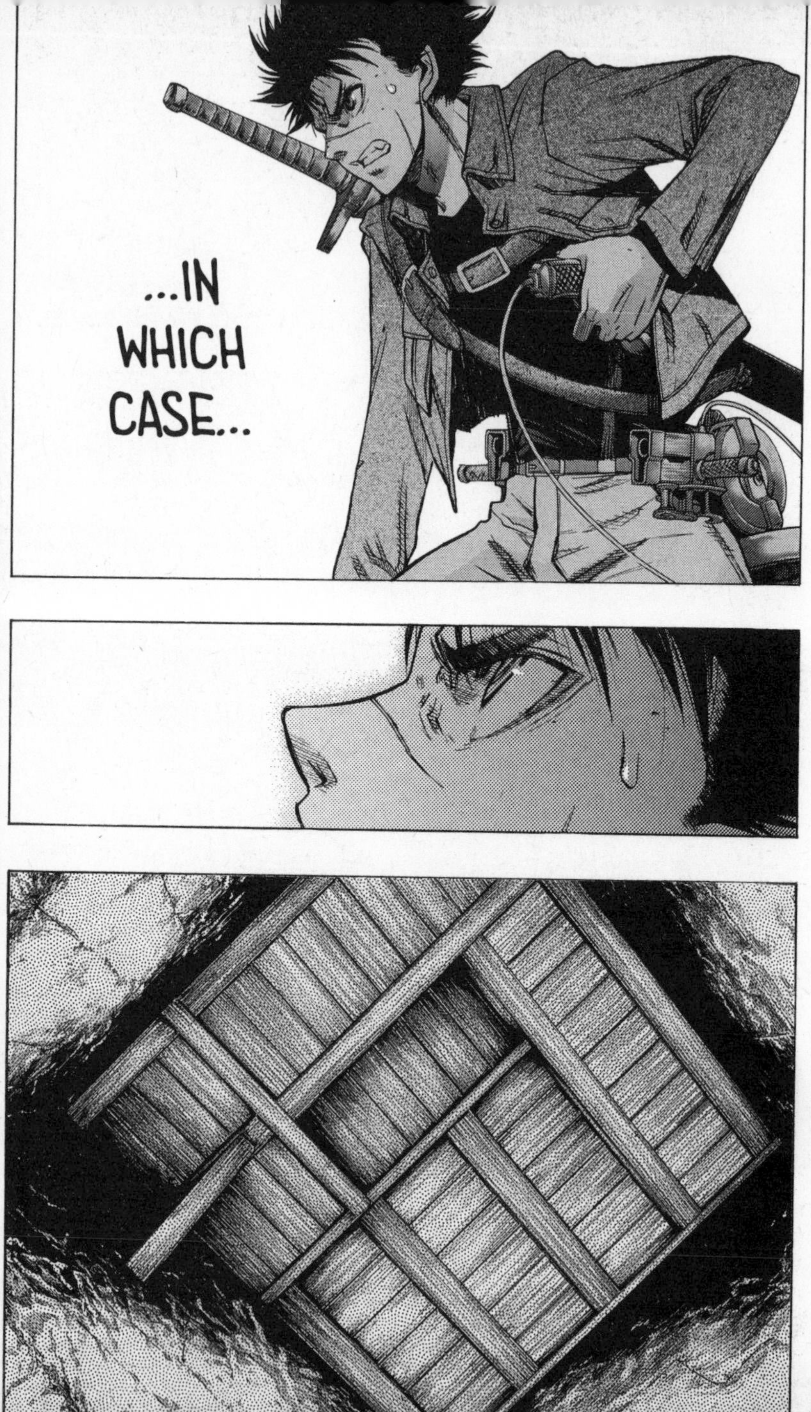
...IN WHICH CASE...

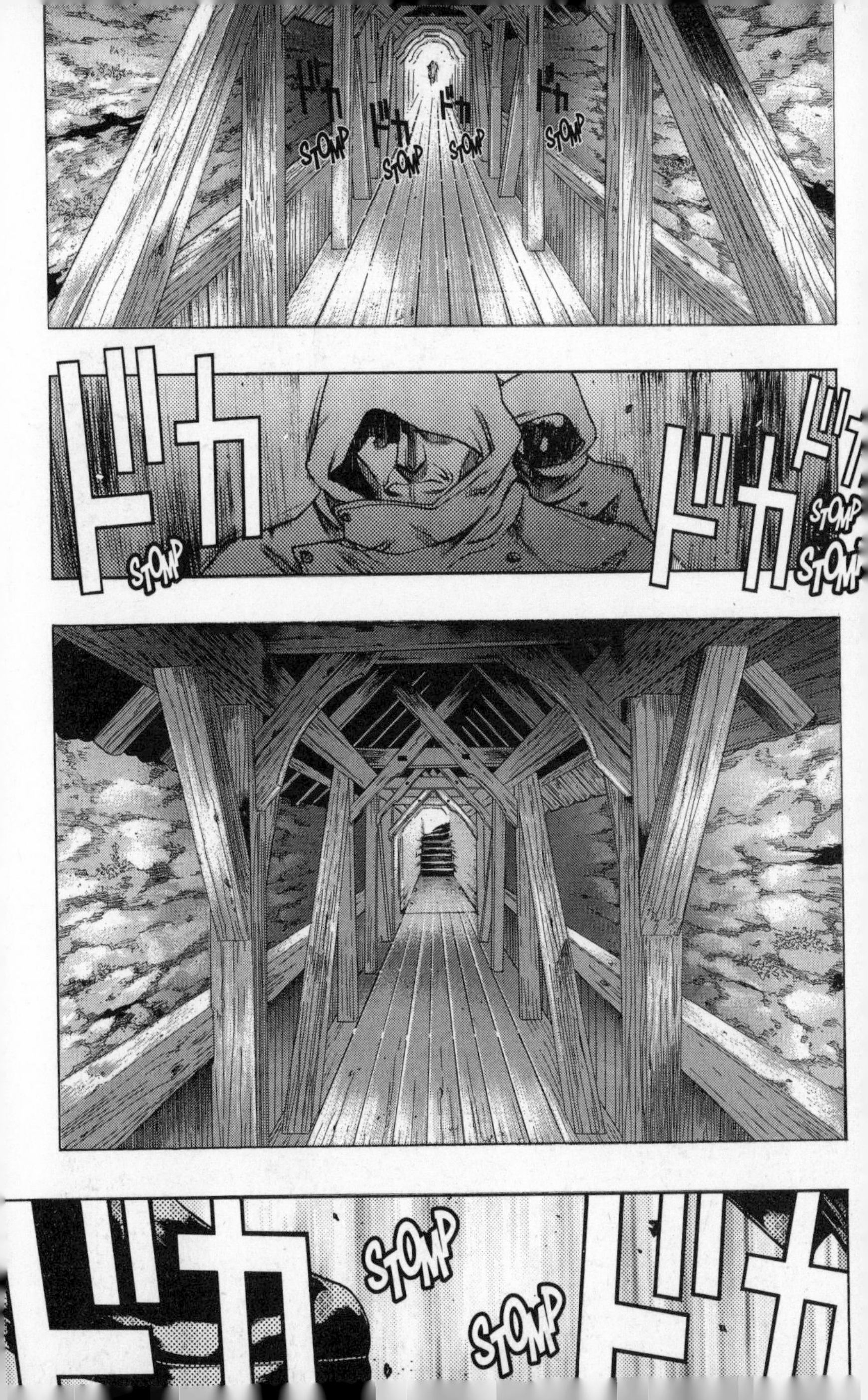
ドカ
STOMP
ドカ
STOMP
ドカ
STOMP
ドカ
STOMP
ドカ
STOMP
STOMP
ドカ
ドカ
STOMP
ドカ
STOMP
STOMP
ドカ

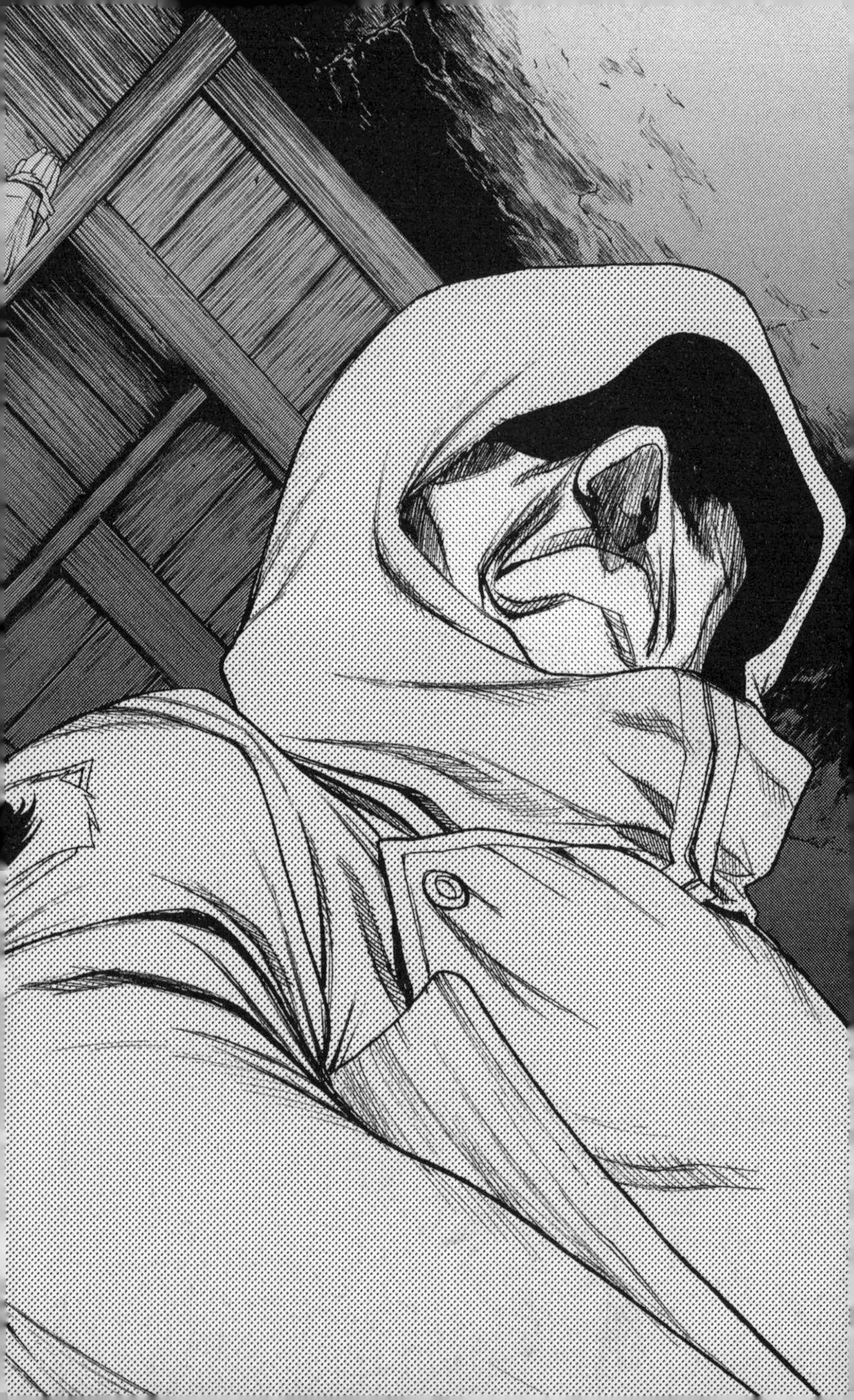

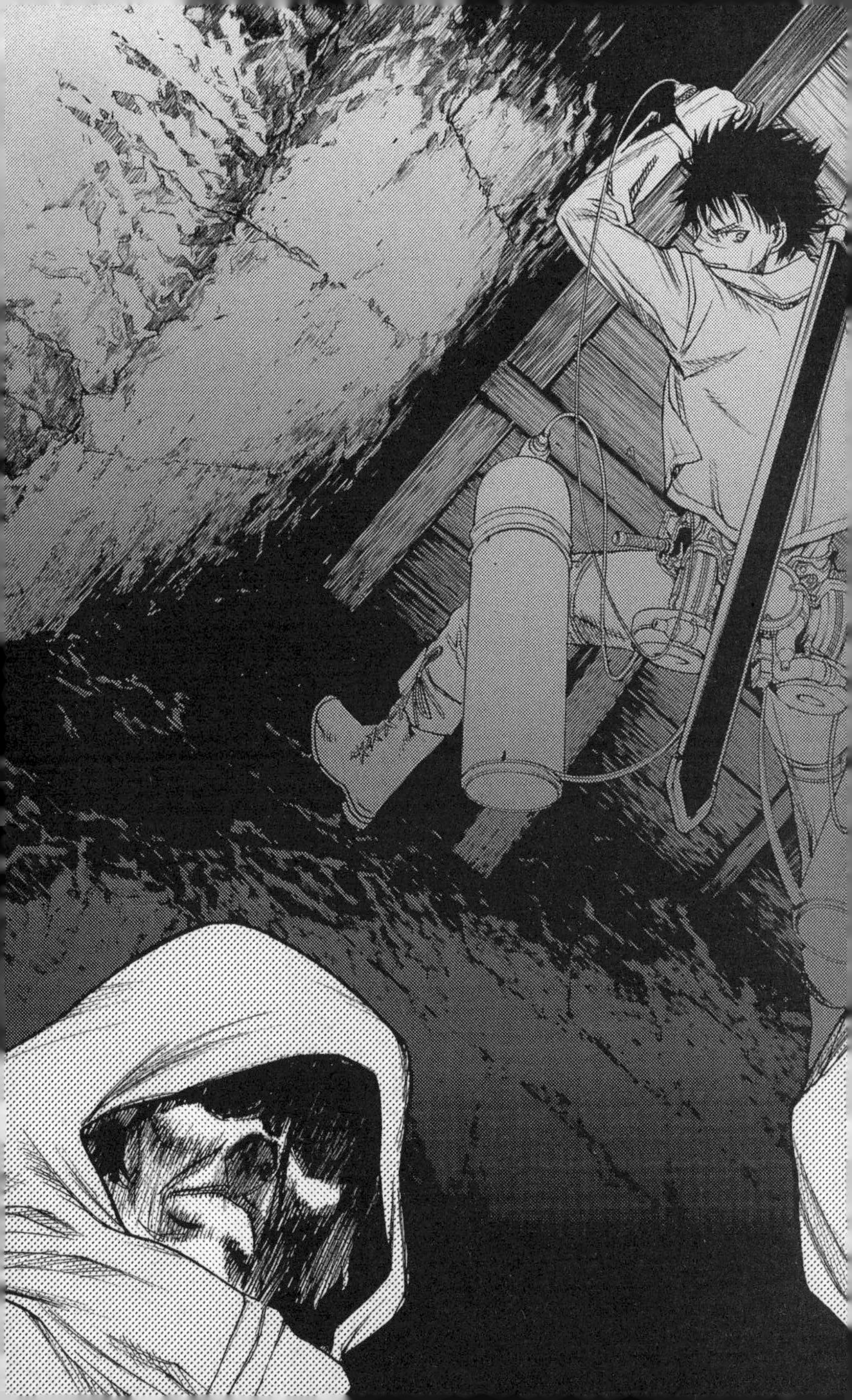

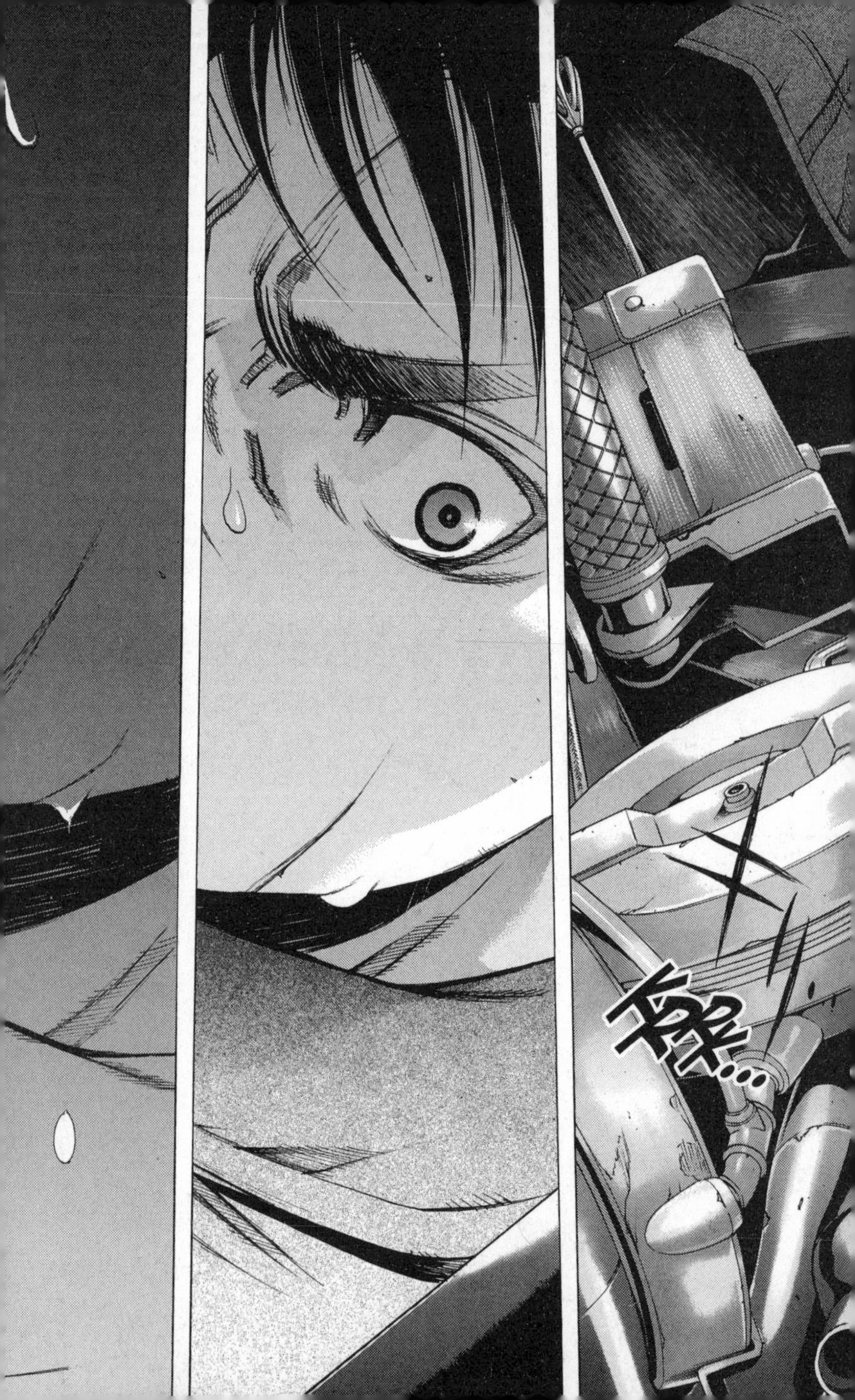
KRRK...

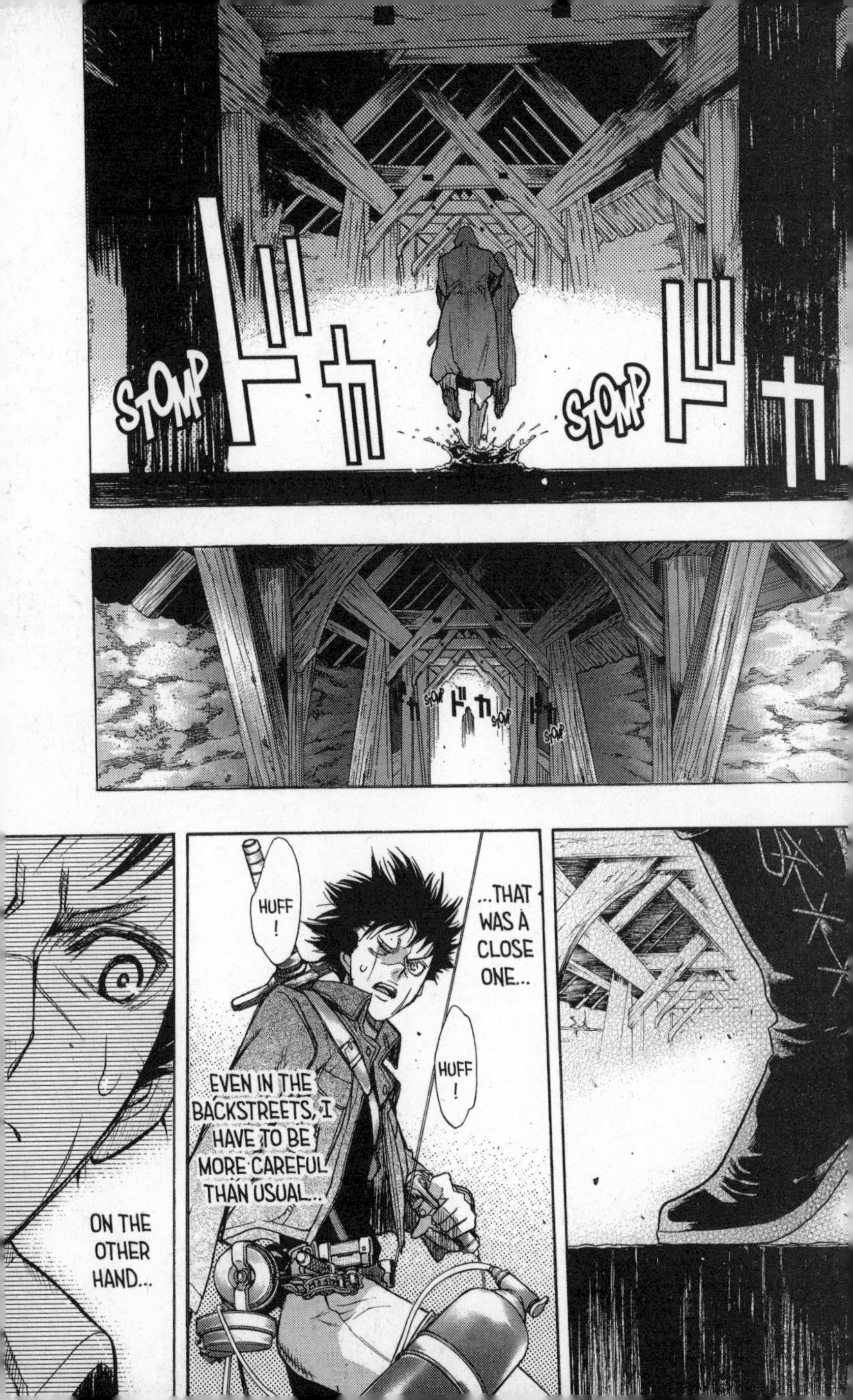
STOMP
ドカ
STOMP
ドカ
...THAT WAS A CLOSE ONE...
HUFF !
HUFF !
EVEN IN THE BACKSTREETS, I HAVE TO BE MORE CAREFUL THAN USUAL...
ON THE OTHER HAND...

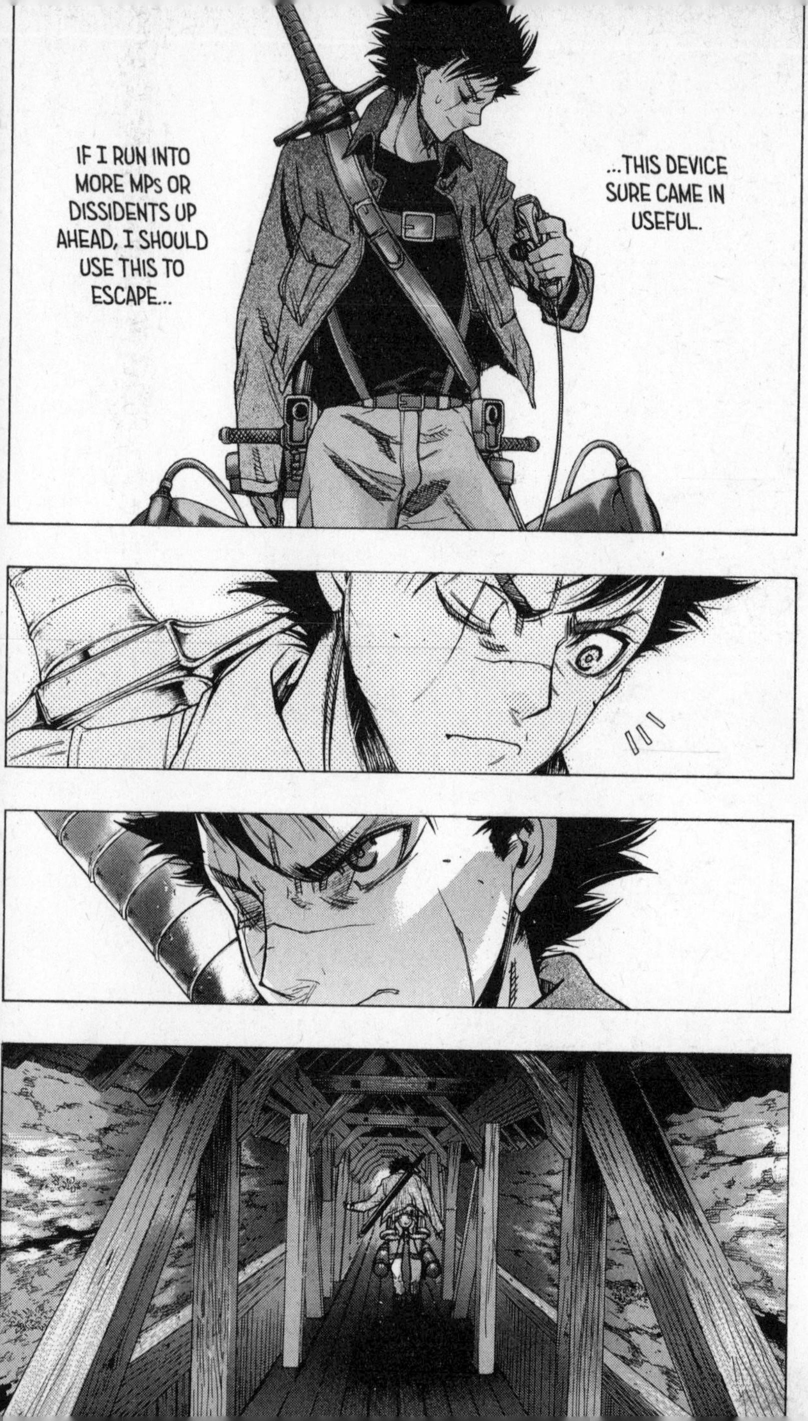
...THIS DEVICE SURE CAME IN USEFUL.
IF I RUN INTO MORE MPs OR DISSIDENTS UP AHEAD, I SHOULD USE THIS TO ESCAPE...

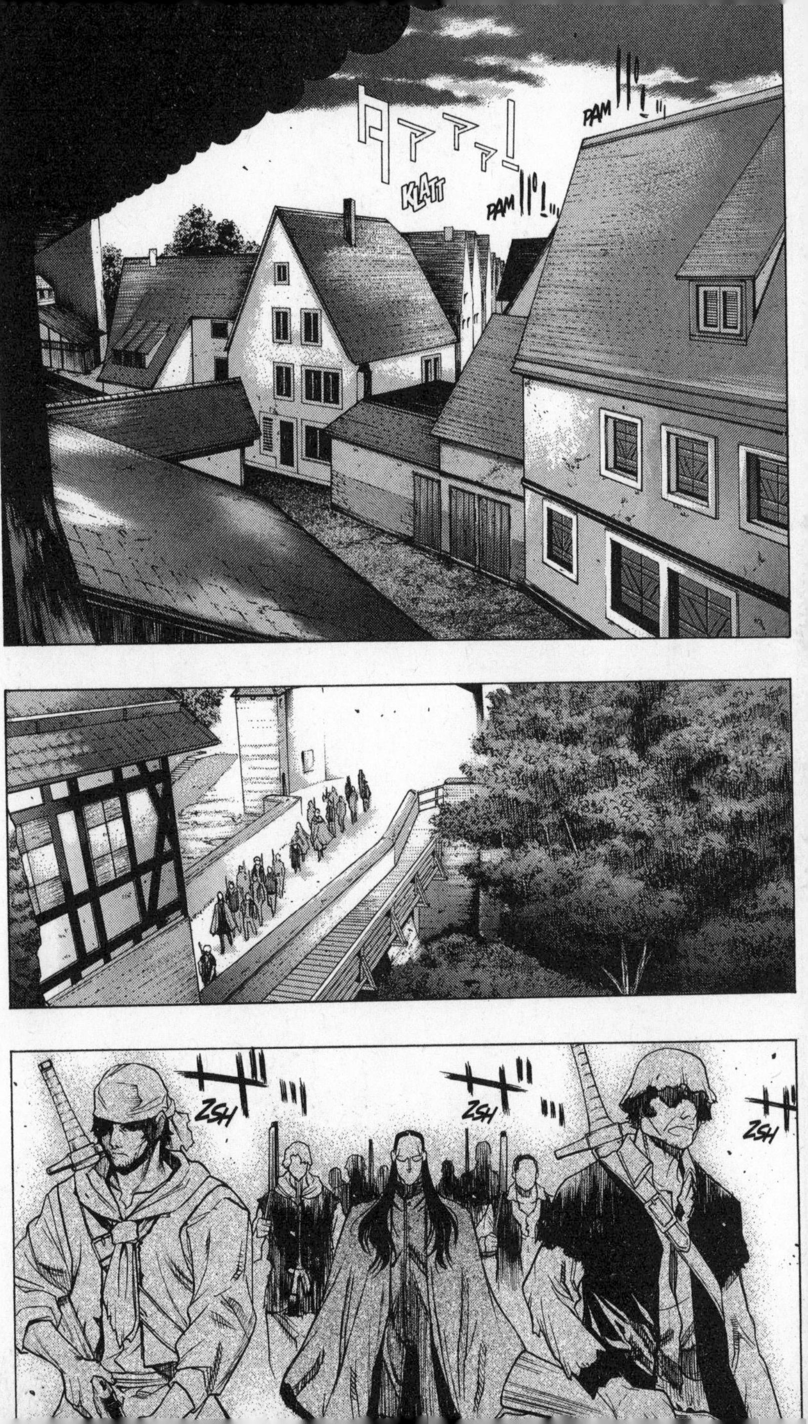
PAM
PAM
KLATT
ZSH
ZSH
ZSH

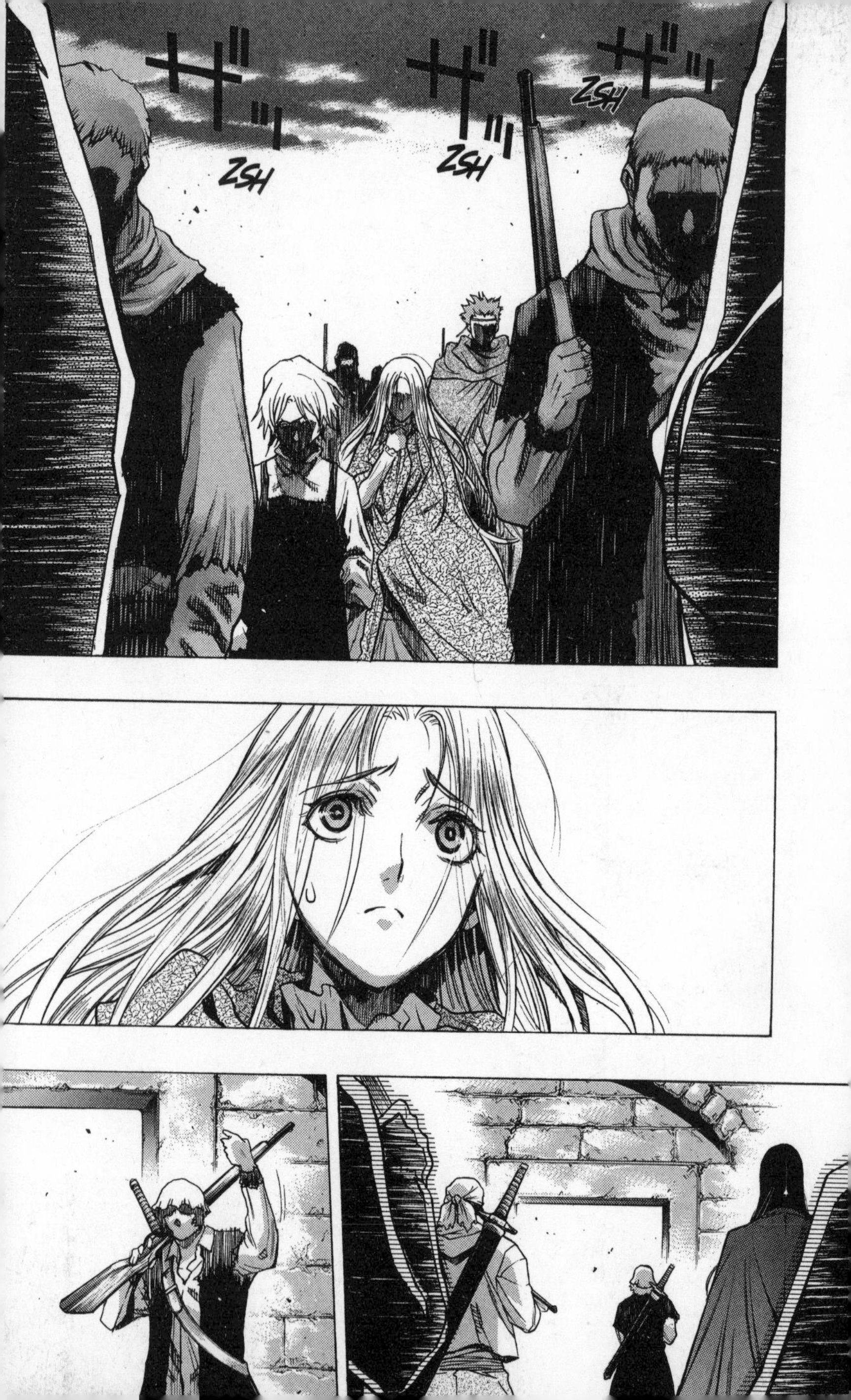
ZSH
ZSH
ZSH

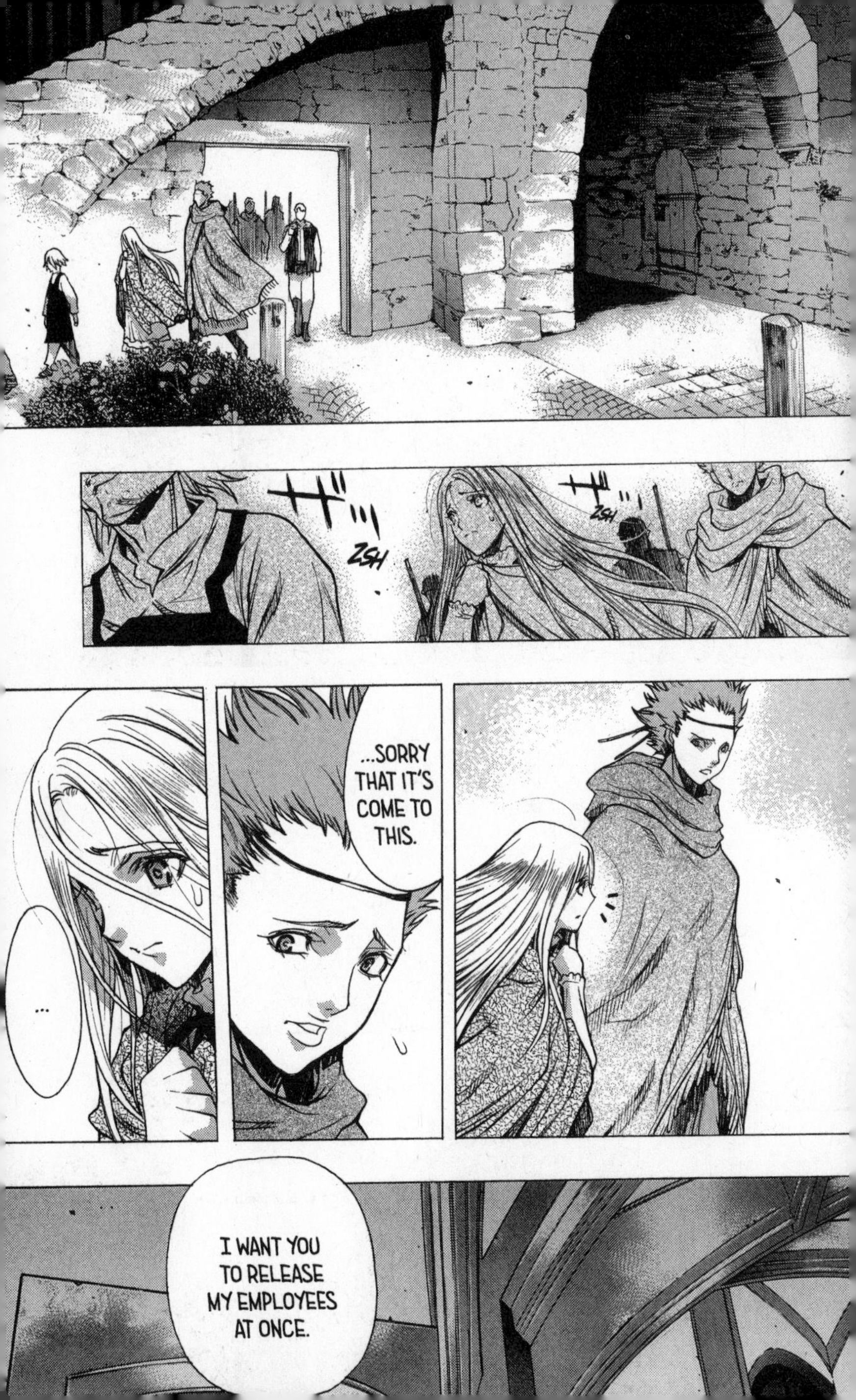
ZSH
ZSH
...SORRY THAT IT'S COME TO THIS.
...
I WANT YOU TO RELEASE MY EMPLOYEES AT ONCE.

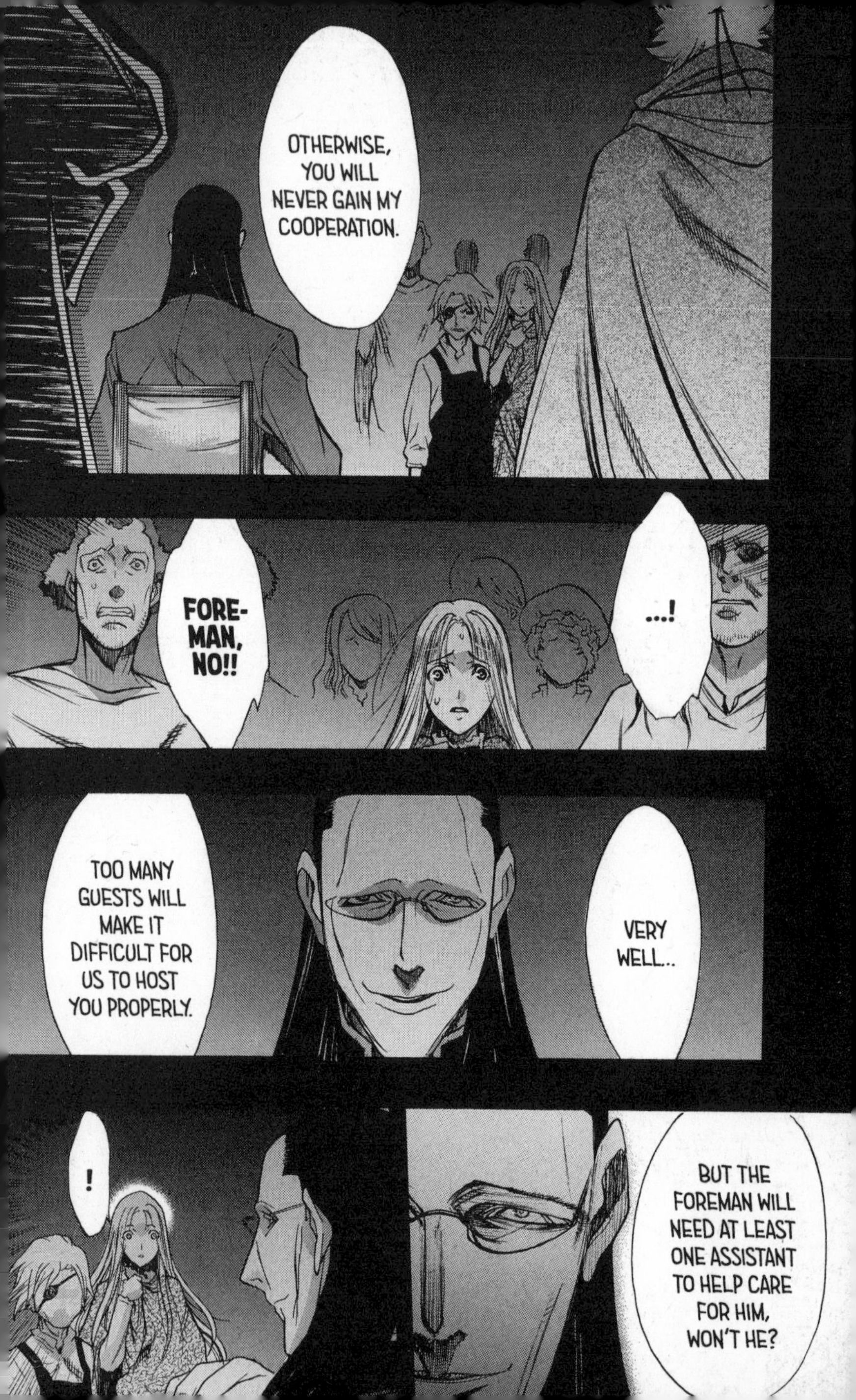
OTHERWISE, YOU WILL NEVER GAIN MY COOPERATION.
...!
FORE-MAN, NO!!
VERY WELL...
TOO MANY GUESTS WILL MAKE IT DIFFICULT FOR US TO HOST YOU PROPERLY.
BUT THE FOREMAN WILL NEED AT LEAST ONE ASSISTANT TO HELP CARE FOR HIM, WON'T HE?
!

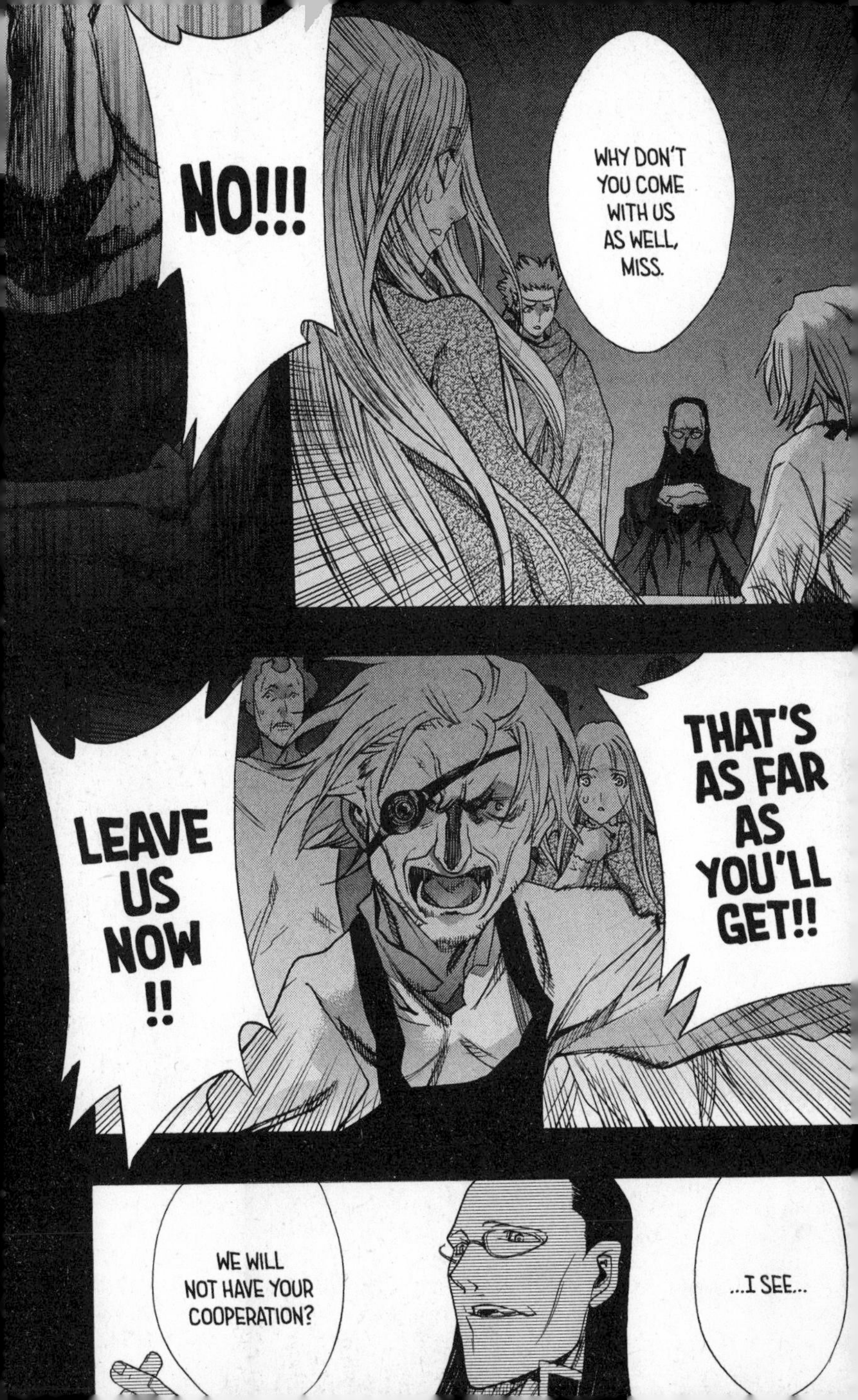
WHY DON'T YOU COME WITH US AS WELL, MISS.
NO!!!
THAT'S AS FAR AS YOU'LL GET!!
LEAVE US NOW !!
...I SEE...
WE WILL NOT HAVE YOUR COOPERATION?

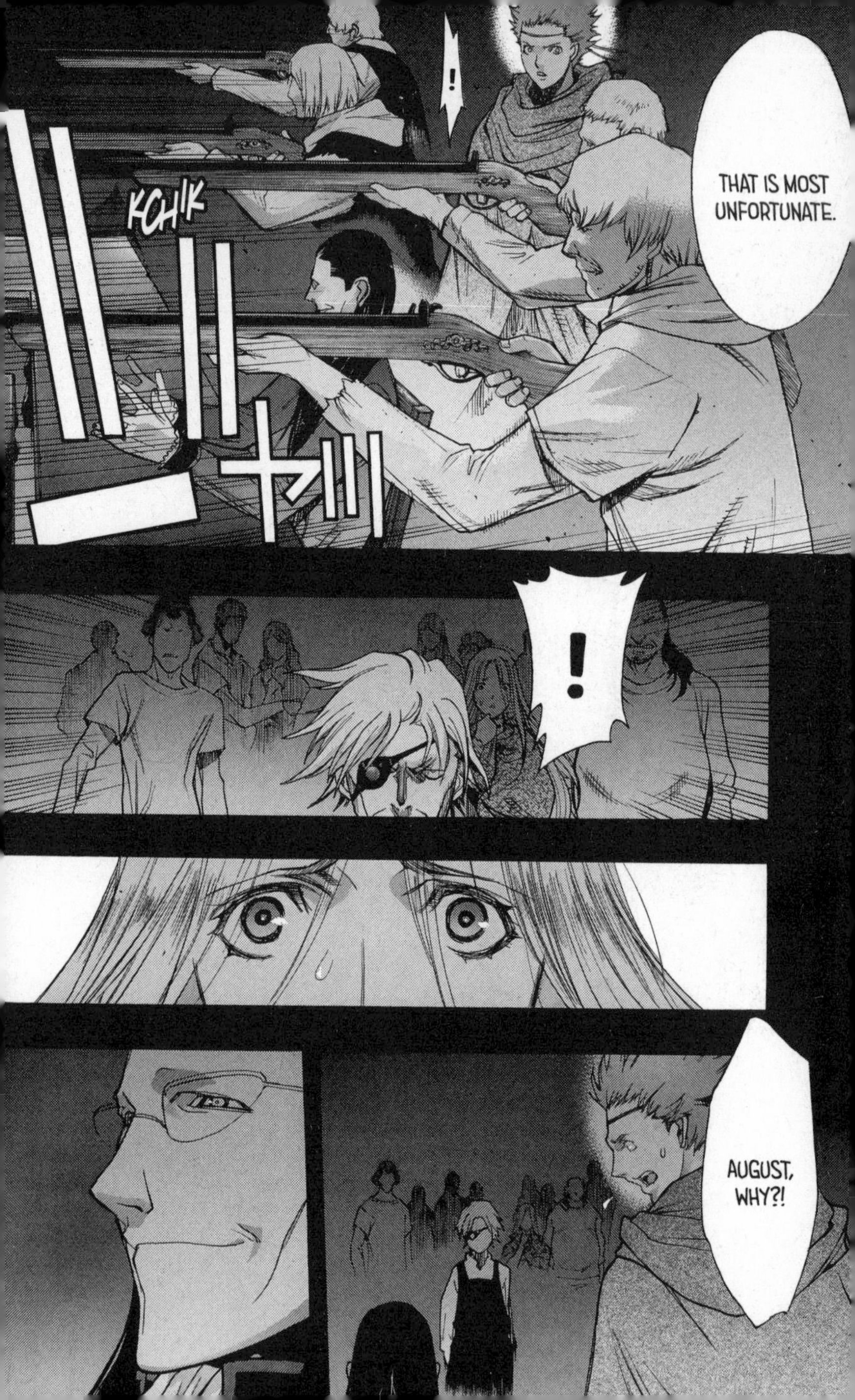
THAT IS MOST UNFORTUNATE.
!
KCHIK
!
AUGUST, WHY?!

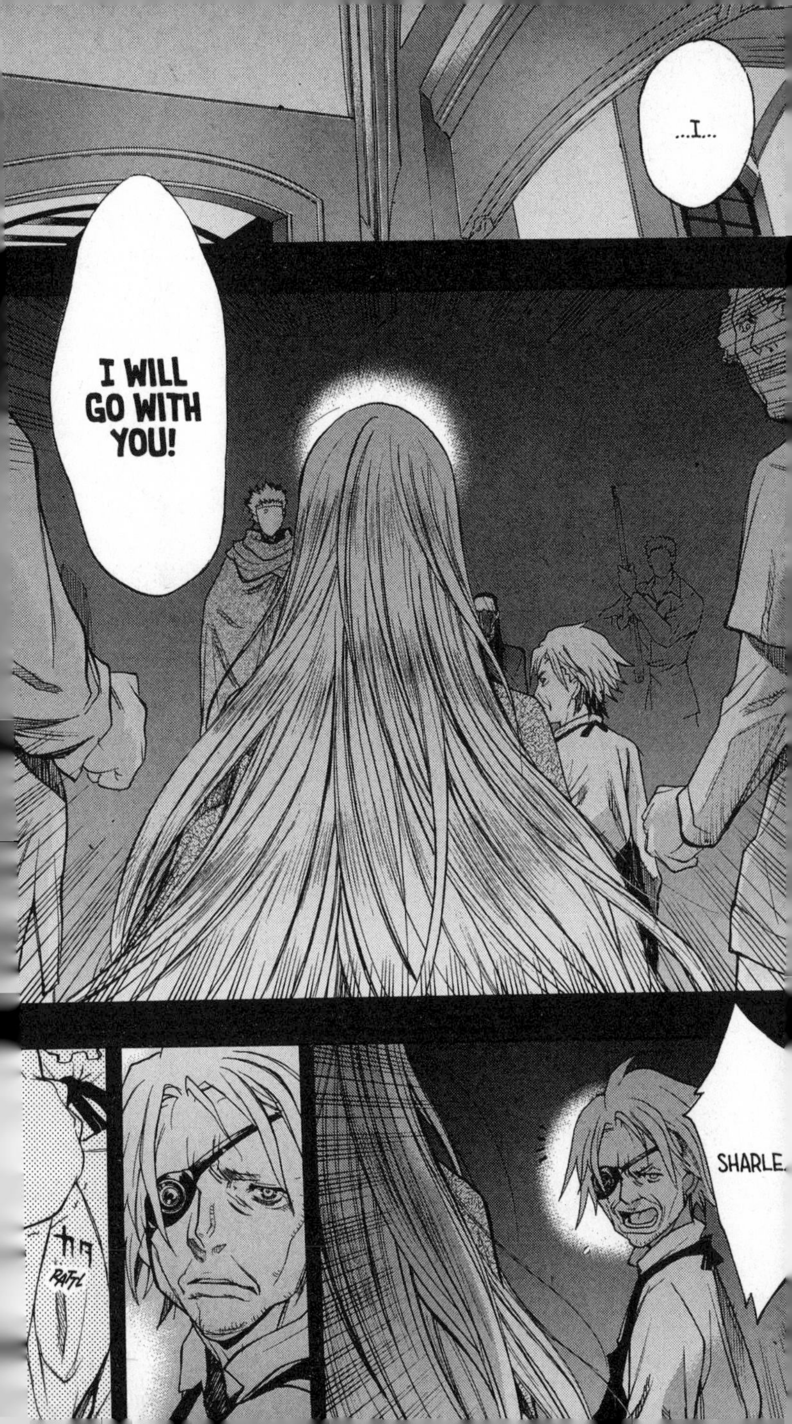
...I...
I WILL GO WITH YOU!
SHARLE.
カタ
RATTL

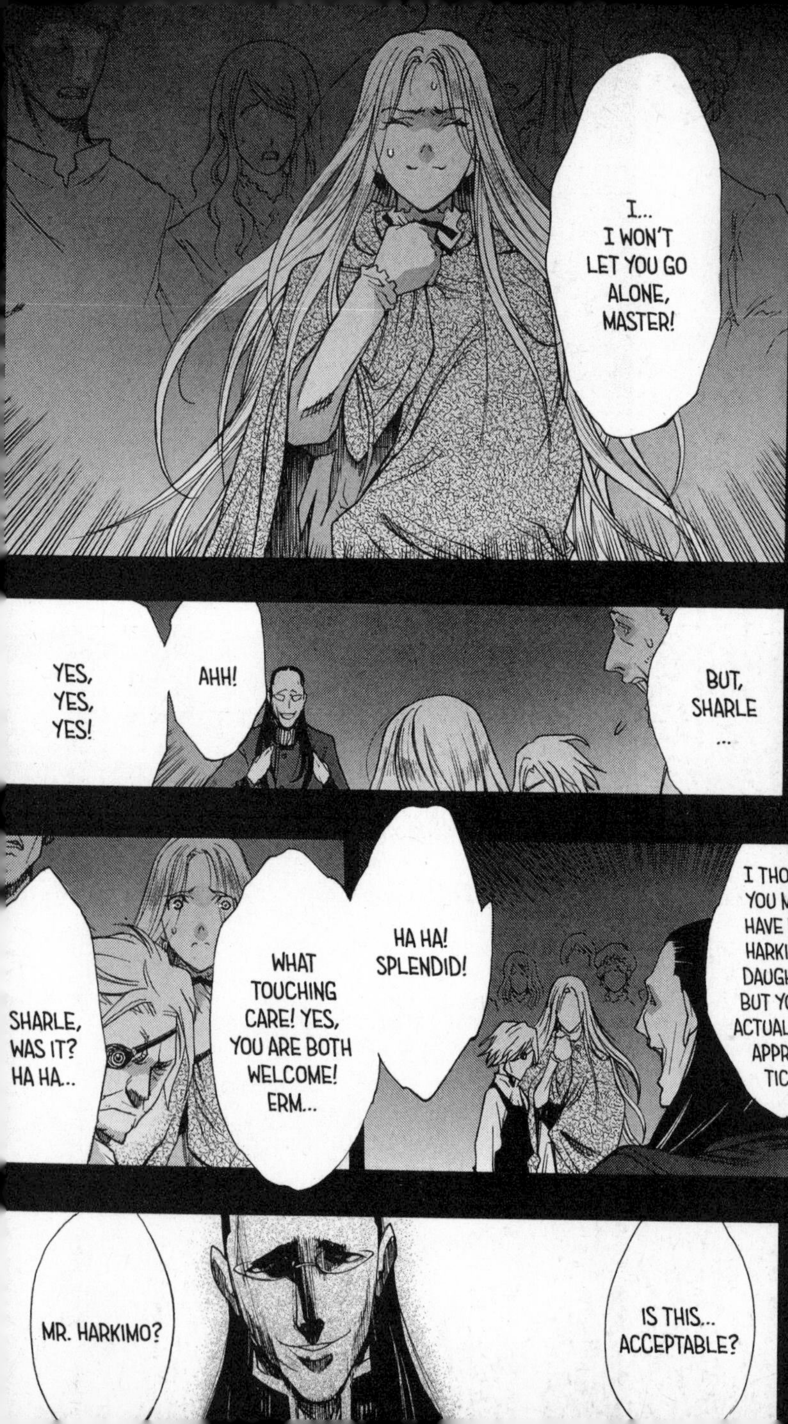
I...
I WON'T
LET YOU GO
ALONE,
MASTER!
BUT,
SHARLE
...
AHH!
YES,
YES,
YES!
I THOUGHT
YOU MIGHT
HAVE BEEN
HARKIMO'S
DAUGHTER,
BUT YOU'RE
ACTUALLY HIS
APPREN-
TICE!
HA HA!
SPLENDID!
WHAT
TOUCHING
CARE! YES,
YOU ARE BOTH
WELCOME!
ERM...
SHARLE,
WAS IT?
HA HA...
IS THIS...
ACCEPTABLE?
MR. HARKIMO?

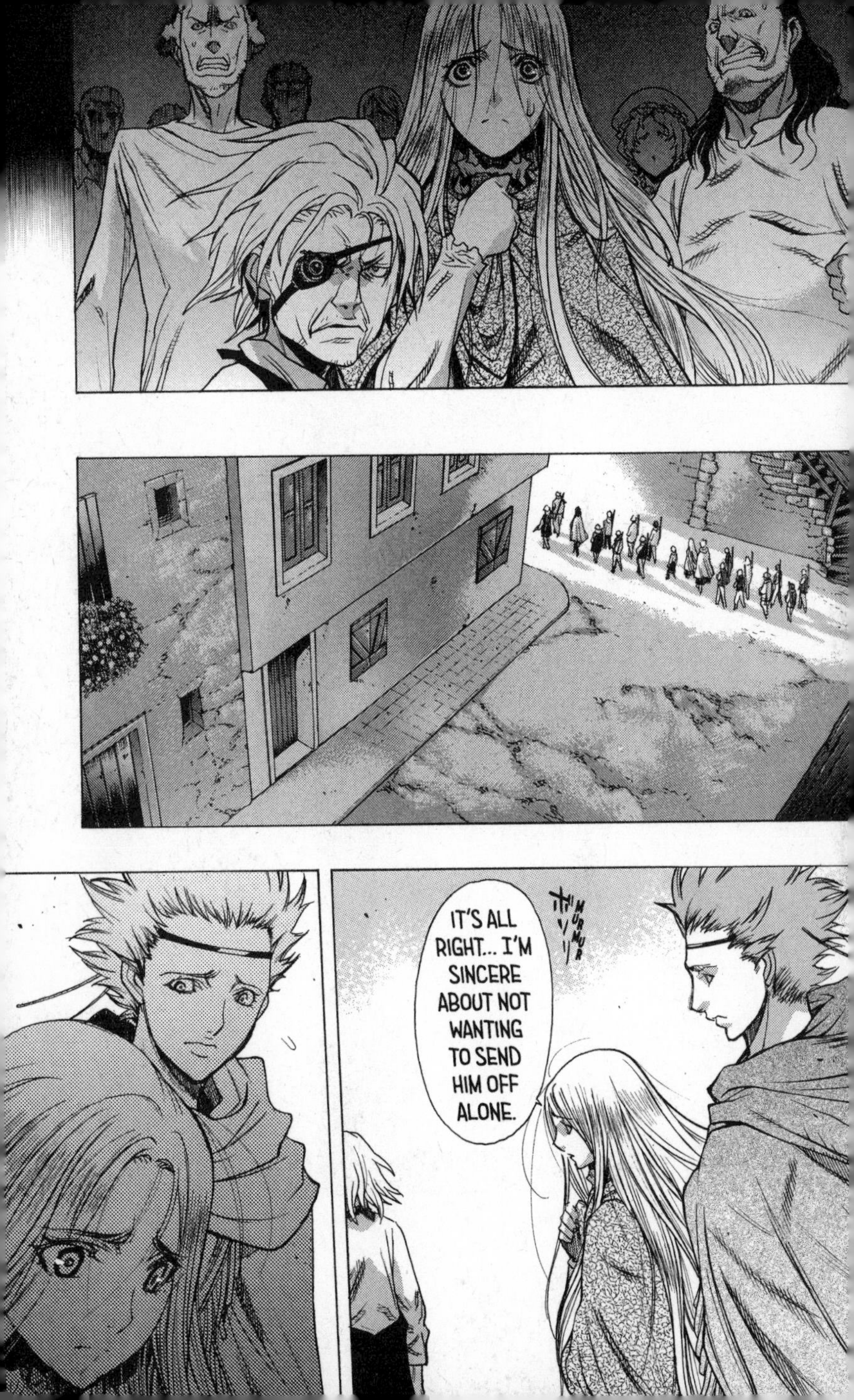
MURMUR
IT'S ALL RIGHT... I'M SINCERE ABOUT NOT WANTING TO SEND HIM OFF ALONE.

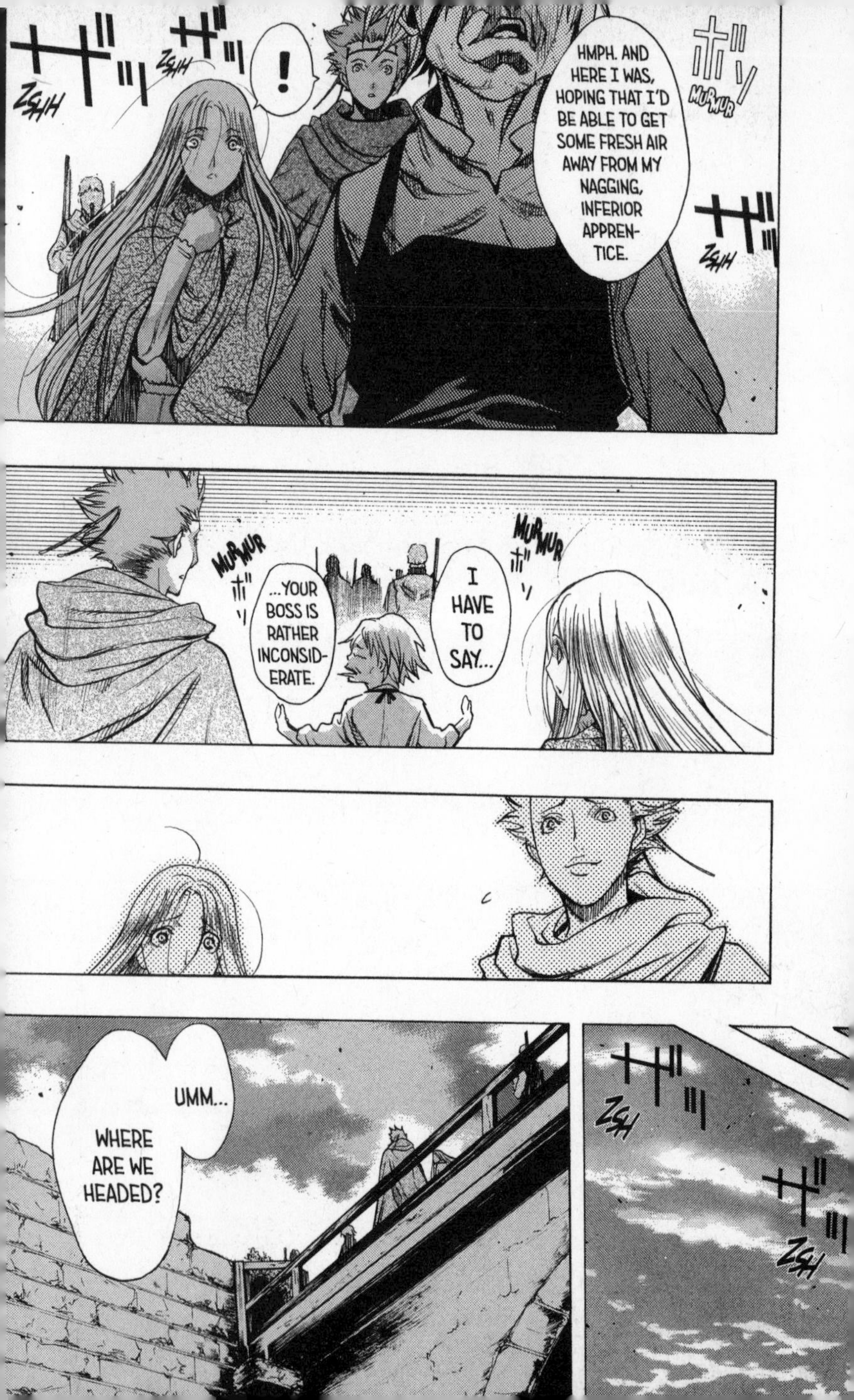
HMPH. AND HERE I WAS, HOPING THAT I'D BE ABLE TO GET SOME FRESH AIR AWAY FROM MY NAGGING, INFERIOR APPREN-TICE.
MURMUR
ZSHH
!
ZSHH
ZSHH
MURMUR
I HAVE TO SAY...
...YOUR BOSS IS RATHER INCONSID-ERATE.
MURMUR
ZSH
ZSH
UMM...
WHERE ARE WE HEADED?

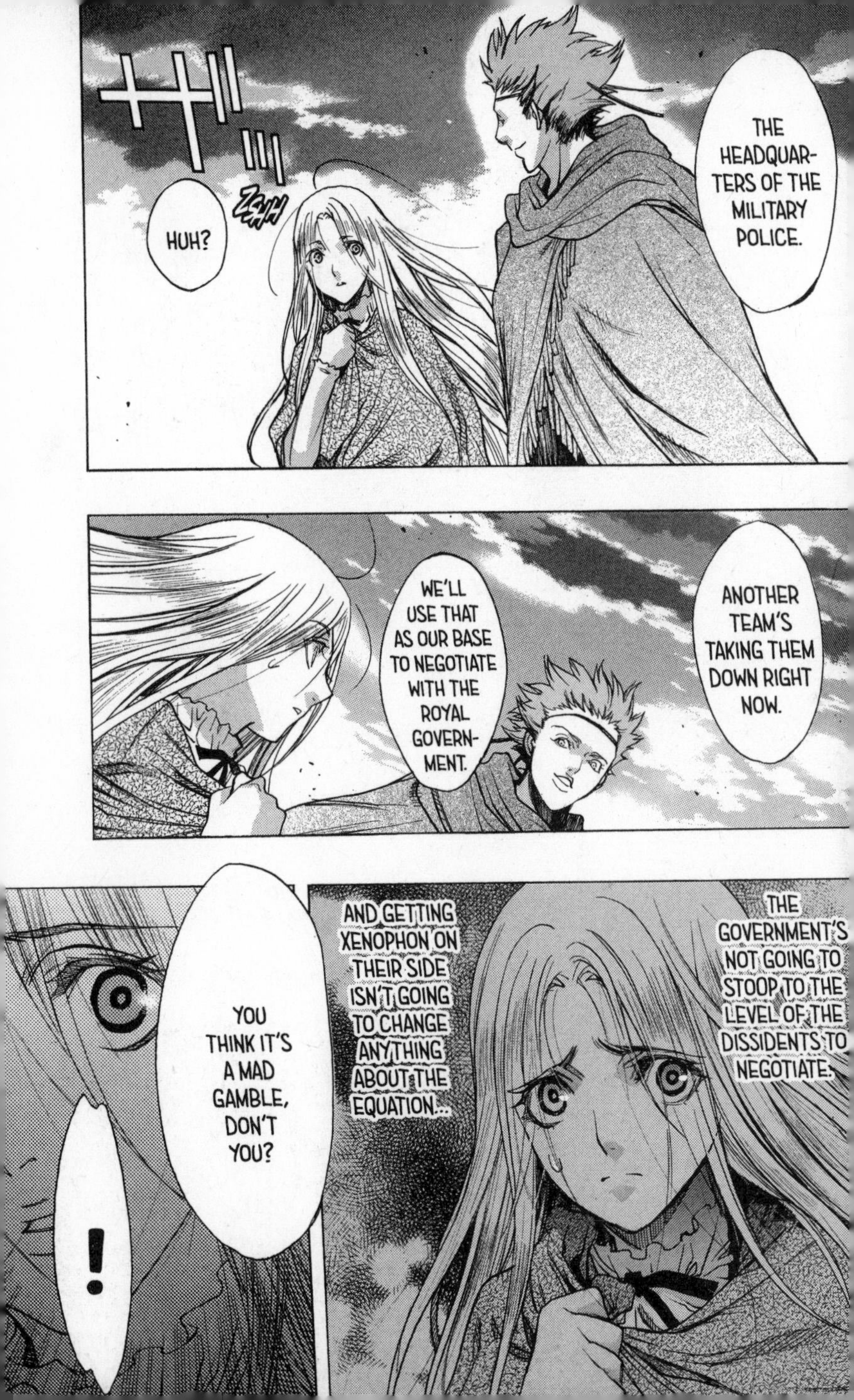
THE HEADQUARTERS OF THE MILITARY POLICE.
ZSHH
HUH?
ANOTHER TEAM'S TAKING THEM DOWN RIGHT NOW.
WE'LL USE THAT AS OUR BASE TO NEGOTIATE WITH THE ROYAL GOVERNMENT.
THE GOVERNMENT'S NOT GOING TO STOOP TO THE LEVEL OF THE DISSIDENTS TO NEGOTIATE.
AND GETTING XENOPHON ON THEIR SIDE ISN'T GOING TO CHANGE ANYTHING ABOUT THE EQUATION...
YOU THINK IT'S A MAD GAMBLE, DON'T YOU?
!

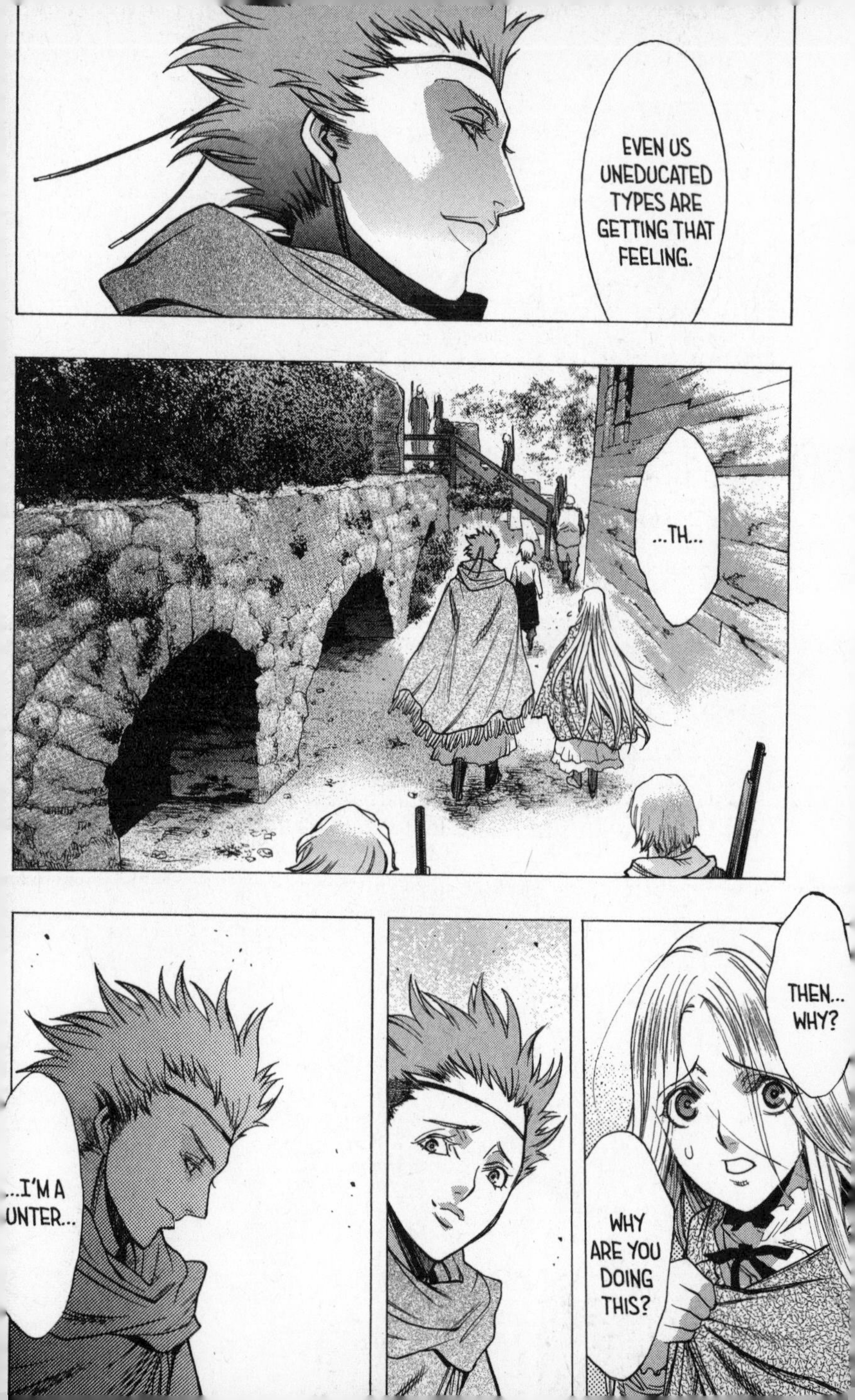
EVEN US UNEDUCATED TYPES ARE GETTING THAT FEELING.
...TH...
THEN... WHY?
WHY ARE YOU DOING THIS?
...I'M A UNTER...

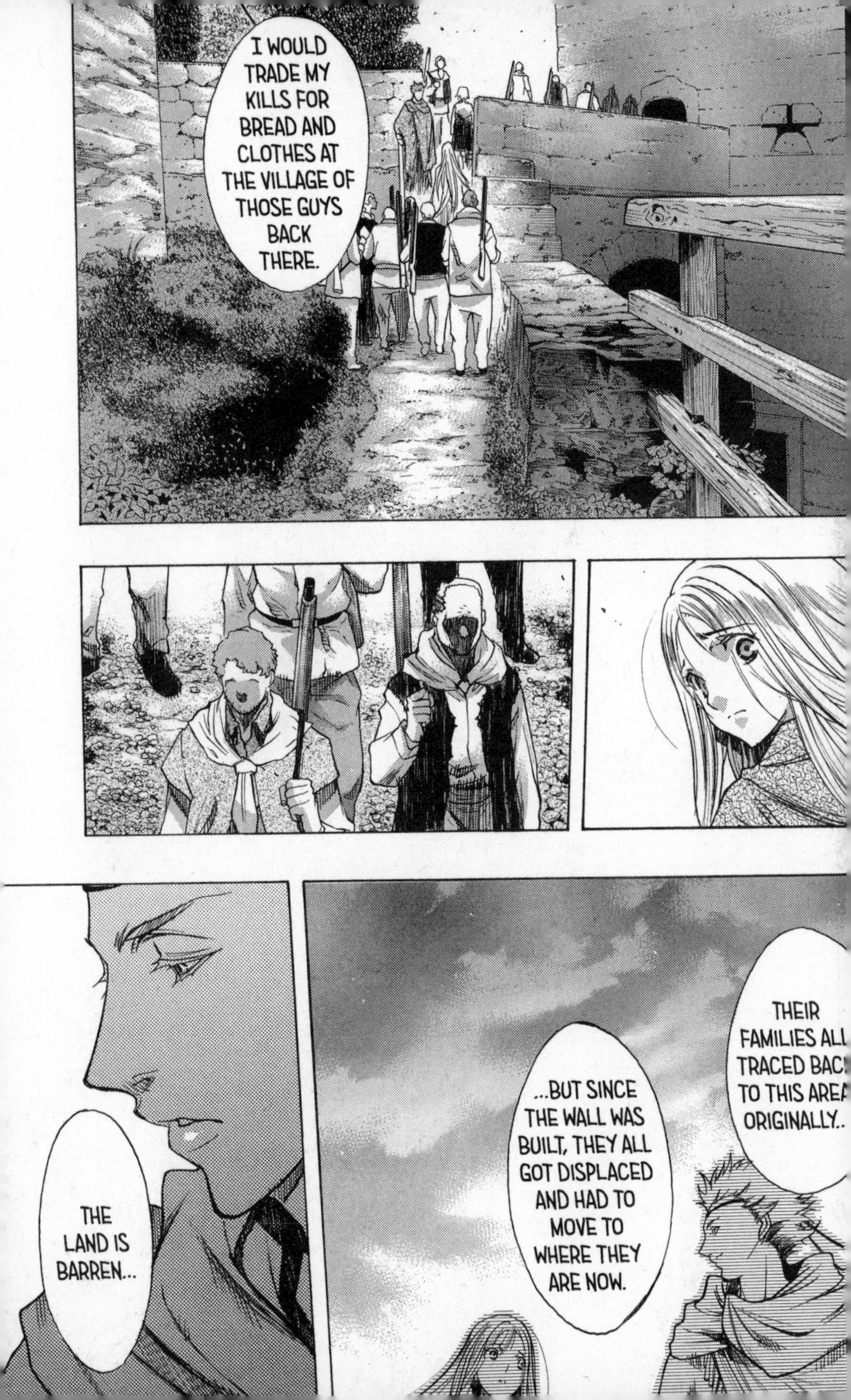
I WOULD TRADE MY KILLS FOR BREAD AND CLOTHES AT THE VILLAGE OF THOSE GUYS BACK THERE.
THEIR FAMILIES ALL TRACED BACK TO THIS AREA ORIGINALLY..
...BUT SINCE THE WALL WAS BUILT, THEY ALL GOT DISPLACED AND HAD TO MOVE TO WHERE THEY ARE NOW.
THE LAND IS BARREN...

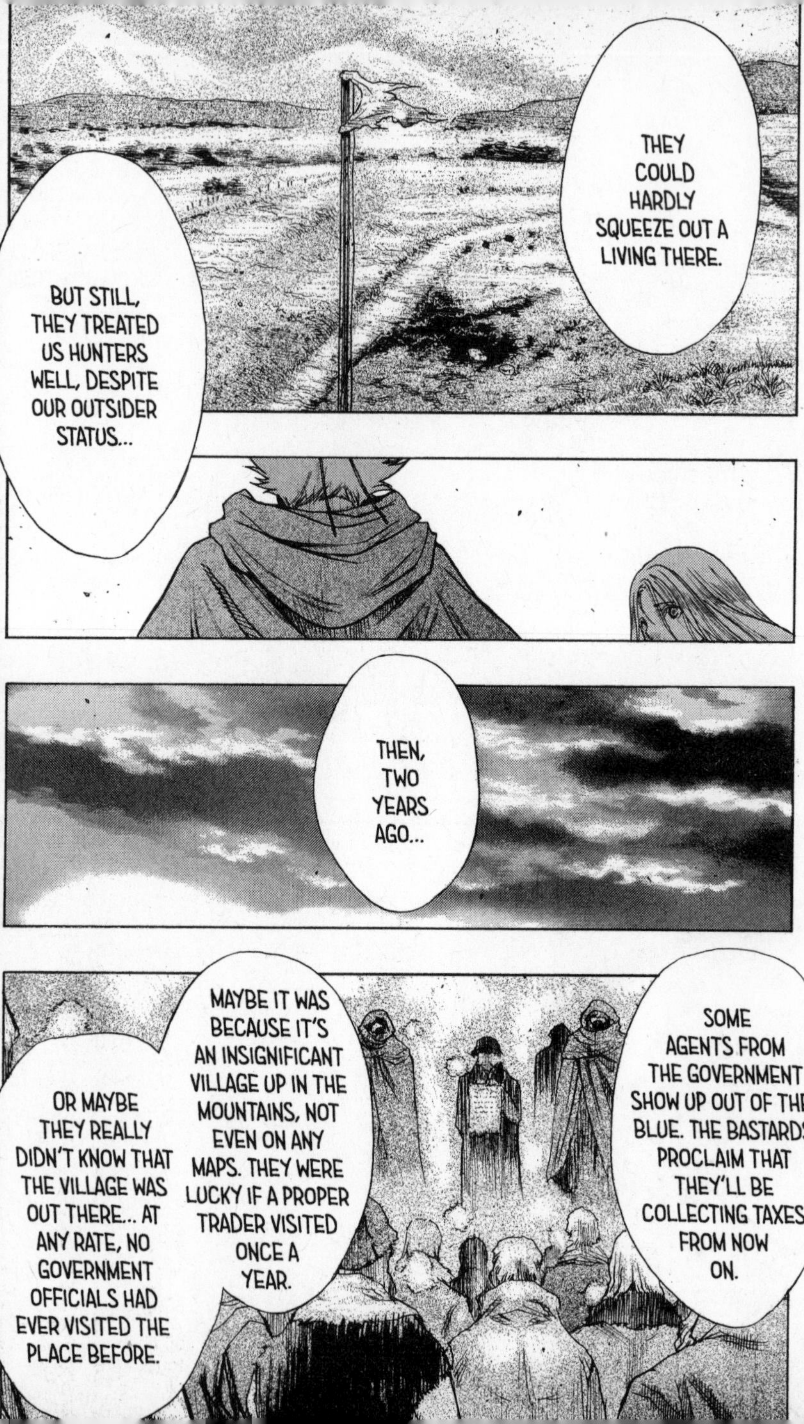
THEY COULD HARDLY SQUEEZE OUT A LIVING THERE.
BUT STILL, THEY TREATED US HUNTERS WELL, DESPITE OUR OUTSIDER STATUS...
THEN, TWO YEARS AGO...
SOME AGENTS FROM THE GOVERNMENT SHOW UP OUT OF THE BLUE. THE BASTARDS PROCLAIM THAT THEY'LL BE COLLECTING TAXES FROM NOW ON.
MAYBE IT WAS BECAUSE IT'S AN INSIGNIFICANT VILLAGE UP IN THE MOUNTAINS, NOT EVEN ON ANY MAPS. THEY WERE LUCKY IF A PROPER TRADER VISITED ONCE A YEAR.
OR MAYBE THEY REALLY DIDN'T KNOW THAT THE VILLAGE WAS OUT THERE... AT ANY RATE, NO GOVERNMENT OFFICIALS HAD EVER VISITED THE PLACE BEFORE.

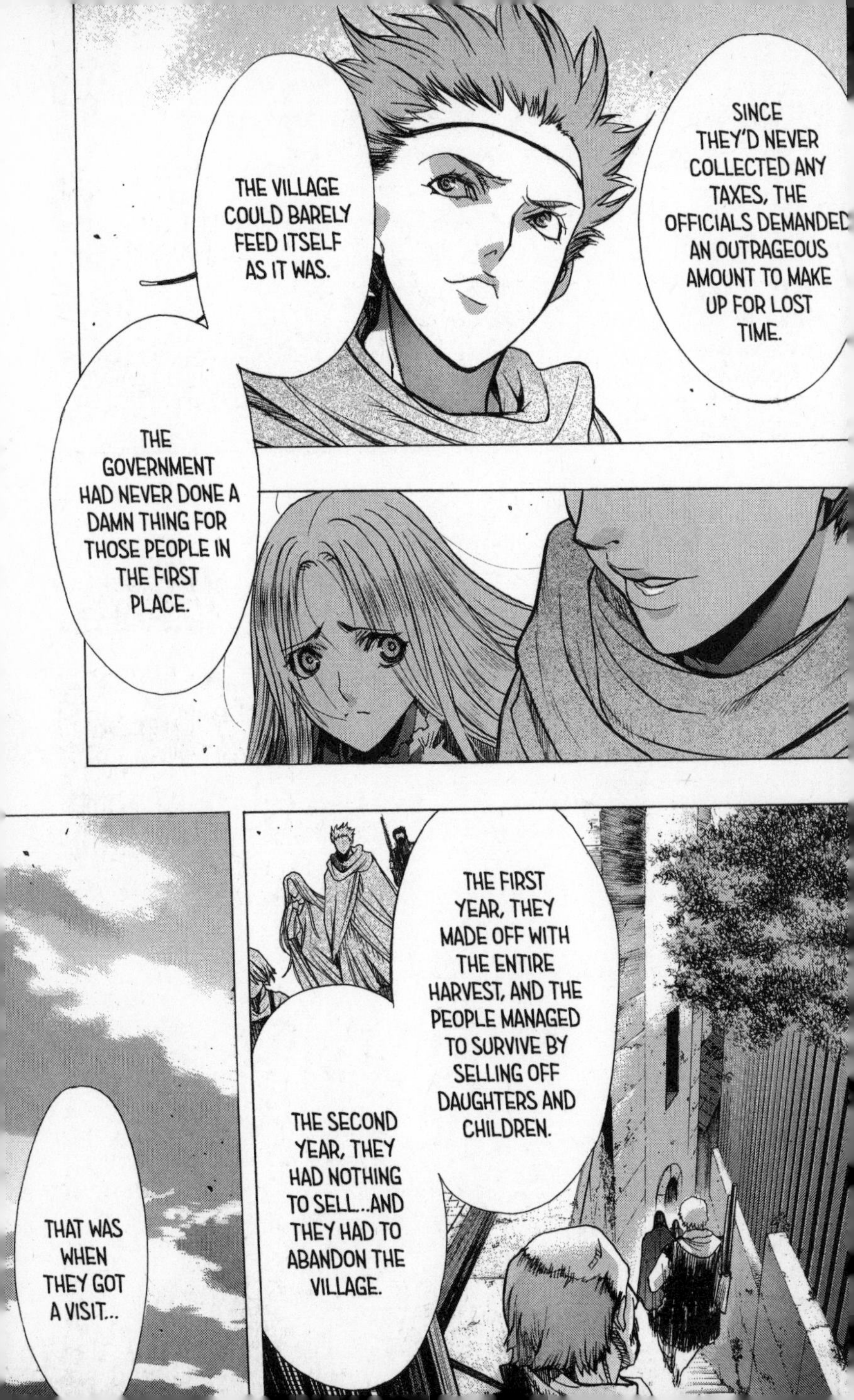
SINCE THEY'D NEVER COLLECTED ANY TAXES, THE OFFICIALS DEMANDED AN OUTRAGEOUS AMOUNT TO MAKE UP FOR LOST TIME.
THE VILLAGE COULD BARELY FEED ITSELF AS IT WAS.
THE GOVERNMENT HAD NEVER DONE A DAMN THING FOR THOSE PEOPLE IN THE FIRST PLACE.
THE FIRST YEAR, THEY MADE OFF WITH THE ENTIRE HARVEST, AND THE PEOPLE MANAGED TO SURVIVE BY SELLING OFF DAUGHTERS AND CHILDREN.
THE SECOND YEAR, THEY HAD NOTHING TO SELL...AND THEY HAD TO ABANDON THE VILLAGE.
THAT WAS WHEN THEY GOT A VISIT...

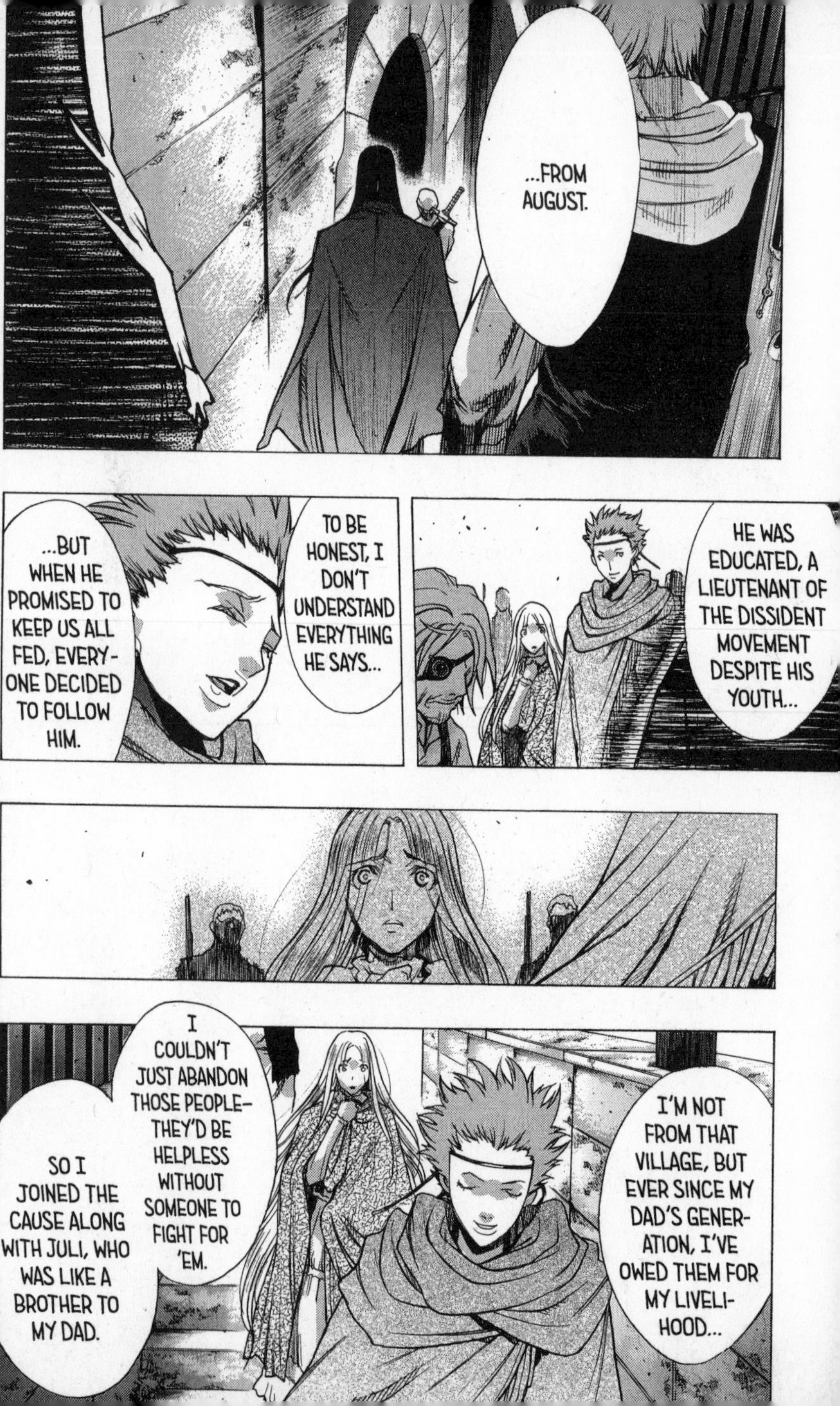
...FROM AUGUST.
HE WAS EDUCATED, A LIEUTENANT OF THE DISSIDENT MOVEMENT DESPITE HIS YOUTH...
TO BE HONEST, I DON'T UNDERSTAND EVERYTHING HE SAYS...
...BUT WHEN HE PROMISED TO KEEP US ALL FED, EVERYONE DECIDED TO FOLLOW HIM.
I'M NOT FROM THAT VILLAGE, BUT EVER SINCE MY DAD'S GENERATION, I'VE OWED THEM FOR MY LIVELIHOOD...
I COULDN'T JUST ABANDON THOSE PEOPLE—THEY'D BE HELPLESS WITHOUT SOMEONE TO FIGHT FOR 'EM.
SO I JOINED THE CAUSE ALONG WITH JULI, WHO WAS LIKE A BROTHER TO MY DAD.

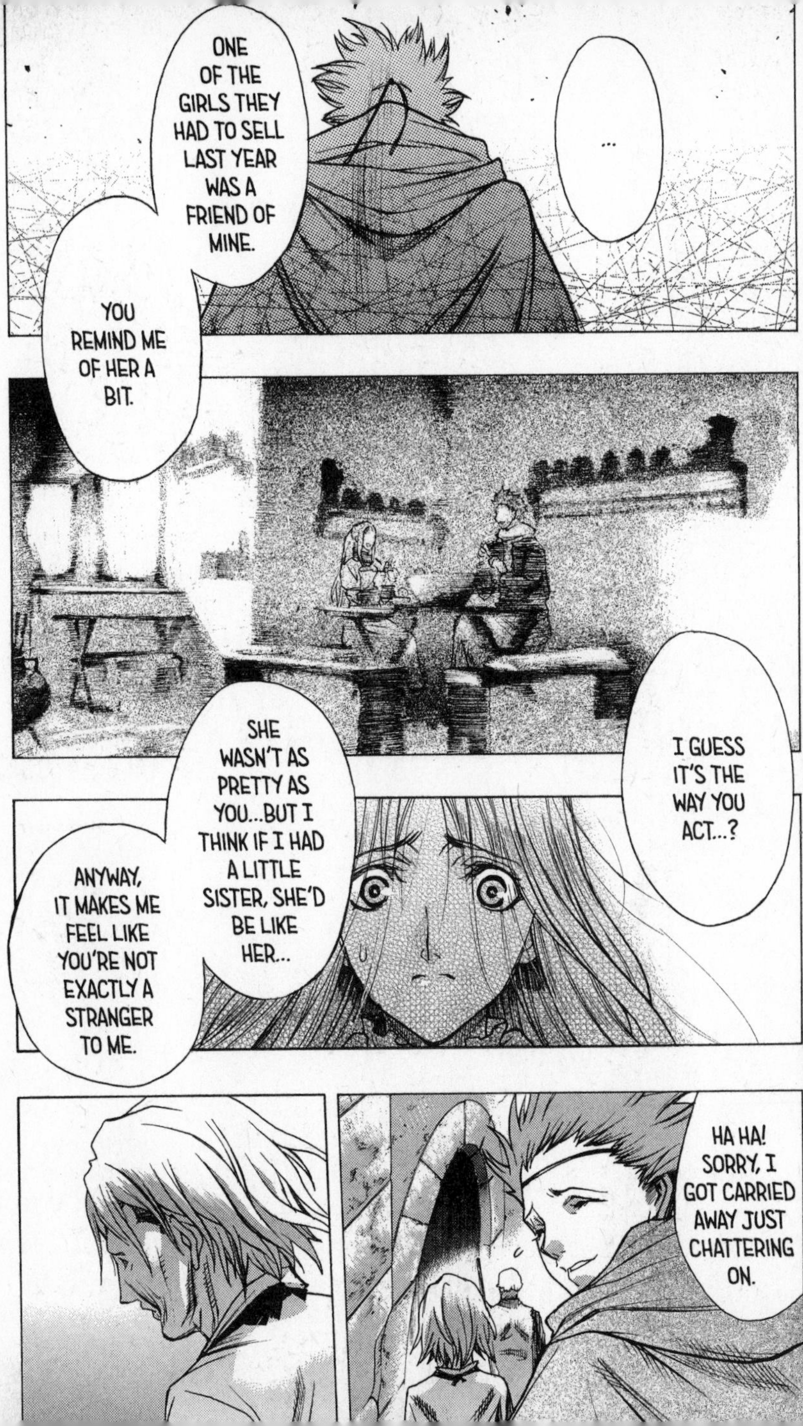
...
ONE OF THE GIRLS THEY HAD TO SELL LAST YEAR WAS A FRIEND OF MINE.
YOU REMIND ME OF HER A BIT.
I GUESS IT'S THE WAY YOU ACT...?
SHE WASN'T AS PRETTY AS YOU...BUT I THINK IF I HAD A LITTLE SISTER, SHE'D BE LIKE HER...
ANYWAY, IT MAKES ME FEEL LIKE YOU'RE NOT EXACTLY A STRANGER TO ME.
HA HA! SORRY, I GOT CARRIED AWAY JUST CHATTERING ON.

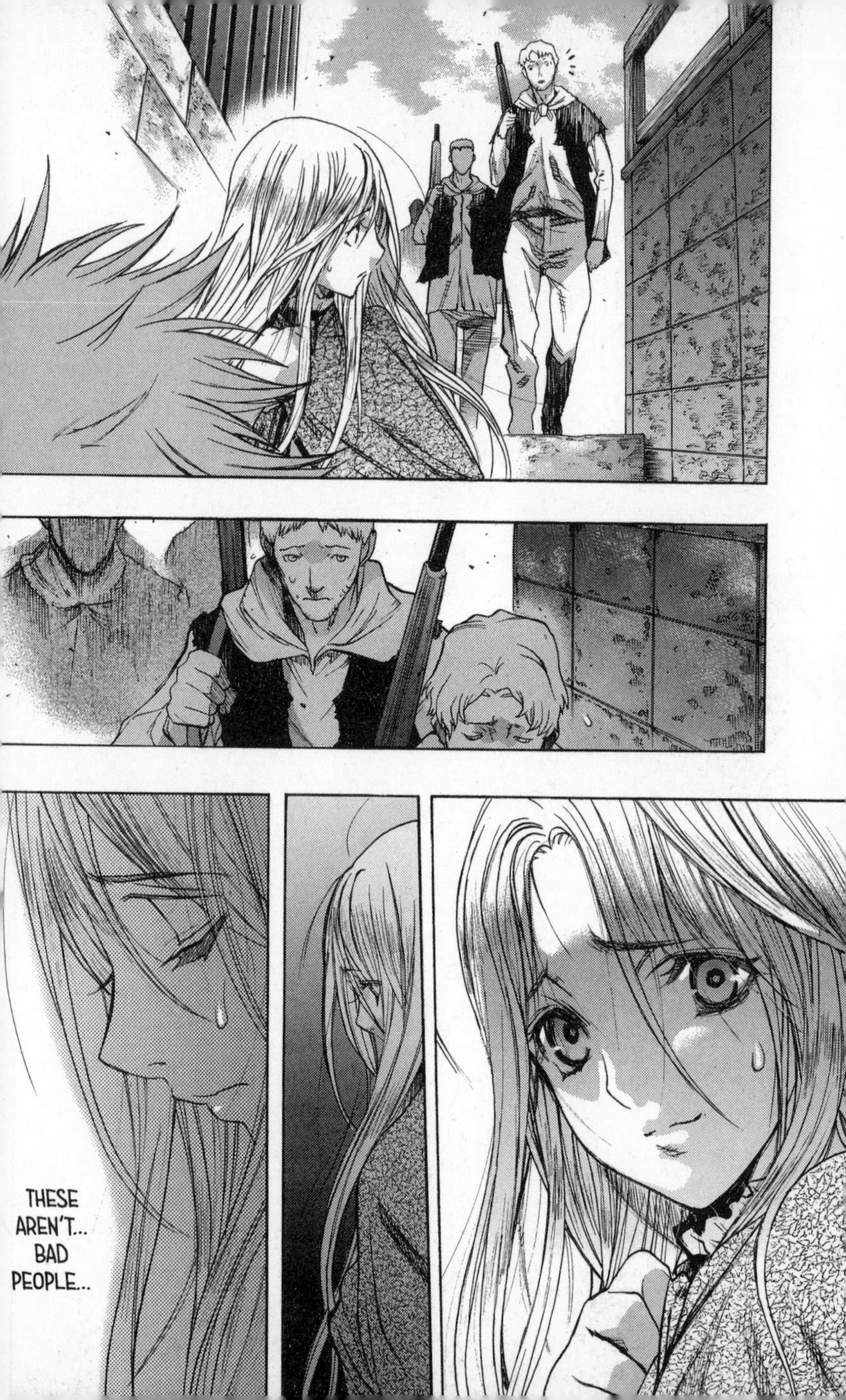
THESE AREN'T... BAD PEOPLE...

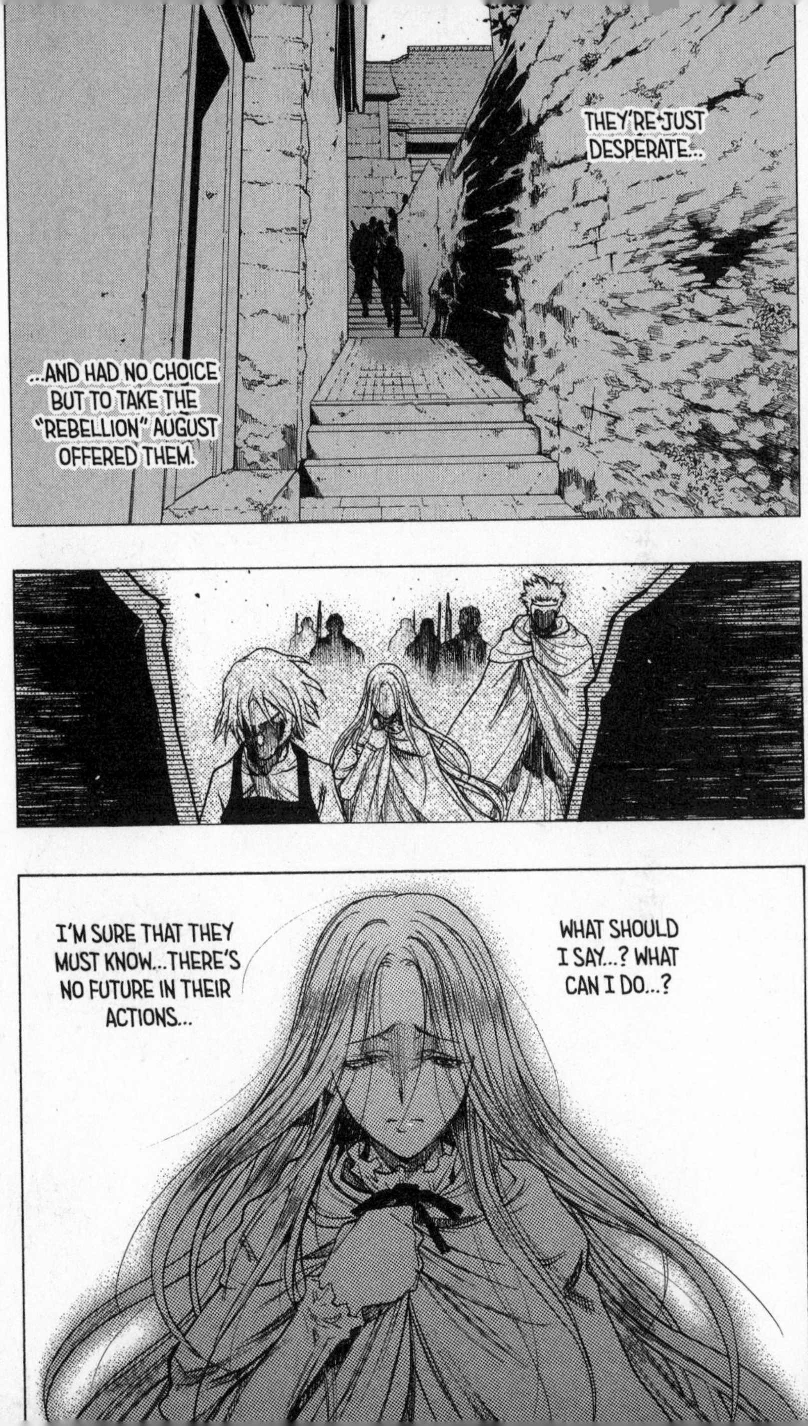
THEY'RE JUST DESPERATE...
...AND HAD NO CHOICE BUT TO TAKE THE "REBELLION" AUGUST OFFERED THEM.
WHAT SHOULD I SAY...? WHAT CAN I DO...?
I'M SURE THAT THEY MUST KNOW...THERE'S NO FUTURE IN THEIR ACTIONS...

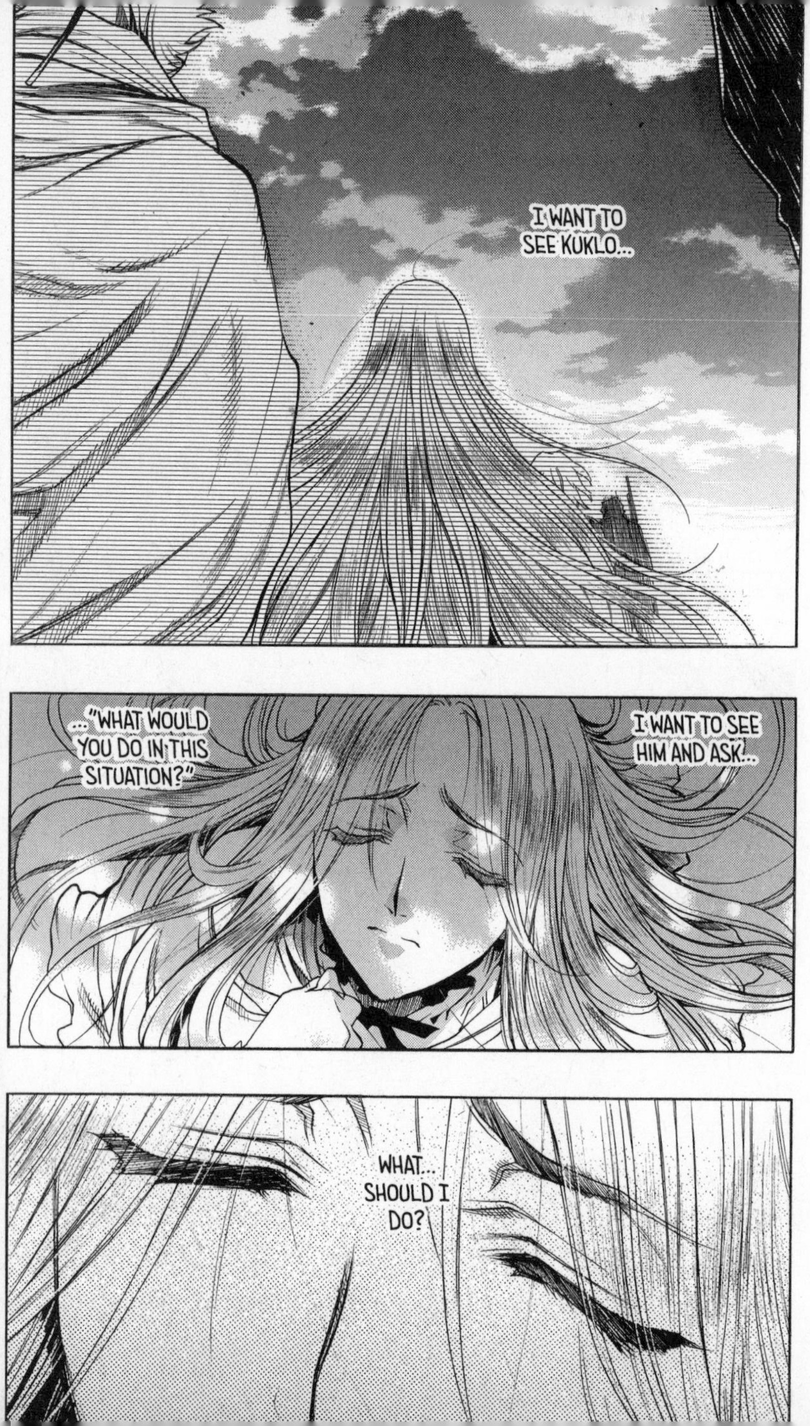
I WANT TO SEE KUKLO...
I WANT TO SEE HIM AND ASK...
..."WHAT WOULD YOU DO IN THIS SITUATION?"
WHAT... SHOULD I DO?

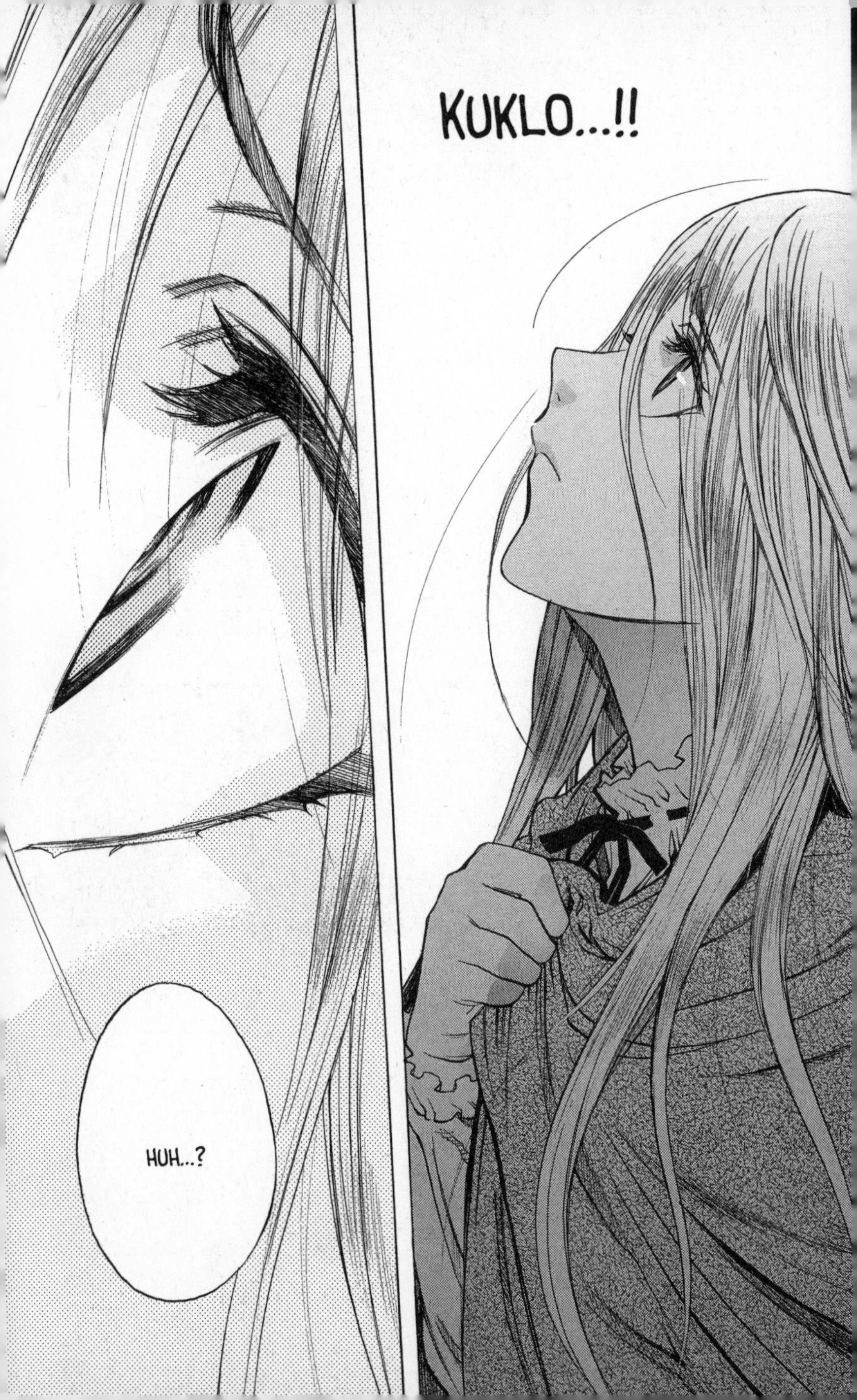
KUKLO...!!
HUH...?

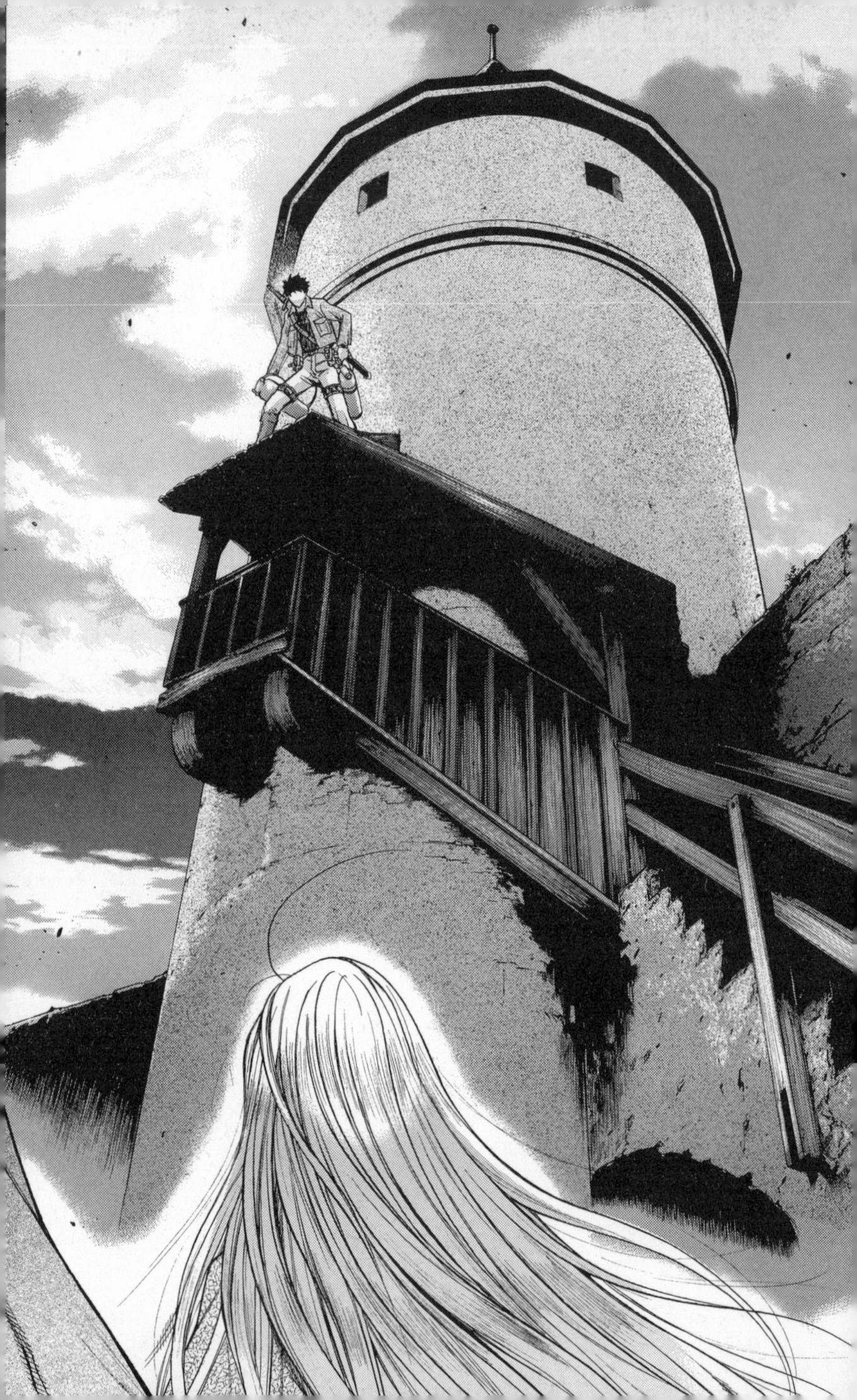

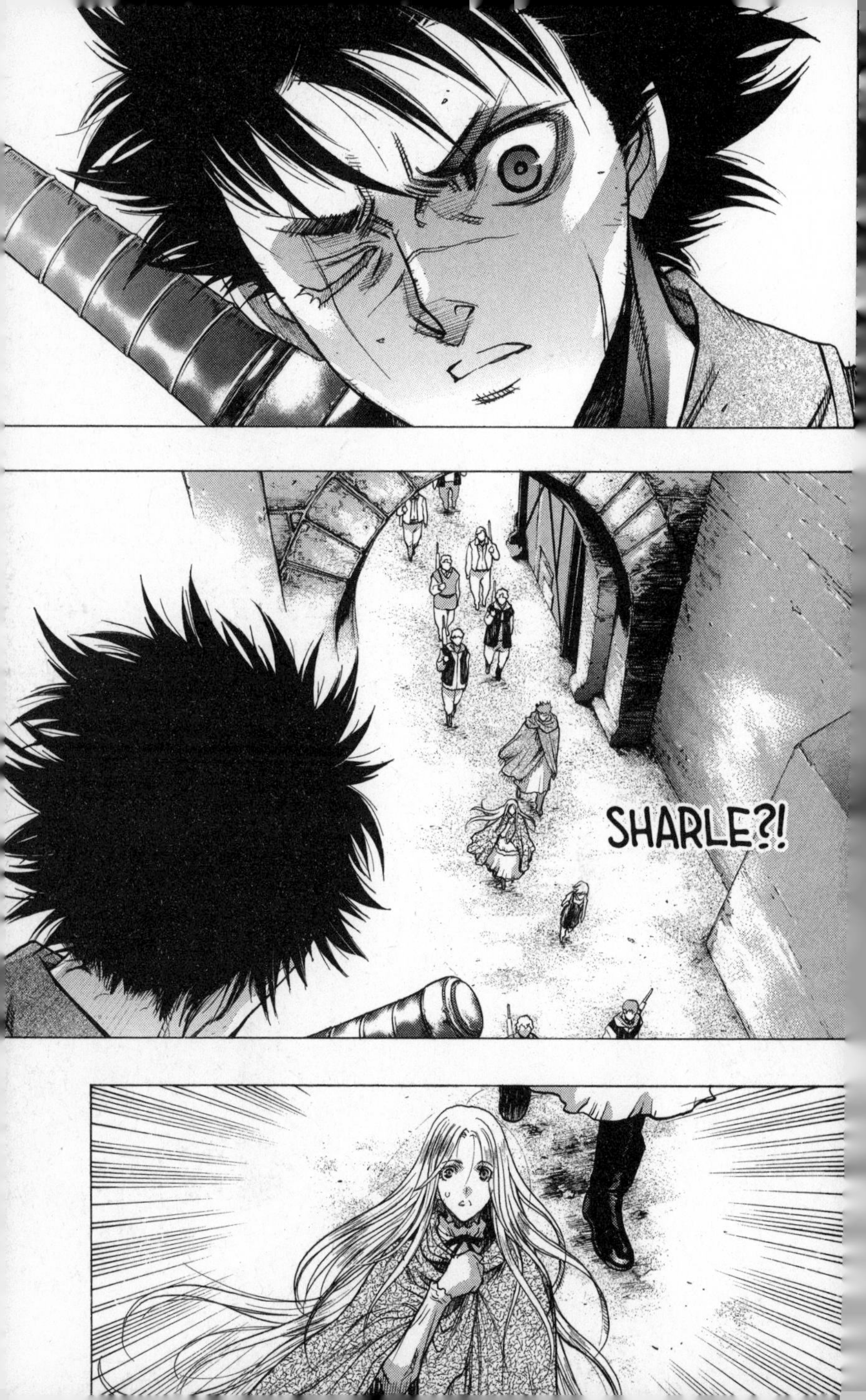
SHARLE?!

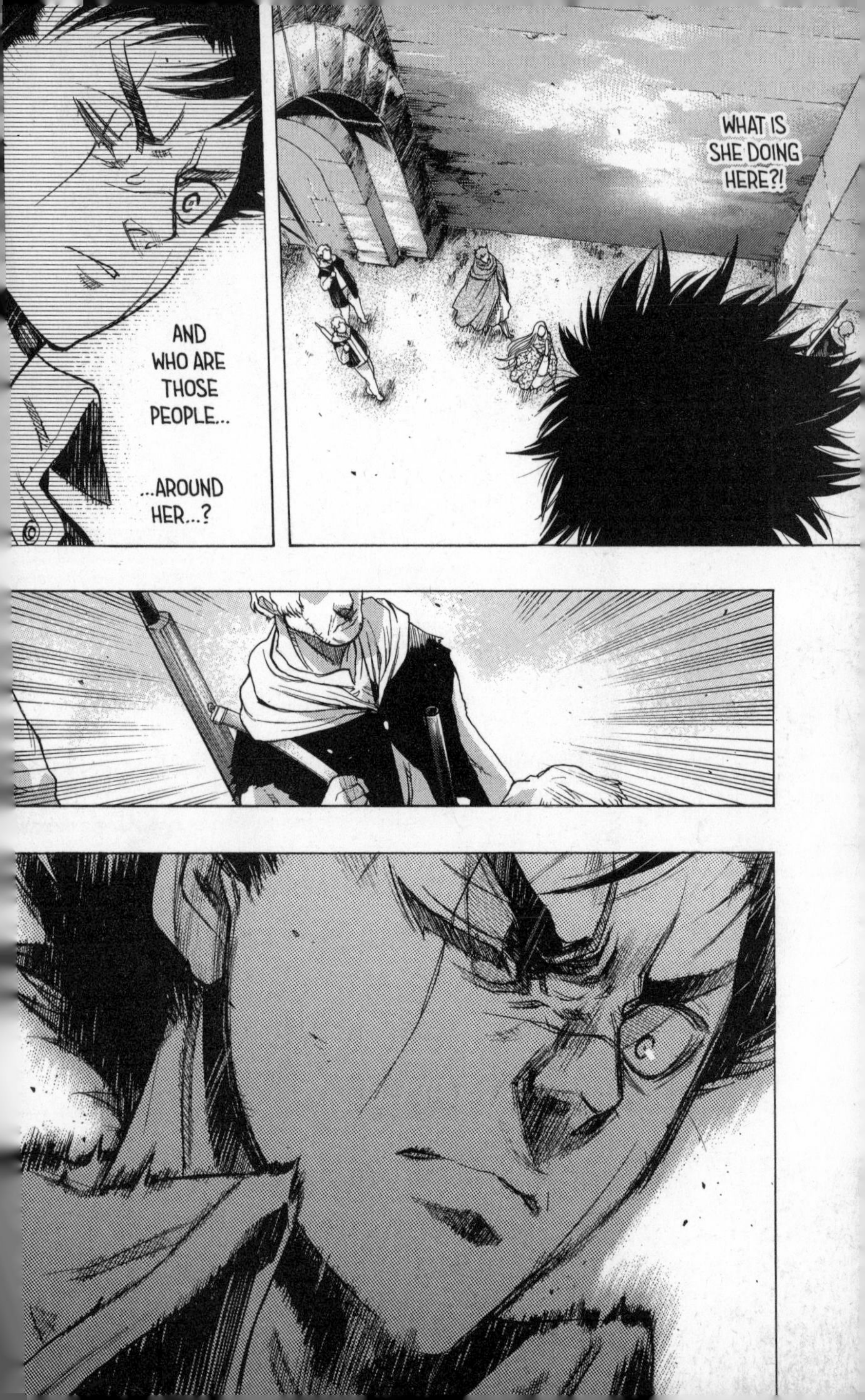
WHAT IS SHE DOING HERE?!
AND WHO ARE THOSE PEOPLE...
...AROUND HER...?

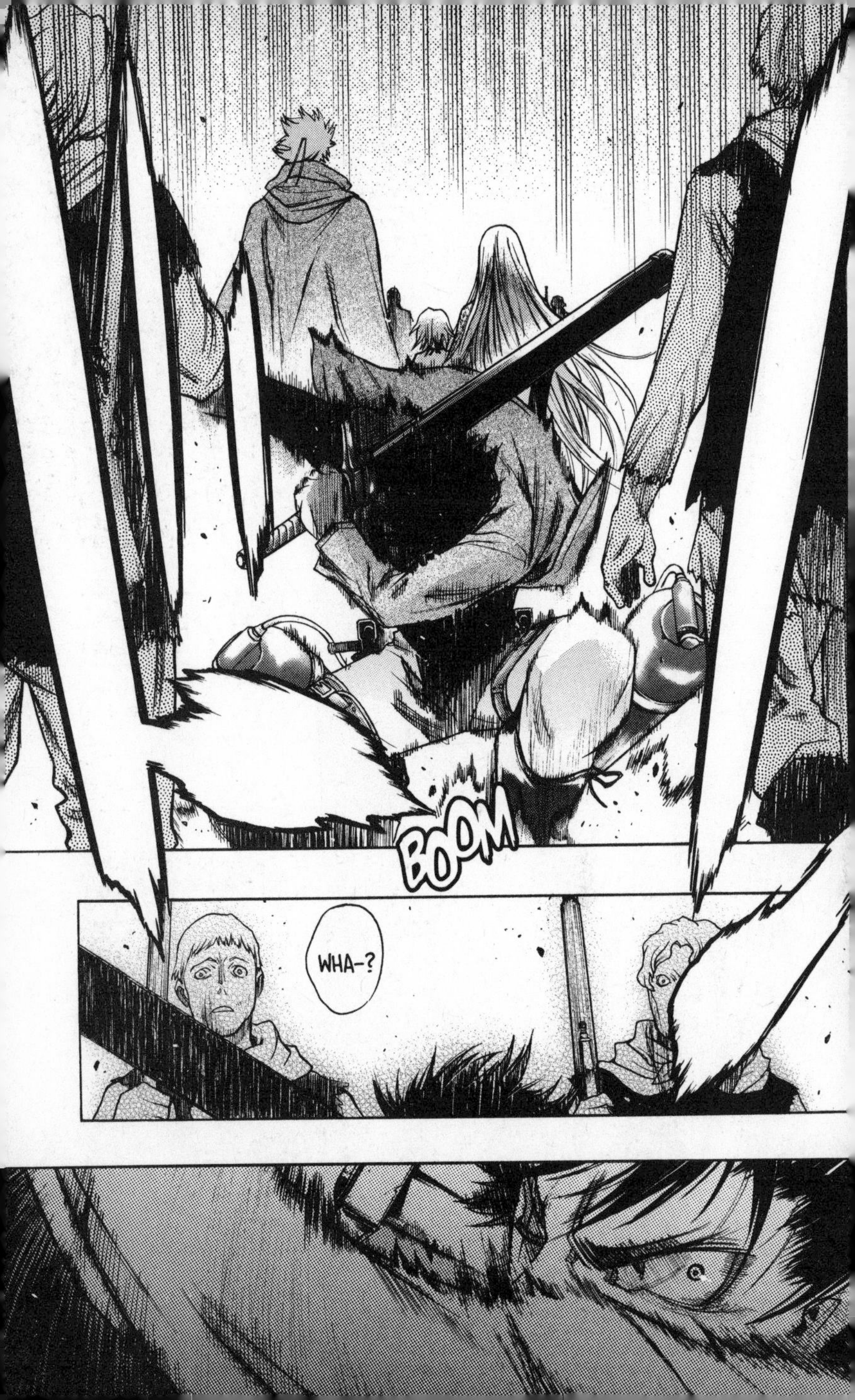
BOOM
WHA-?

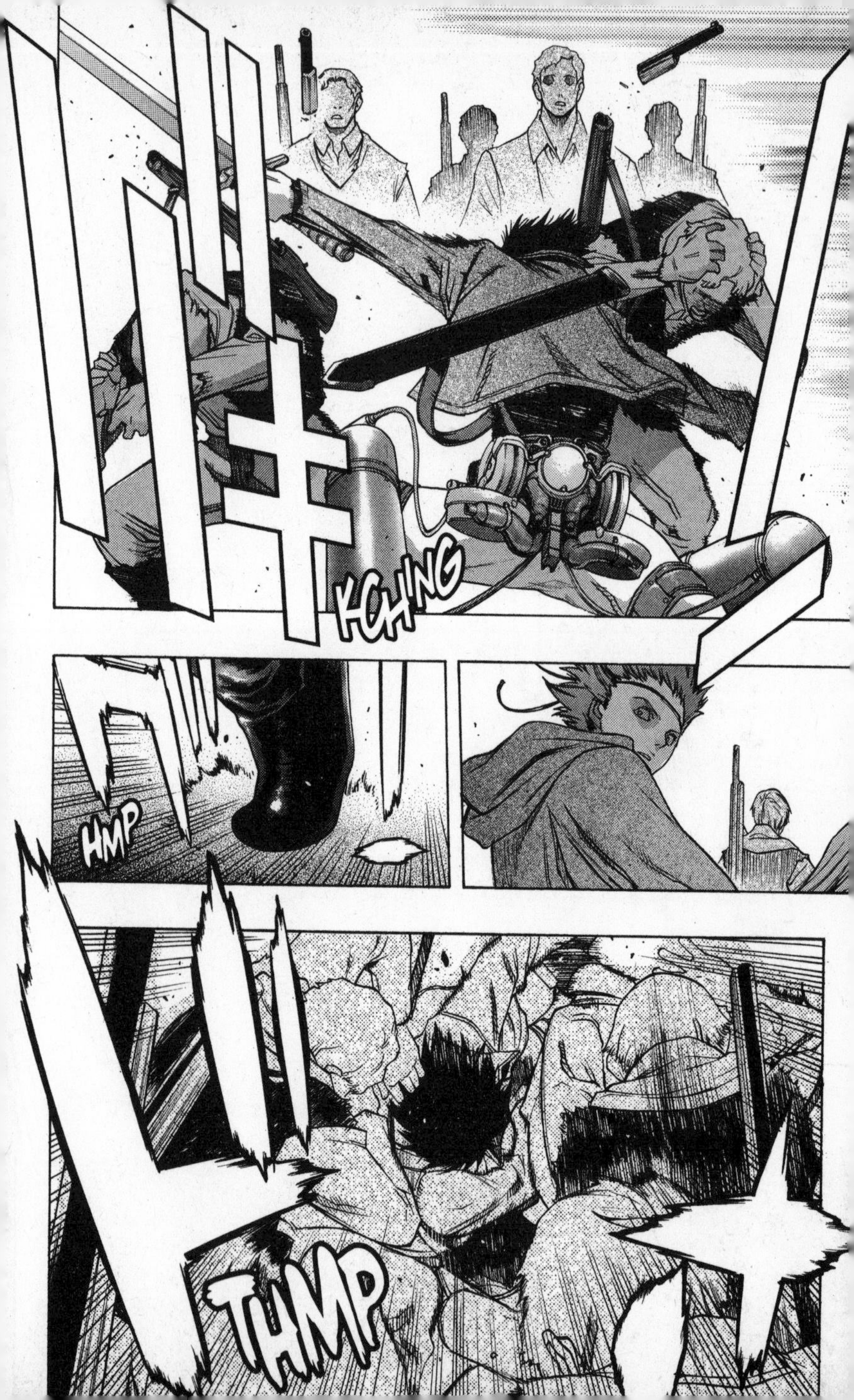
KCHING
HMP
THMP

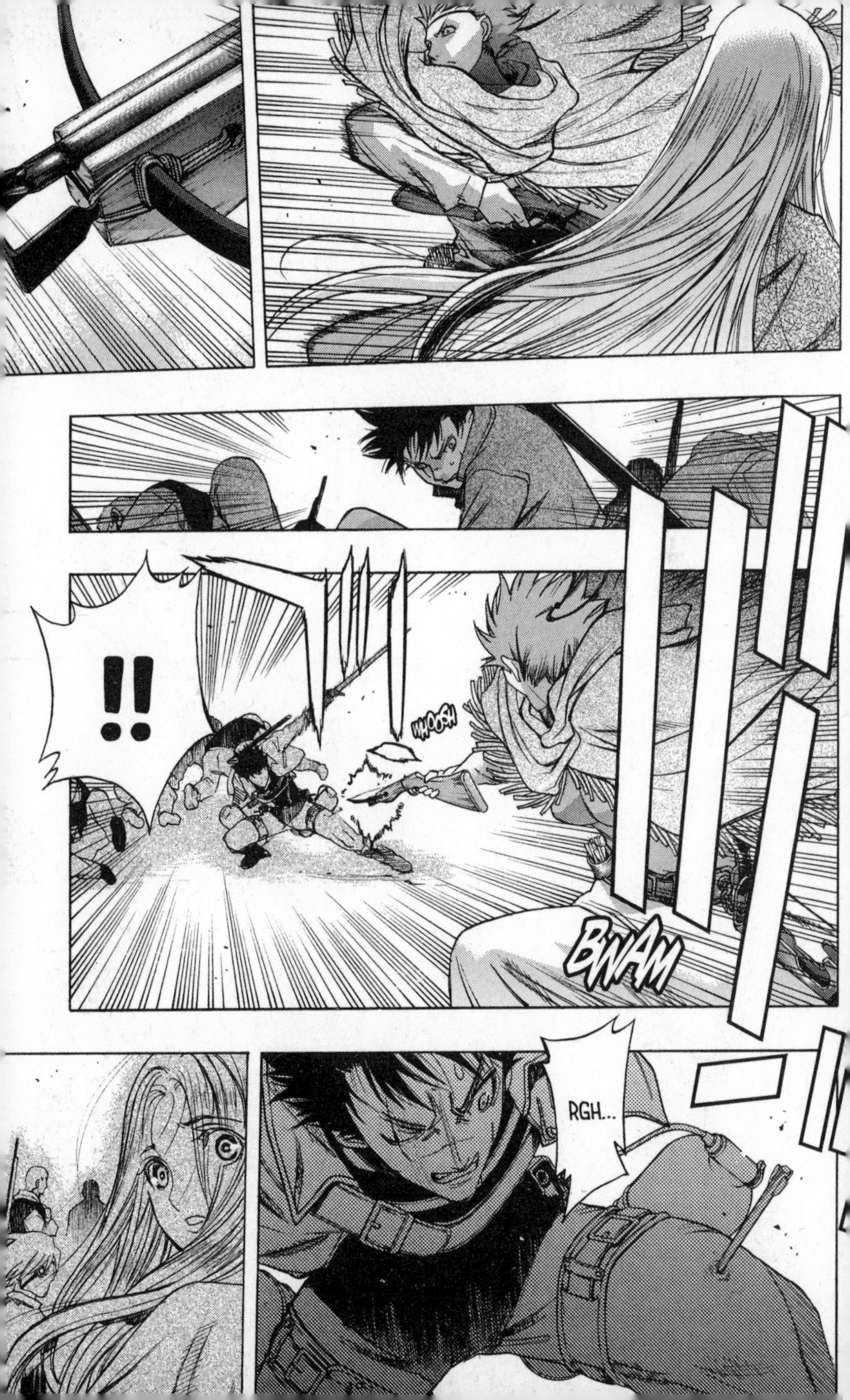
!!
WHOOSH
BWAM
RGH...

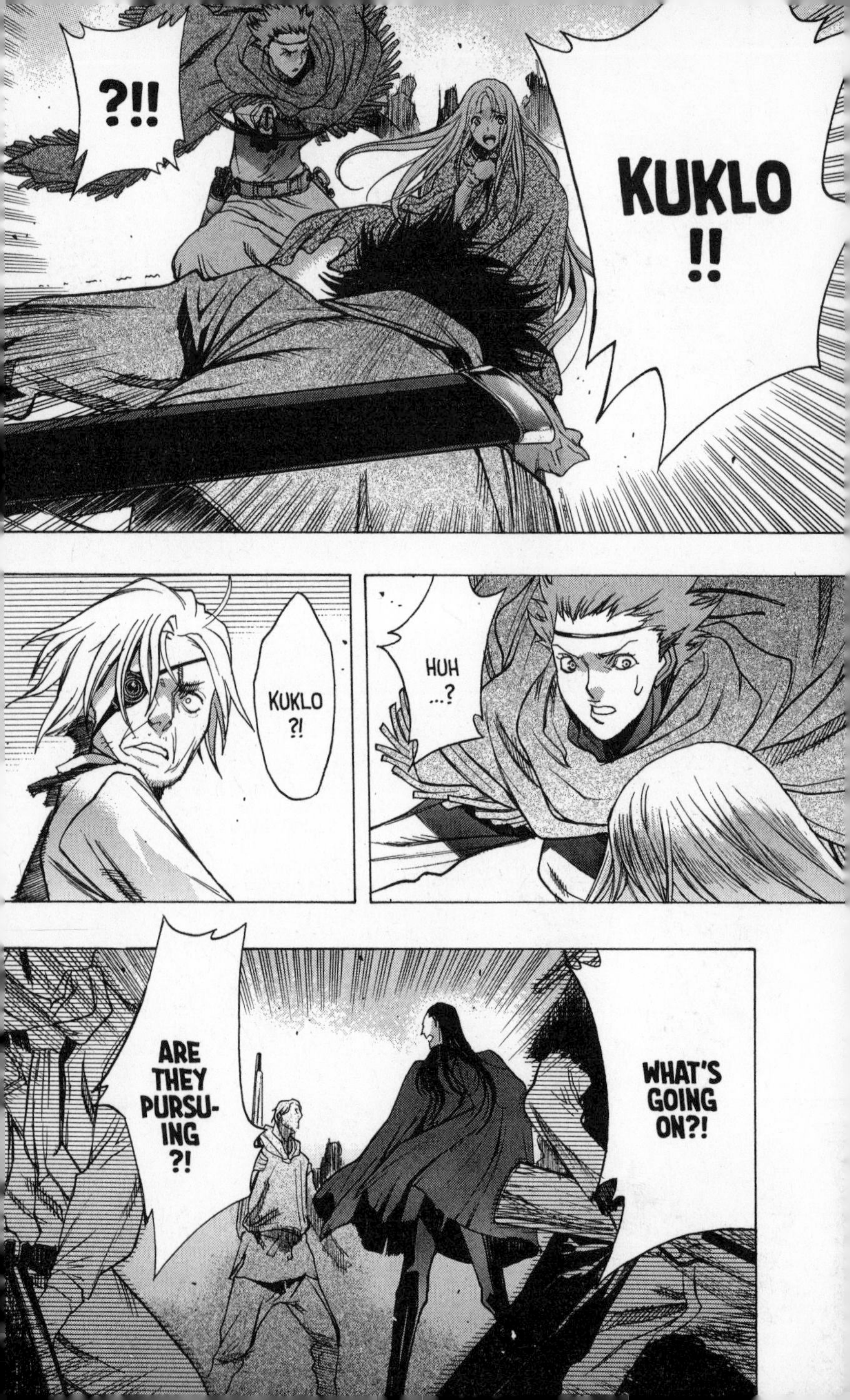
KUKLO !!
?!!
HUH ...?
KUKLO ?!
WHAT'S GOING ON?!
ARE THEY PURSU-ING ?!

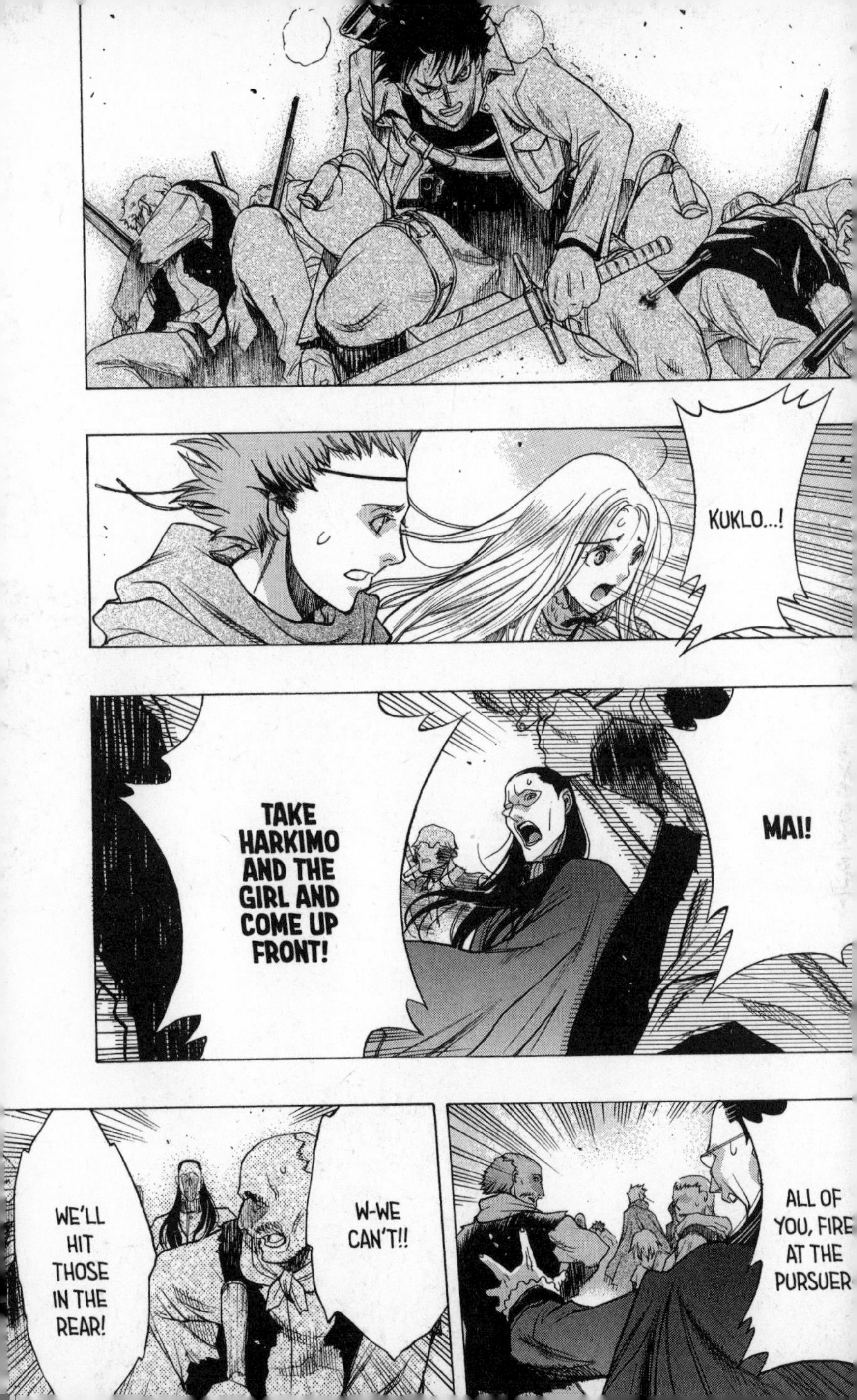
KUKLO...!
MAI!
TAKE HARKIMO AND THE GIRL AND COME UP FRONT!
ALL OF YOU, FIRE AT THE PURSUER
W-WE CAN'T!!
WE'LL HIT THOSE IN THE REAR!

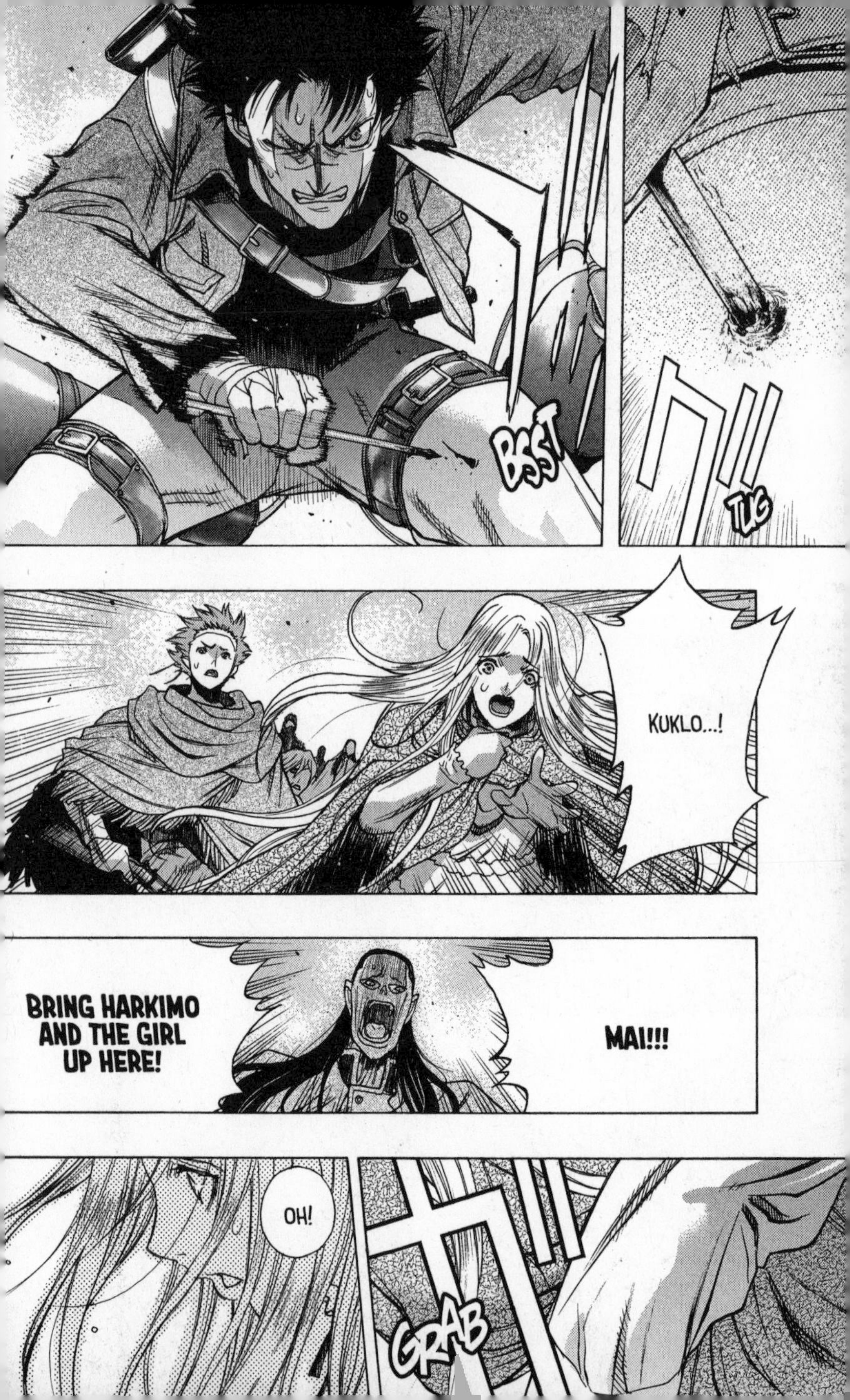

TUG
BSST
KUKLO...!
MAI!!!
BRING HARKIMO AND THE GIRL UP HERE!
GRAB
OH!

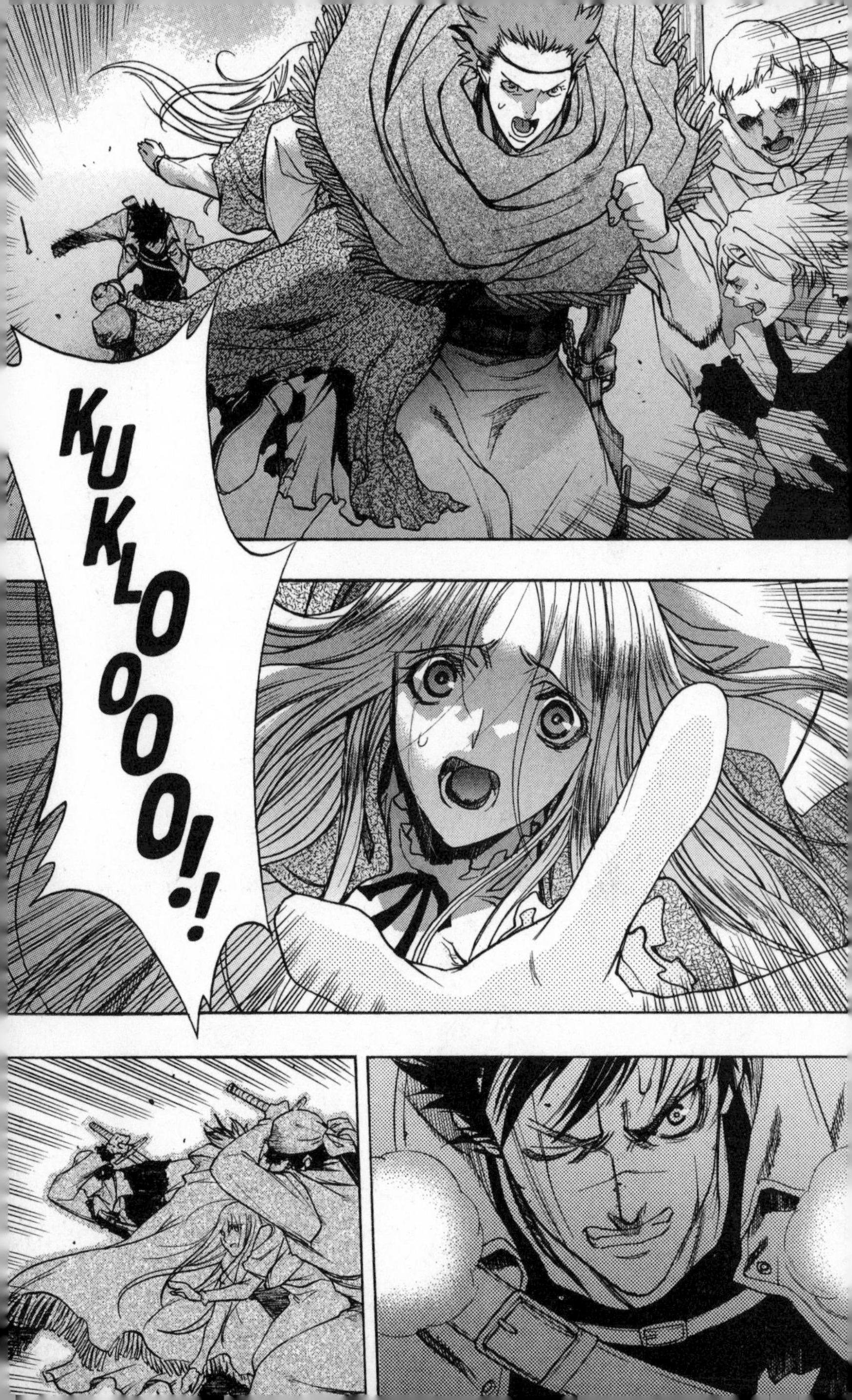
KUKLOOOO!!

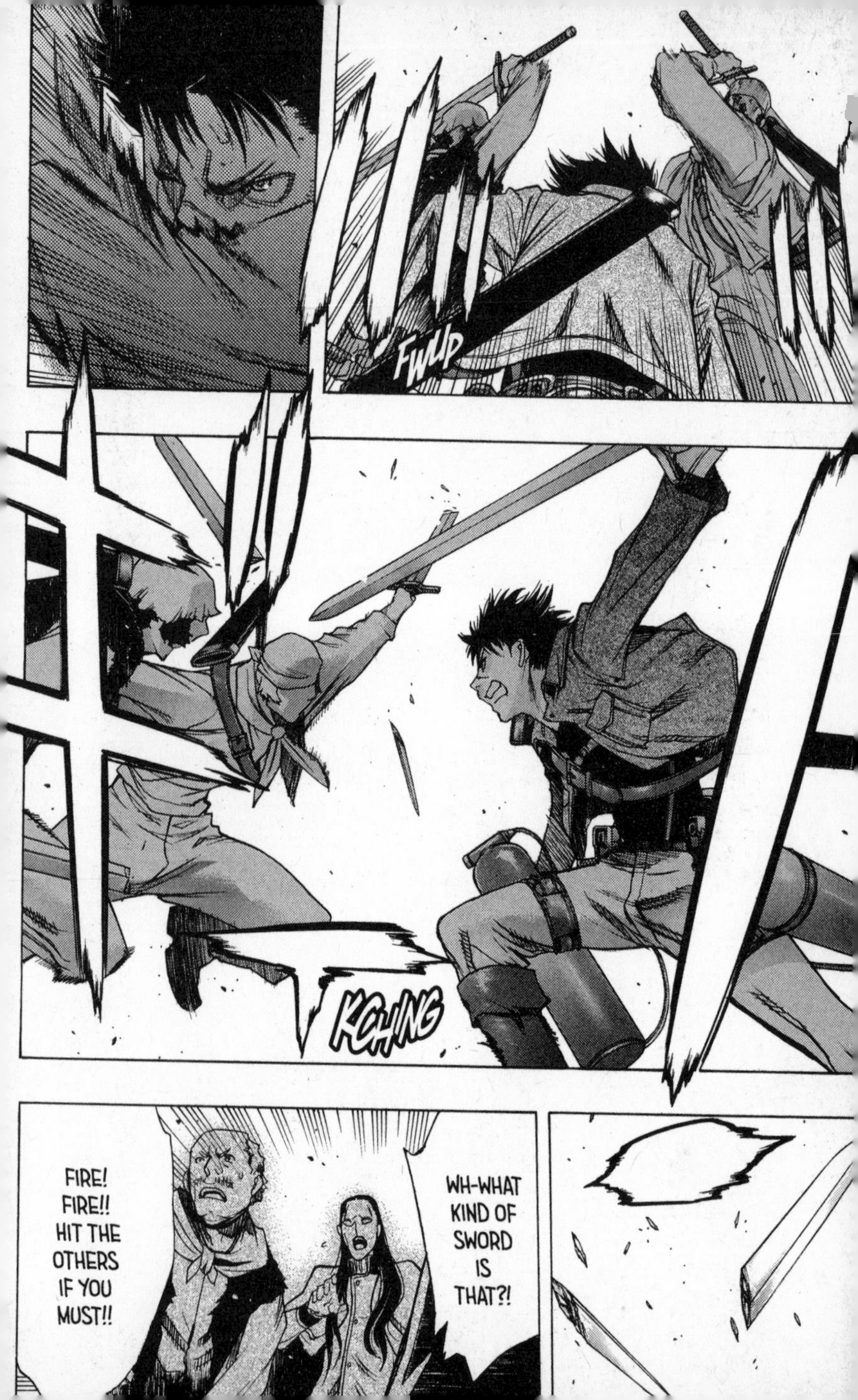
FWUP
KCHING
WH-WHAT KIND OF SWORD IS THAT?!
FIRE! FIRE!! HIT THE OTHERS IF YOU MUST!!

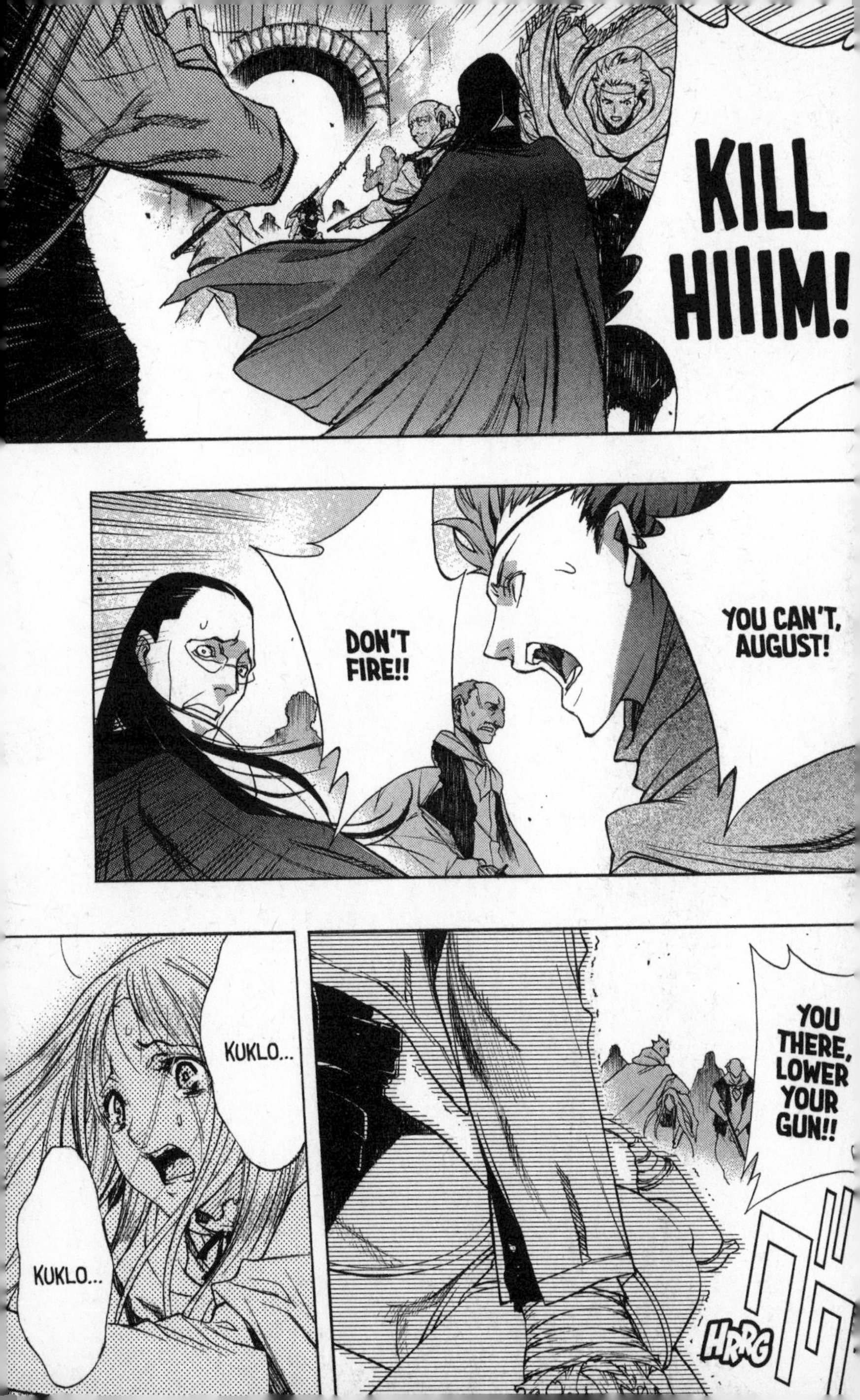
KILL HIIIM!
YOU CAN'T, AUGUST!
DON'T FIRE!!
YOU THERE, LOWER YOUR GUN!!
HRRG
KUKLO...
KUKLO...

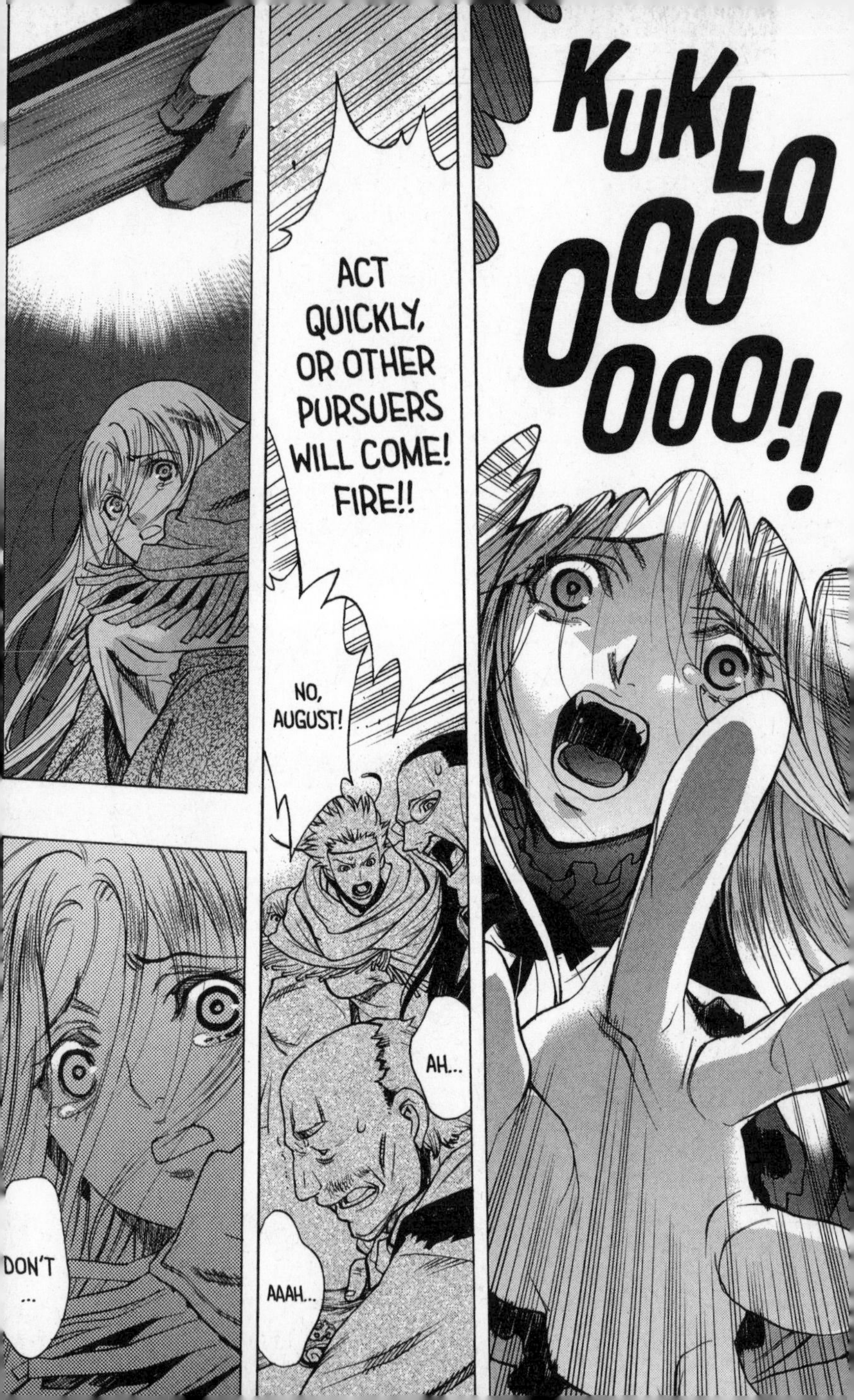
KUKLOOOOOOO!!
ACT QUICKLY, OR OTHER PURSUERS WILL COME! FIRE!!
NO, AUGUST!
AH...
AAAH...
DON'T ...

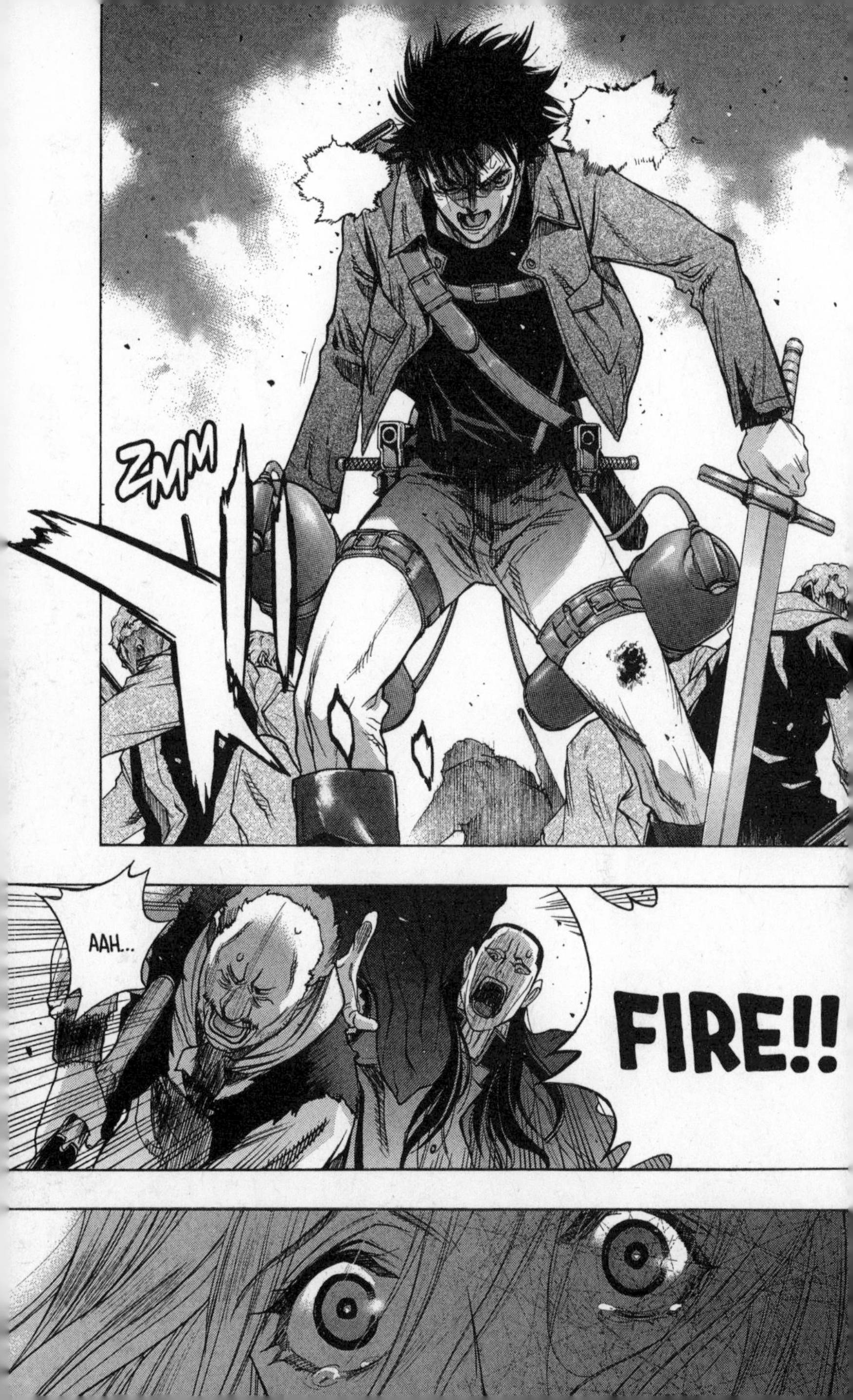
ZMM
FIRE!!
AAH...

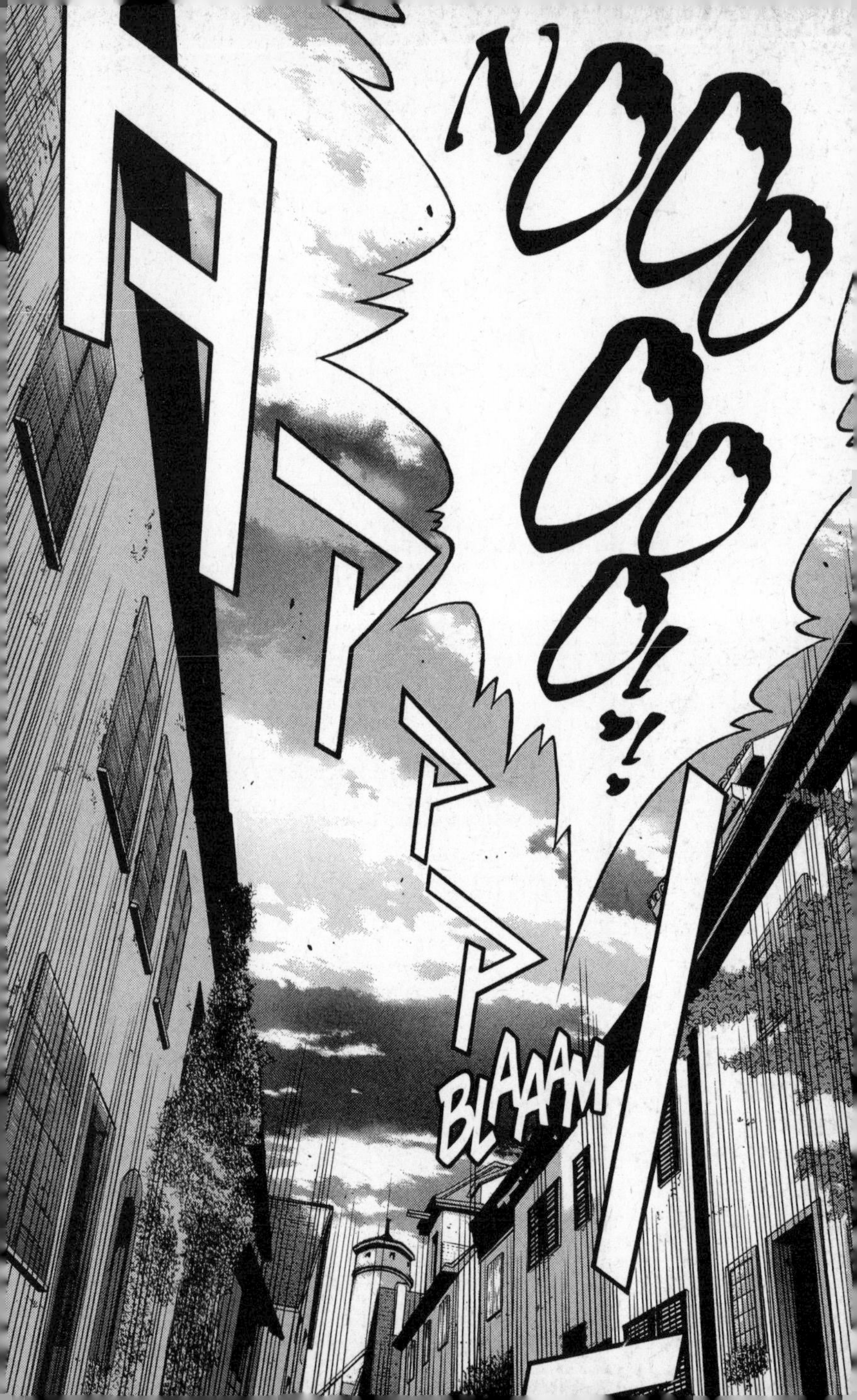
NOOOOOO!!
BLAAAM

Chapter 29: Disturbance in the City · End

ATTACK on TITAN

BEFORE THE FALL

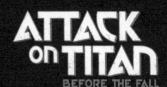

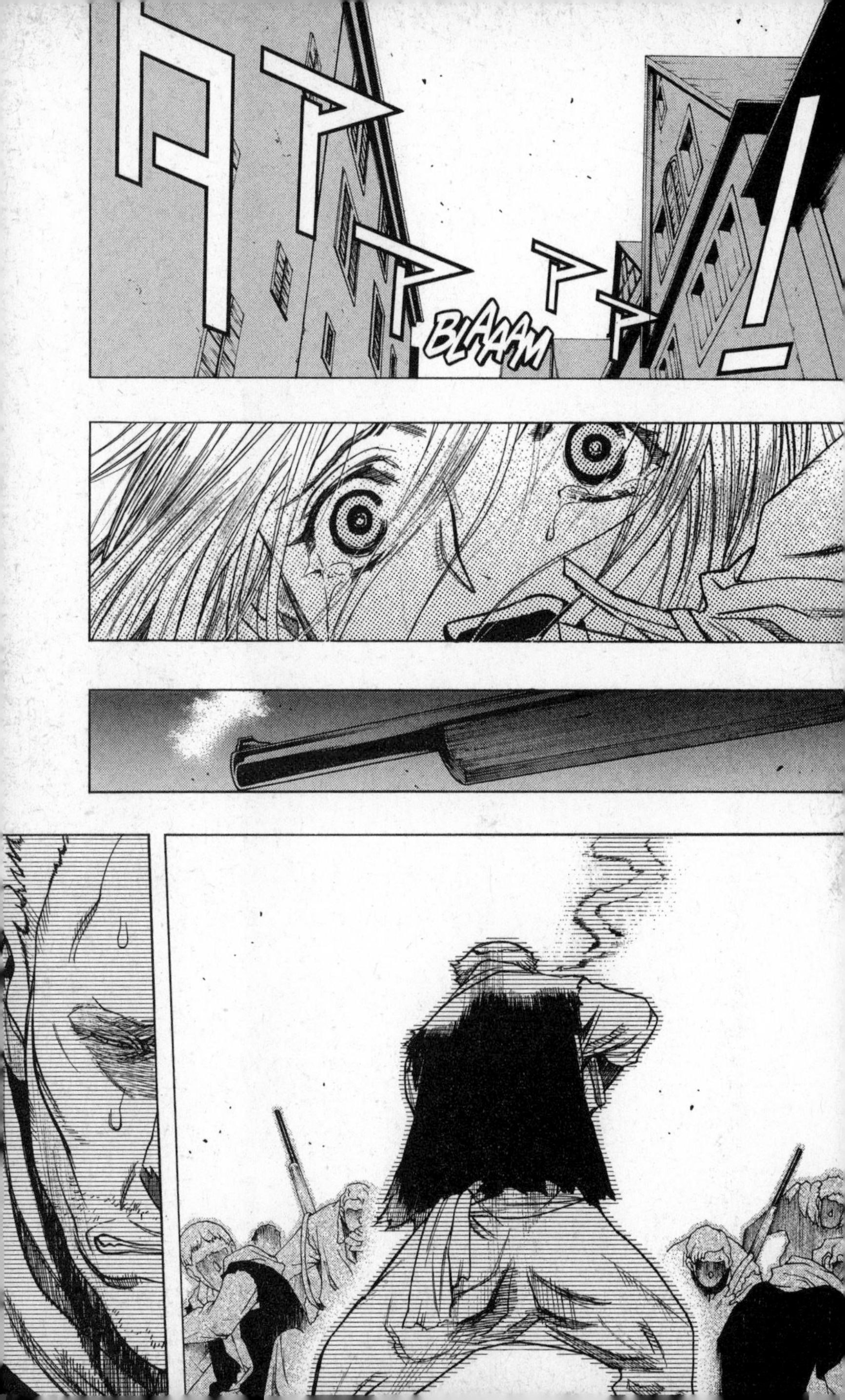

BLAAAM

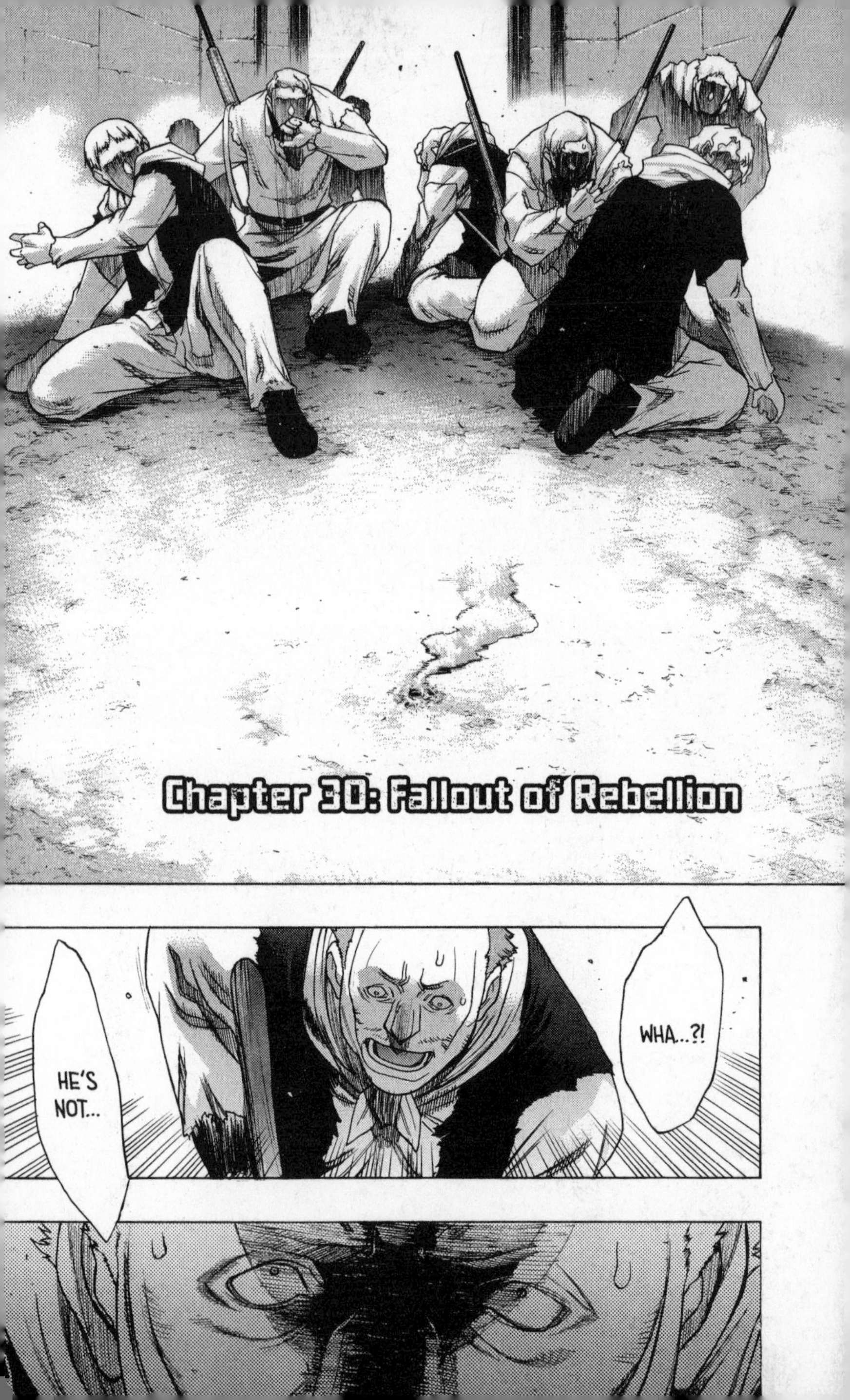
Chapter 30: Fallout of Rebellion
WHA...?!
HE'S NOT...

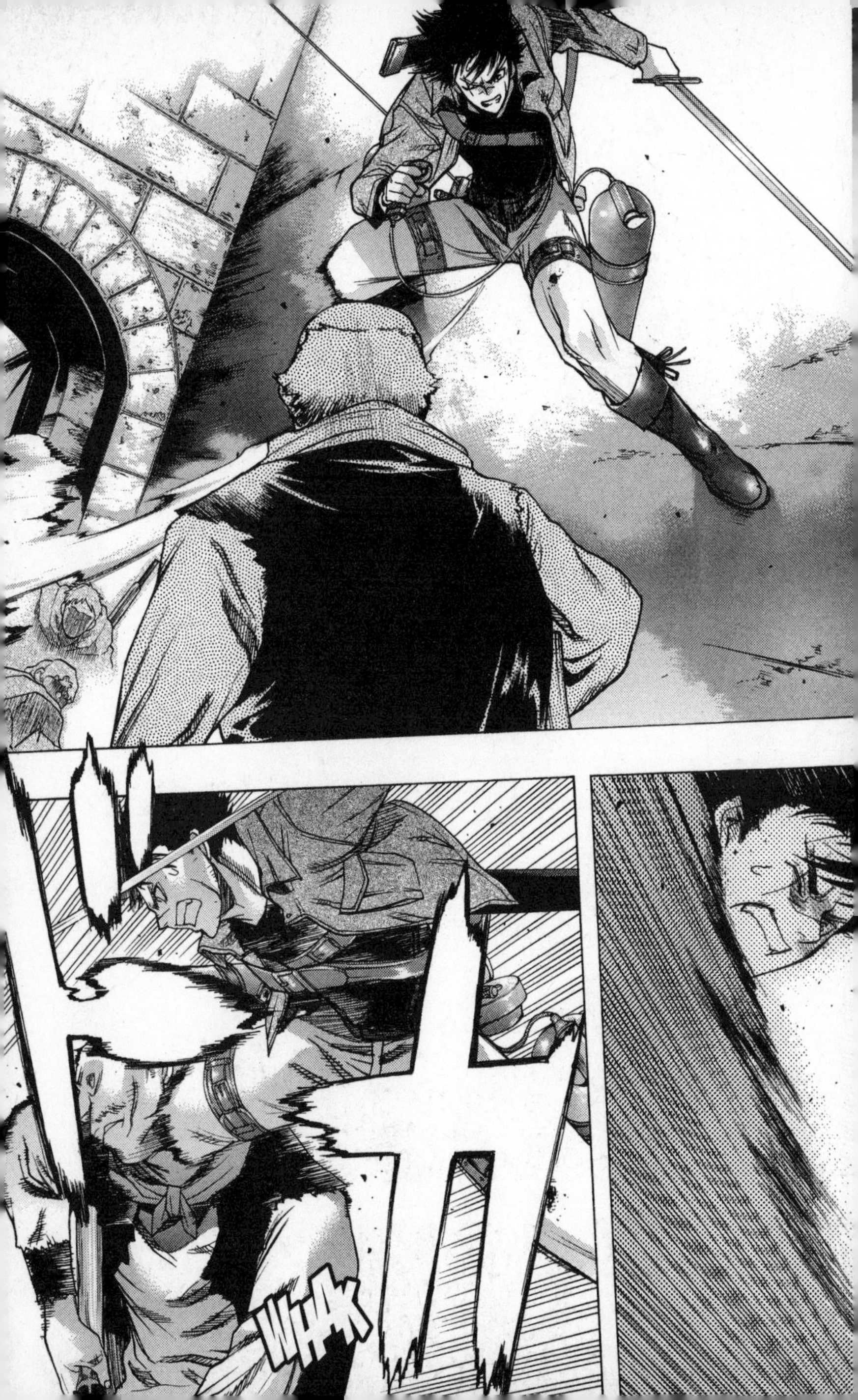
WHAK

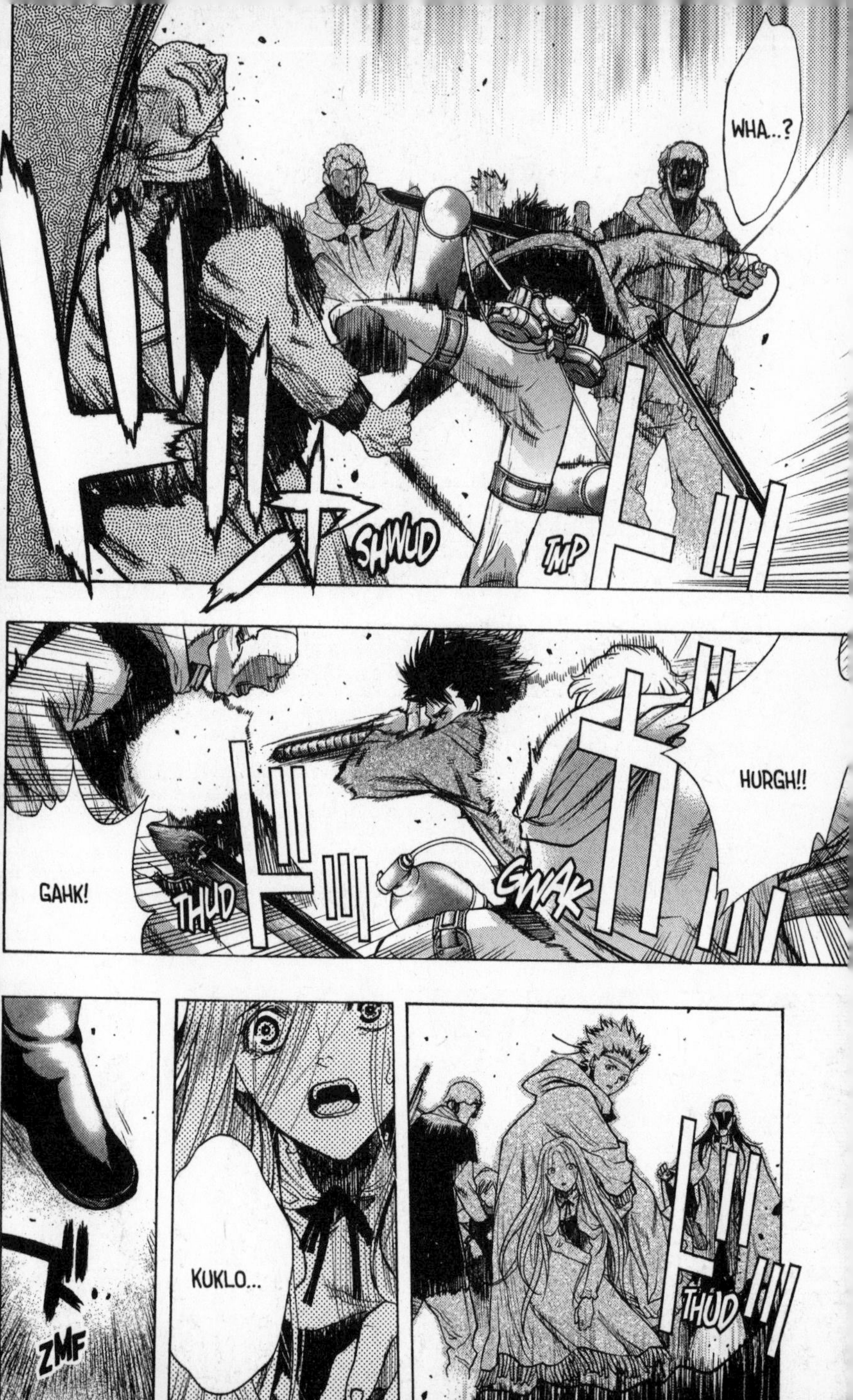
WHA...?
TMP
SHWUD
HURGH!!
GWAK
THUD
GAHK!
THUD
KUKLO...
ZMF

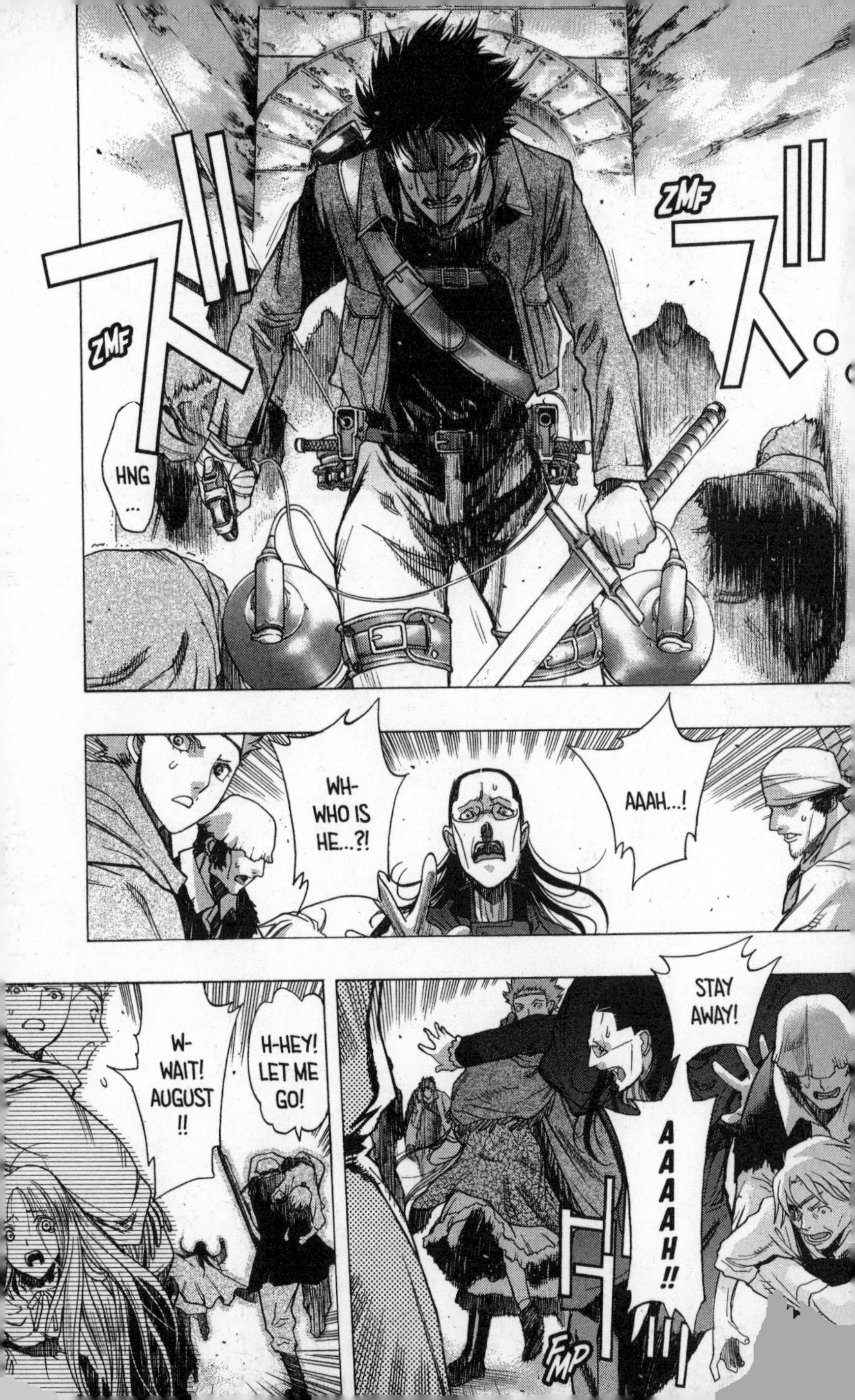
ZMF
ZMF
HNG ...
AAAH...!
WH- WHO IS HE...?!
STAY AWAY!
AAAAAH!!
FMP
H-HEY! LET ME GO!
W- WAIT! AUGUST !!

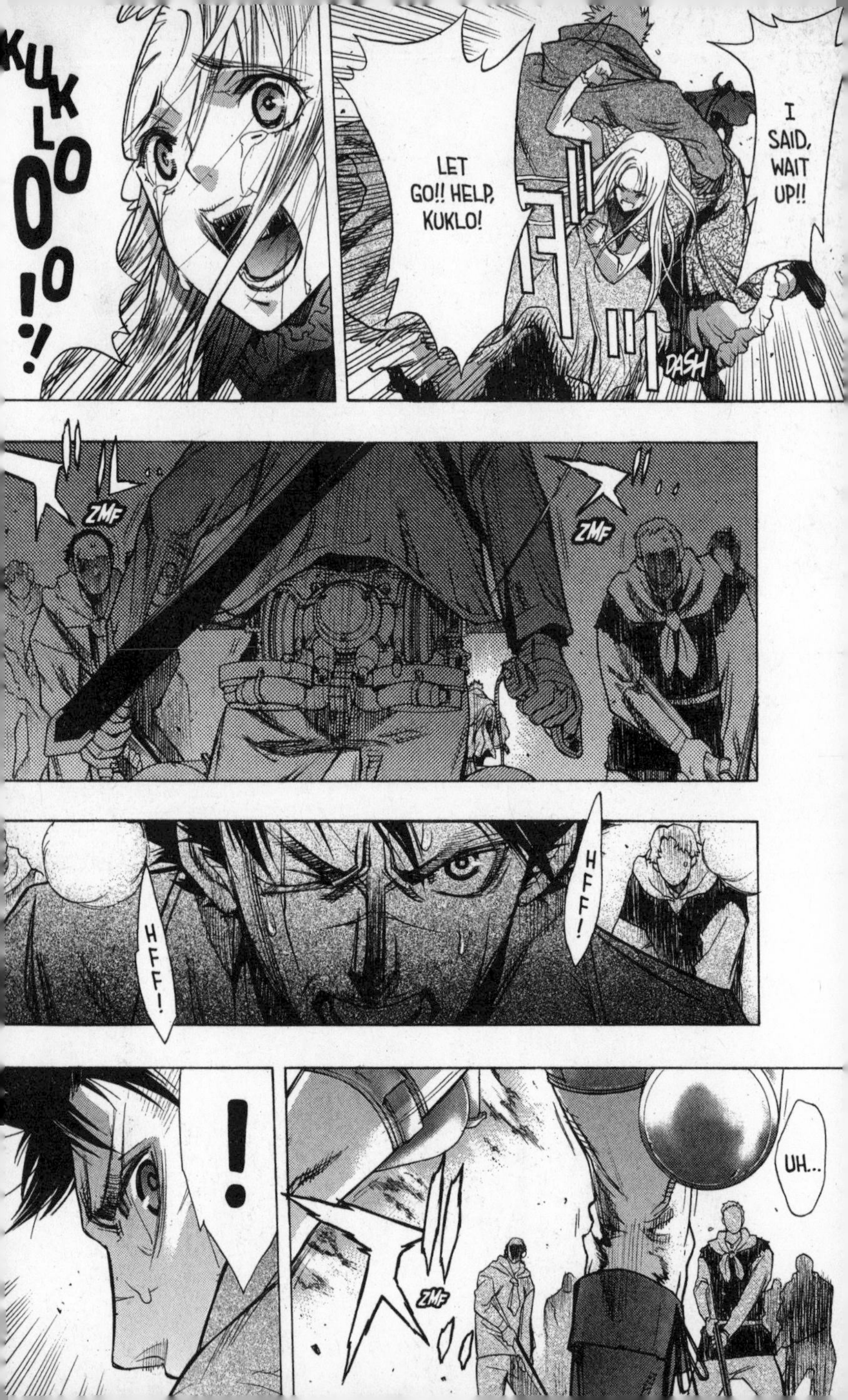
I SAID, WAIT UP!!
LET GO!! HELP, KUKLO!
DASH
KUKLOOO!!
ZMF
ZMF
HFF!
HFF!
UH...
ZMF
!

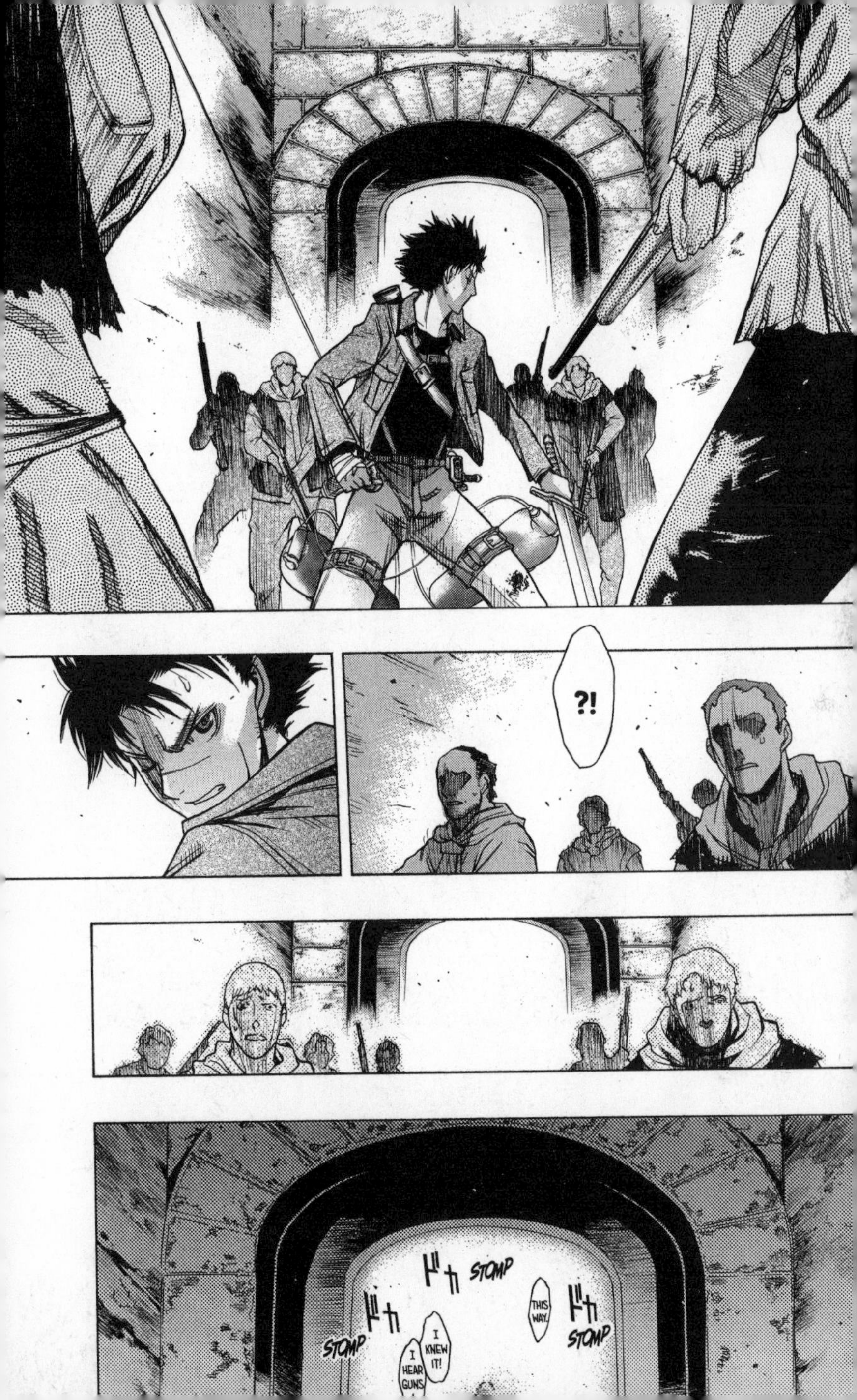
?!
ドカ STOMP
THIS WAY.
ドカ STOMP
ドカ STOMP
I KNEW IT!
I HEAR GUNS

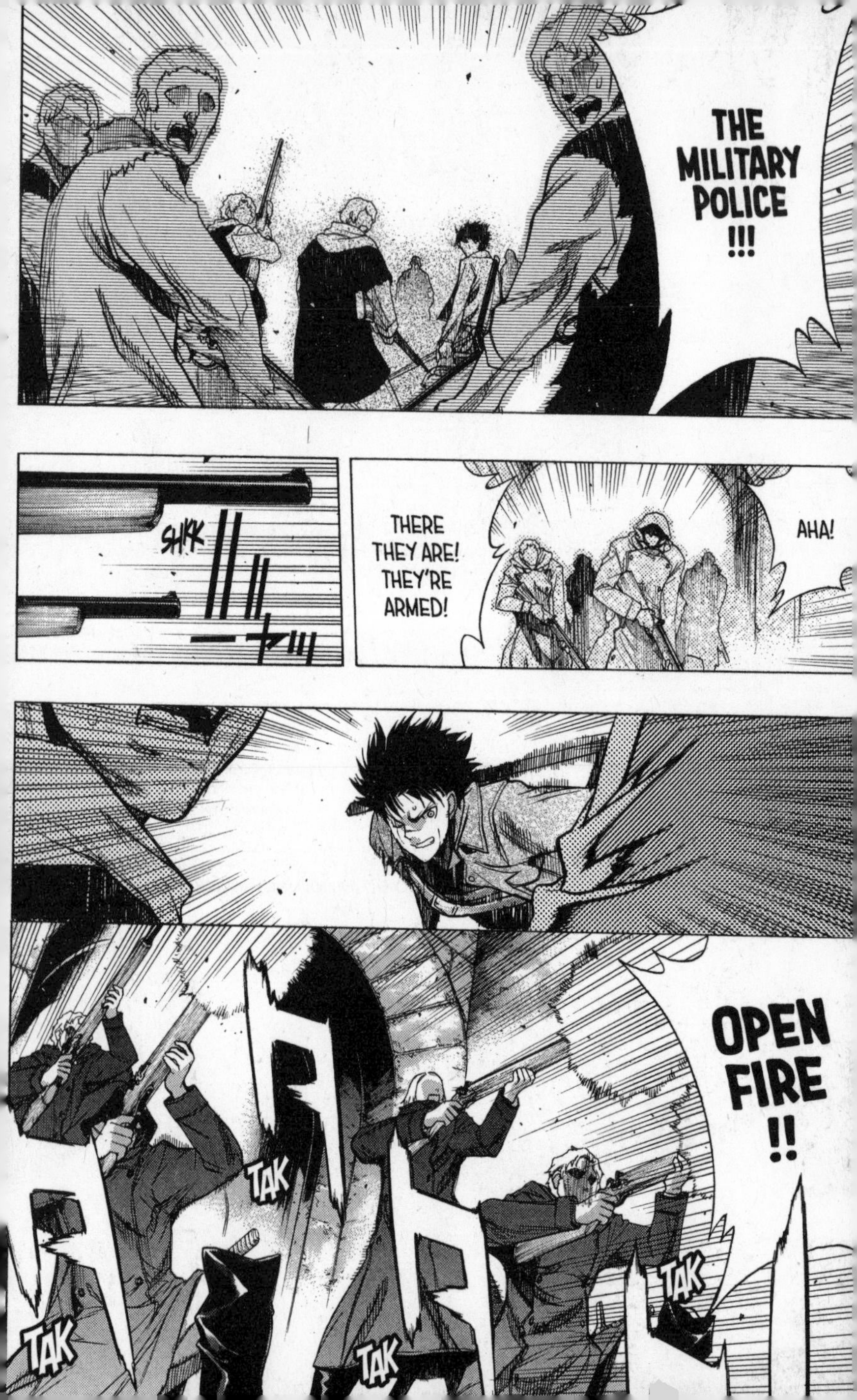
THE MILITARY POLICE !!!
AHA!
THERE THEY ARE! THEY'RE ARMED!
SHKK
OPEN FIRE !!
TAK
TAK
TAK
TAK

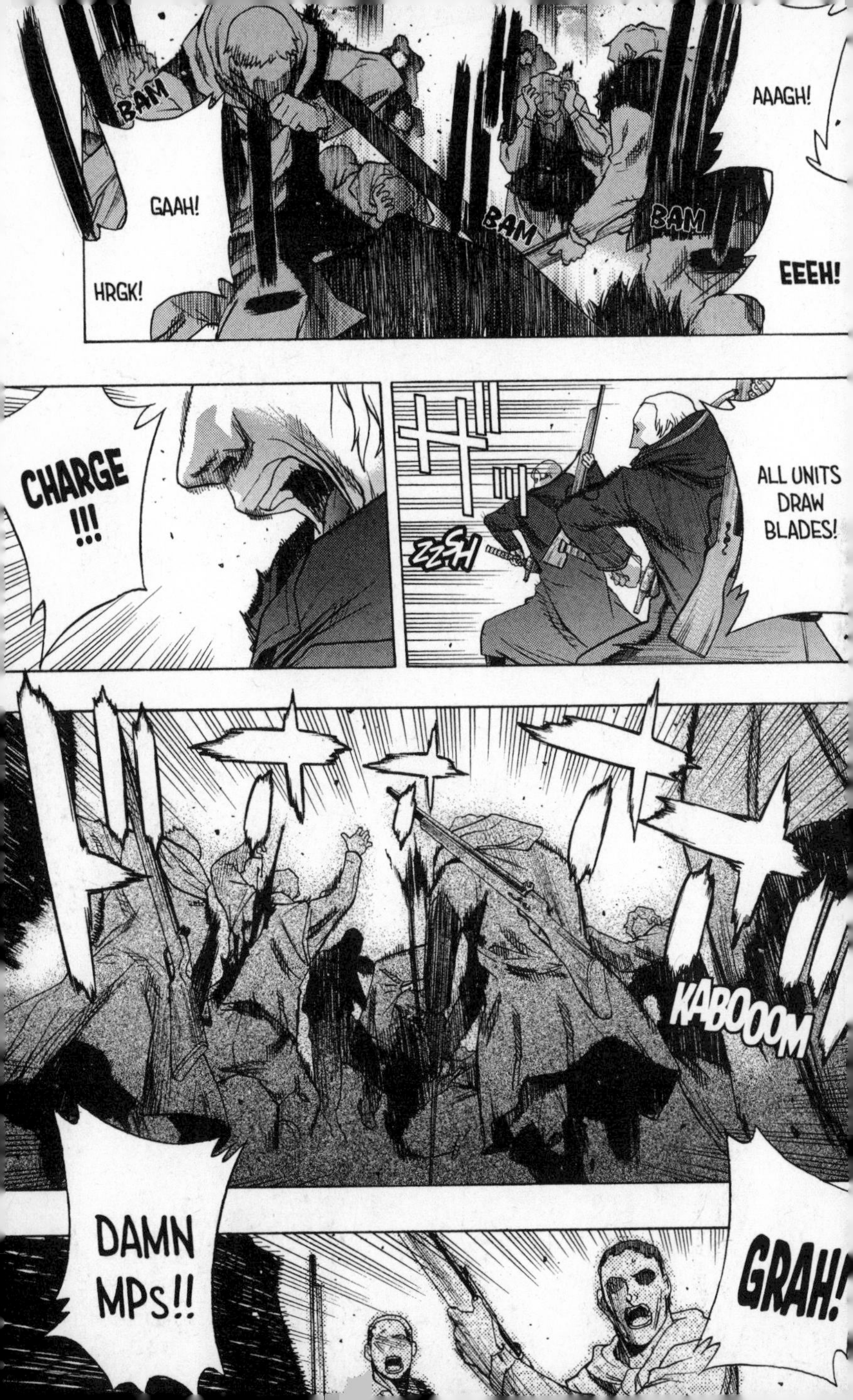
AAAGH!
BAM
EEEH!
BAM
BAM
GAAH!
HRGK!
ALL UNITS DRAW BLADES!
HSZZ
CHARGE!!!
KABOOOM
GRAH!
DAMN MPs!!

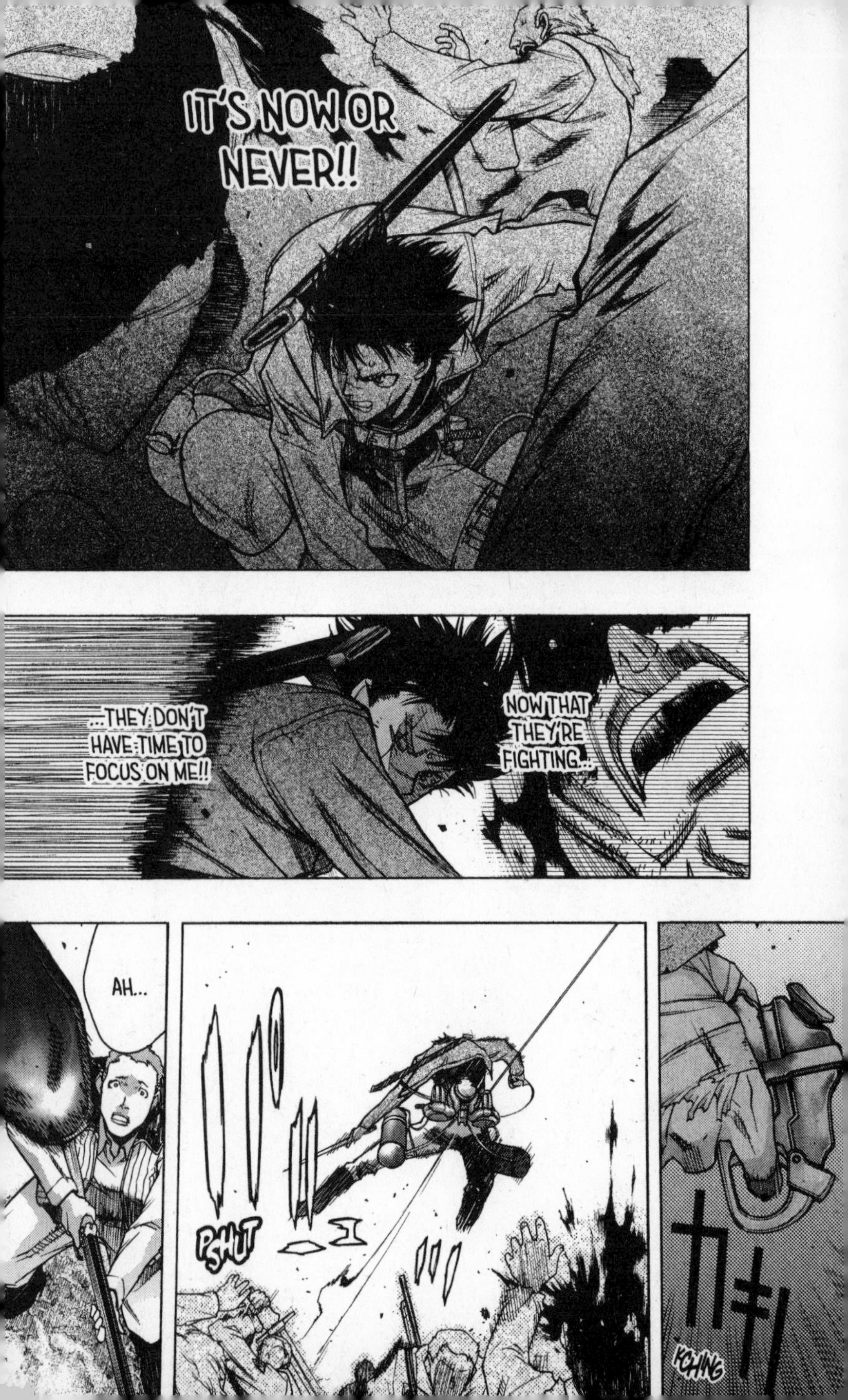
IT'S NOW OR NEVER!!
NOW THAT THEY'RE FIGHTING...
...THEY DON'T HAVE TIME TO FOCUS ON ME!!
カキッ
KCHING
PSHUT
AH...

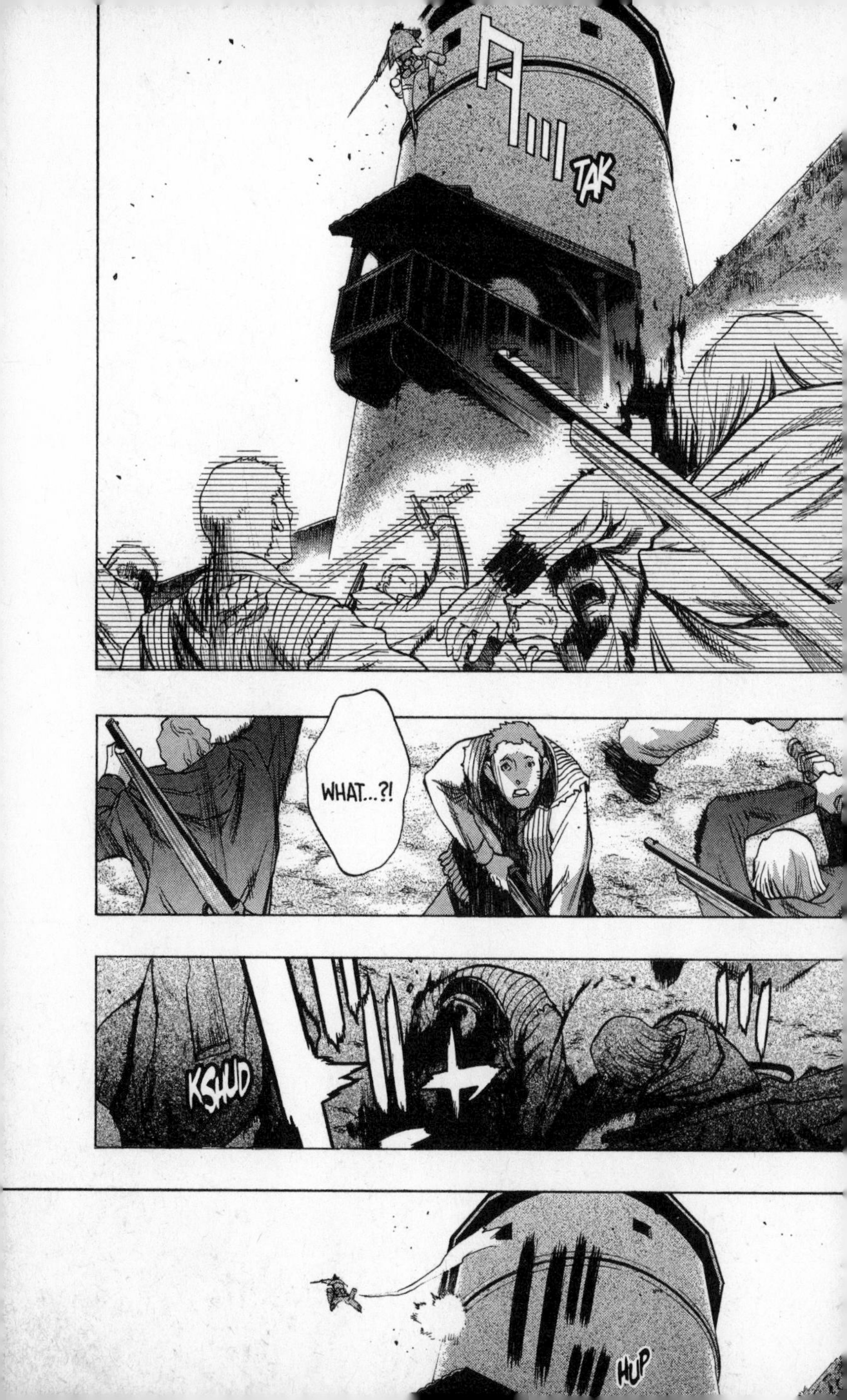
TAK
WHAT...?!
KSHUD
HUP

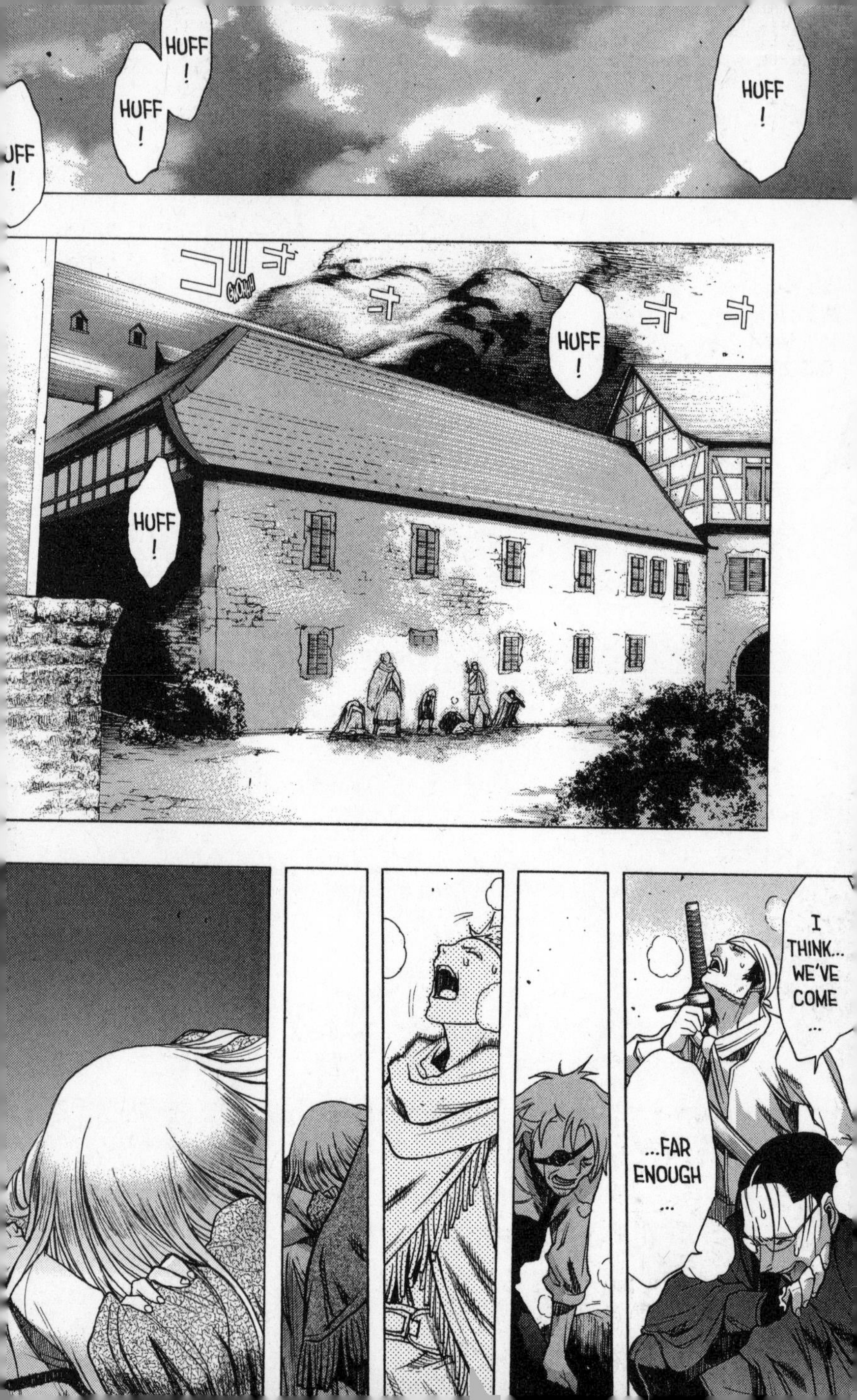
HUFF!
HUFF!
HUFF!
UFF!
GWOAHH
HUFF!
HUFF!
I THINK... WE'VE COME ...
...FAR ENOUGH ...

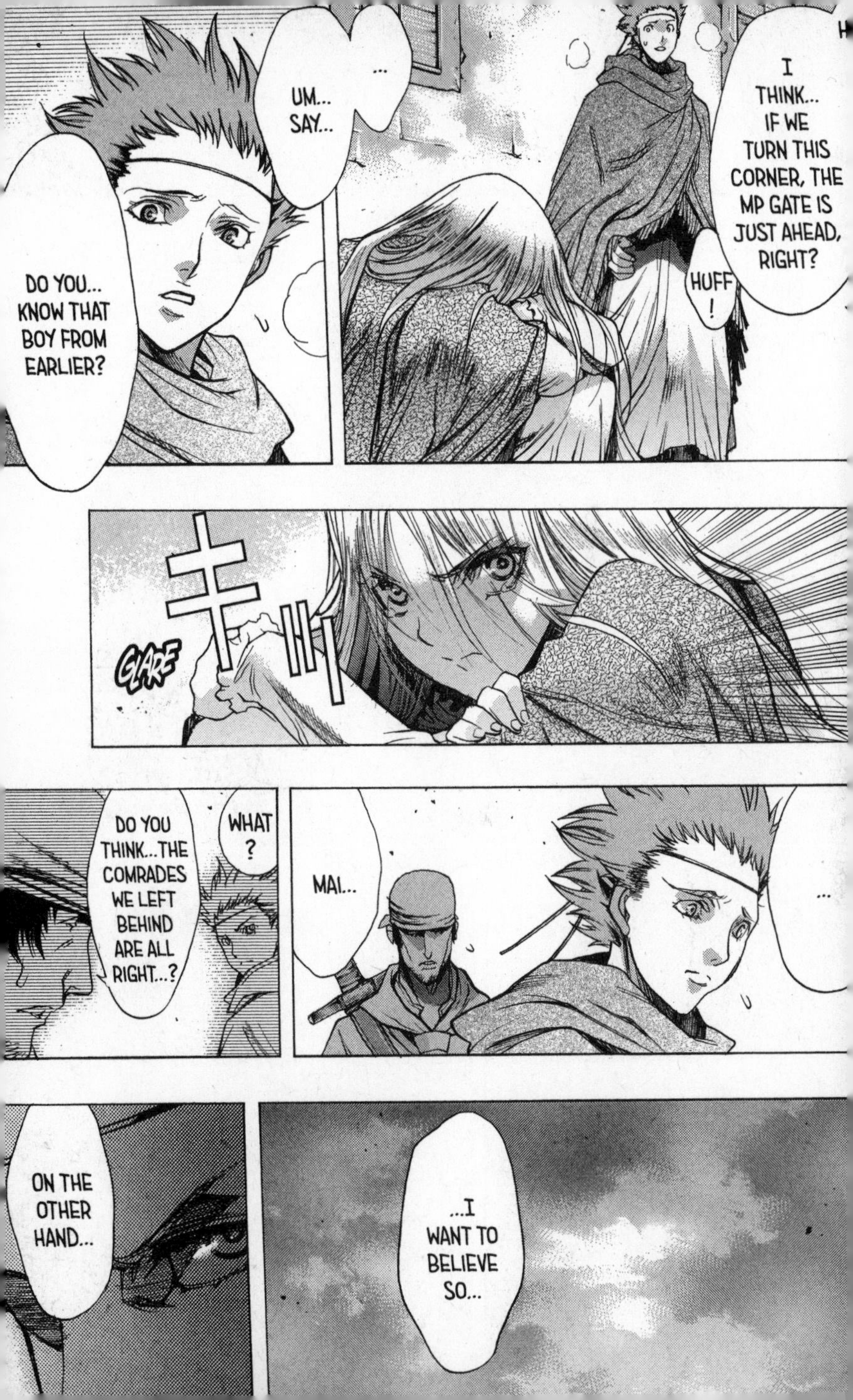
I THINK... IF WE TURN THIS CORNER, THE MP GATE IS JUST AHEAD, RIGHT?
HUFF!
...
UM... SAY...
DO YOU... KNOW THAT BOY FROM EARLIER?
GLARE
...
MAI...
WHAT?
DO YOU THINK...THE COMRADES WE LEFT BEHIND ARE ALL RIGHT...?
...I WANT TO BELIEVE SO...
ON THE OTHER HAND...

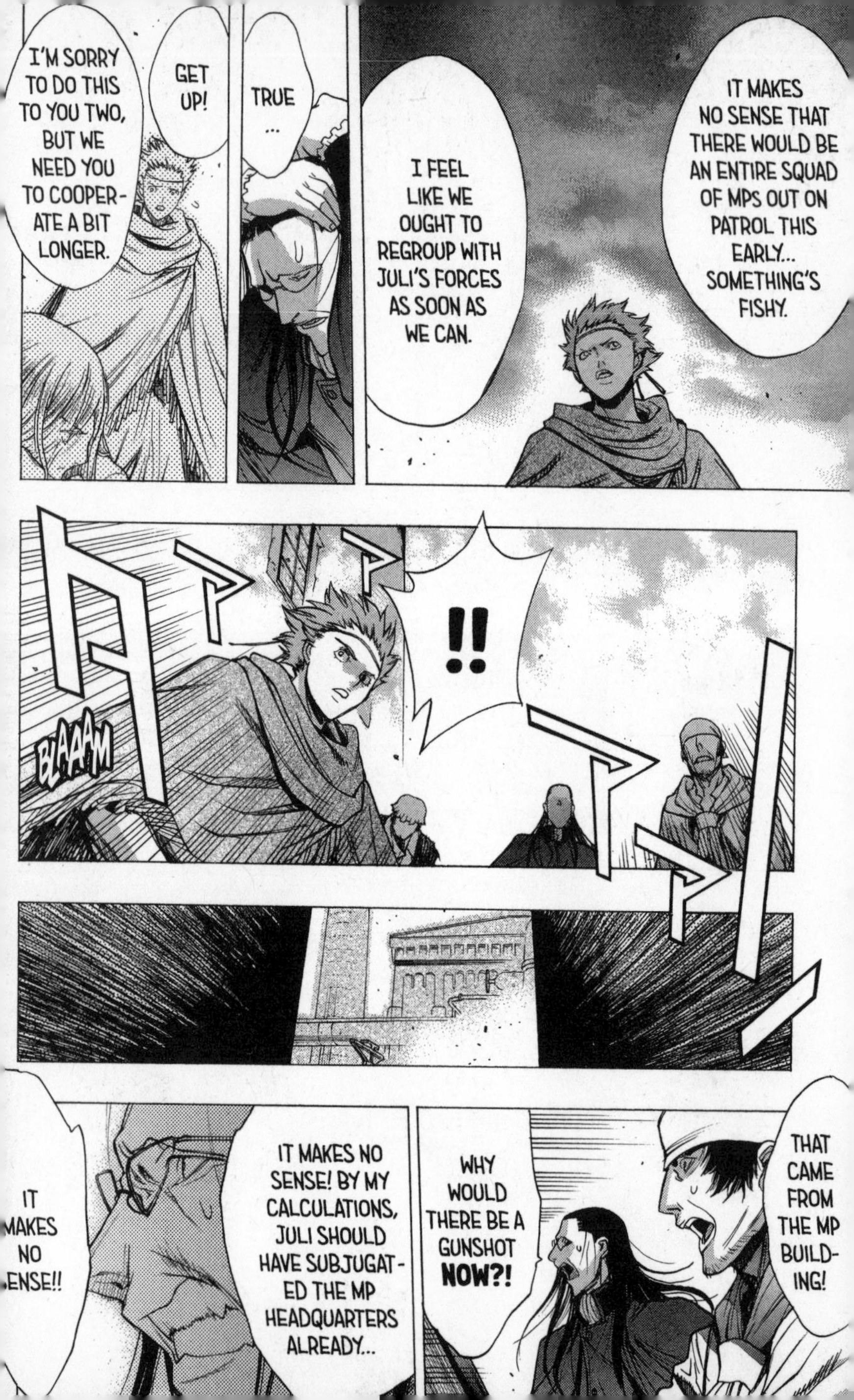
IT MAKES NO SENSE THAT THERE WOULD BE AN ENTIRE SQUAD OF MPS OUT ON PATROL THIS EARLY... SOMETHING'S FISHY.
I FEEL LIKE WE OUGHT TO REGROUP WITH JULI'S FORCES AS SOON AS WE CAN.
TRUE ...
GET UP!
I'M SORRY TO DO THIS TO YOU TWO, BUT WE NEED YOU TO COOPER-ATE A BIT LONGER.
!!
BLAAAM
THAT CAME FROM THE MP BUILD-ING!
WHY WOULD THERE BE A GUNSHOT **NOW?!**
IT MAKES NO SENSE! BY MY CALCULATIONS, JULI SHOULD HAVE SUBJUGAT-ED THE MP HEADQUARTERS ALREADY...
IT MAKES NO SENSE!!

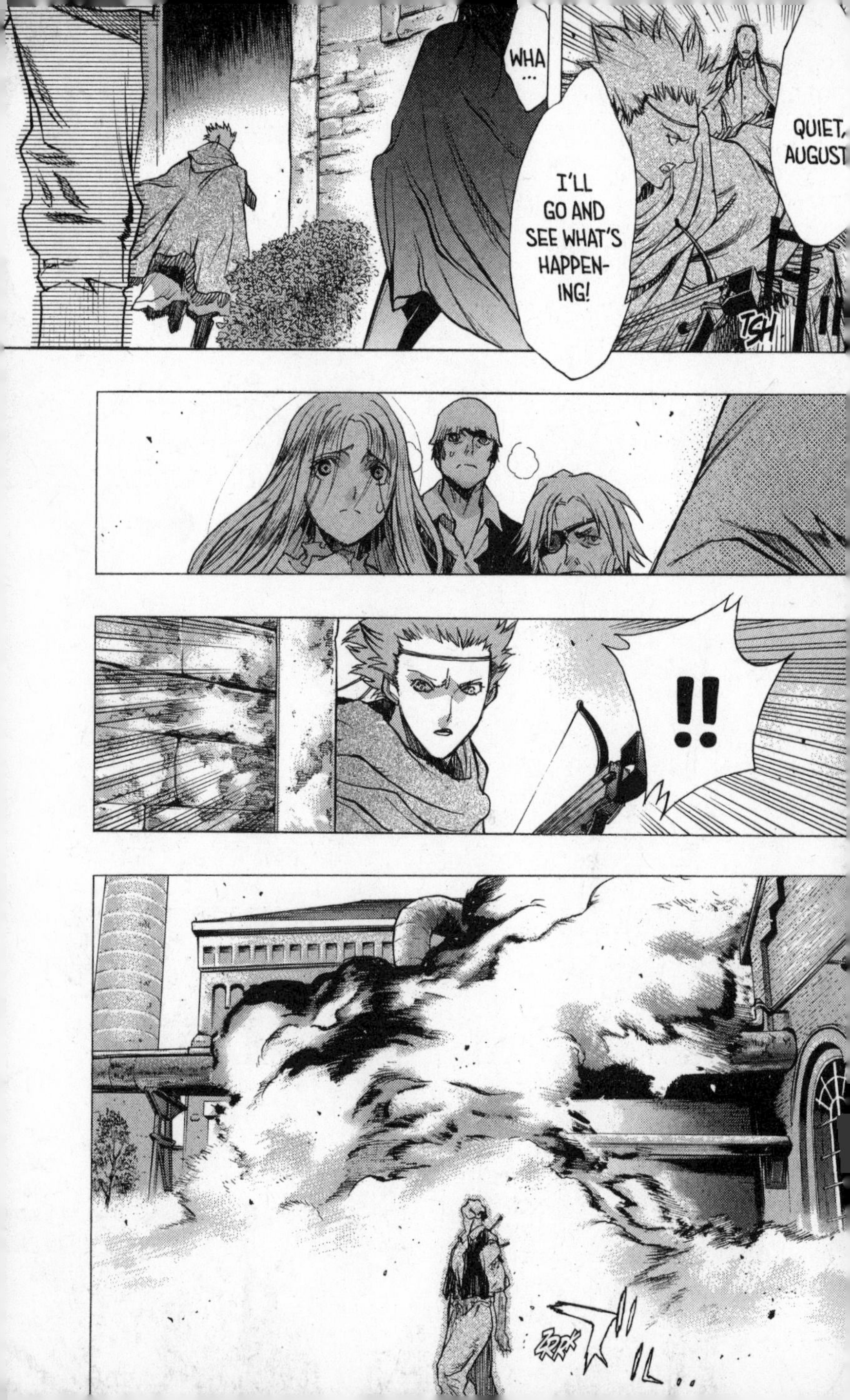
QUIET, AUGUST
I'LL GO AND SEE WHAT'S HAPPEN-ING!
TCH
WHA ...
!!
ZRRK

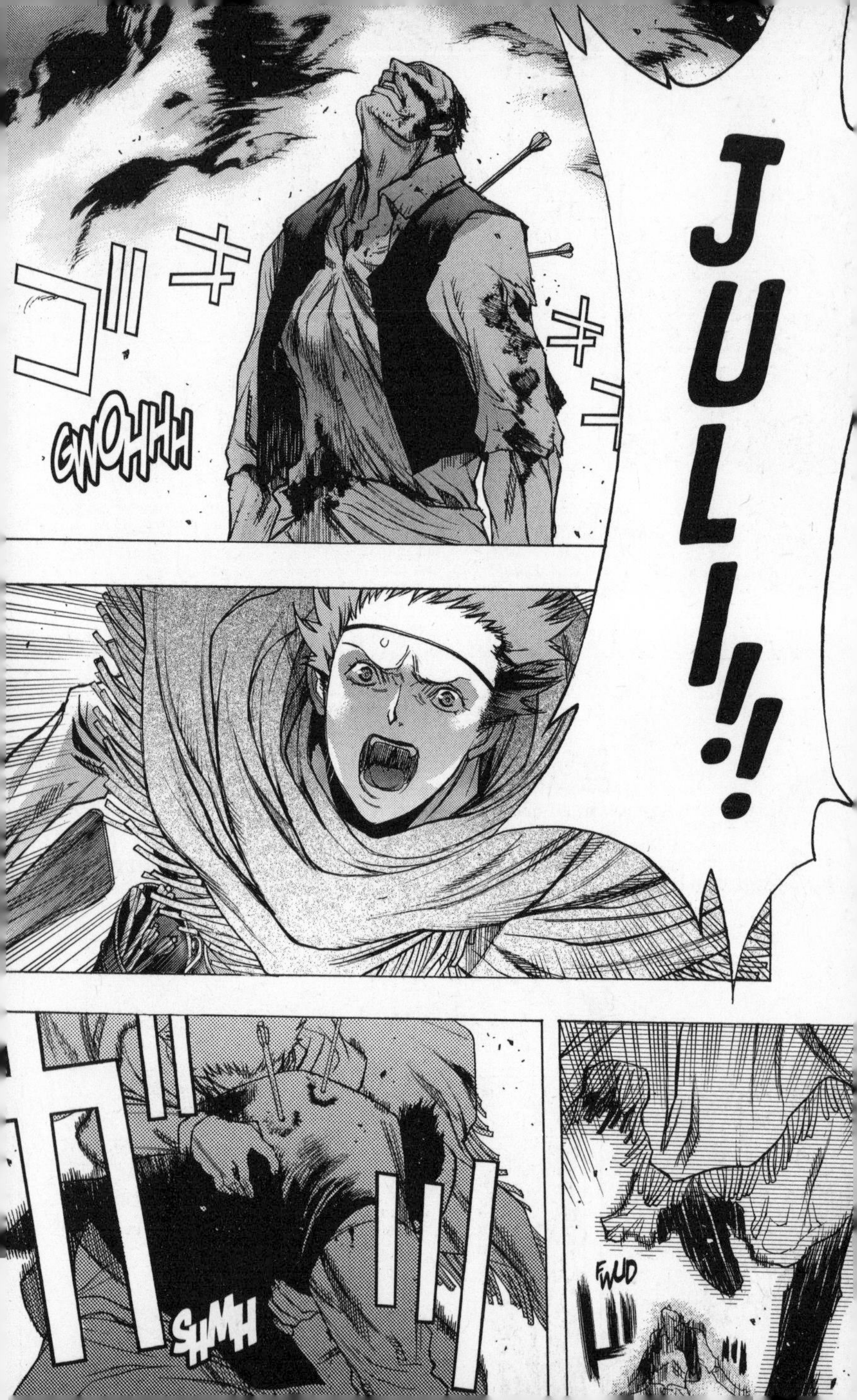

JULI!!!
GWOHHH
SHMH
FWUD

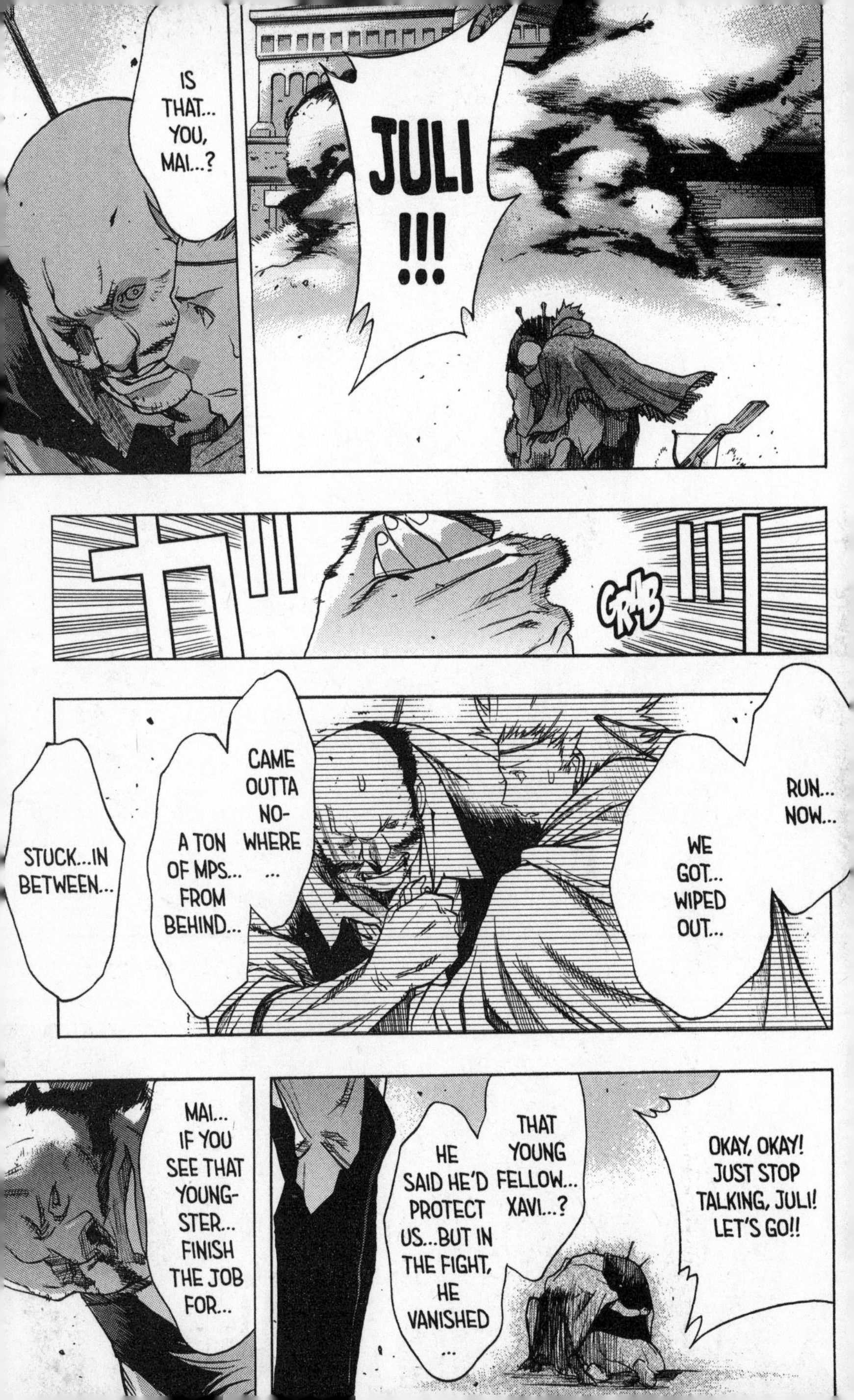
JULI!!!
IS THAT... YOU, MAI...?
GRAB
RUN... NOW...
WE GOT... WIPED OUT...
CAME OUTTA NO-WHERE...
A TON OF MPS... FROM BEHIND...
STUCK...IN BETWEEN...
OKAY, OKAY! JUST STOP TALKING, JULI! LET'S GO!!
THAT YOUNG FELLOW... XAVI...?
HE SAID HE'D PROTECT US...BUT IN THE FIGHT, HE VANISHED...
MAI... IF YOU SEE THAT YOUNG-STER... FINISH THE JOB FOR...

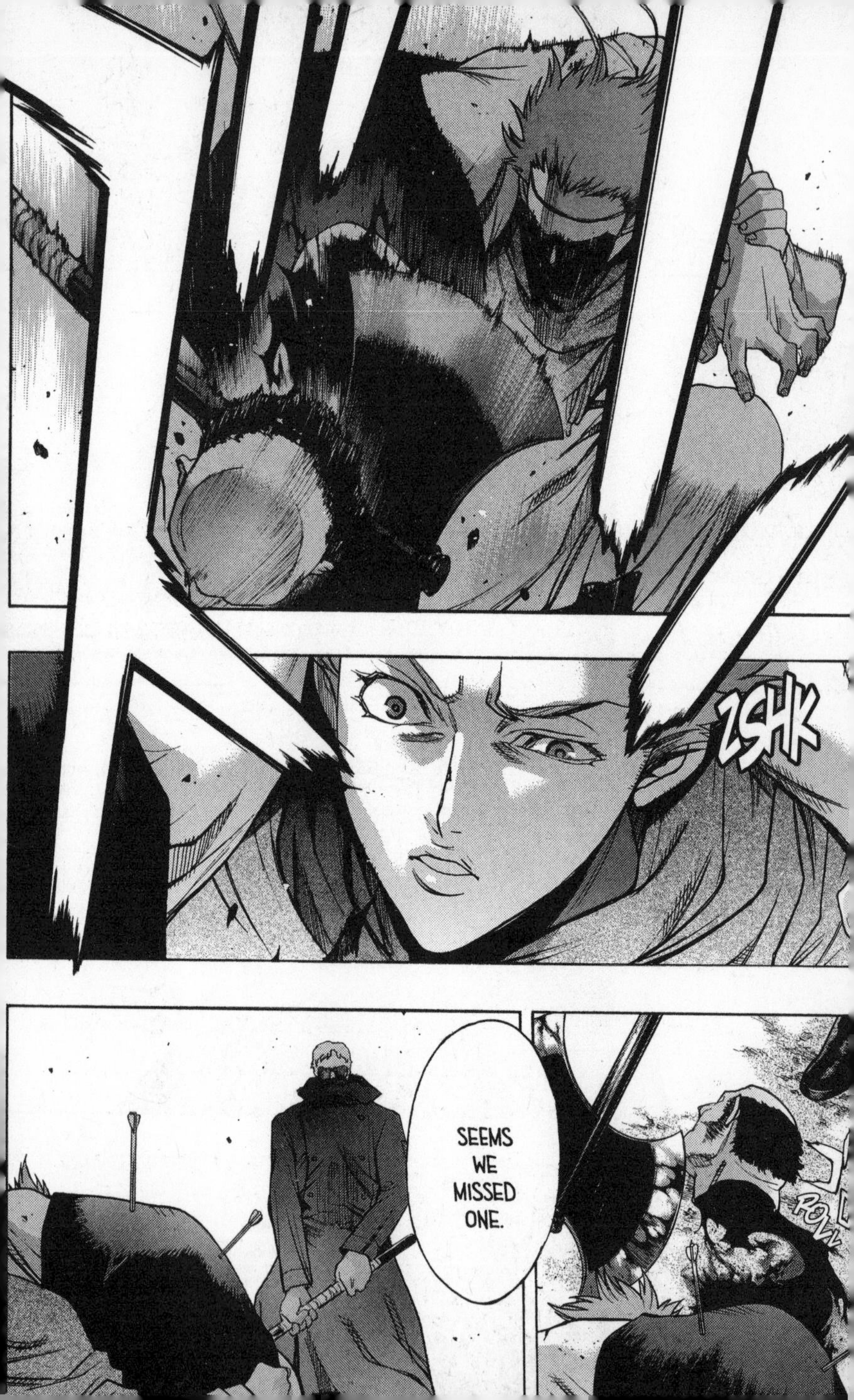
ZSHK
SEEMS WE MISSED ONE.
ROLL

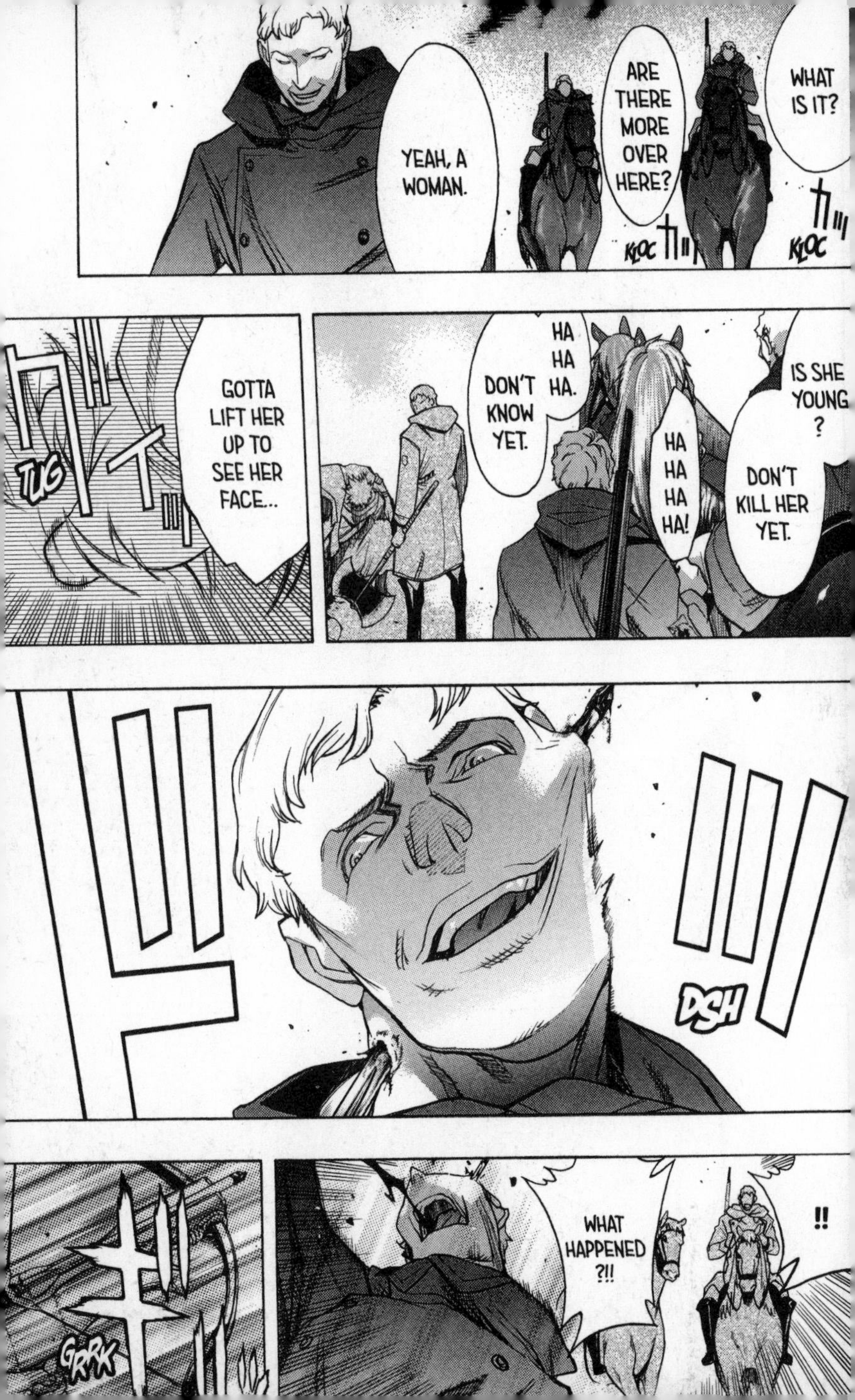
WHAT IS IT?
ARE THERE MORE OVER HERE?
KLOC
KLOC
YEAH, A WOMAN.
IS SHE YOUNG?
DON'T KILL HER YET.
HA HA HA HA!
HA HA HA.
DON'T KNOW YET.
GOTTA LIFT HER UP TO SEE HER FACE...
TUG
DSH
!!
WHAT HAPPENED ?!!
GRRK

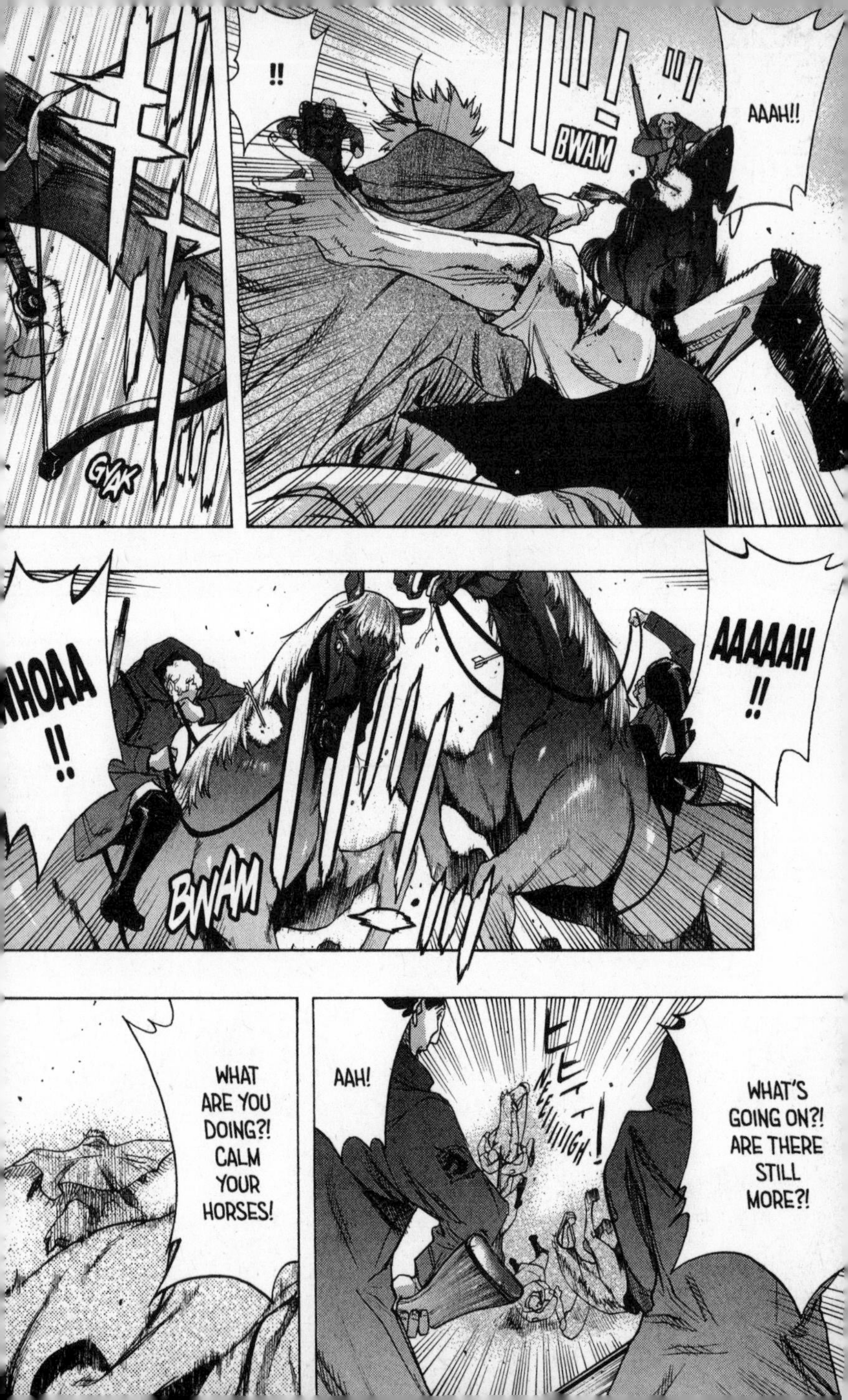
AAAH!!
BWAM
!!
GYAK
AAAAAH!!
WHOAA!!
BWAM
WHAT'S GOING ON?! ARE THERE STILL MORE?!
NEEIIIIIGH!
AAH!
WHAT ARE YOU DOING?! CALM YOUR HORSES!

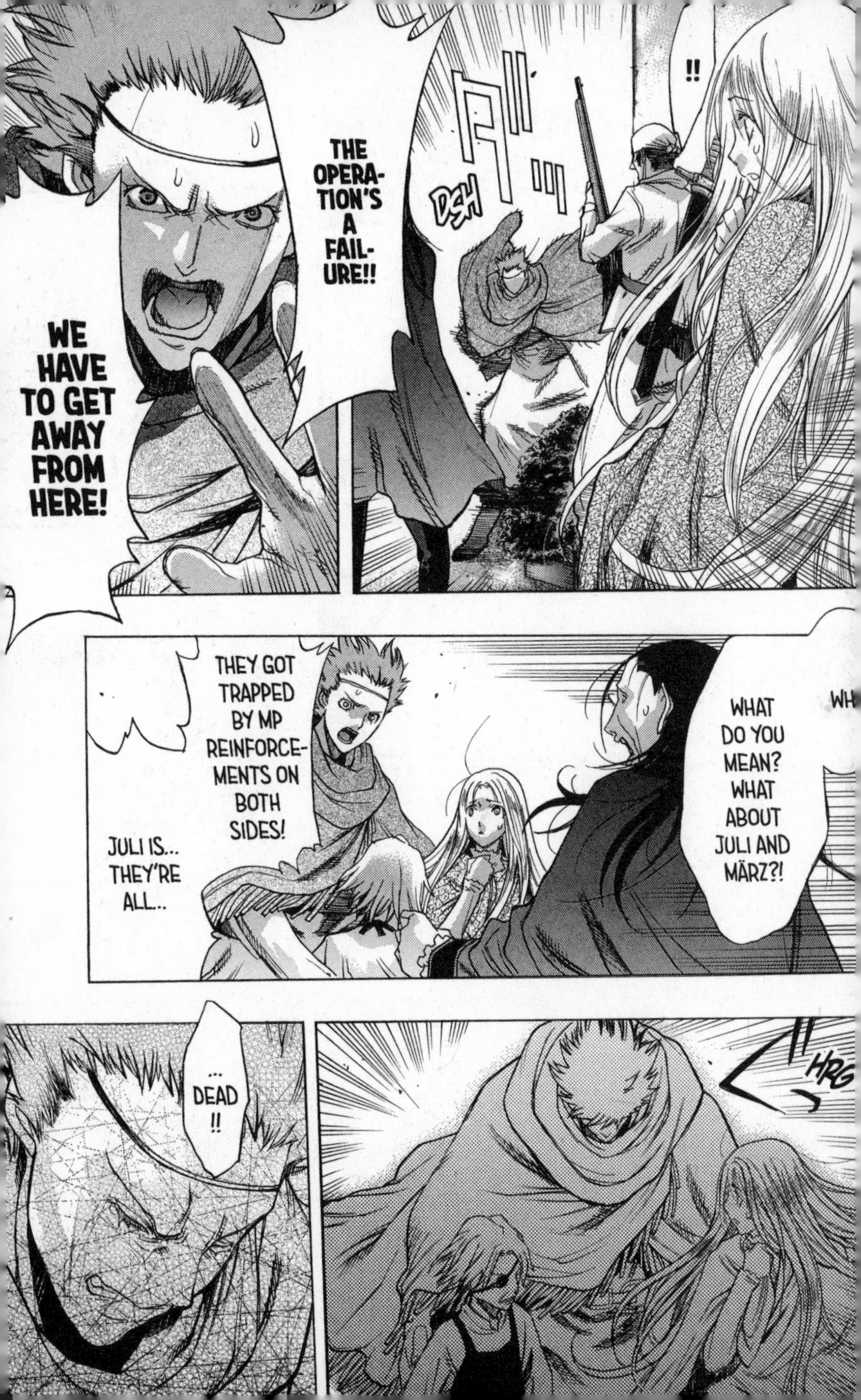
!!
DSH
THE OPERATION'S A FAILURE!!
WE HAVE TO GET AWAY FROM HERE!
WH
WHAT DO YOU MEAN? WHAT ABOUT JULI AND MÄRZ?!
THEY GOT TRAPPED BY MP REINFORCEMENTS ON BOTH SIDES!
JULI IS... THEY'RE ALL..
HRG
...DEAD!!

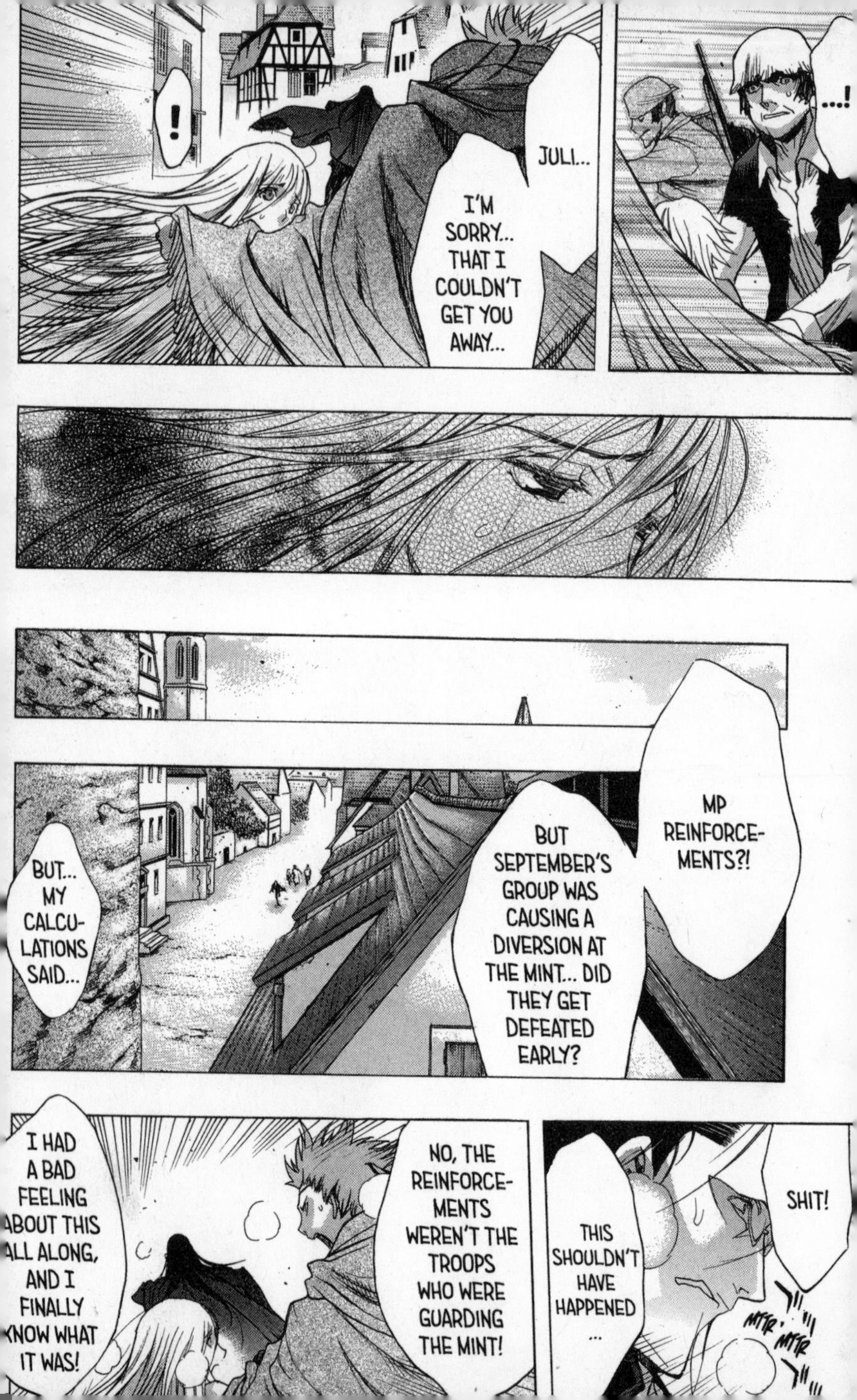
...!
JULI...
I'M SORRY... THAT I COULDN'T GET YOU AWAY...
!
MP REINFORCEMENTS?!
BUT SEPTEMBER'S GROUP WAS CAUSING A DIVERSION AT THE MINT... DID THEY GET DEFEATED EARLY?
BUT... MY CALCULATIONS SAID...
SHIT!
THIS SHOULDN'T HAVE HAPPENED...
MTTR MTTR
NO, THE REINFORCEMENTS WEREN'T THE TROOPS WHO WERE GUARDING THE MINT!
I HAD A BAD FEELING ABOUT THIS ALL ALONG, AND I FINALLY KNOW WHAT IT WAS!

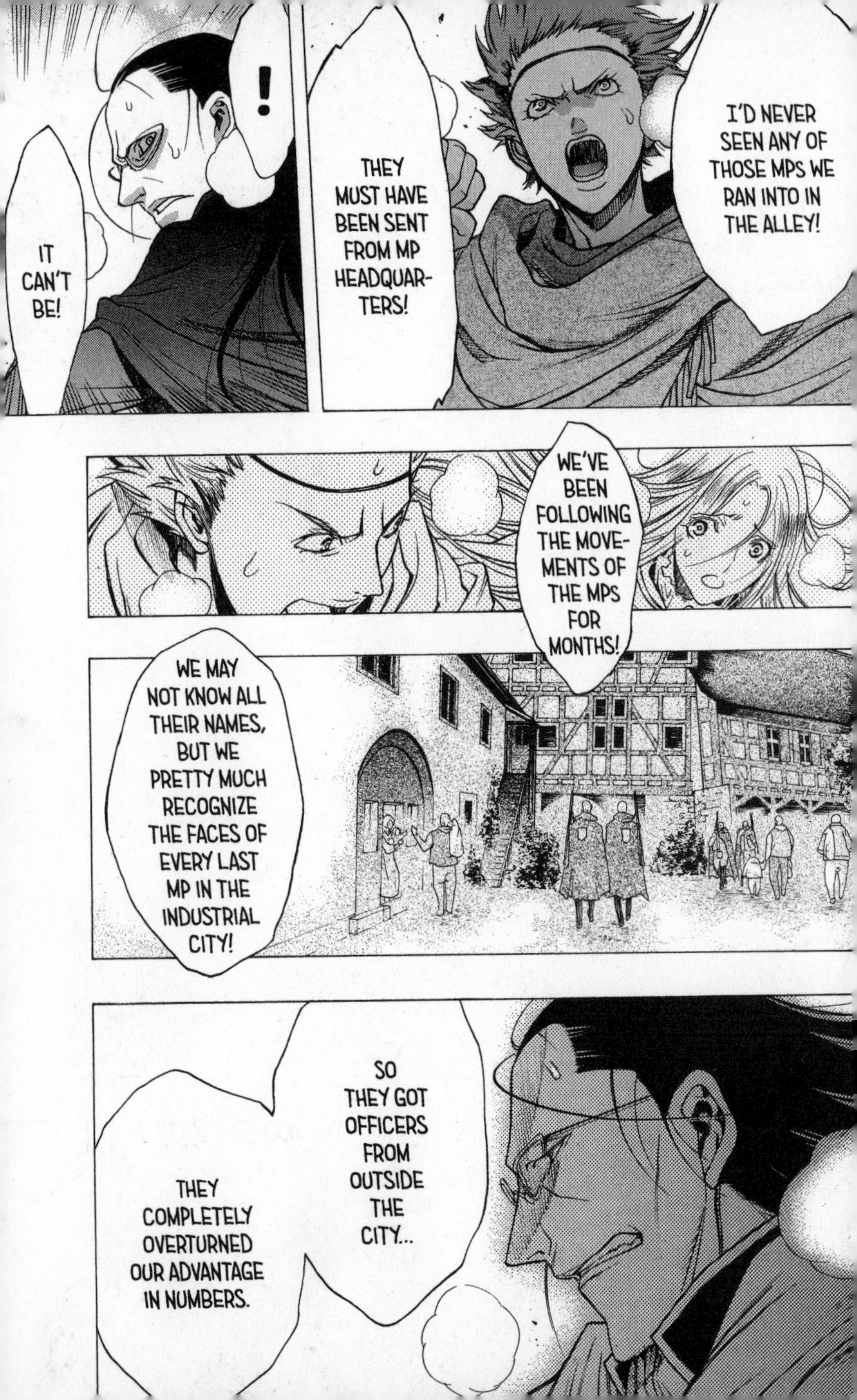
I'D NEVER SEEN ANY OF THOSE MPS WE RAN INTO IN THE ALLEY!
THEY MUST HAVE BEEN SENT FROM MP HEADQUARTERS!
!
IT CAN'T BE!
WE'VE BEEN FOLLOWING THE MOVEMENTS OF THE MPS FOR MONTHS!
WE MAY NOT KNOW ALL THEIR NAMES, BUT WE PRETTY MUCH RECOGNIZE THE FACES OF EVERY LAST MP IN THE INDUSTRIAL CITY!
SO THEY GOT OFFICERS FROM OUTSIDE THE CITY...
THEY COMPLETELY OVERTURNED OUR ADVANTAGE IN NUMBERS.

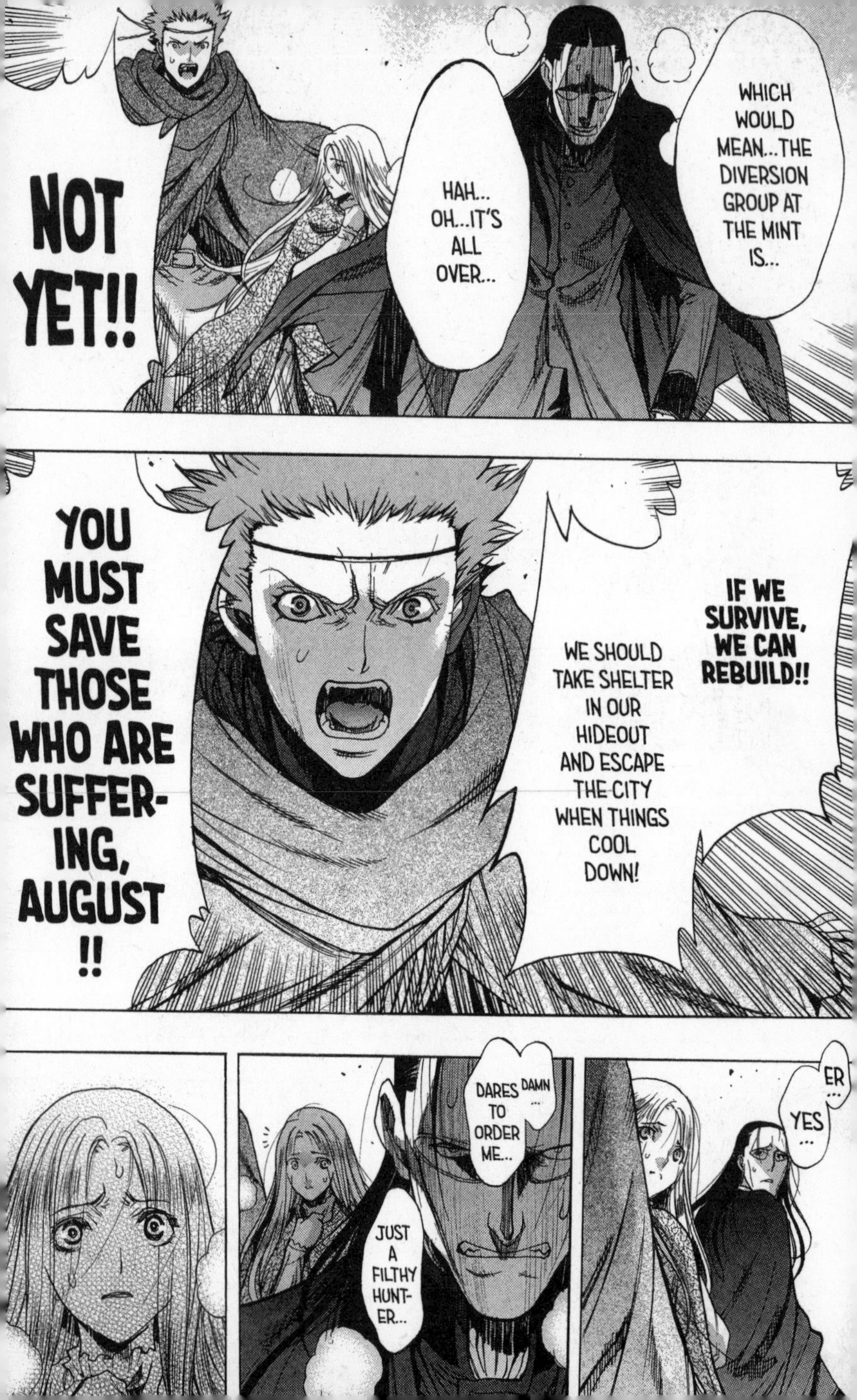
WHICH WOULD MEAN...THE DIVERSION GROUP AT THE MINT IS...
HAH... OH...IT'S ALL OVER...
NOT YET!!
IF WE SURVIVE, WE CAN REBUILD!!
WE SHOULD TAKE SHELTER IN OUR HIDEOUT AND ESCAPE THE CITY WHEN THINGS COOL DOWN!
YOU MUST SAVE THOSE WHO ARE SUFFER-ING, AUGUST!!
ER... YES...
DAMN...
DARES TO ORDER ME...
JUST A FILTHY HUNT-ER...

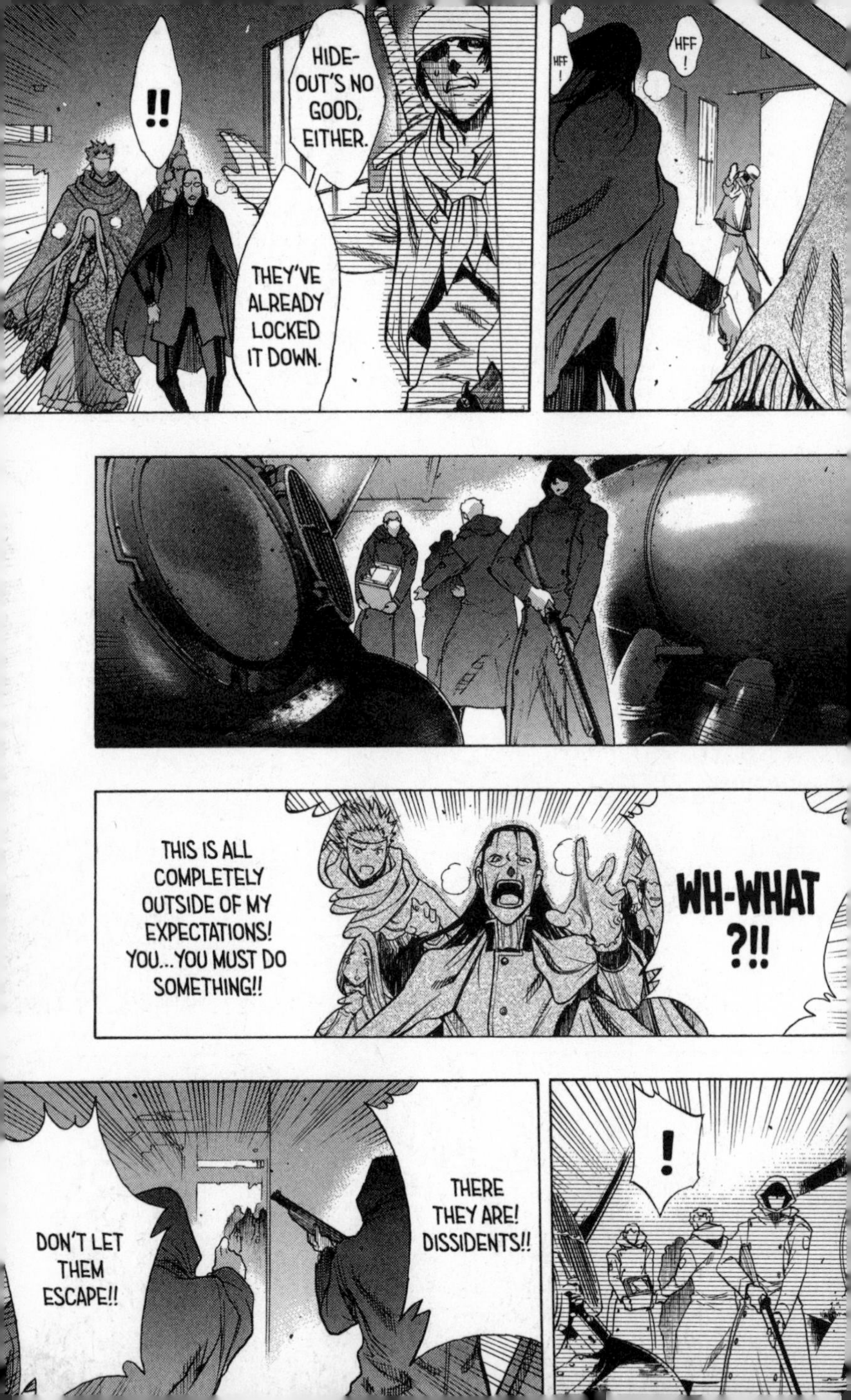
HFF!
HFF!
HIDE-OUT'S NO GOOD, EITHER.
THEY'VE ALREADY LOCKED IT DOWN.
!!
WH-WHAT?!!
THIS IS ALL COMPLETELY OUTSIDE OF MY EXPECTATIONS! YOU...YOU MUST DO SOMETHING!!
!
THERE THEY ARE! DISSIDENTS!!
DON'T LET THEM ESCAPE!!

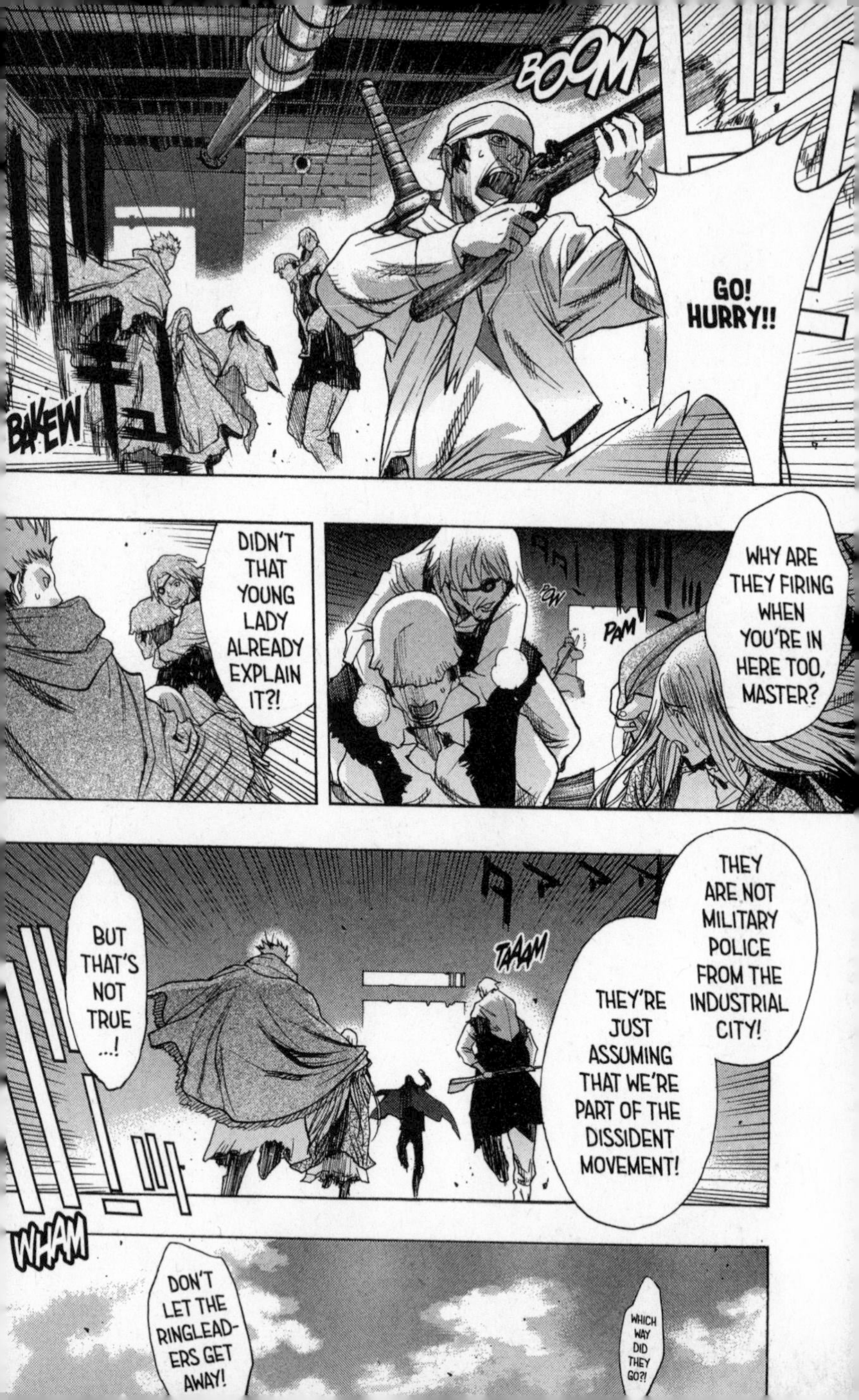
BOOM
GO! HURRY!!
BAKEW
WHY ARE THEY FIRING WHEN YOU'RE IN HERE TOO, MASTER?
PAM
POW
DIDN'T THAT YOUNG LADY ALREADY EXPLAIN IT?!
THEY ARE NOT MILITARY POLICE FROM THE INDUSTRIAL CITY!
THEY'RE JUST ASSUMING THAT WE'RE PART OF THE DISSIDENT MOVEMENT!
TAAAM
BUT THAT'S NOT TRUE ...!
WHAM
WHICH WAY DID THEY GO?!
DON'T LET THE RINGLEAD-ERS GET AWAY!

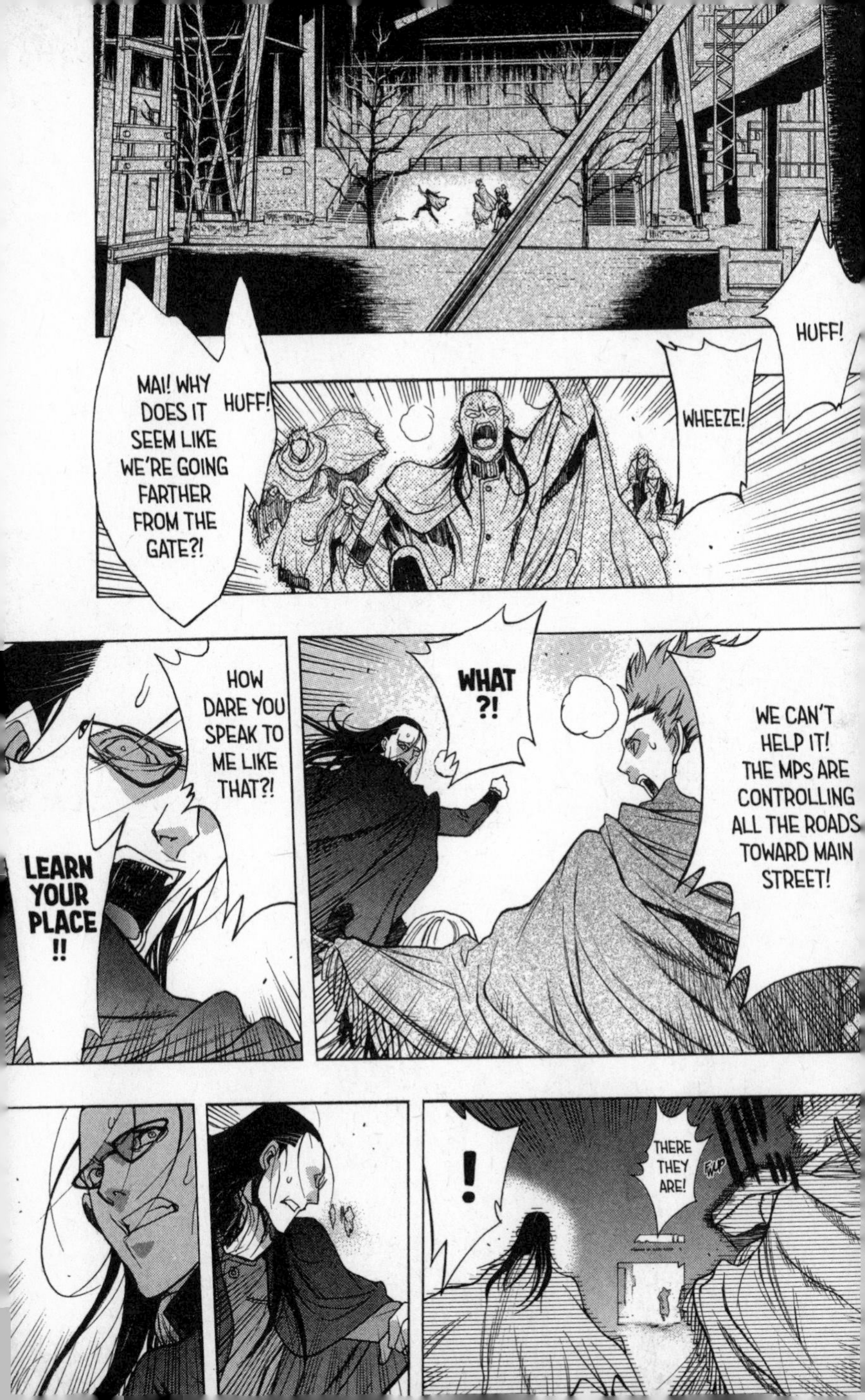
HUFF!
WHEEZE!
HUFF!
MAI! WHY DOES IT SEEM LIKE WE'RE GOING FARTHER FROM THE GATE?!
WE CAN'T HELP IT! THE MPS ARE CONTROLLING ALL THE ROADS TOWARD MAIN STREET!
WHAT ?!
HOW DARE YOU SPEAK TO ME LIKE THAT?!
LEARN YOUR PLACE !!
THERE THEY ARE!
FWUP
!

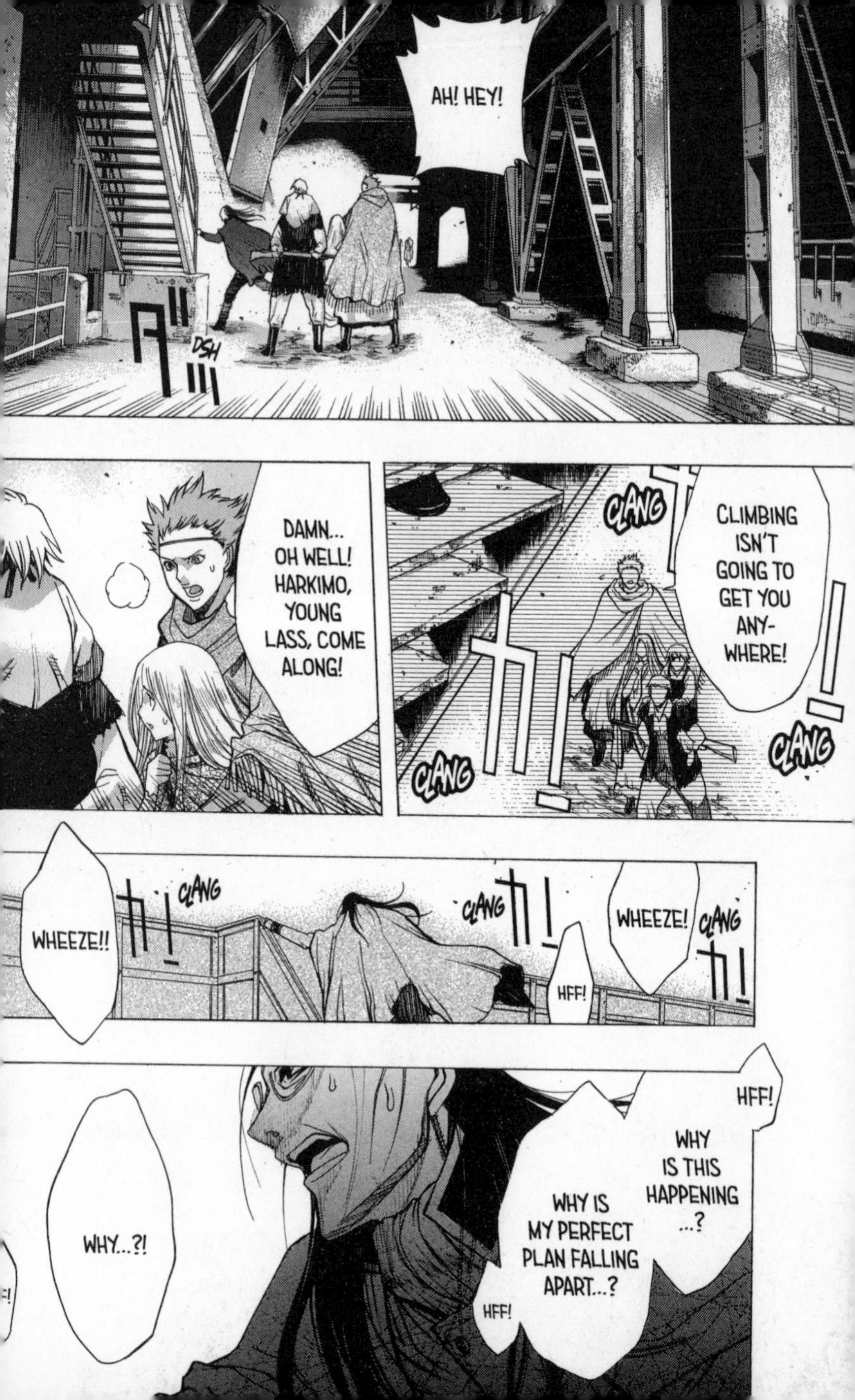
AH! HEY!
DSH
CLANG
CLIMBING ISN'T GOING TO GET YOU ANY-WHERE!
CLANG
CLANG
DAMN... OH WELL! HARKIMO, YOUNG LASS, COME ALONG!
CLANG
WHEEZE!
HFF!
CLANG
CLANG
WHEEZE!!
HFF!
WHY IS THIS HAPPENING ...?
WHY IS MY PERFECT PLAN FALLING APART...?
HFF!
WHY...?!

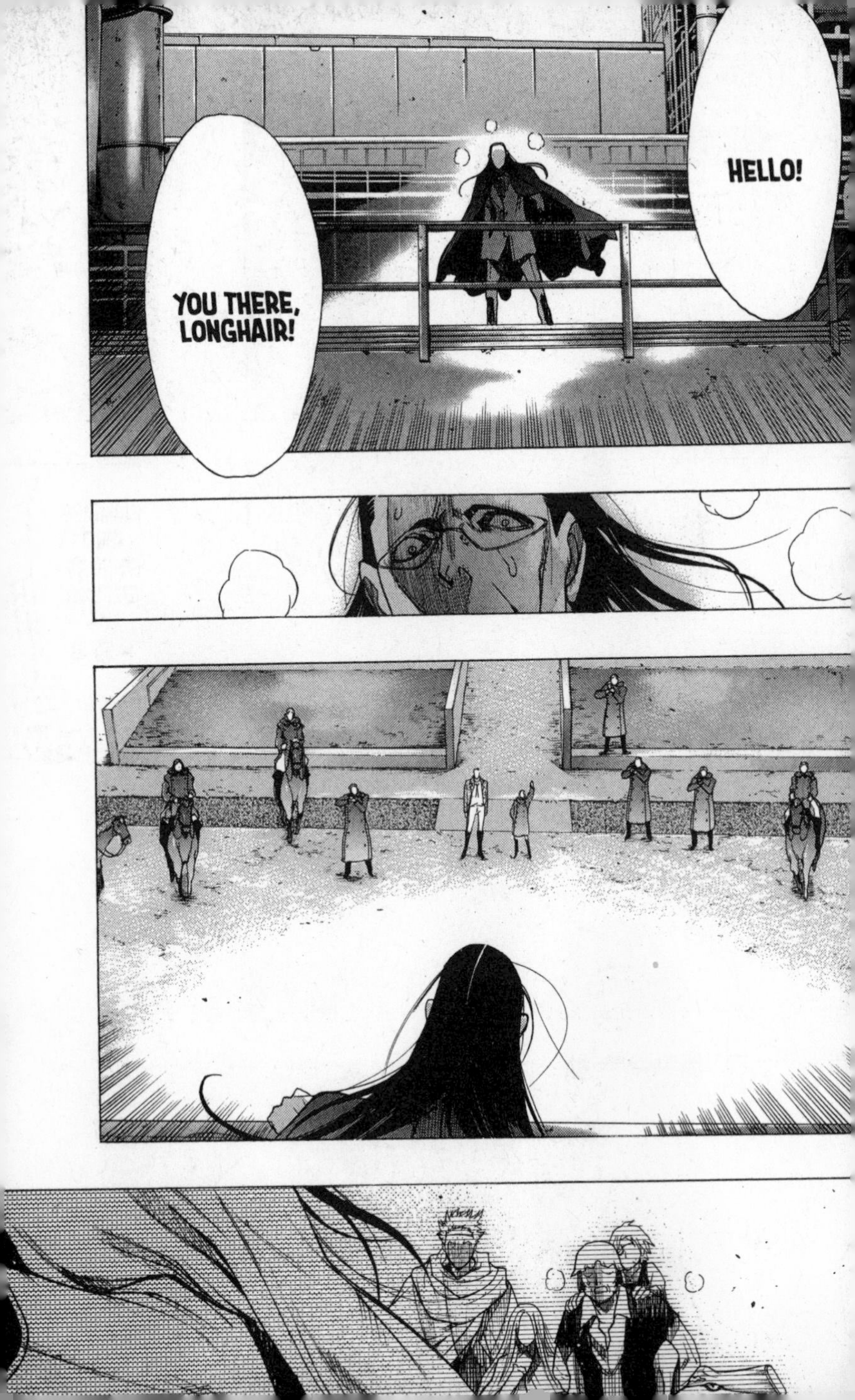
HELLO!
YOU THERE, LONGHAIR!

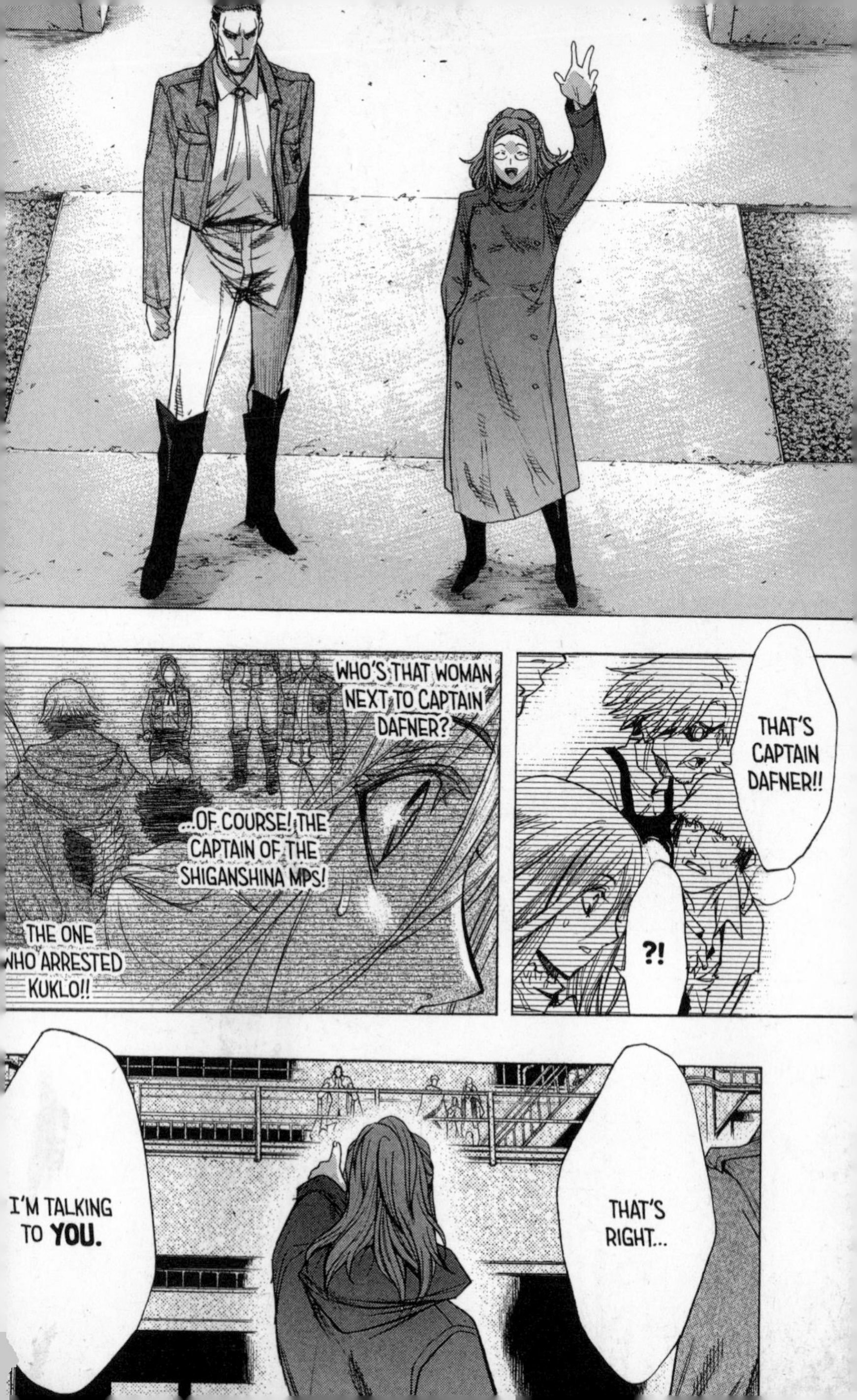
THAT'S CAPTAIN DAFNER!!
?!
WHO'S THAT WOMAN NEXT TO CAPTAIN DAFNER?
...OF COURSE! THE CAPTAIN OF THE SHIGANSHINA MPS!
THE ONE WHO ARRESTED KUKLO!!
THAT'S RIGHT...
I'M TALKING TO YOU.

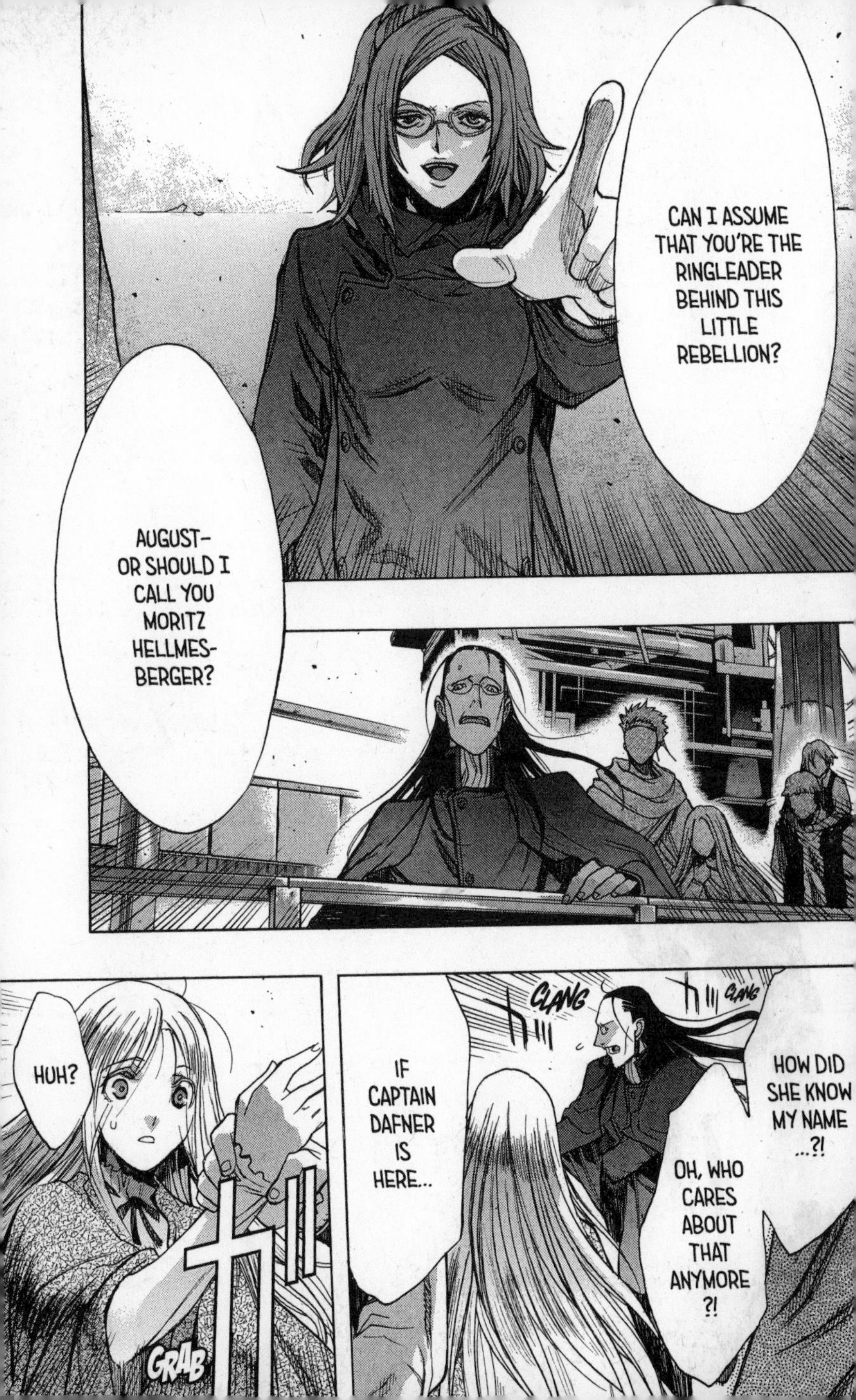
CAN I ASSUME THAT YOU'RE THE RINGLEADER BEHIND THIS LITTLE REBELLION?
AUGUST– OR SHOULD I CALL YOU MORITZ HELLMES-BERGER?
CLANG
HOW DID SHE KNOW MY NAME ...?!
CLANG
OH, WHO CARES ABOUT THAT ANYMORE ?!
IF CAPTAIN DAFNER IS HERE...
HUH?
GRAB

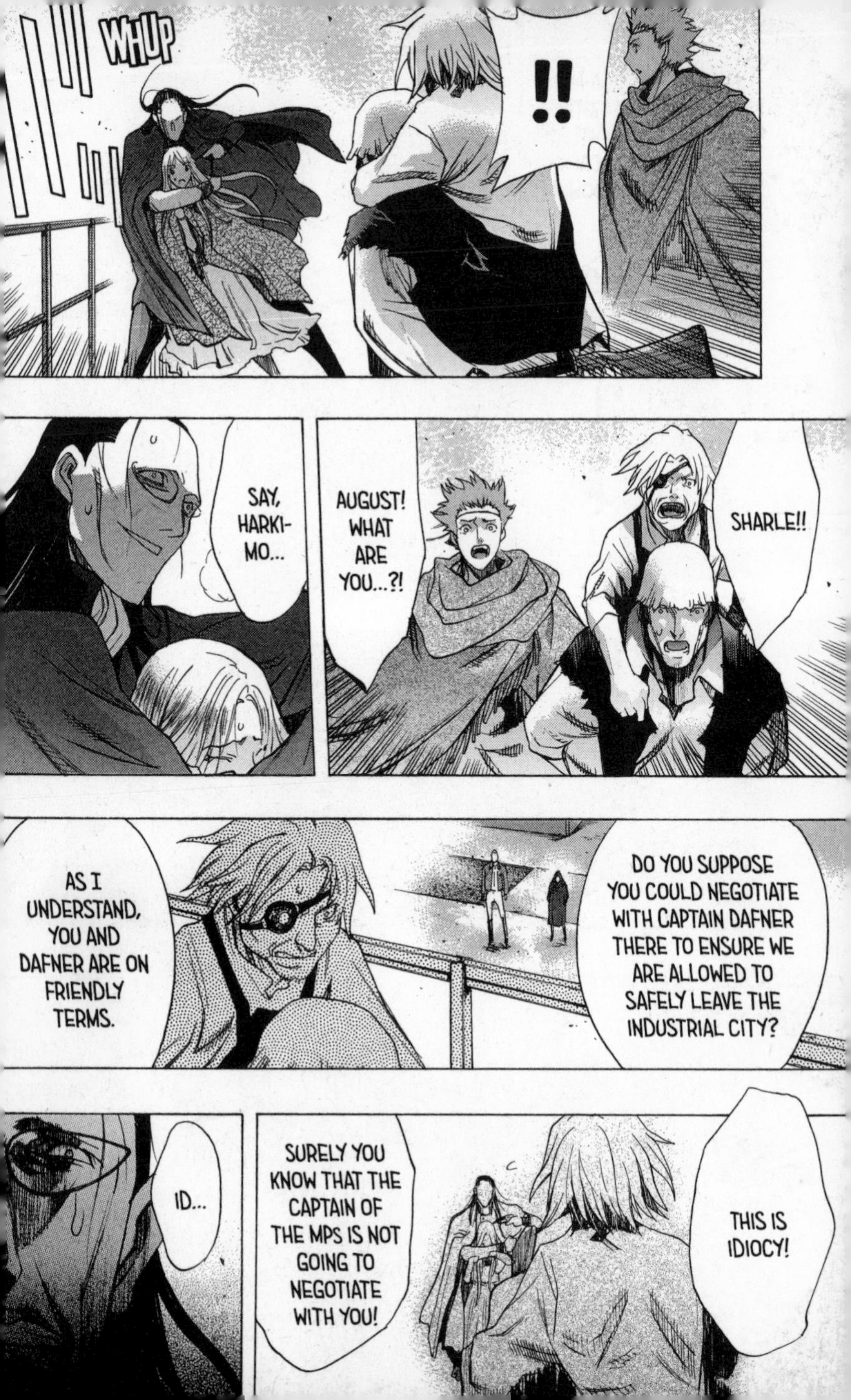
WHUP
!!
SHARLE!!
AUGUST! WHAT ARE YOU...?!
SAY, HARKI-MO...
DO YOU SUPPOSE YOU COULD NEGOTIATE WITH CAPTAIN DAFNER THERE TO ENSURE WE ARE ALLOWED TO SAFELY LEAVE THE INDUSTRIAL CITY?
AS I UNDERSTAND, YOU AND DAFNER ARE ON FRIENDLY TERMS.
THIS IS IDIOCY!
SURELY YOU KNOW THAT THE CAPTAIN OF THE MPS IS NOT GOING TO NEGOTIATE WITH YOU!
ID...

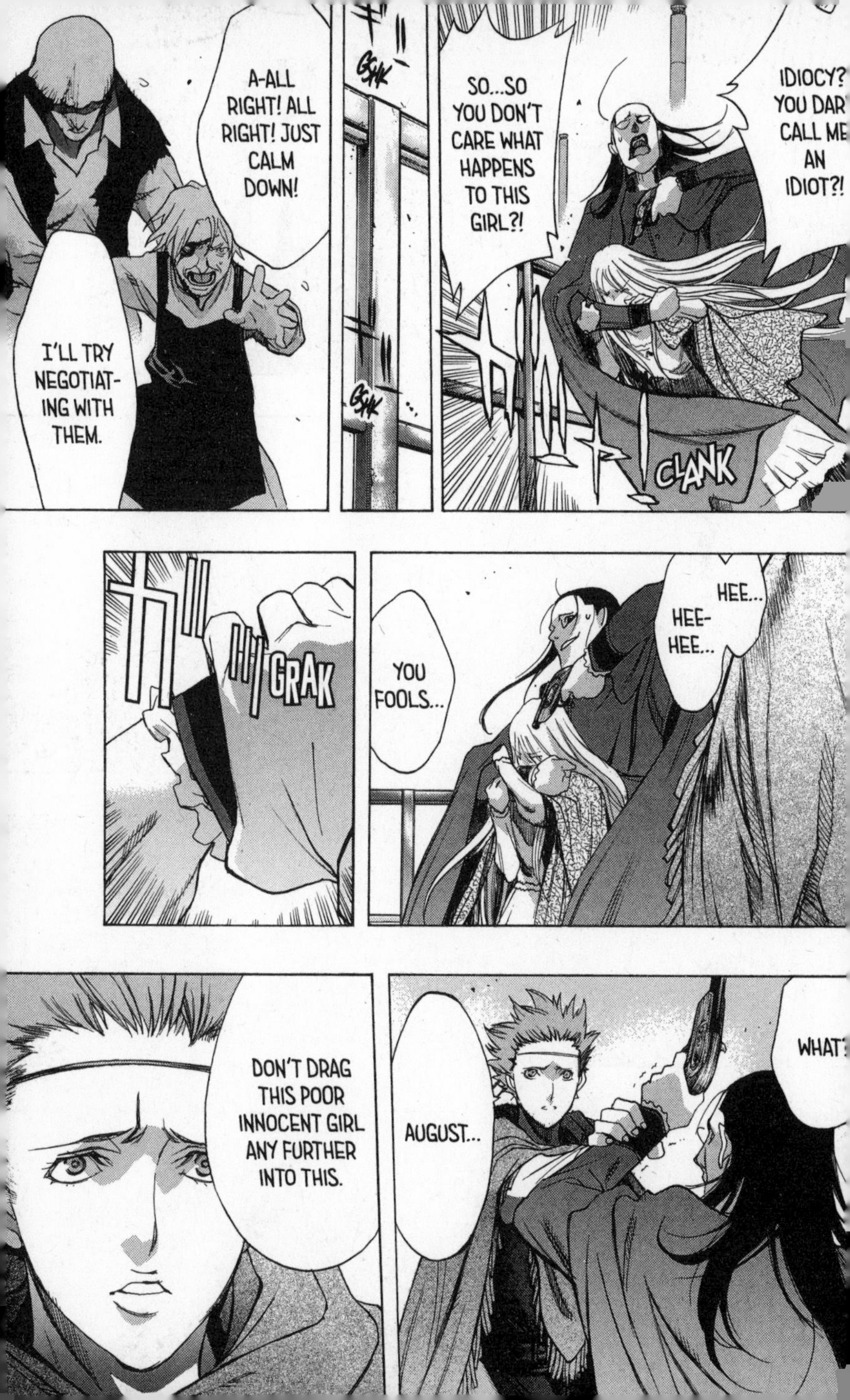

IDIOCY? YOU DAR CALL ME AN IDIOT?!
SO...SO YOU DON'T CARE WHAT HAPPENS TO THIS GIRL?!
CLANK
GSHK
GSHK
A-ALL RIGHT! ALL RIGHT! JUST CALM DOWN!
I'LL TRY NEGOTIATING WITH THEM.
HEE... HEE-HEE...
YOU FOOLS...
GRAK
WHAT
AUGUST...
DON'T DRAG THIS POOR INNOCENT GIRL ANY FURTHER INTO THIS.

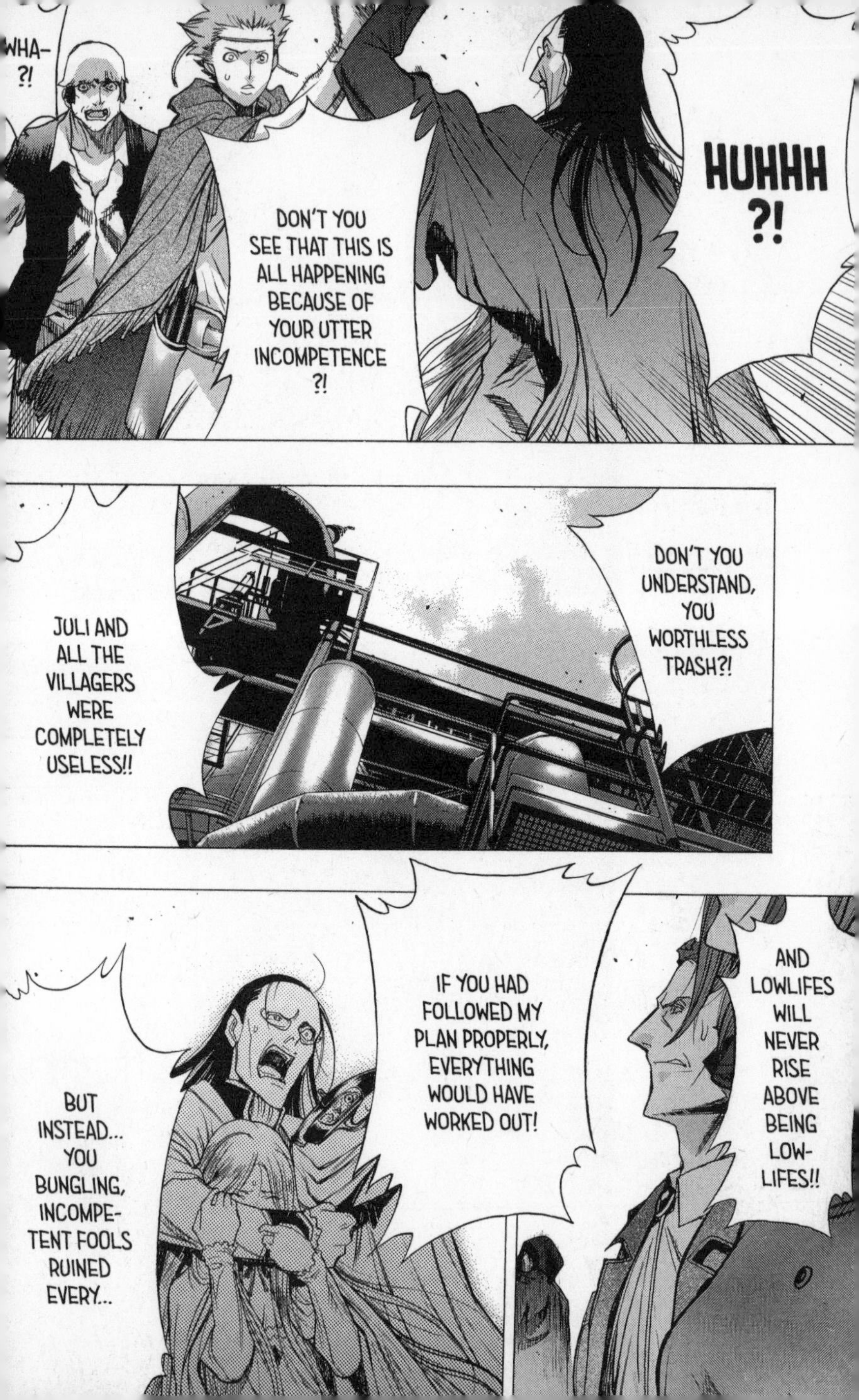
HUHHH ?!
DON'T YOU SEE THAT THIS IS ALL HAPPENING BECAUSE OF YOUR UTTER INCOMPETENCE ?!
WHA- ?!
DON'T YOU UNDERSTAND, YOU WORTHLESS TRASH?!
JULI AND ALL THE VILLAGERS WERE COMPLETELY USELESS!!
AND LOWLIFES WILL NEVER RISE ABOVE BEING LOW-LIFES!!
IF YOU HAD FOLLOWED MY PLAN PROPERLY, EVERYTHING WOULD HAVE WORKED OUT!
BUT INSTEAD... YOU BUNGLING, INCOMPE-TENT FOOLS RUINED EVERY...

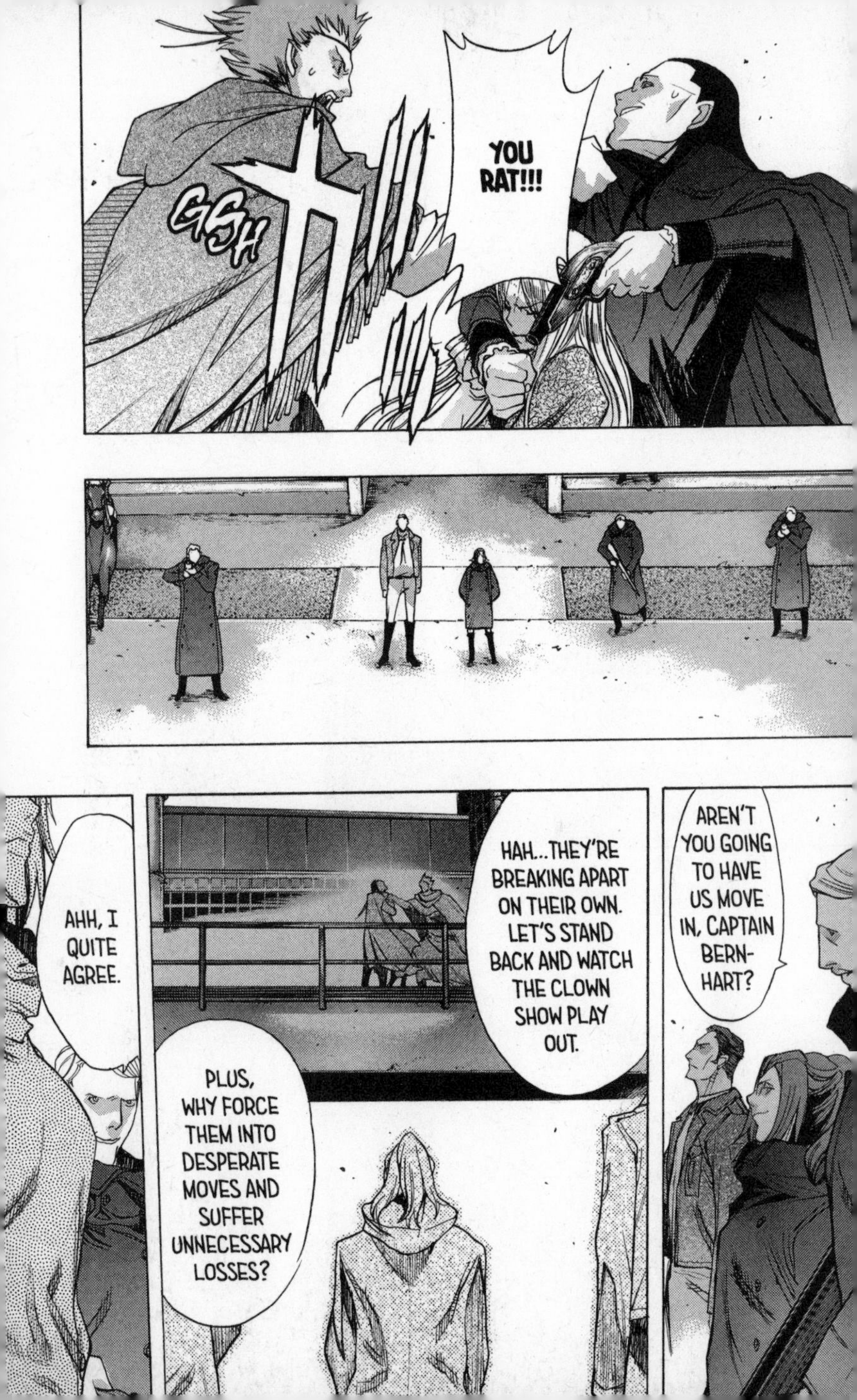
YOU RAT!!!
GSH
AREN'T YOU GOING TO HAVE US MOVE IN, CAPTAIN BERN-HART?
HAH...THEY'RE BREAKING APART ON THEIR OWN. LET'S STAND BACK AND WATCH THE CLOWN SHOW PLAY OUT.
PLUS, WHY FORCE THEM INTO DESPERATE MOVES AND SUFFER UNNECESSARY LOSSES?
AHH, I QUITE AGREE.

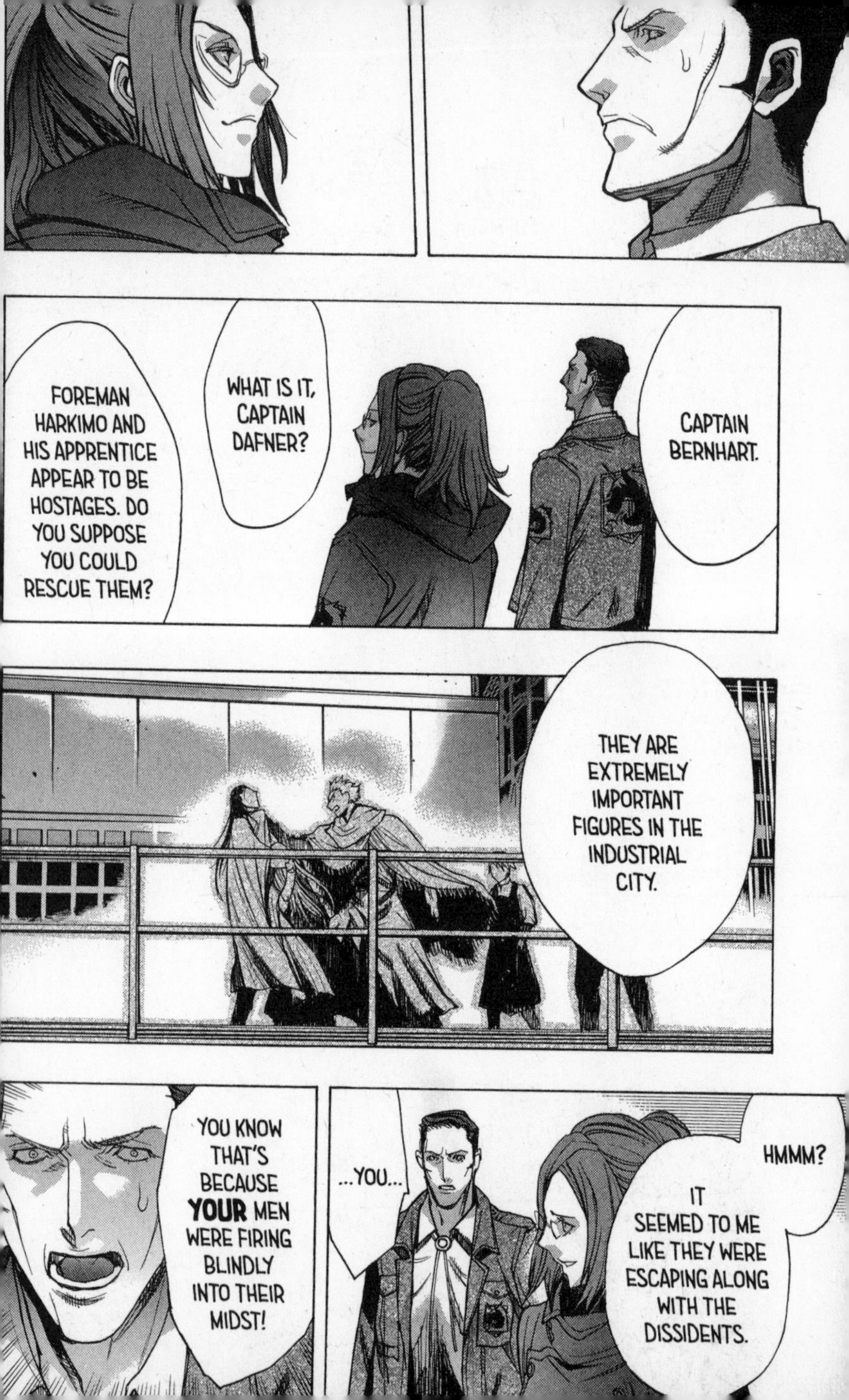
CAPTAIN BERNHART.
WHAT IS IT, CAPTAIN DAFNER?
FOREMAN HARKIMO AND HIS APPRENTICE APPEAR TO BE HOSTAGES. DO YOU SUPPOSE YOU COULD RESCUE THEM?
THEY ARE EXTREMELY IMPORTANT FIGURES IN THE INDUSTRIAL CITY.
HMMM?
IT SEEMED TO ME LIKE THEY WERE ESCAPING ALONG WITH THE DISSIDENTS.
...YOU...
YOU KNOW THAT'S BECAUSE **YOUR** MEN WERE FIRING BLINDLY INTO THEIR MIDST!

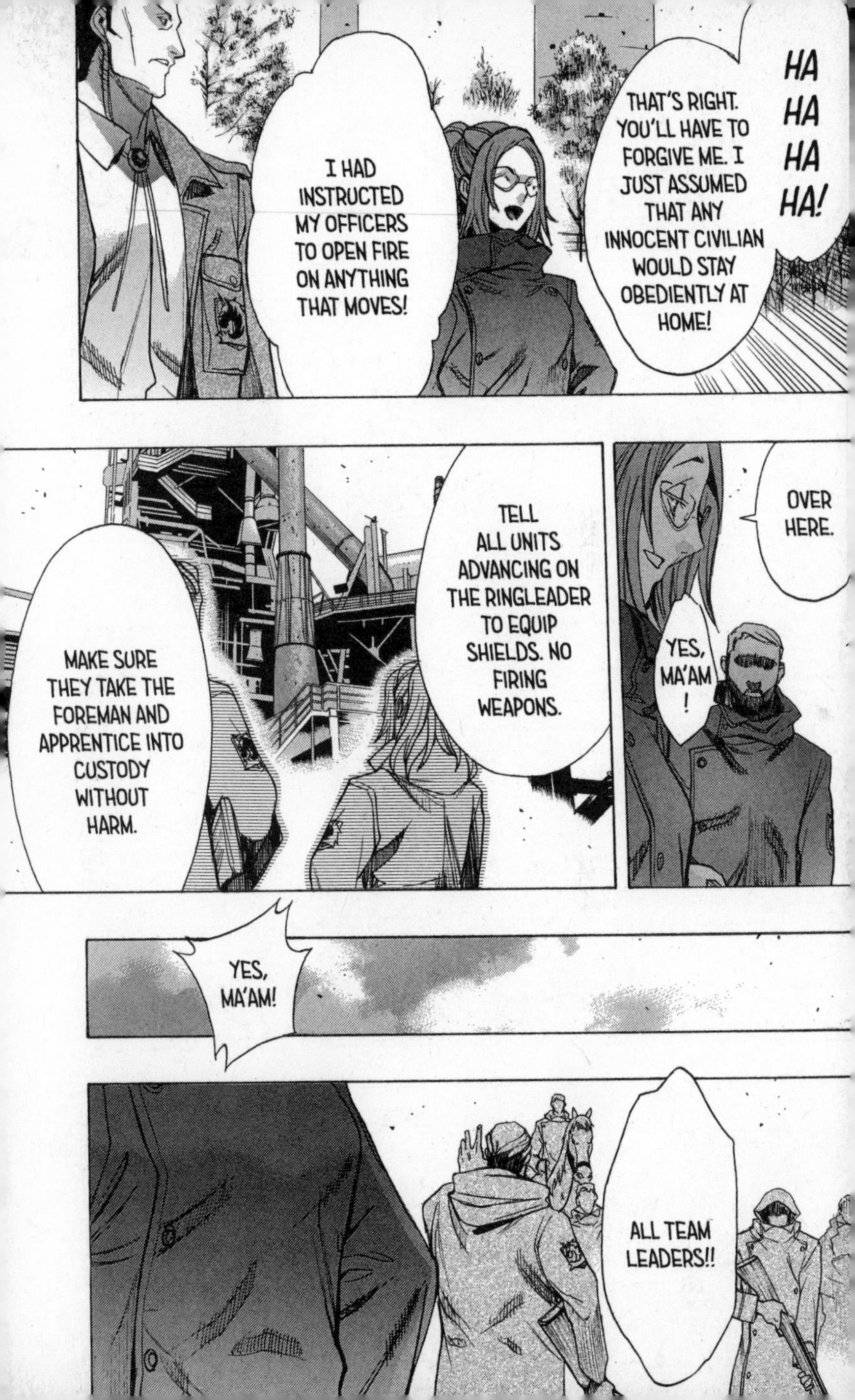
HA HA HA HA!
THAT'S RIGHT. YOU'LL HAVE TO FORGIVE ME. I JUST ASSUMED THAT ANY INNOCENT CIVILIAN WOULD STAY OBEDIENTLY AT HOME!
I HAD INSTRUCTED MY OFFICERS TO OPEN FIRE ON ANYTHING THAT MOVES!
OVER HERE.
YES, MA'AM!
TELL ALL UNITS ADVANCING ON THE RINGLEADER TO EQUIP SHIELDS. NO FIRING WEAPONS.
MAKE SURE THEY TAKE THE FOREMAN AND APPRENTICE INTO CUSTODY WITHOUT HARM.
YES, MA'AM!
ALL TEAM LEADERS!!

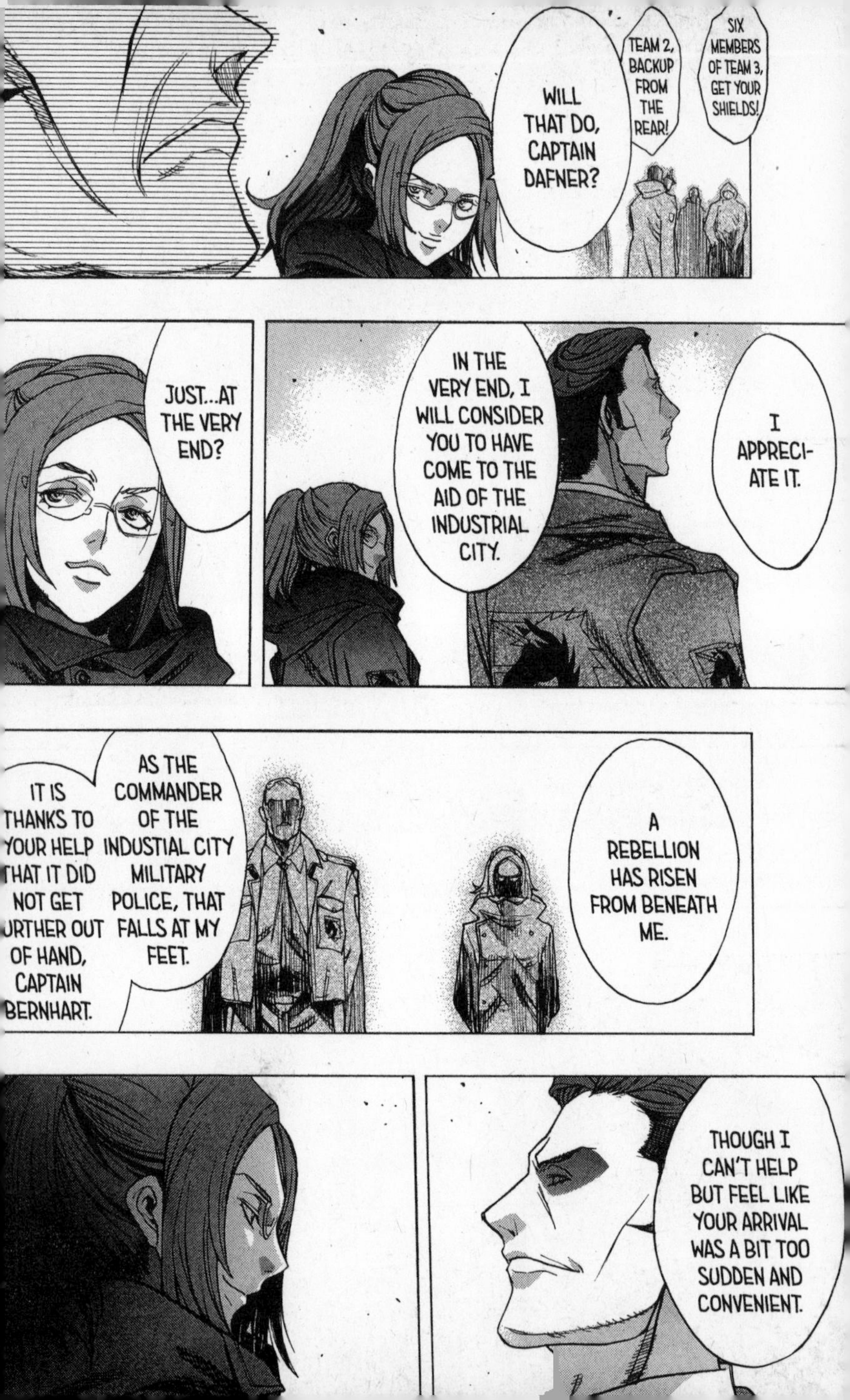
SIX MEMBERS OF TEAM 3, GET YOUR SHIELDS!
TEAM 2, BACKUP FROM THE REAR!
WILL THAT DO, CAPTAIN DAFNER?
I APPRECI-ATE IT.
IN THE VERY END, I WILL CONSIDER YOU TO HAVE COME TO THE AID OF THE INDUSTRIAL CITY.
JUST...AT THE VERY END?
A REBELLION HAS RISEN FROM BENEATH ME.
AS THE COMMANDER OF THE INDUSTIAL CITY MILITARY POLICE, THAT FALLS AT MY FEET.
IT IS THANKS TO YOUR HELP THAT IT DID NOT GET URTHER OUT OF HAND, CAPTAIN BERNHART.
THOUGH I CAN'T HELP BUT FEEL LIKE YOUR ARRIVAL WAS A BIT TOO SUDDEN AND CONVENIENT.
...

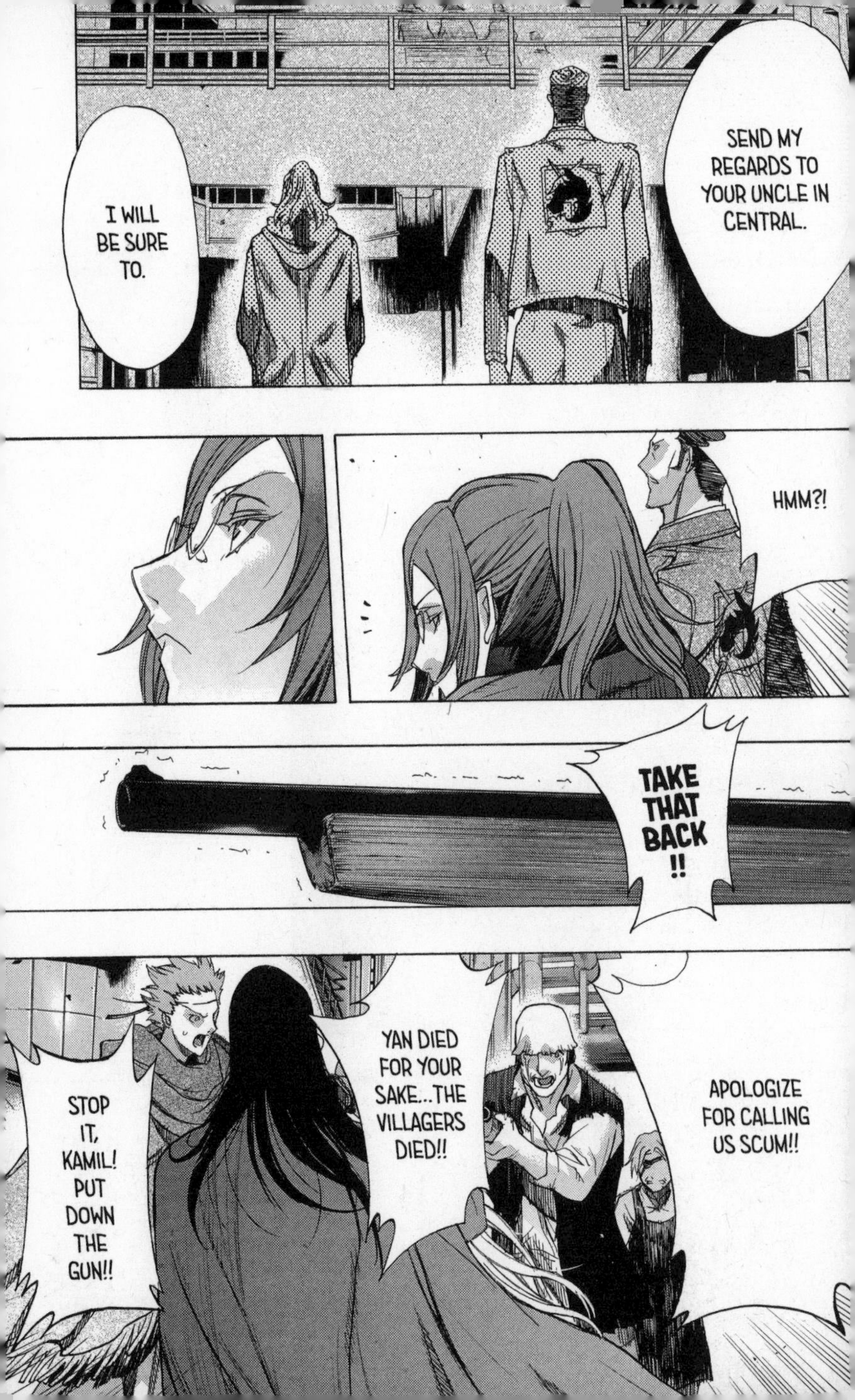
SEND MY REGARDS TO YOUR UNCLE IN CENTRAL.
I WILL BE SURE TO.
HMM?!
TAKE THAT BACK!!
APOLOGIZE FOR CALLING US SCUM!!
YAN DIED FOR YOUR SAKE...THE VILLAGERS DIED!!
STOP IT, KAMIL! PUT DOWN THE GUN!!

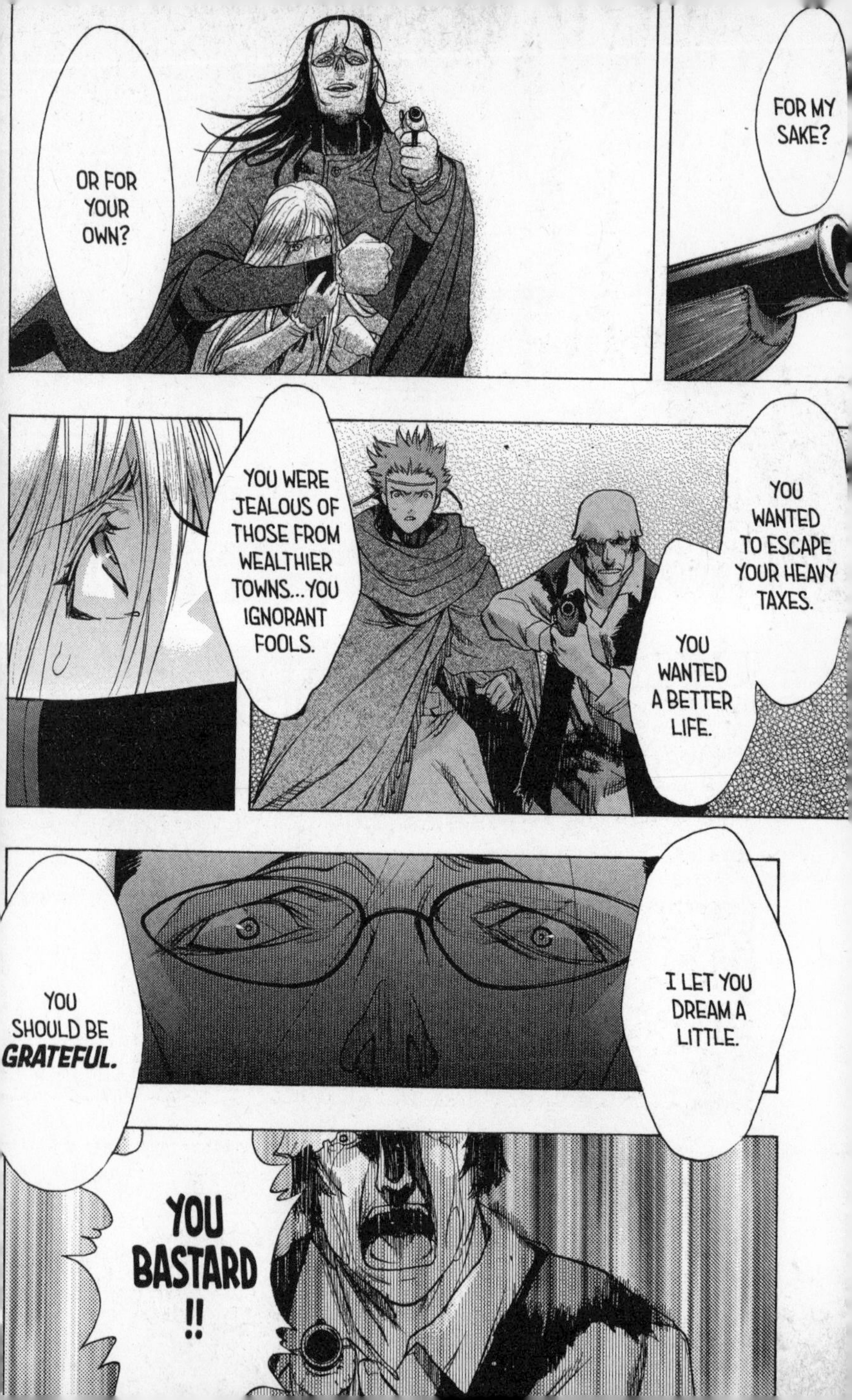
FOR MY SAKE?
OR FOR YOUR OWN?
YOU WANTED TO ESCAPE YOUR HEAVY TAXES.
YOU WANTED A BETTER LIFE.
YOU WERE JEALOUS OF THOSE FROM WEALTHIER TOWNS...YOU IGNORANT FOOLS.
I LET YOU DREAM A LITTLE.
YOU SHOULD BE GRATEFUL.
YOU BASTARD !!

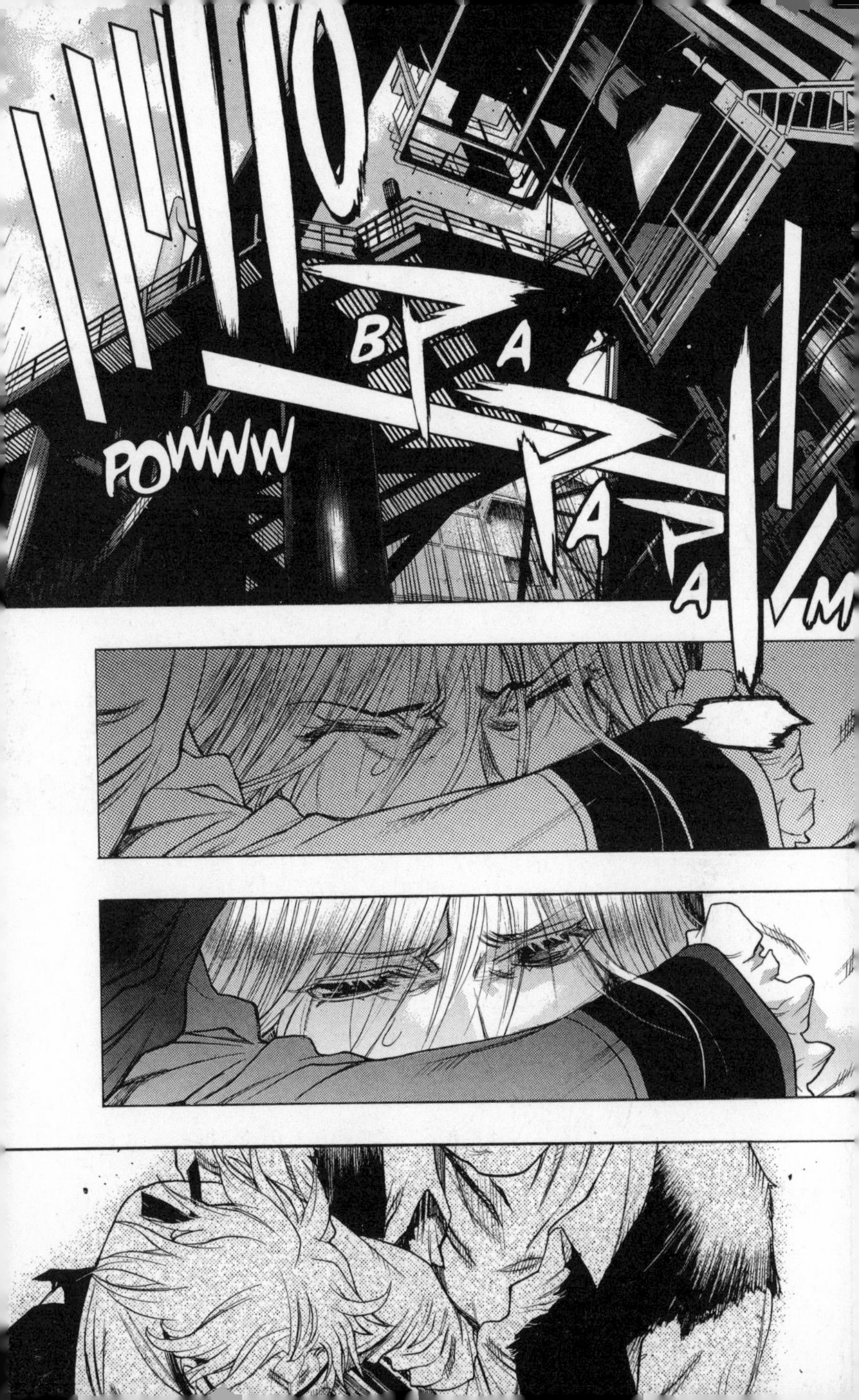
POWWW

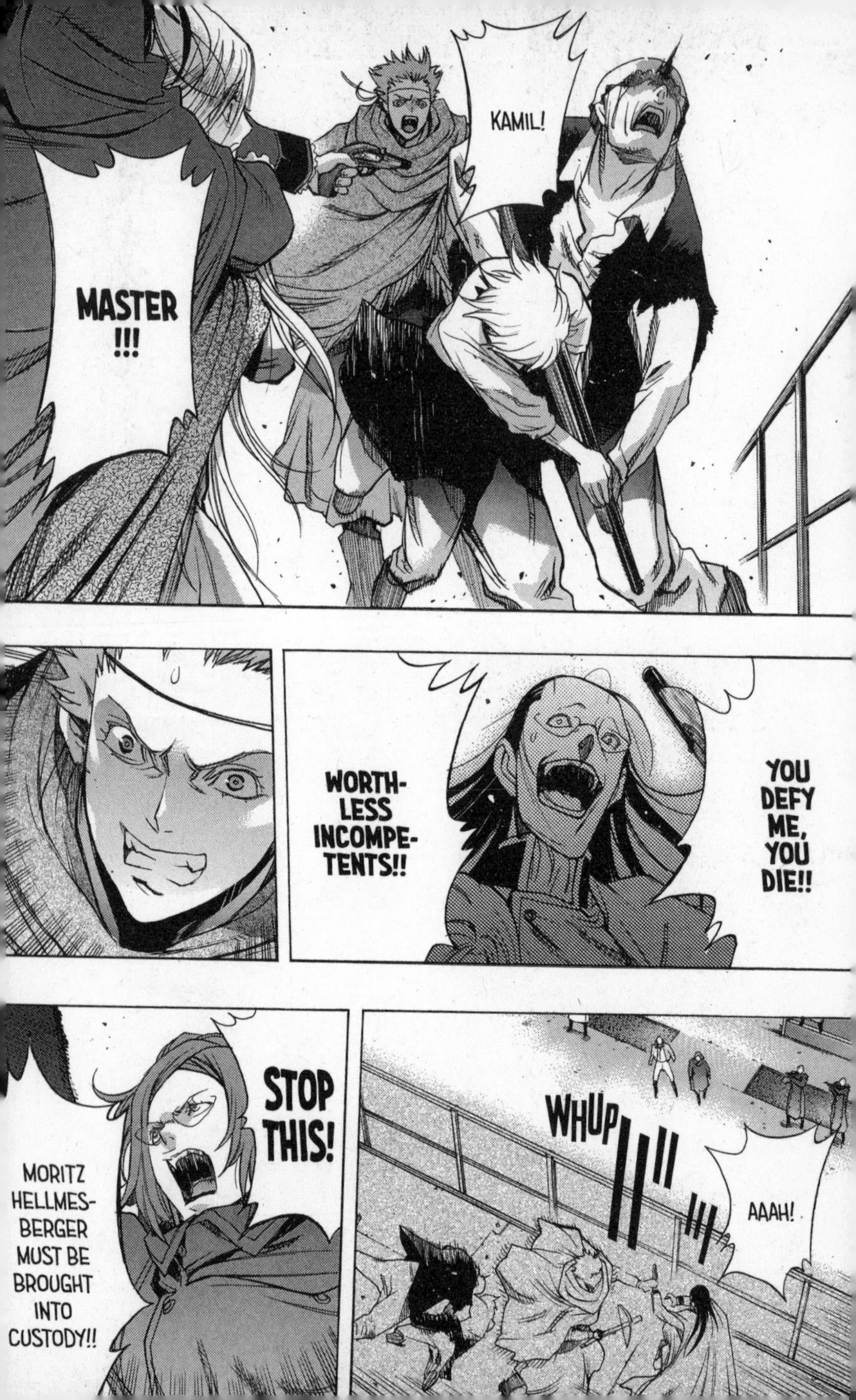
KAMIL!
MASTER !!!
YOU DEFY ME, YOU DIE!!
WORTH-LESS INCOMPE-TENTS!!
WHUP
AAAH!
STOP THIS!
MORITZ HELLMES-BERGER MUST BE BROUGHT INTO CUSTODY!!

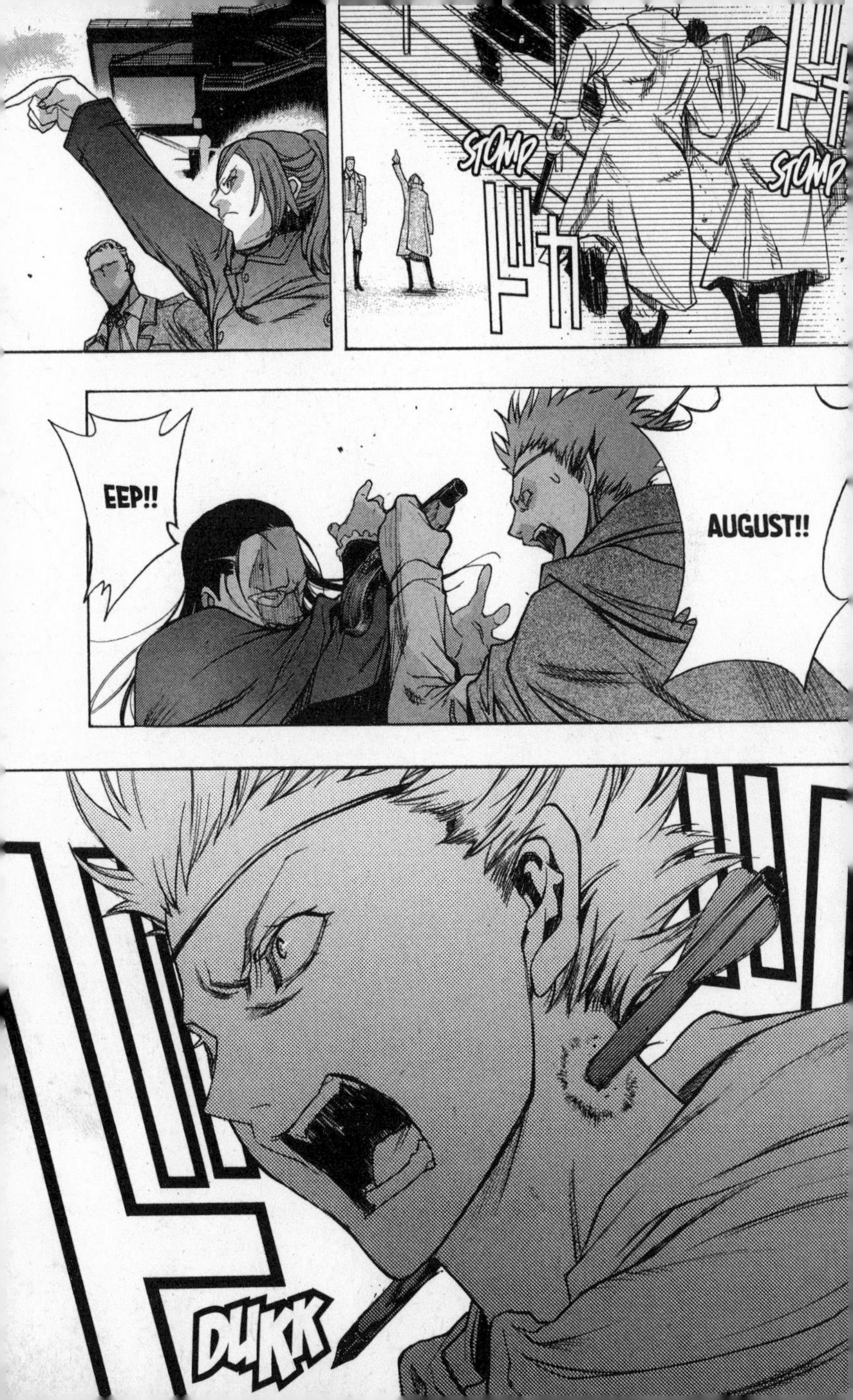
STOMP
STOMP
AUGUST!!
EEP!!
DUKK

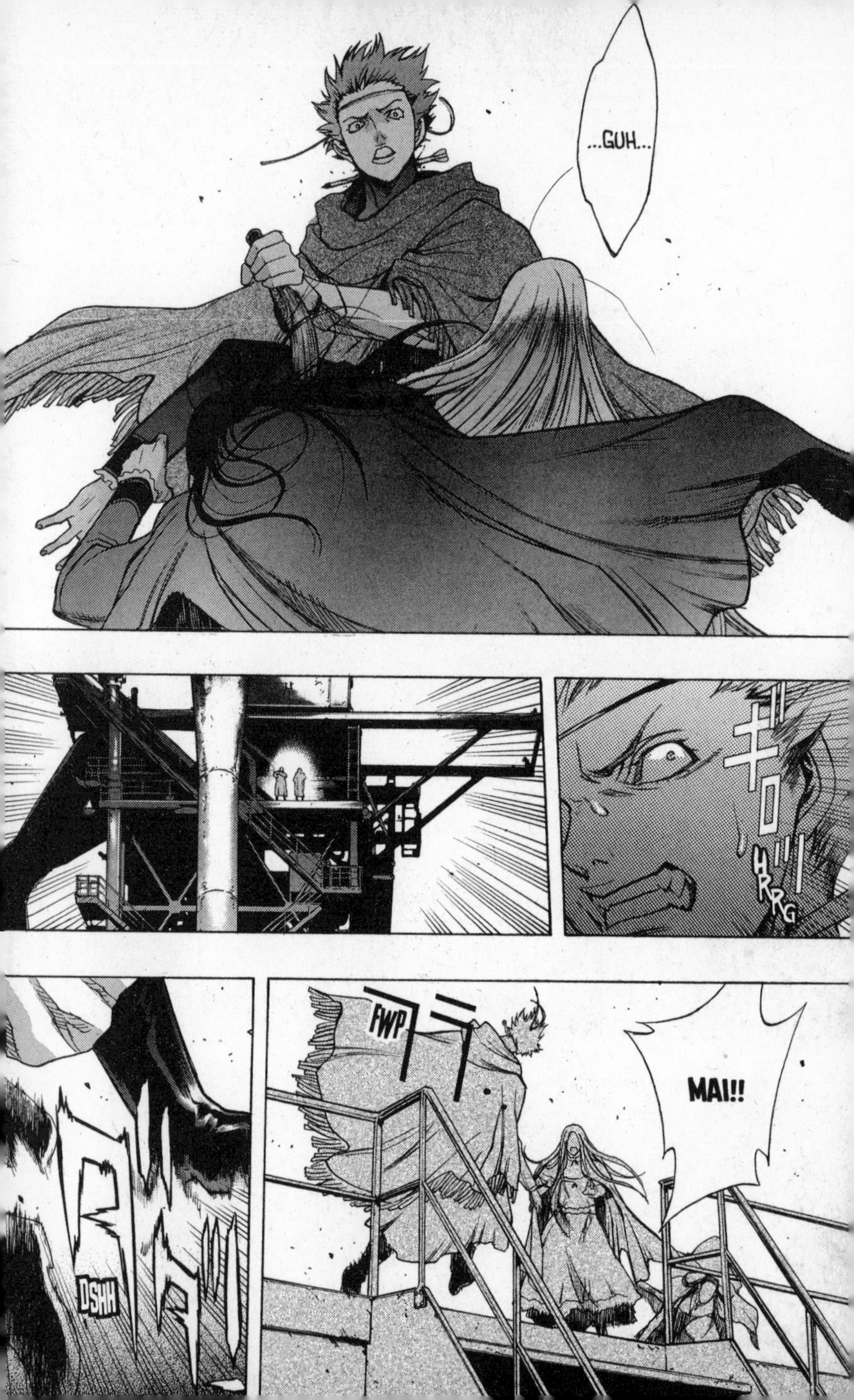
...GUH...
ギロッ
HRRG
FWP
MAI!!
DSHH

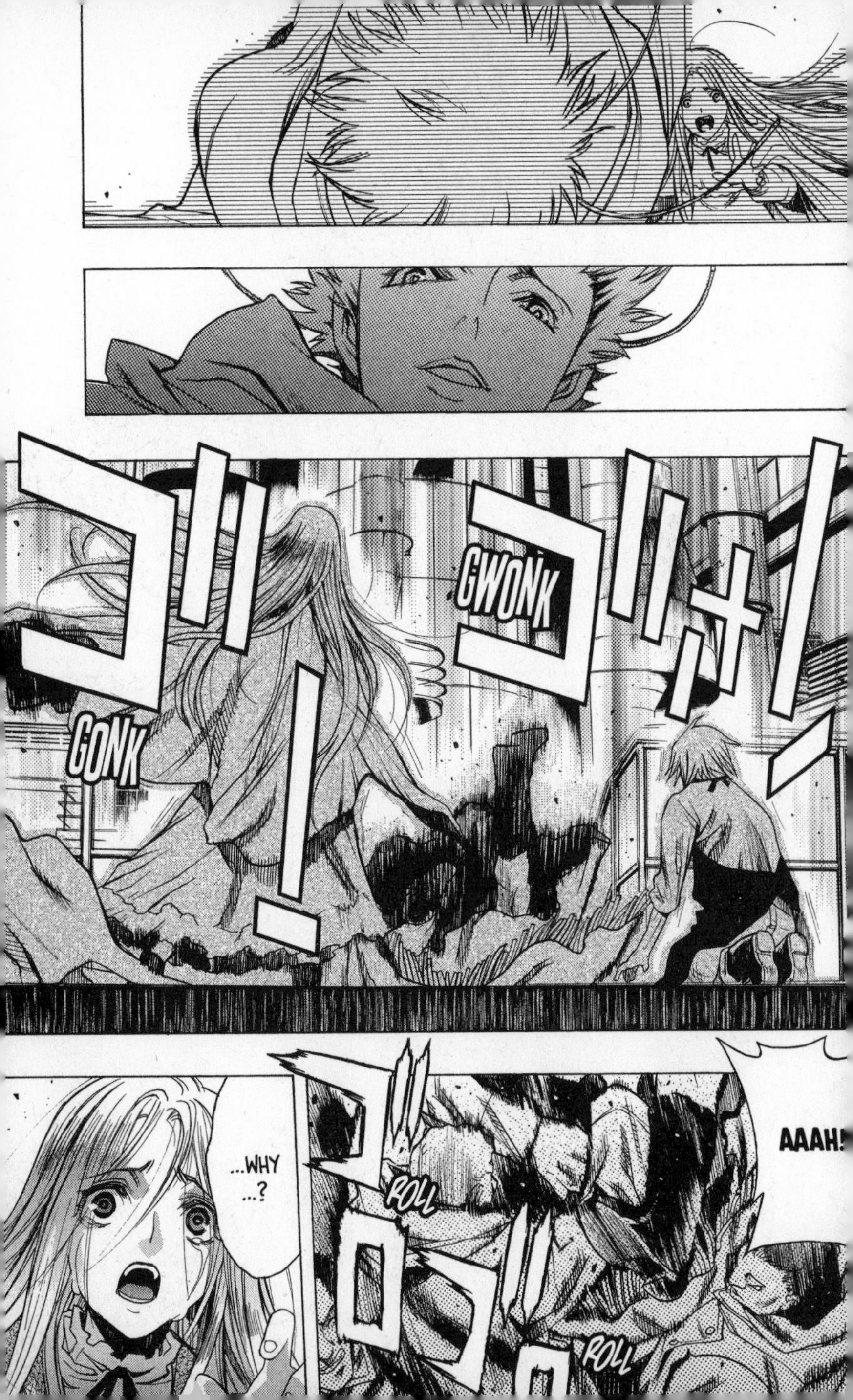
GWONK
GONK
AAAH!
ROLL
ROLL
...WHY ...?

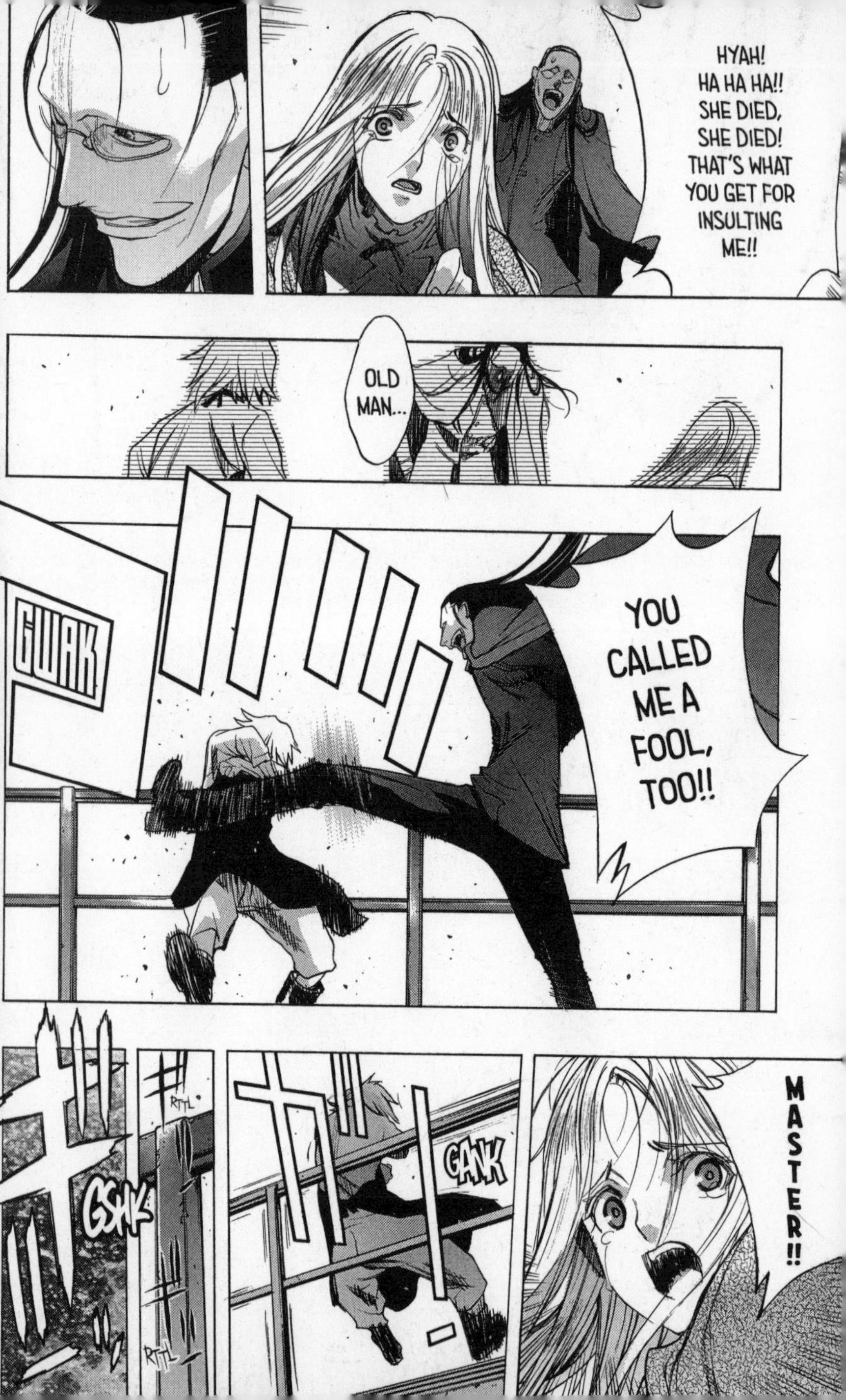
HYAH! HA HA HA!! SHE DIED, SHE DIED! THAT'S WHAT YOU GET FOR INSULTING ME!!
OLD MAN...
YOU CALLED ME A FOOL, TOO!!
GWAK
MASTER!!
GANK
GSHK

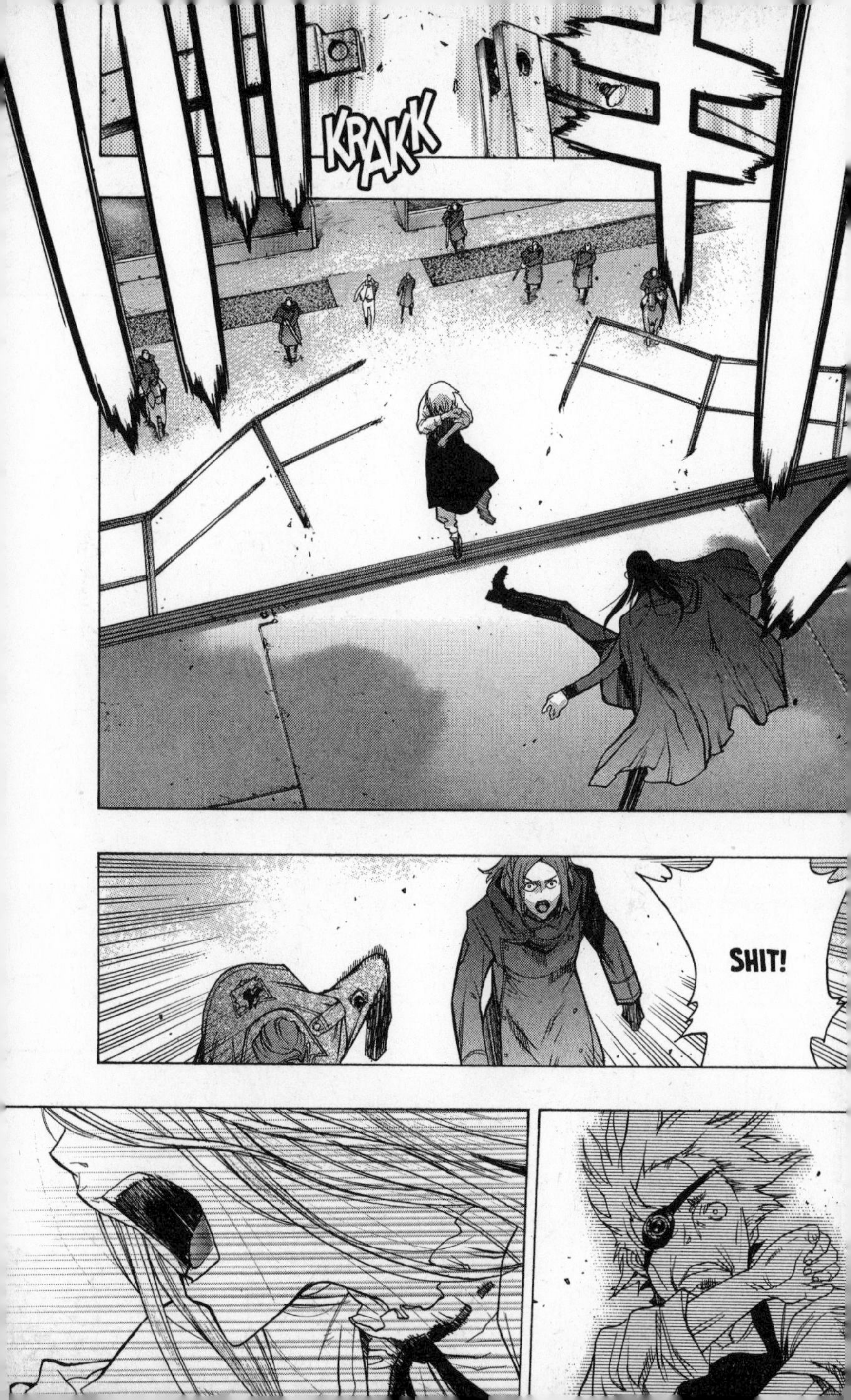
KRAKK
SHIT!

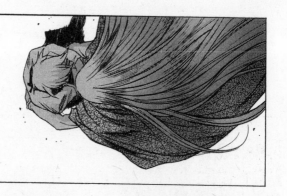

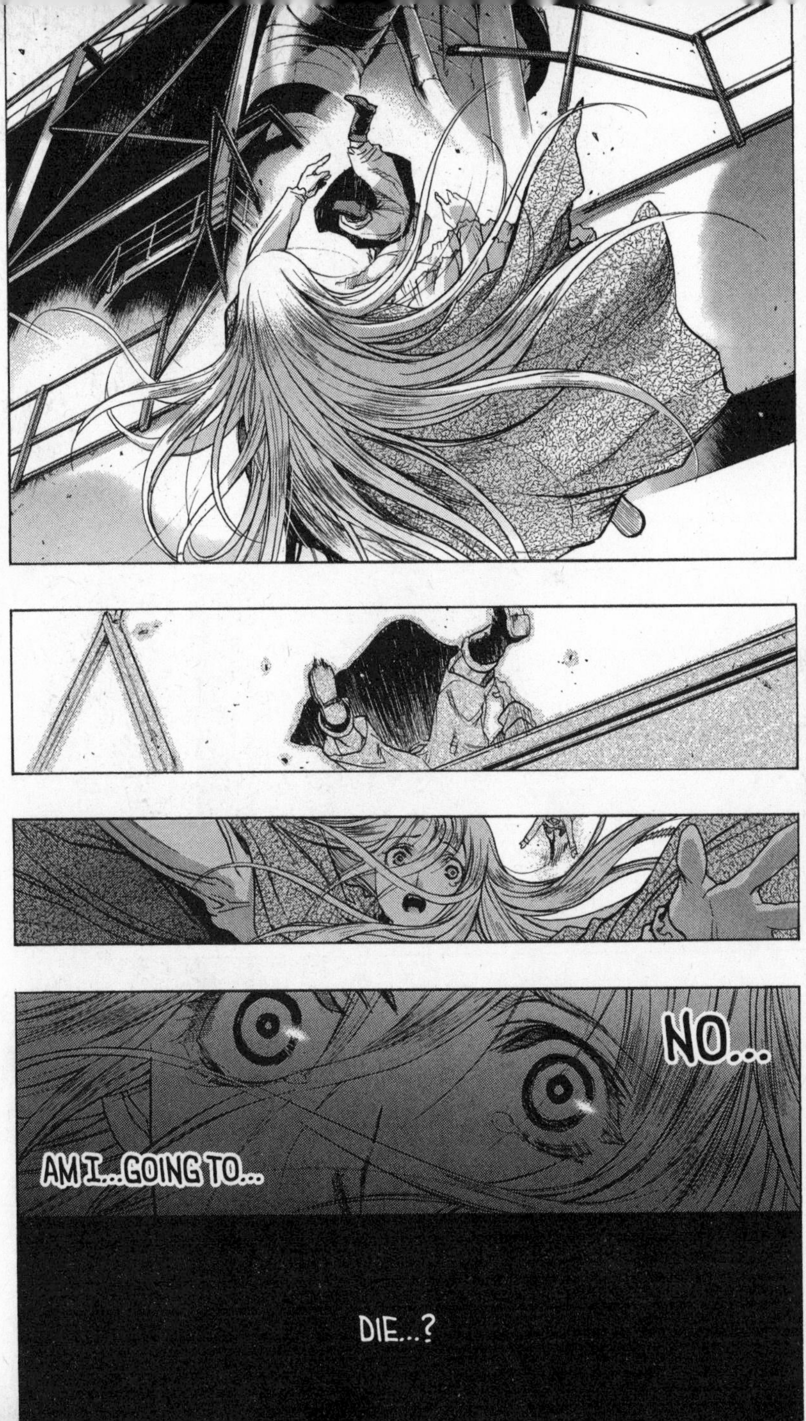
NO...
AM I...GOING TO...
DIE...?

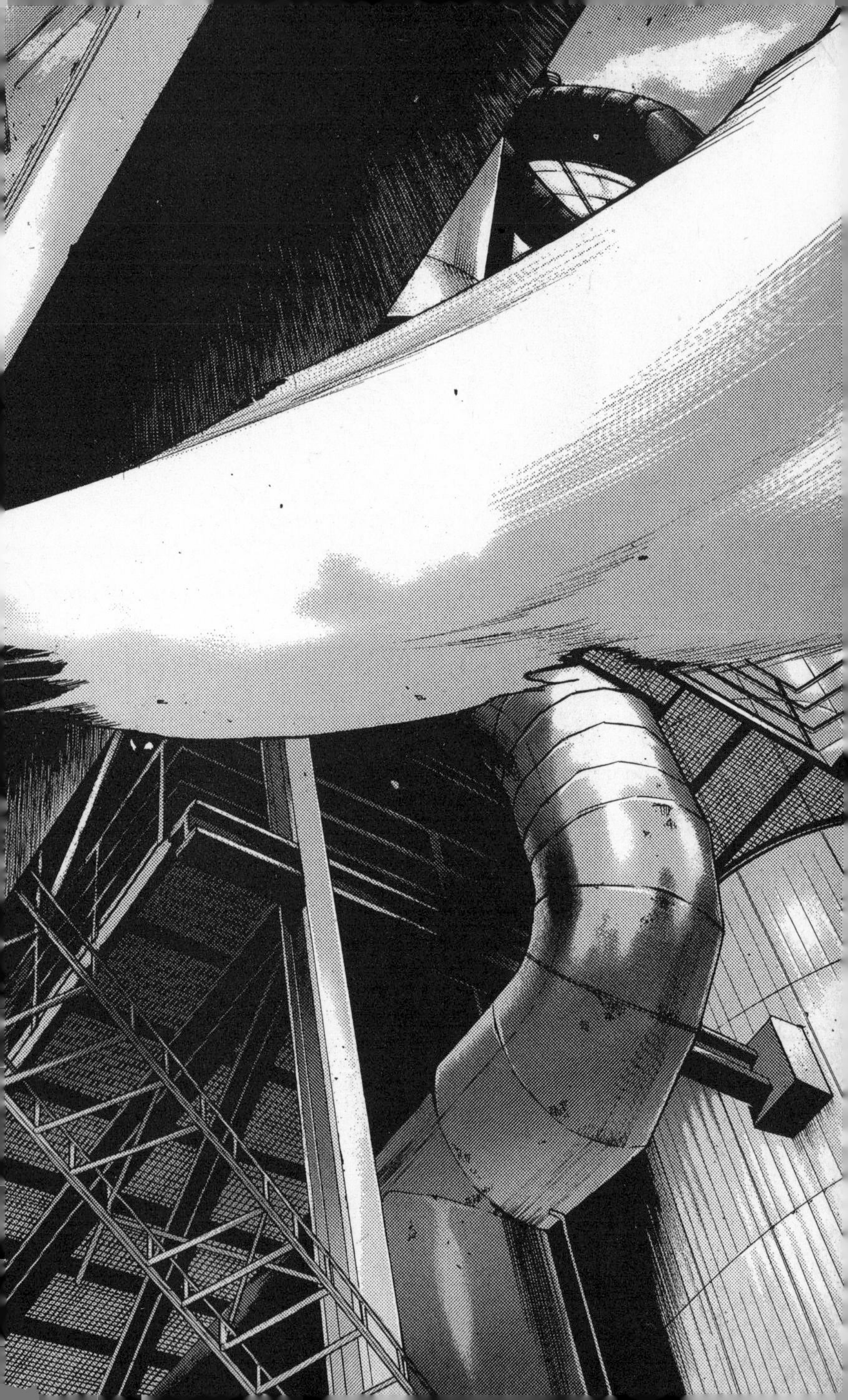

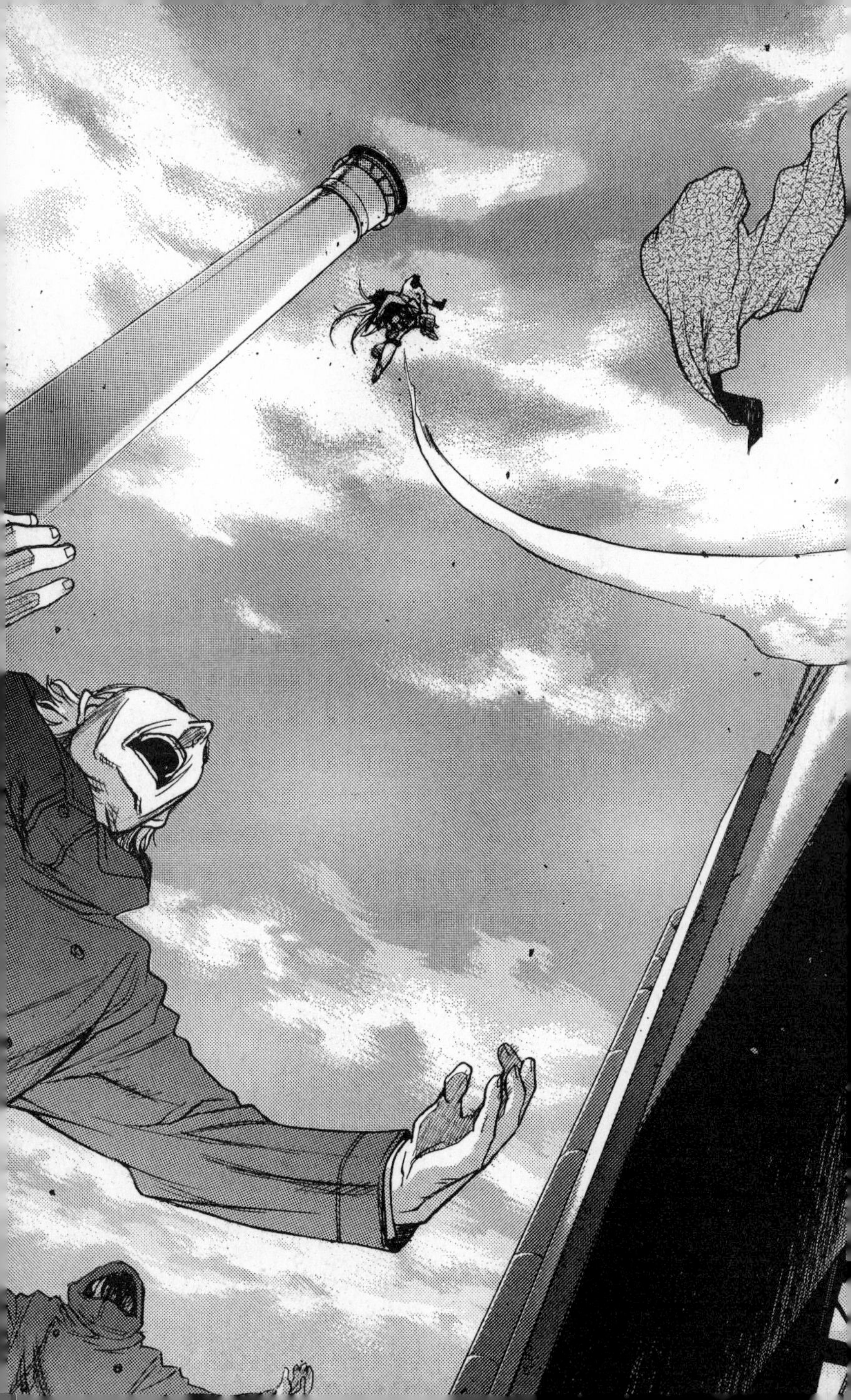

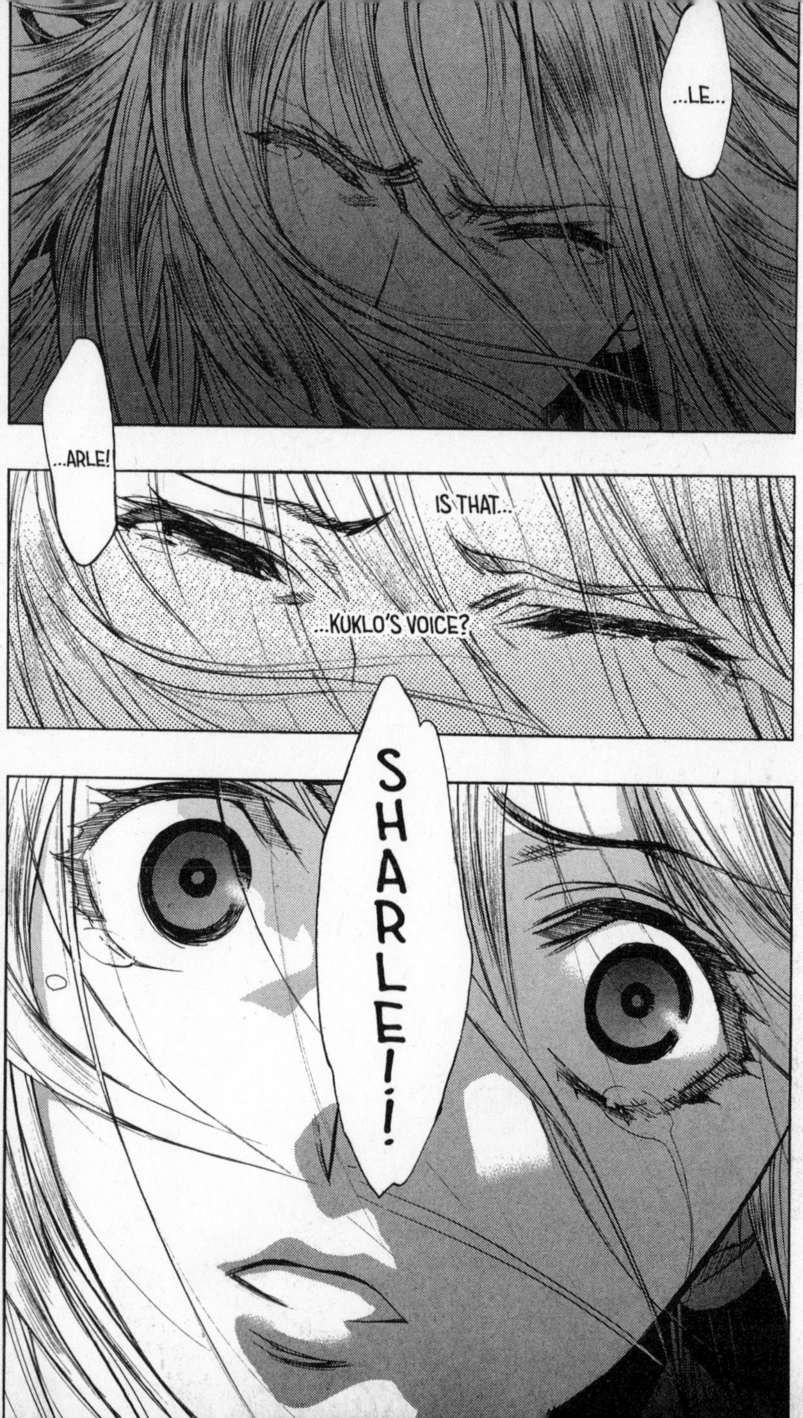
...LE...
...ARLE!
IS THAT...
...KUKLO'S VOICE?
SHARLE!!

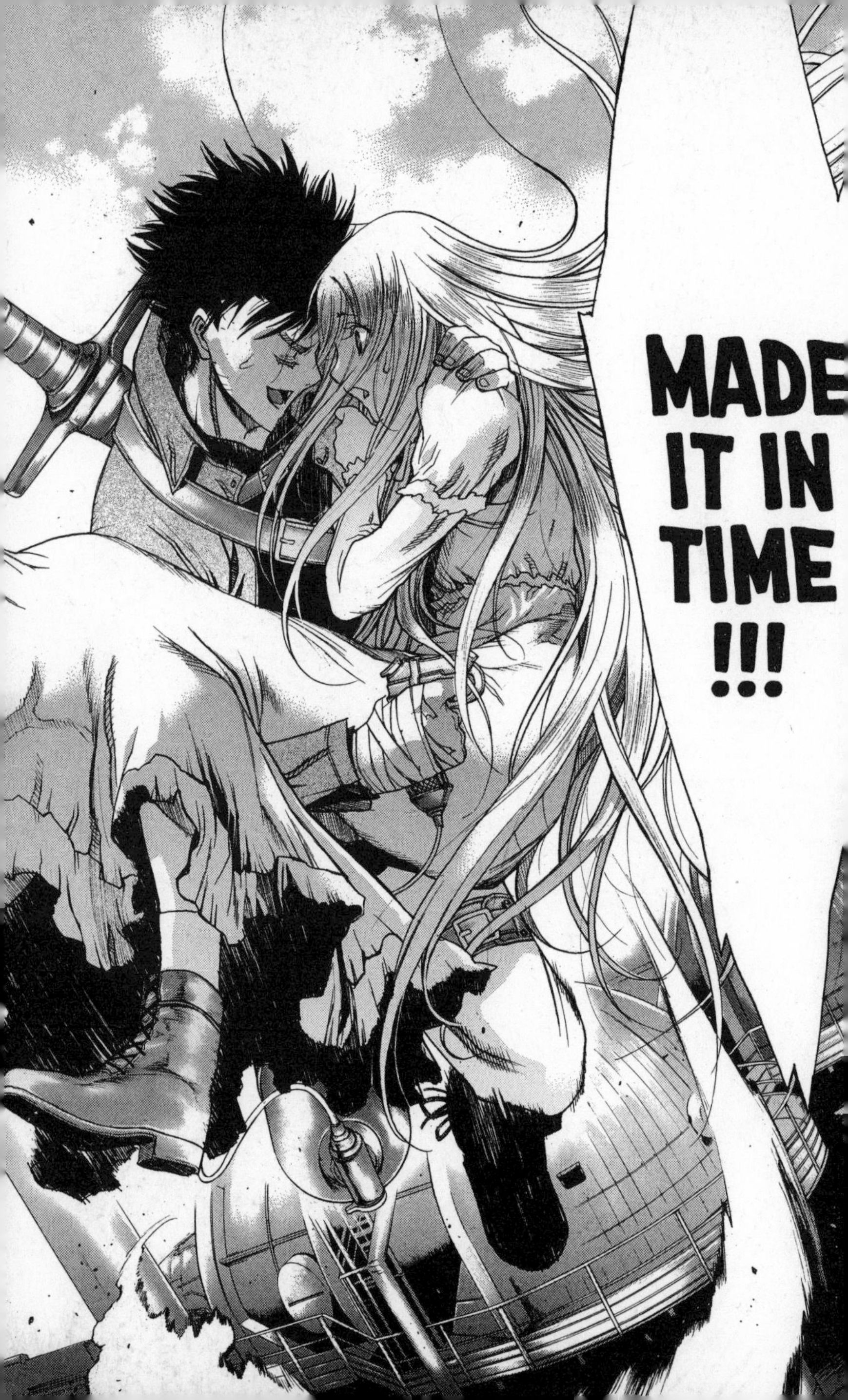
MADE IT IN TIME !!!

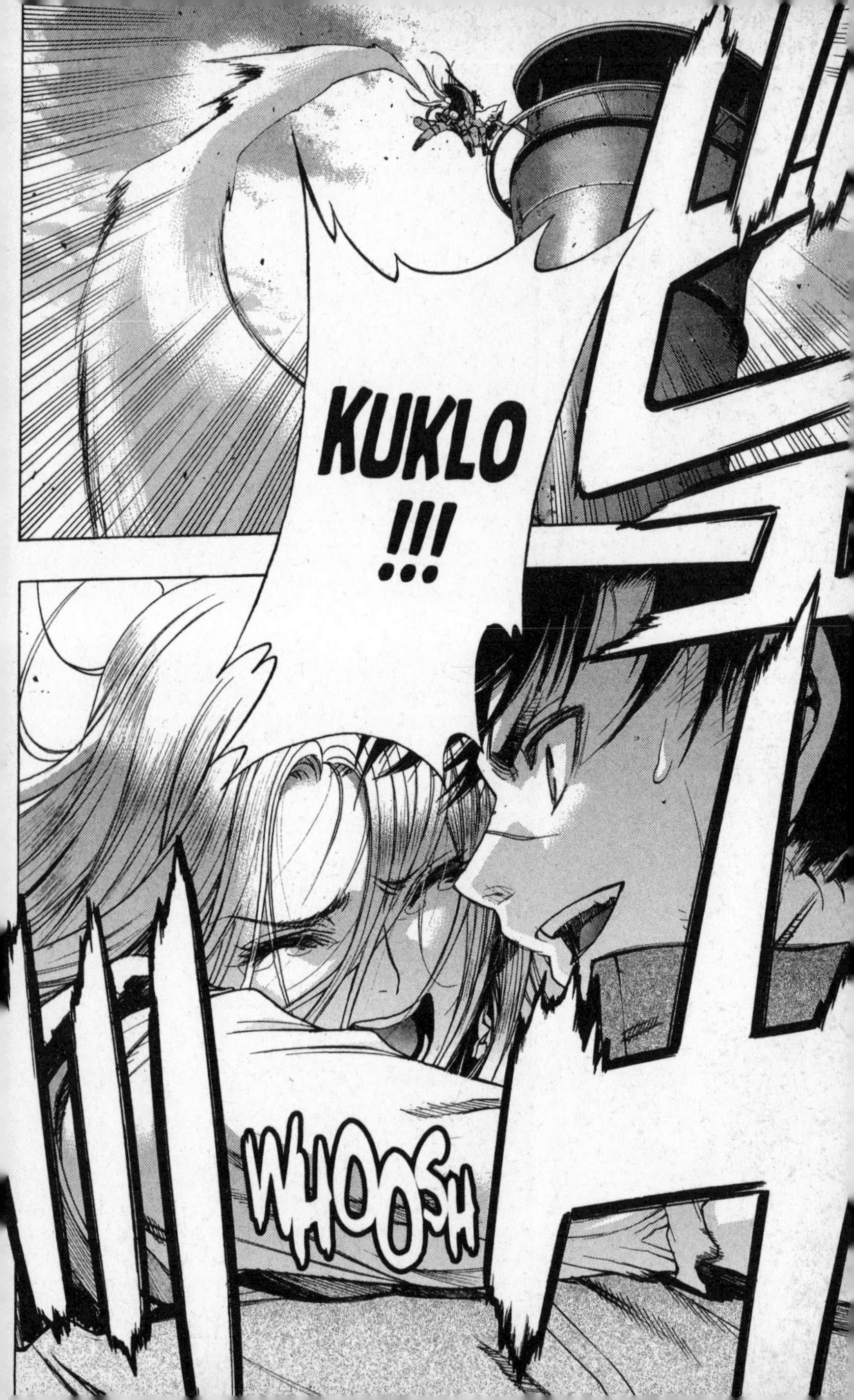
KUKLO !!!
WHOOSH

Chapter 30: Fallout of Rebellion · End

ATTACK on TITAN
BEFORE THE FALL

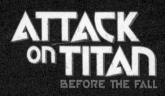

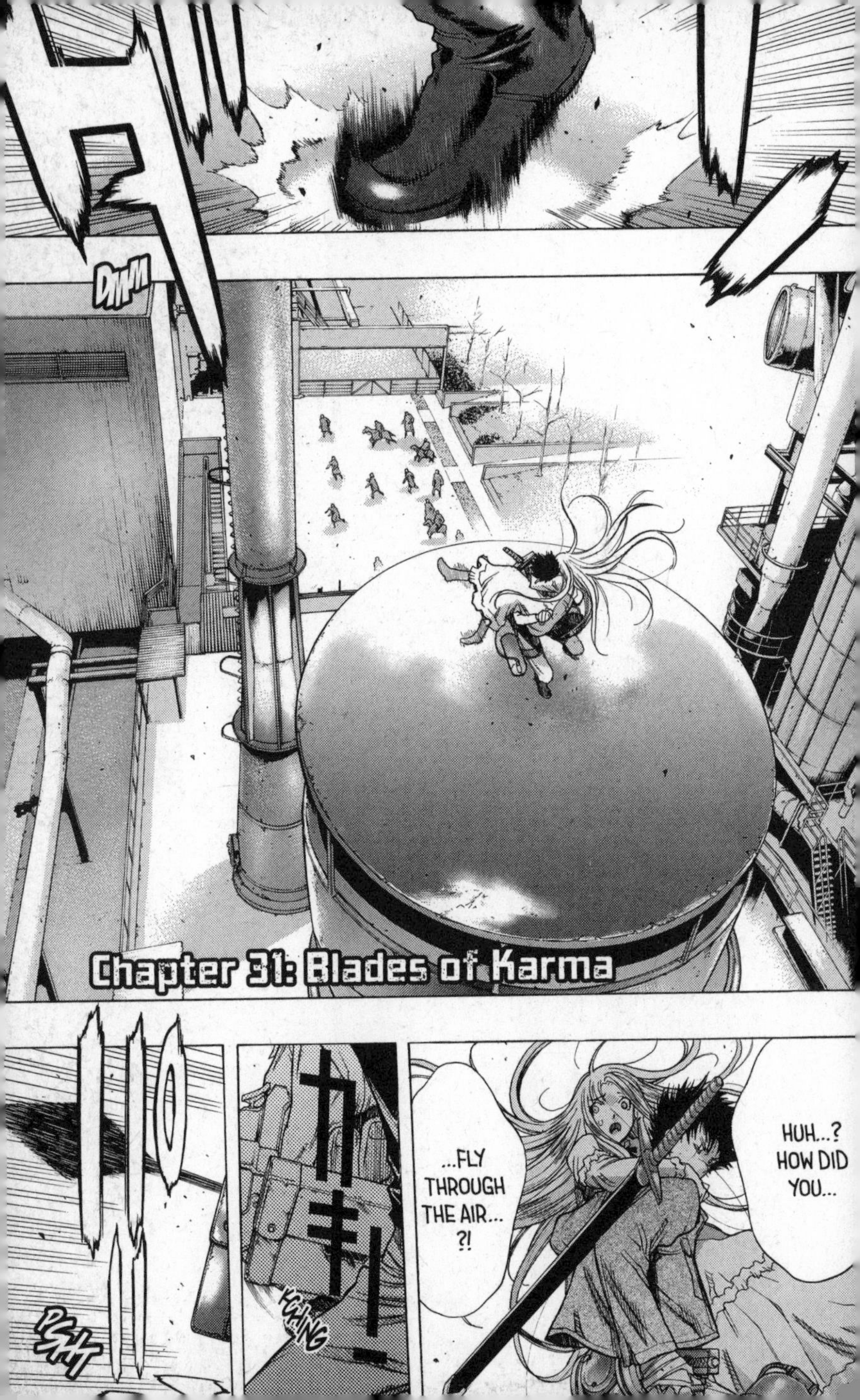
DMM
Chapter 31: Blades of Karma
HUH...? HOW DID YOU...
...FLY THROUGH THE AIR...?!
KCHING
PSHT

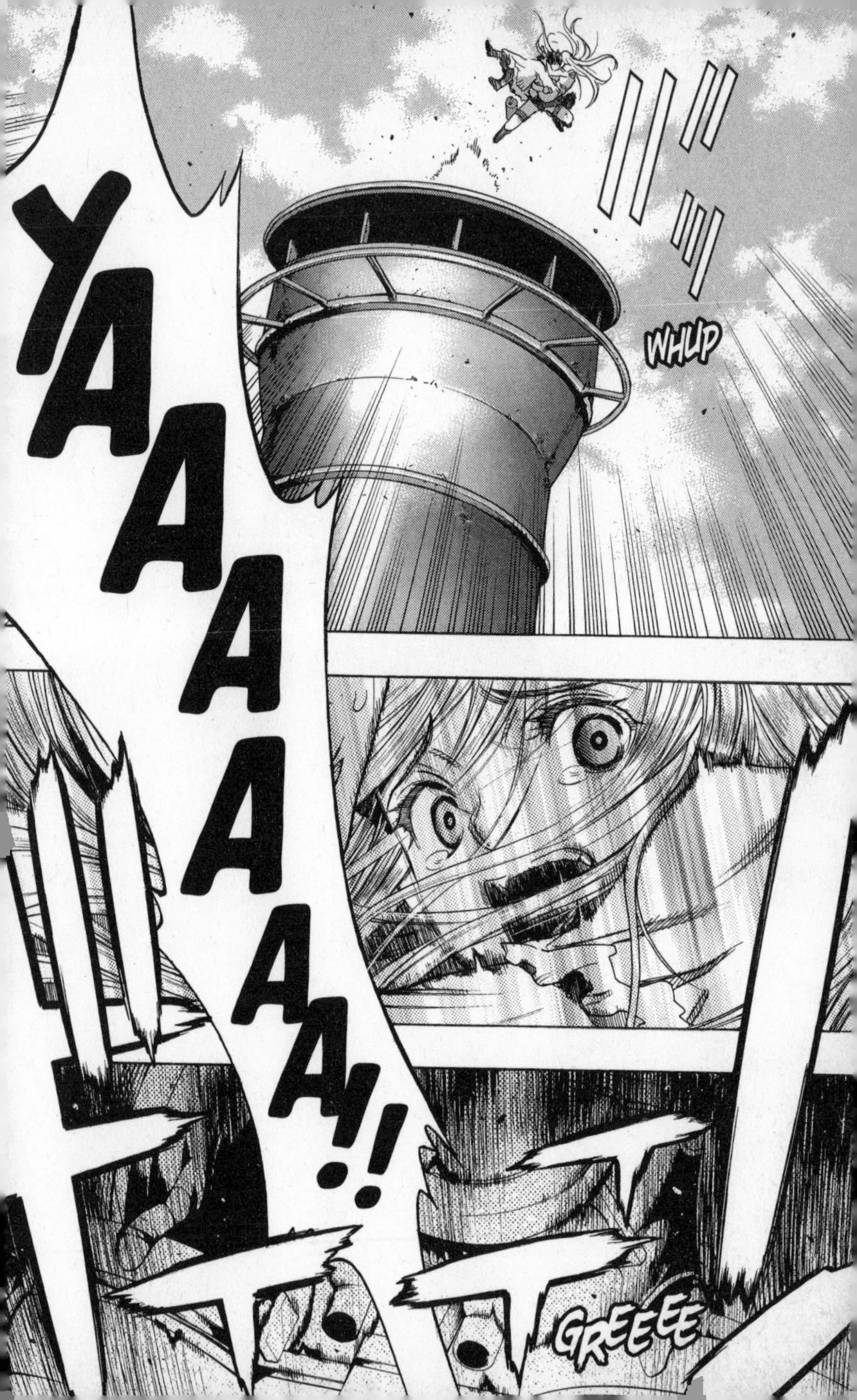
WHUP
YAAAAAAAAH!!
GREEEE

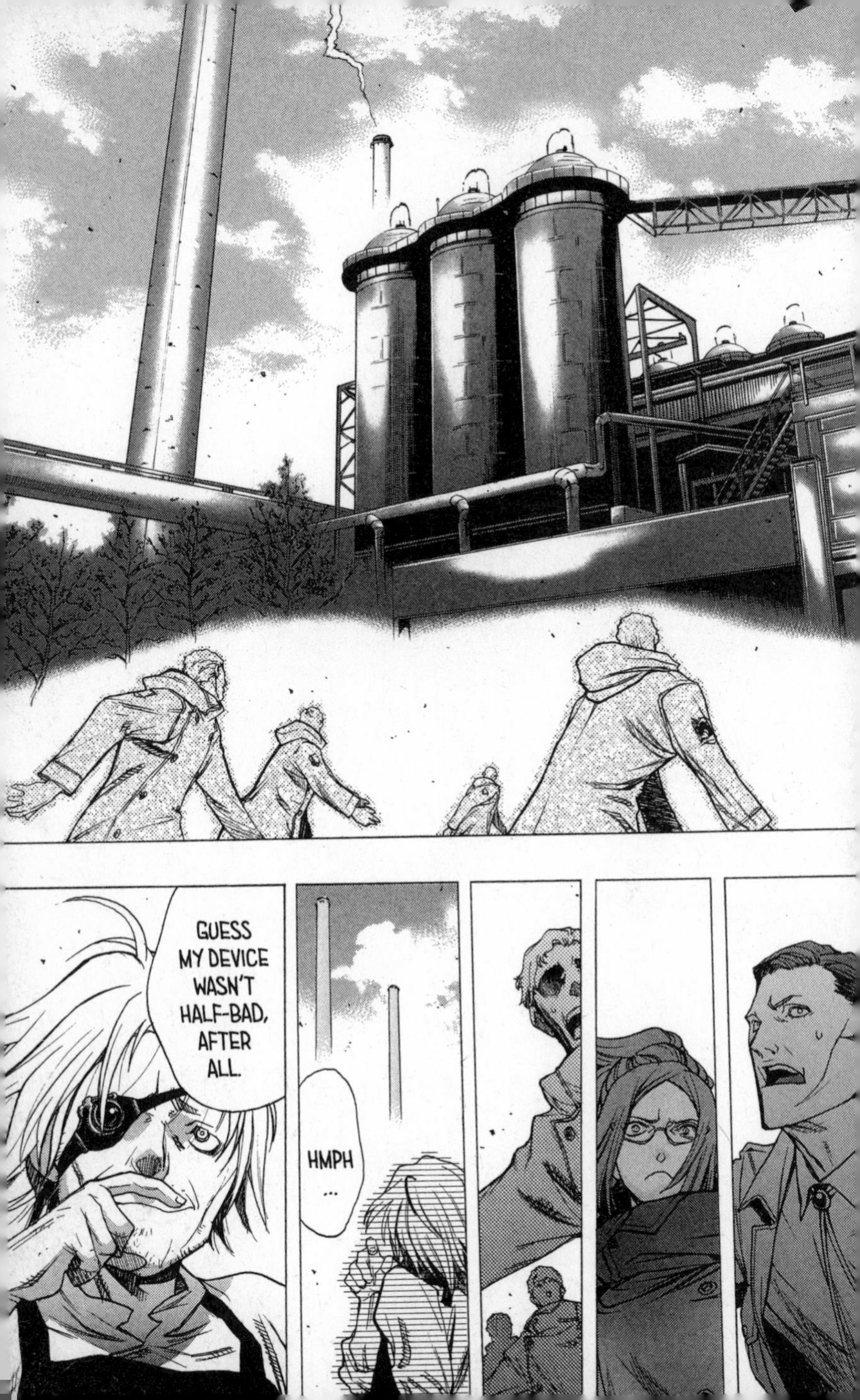
HMPH ...
GUESS MY DEVICE WASN'T HALF-BAD, AFTER ALL.

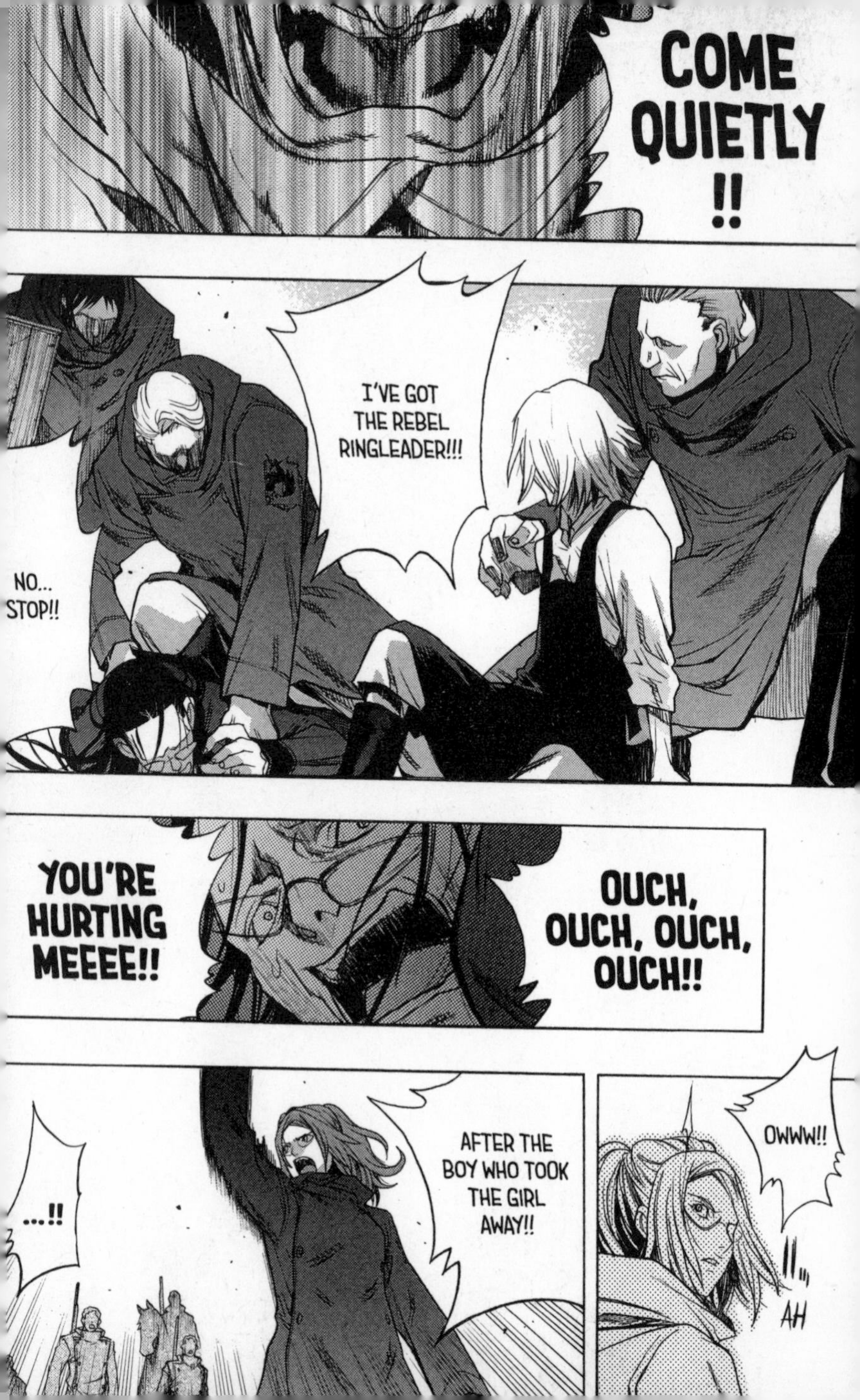
COME QUIETLY!!
I'VE GOT THE REBEL RINGLEADER!!!
NO... STOP!!
OUCH, OUCH, OUCH, OUCH!!
YOU'RE HURTING MEEEE!!
OWWW!!
AH
AFTER THE BOY WHO TOOK THE GIRL AWAY!!
...!!

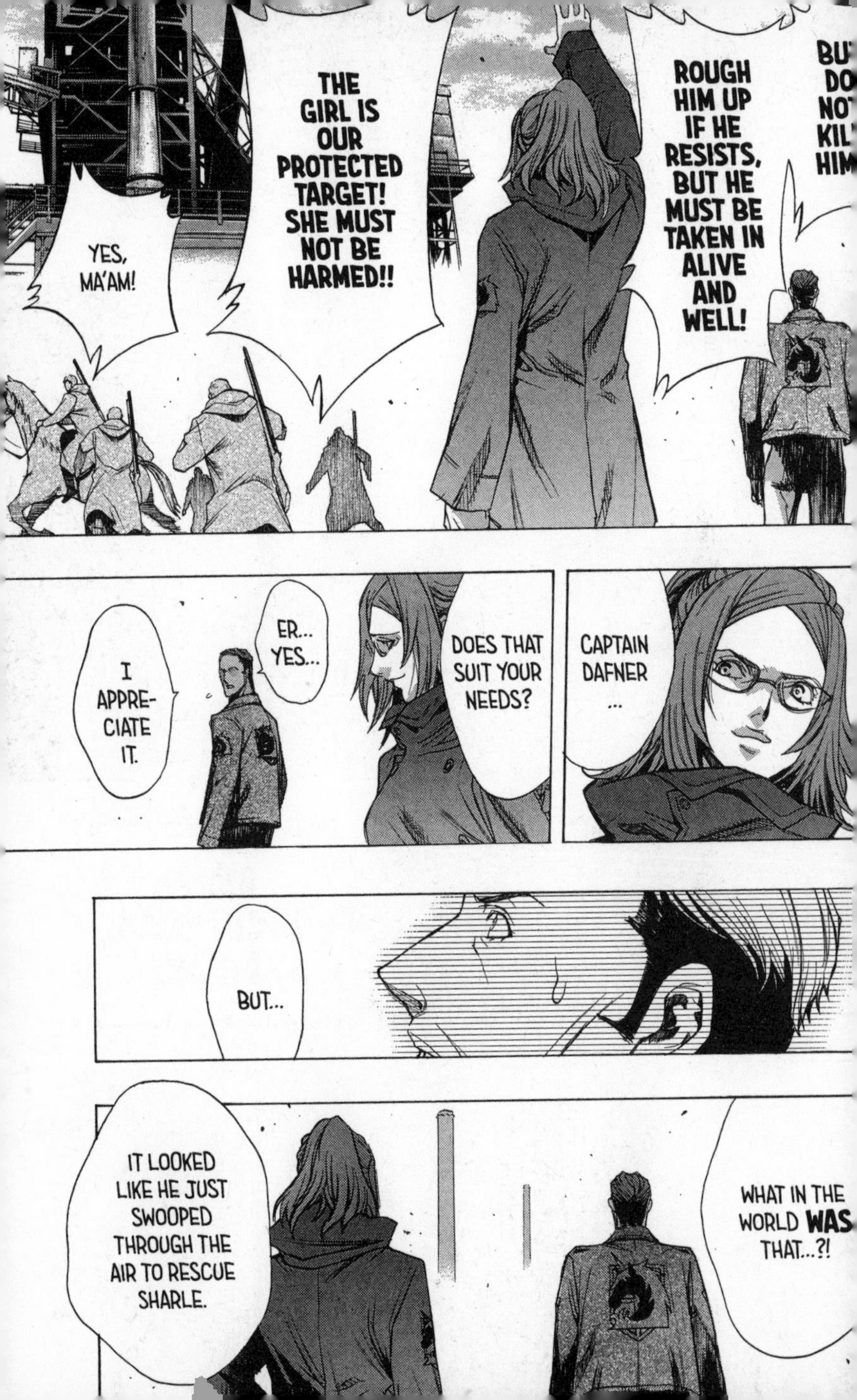
BU DO NO KIL HIM
ROUGH HIM UP IF HE RESISTS, BUT HE MUST BE TAKEN IN ALIVE AND WELL!
THE GIRL IS OUR PROTECTED TARGET! SHE MUST NOT BE HARMED!!
YES, MA'AM!
CAPTAIN DAFNER ...
DOES THAT SUIT YOUR NEEDS?
ER... YES...
I APPRE-CIATE IT.
BUT...
WHAT IN THE WORLD **WAS** THAT...?!
IT LOOKED LIKE HE JUST SWOOPED THROUGH THE AIR TO RESCUE SHARLE.

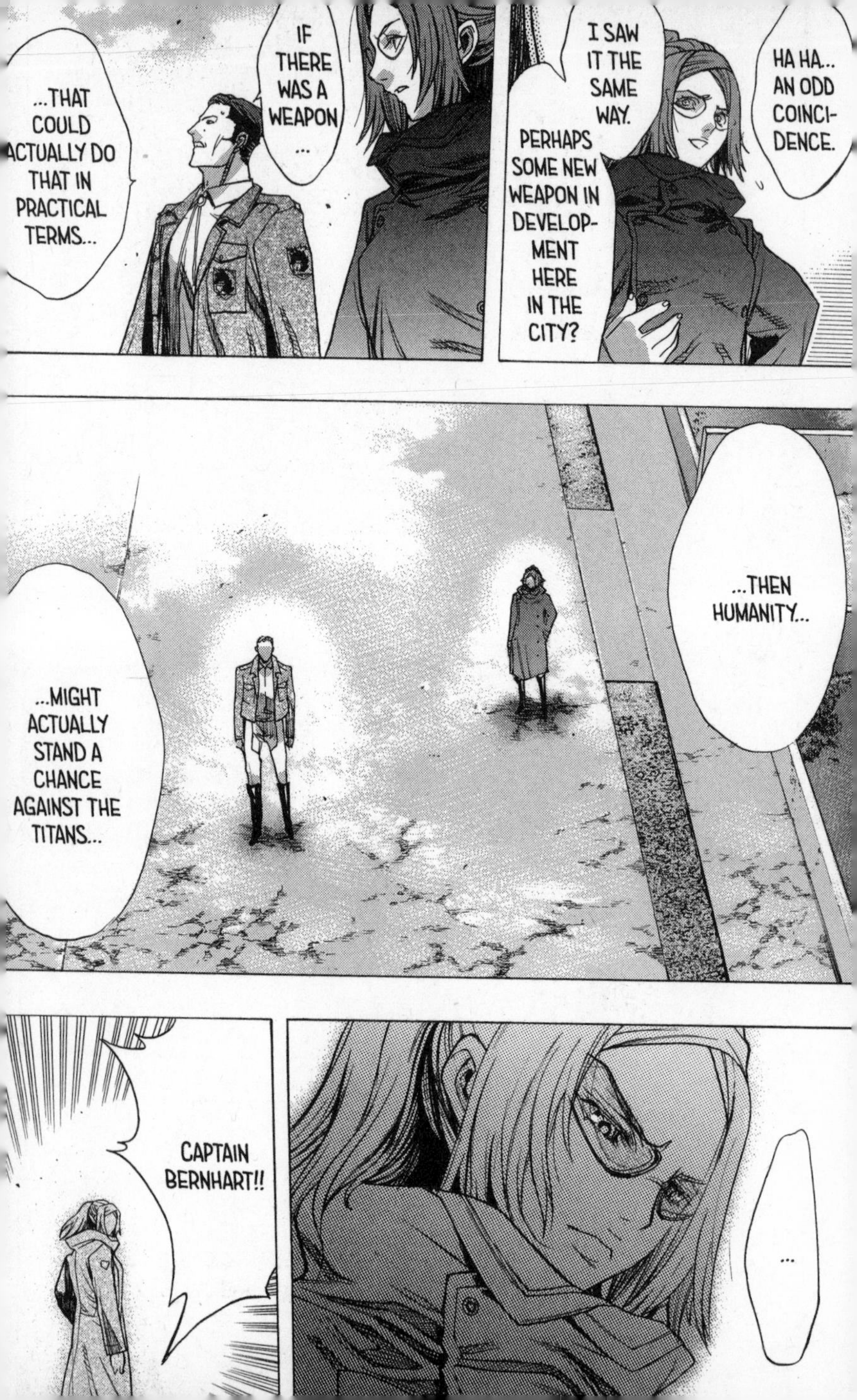
HA HA... AN ODD COINCIDENCE.
I SAW IT THE SAME WAY.
PERHAPS SOME NEW WEAPON IN DEVELOPMENT HERE IN THE CITY?
IF THERE WAS A WEAPON...
...THAT COULD ACTUALLY DO THAT IN PRACTICAL TERMS...
...THEN HUMANITY...
...MIGHT ACTUALLY STAND A CHANCE AGAINST THE TITANS...
...
CAPTAIN BERNHART!!

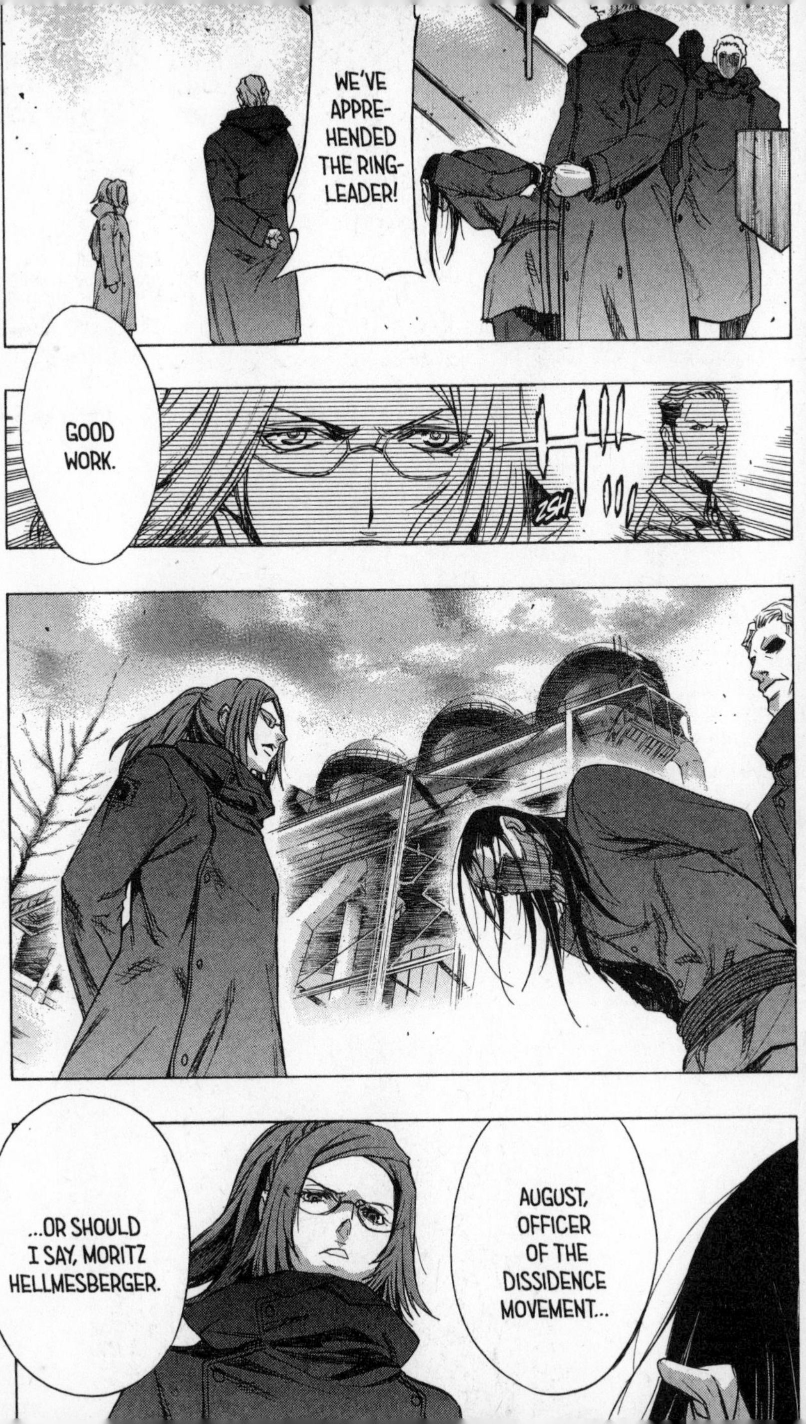
WE'VE APPREHENDED THE RINGLEADER!
GOOD WORK.
ZSH
AUGUST, OFFICER OF THE DISSIDENCE MOVEMENT...
...OR SHOULD I SAY, MORITZ HELLMESBERGER.

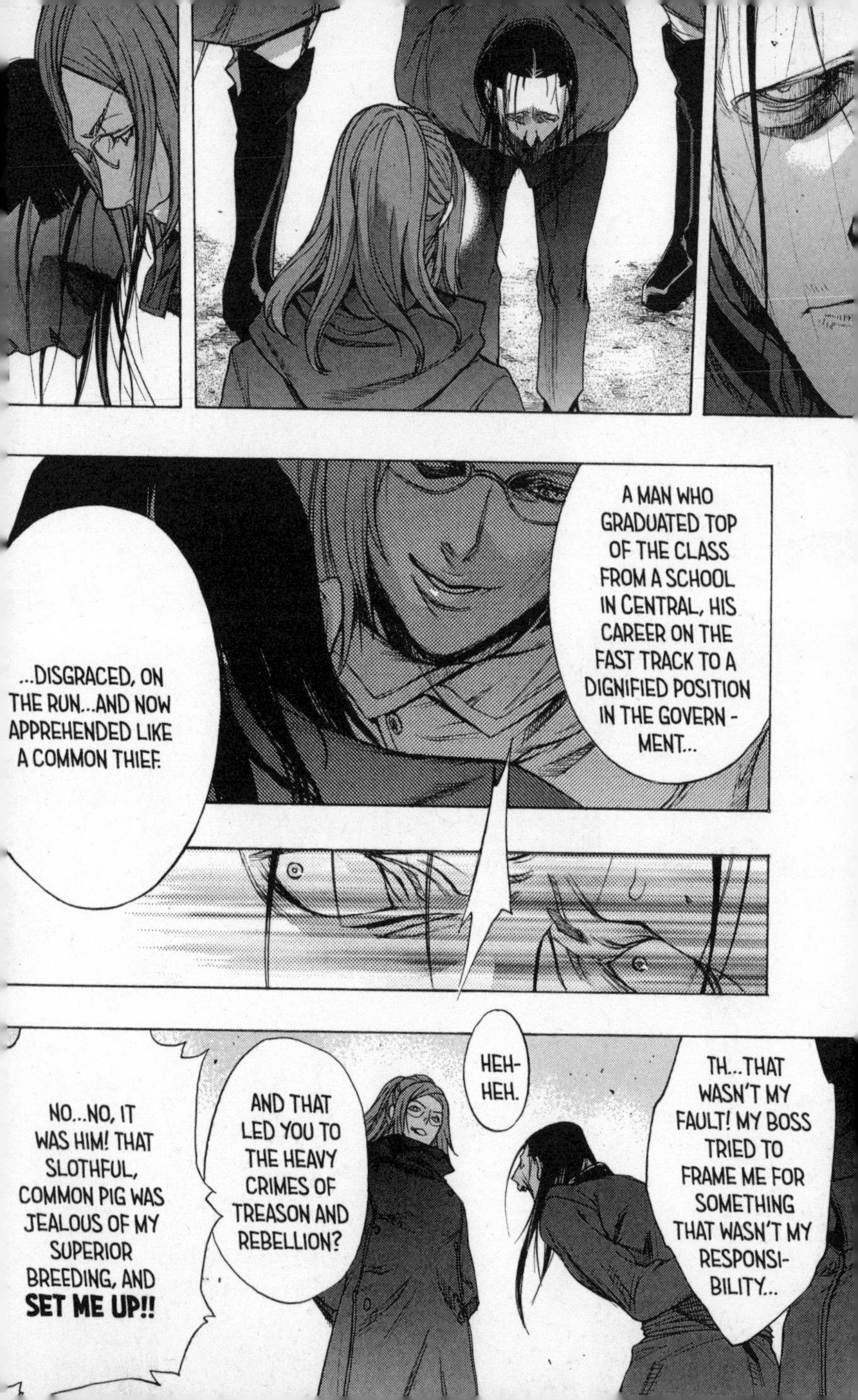

A MAN WHO GRADUATED TOP OF THE CLASS FROM A SCHOOL IN CENTRAL, HIS CAREER ON THE FAST TRACK TO A DIGNIFIED POSITION IN THE GOVERN - MENT...
...DISGRACED, ON THE RUN...AND NOW APPREHENDED LIKE A COMMON THIEF.
TH...THAT WASN'T MY FAULT! MY BOSS TRIED TO FRAME ME FOR SOMETHING THAT WASN'T MY RESPONSI- BILITY...
HEH- HEH.
AND THAT LED YOU TO THE HEAVY CRIMES OF TREASON AND REBELLION?
NO...NO, IT WAS HIM! THAT SLOTHFUL, COMMON PIG WAS JEALOUS OF MY SUPERIOR BREEDING, AND **SET ME UP!!**

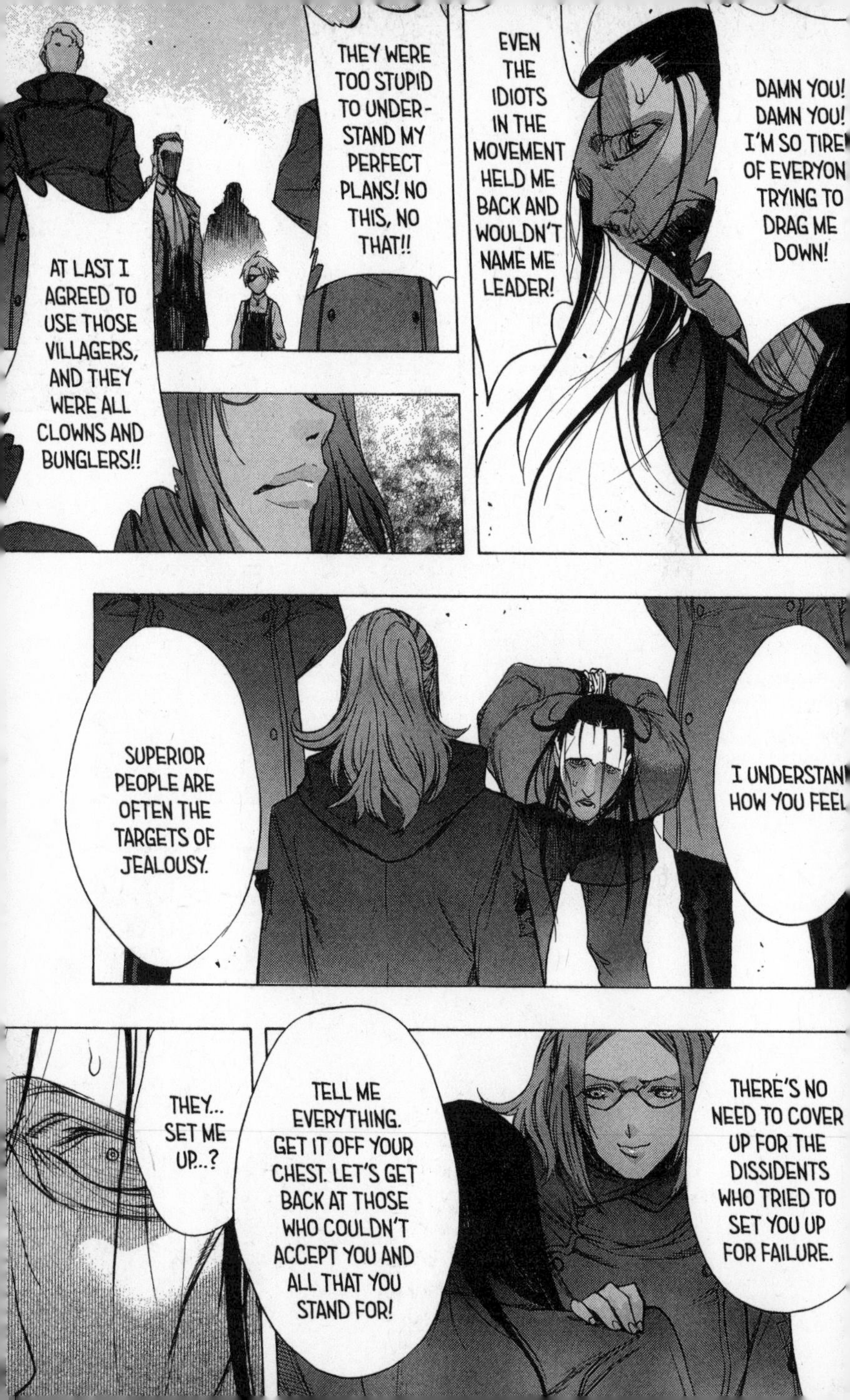
DAMN YOU! DAMN YOU! I'M SO TIRE OF EVERYON TRYING TO DRAG ME DOWN!
EVEN THE IDIOTS IN THE MOVEMENT HELD ME BACK AND WOULDN'T NAME ME LEADER!
THEY WERE TOO STUPID TO UNDER-STAND MY PERFECT PLANS! NO THIS, NO THAT!!
AT LAST I AGREED TO USE THOSE VILLAGERS, AND THEY WERE ALL CLOWNS AND BUNGLERS!!
I UNDERSTAN HOW YOU FEEL
SUPERIOR PEOPLE ARE OFTEN THE TARGETS OF JEALOUSY.
THERE'S NO NEED TO COVER UP FOR THE DISSIDENTS WHO TRIED TO SET YOU UP FOR FAILURE.
TELL ME EVERYTHING. GET IT OFF YOUR CHEST. LET'S GET BACK AT THOSE WHO COULDN'T ACCEPT YOU AND ALL THAT YOU STAND FOR!
THEY... SET ME UP...?

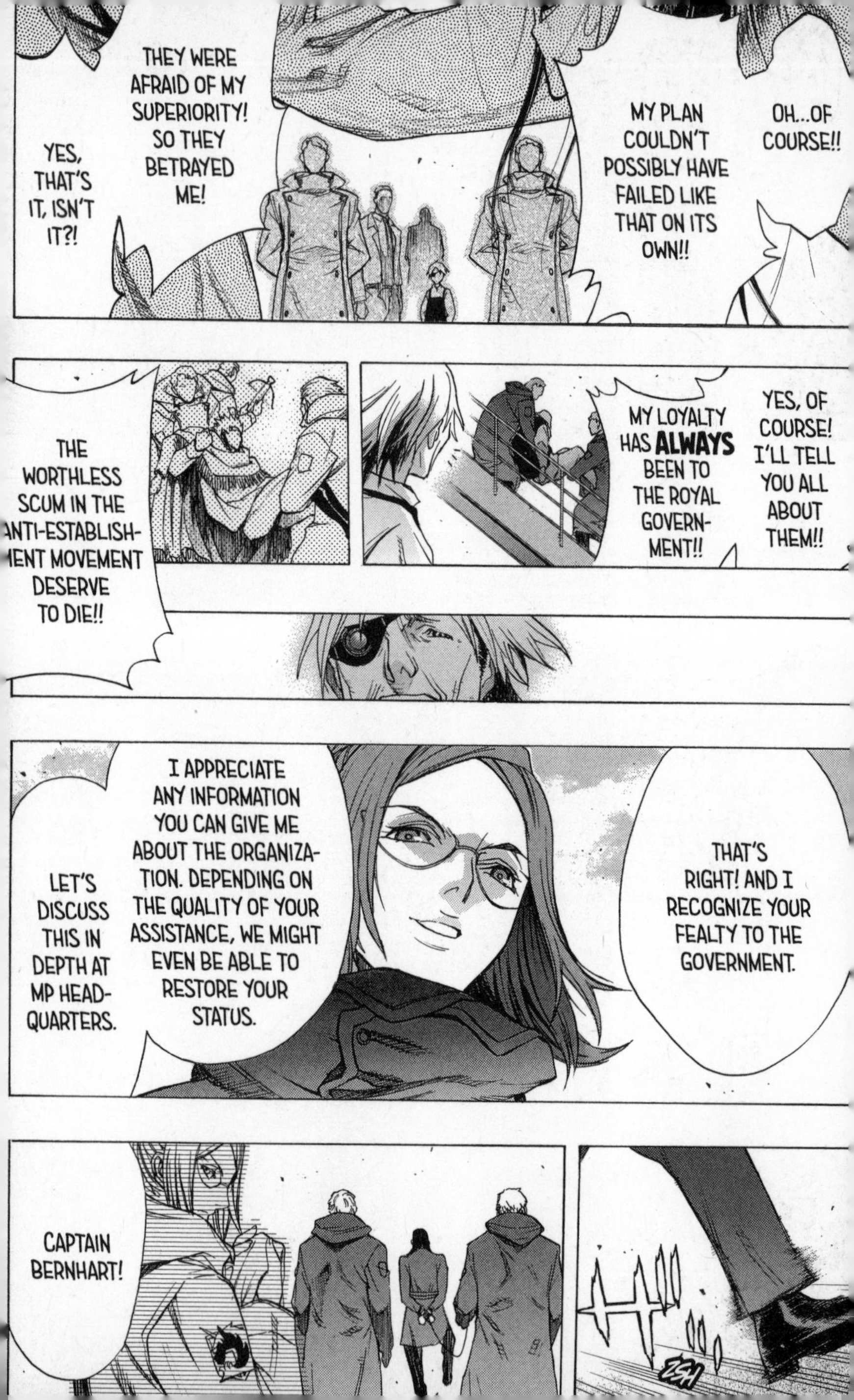
OH...OF COURSE!!
MY PLAN COULDN'T POSSIBLY HAVE FAILED LIKE THAT ON ITS OWN!!
THEY WERE AFRAID OF MY SUPERIORITY! SO THEY BETRAYED ME!
YES, THAT'S IT, ISN'T IT?!
YES, OF COURSE! I'LL TELL YOU ALL ABOUT THEM!!
MY LOYALTY HAS **ALWAYS** BEEN TO THE ROYAL GOVERNMENT!!
THE WORTHLESS SCUM IN THE ANTI-ESTABLISHMENT MOVEMENT DESERVE TO DIE!!
THAT'S RIGHT! AND I RECOGNIZE YOUR FEALTY TO THE GOVERNMENT.
I APPRECIATE ANY INFORMATION YOU CAN GIVE ME ABOUT THE ORGANIZATION. DEPENDING ON THE QUALITY OF YOUR ASSISTANCE, WE MIGHT EVEN BE ABLE TO RESTORE YOUR STATUS.
LET'S DISCUSS THIS IN DEPTH AT MP HEADQUARTERS.
ZSH
CAPTAIN BERNHART!

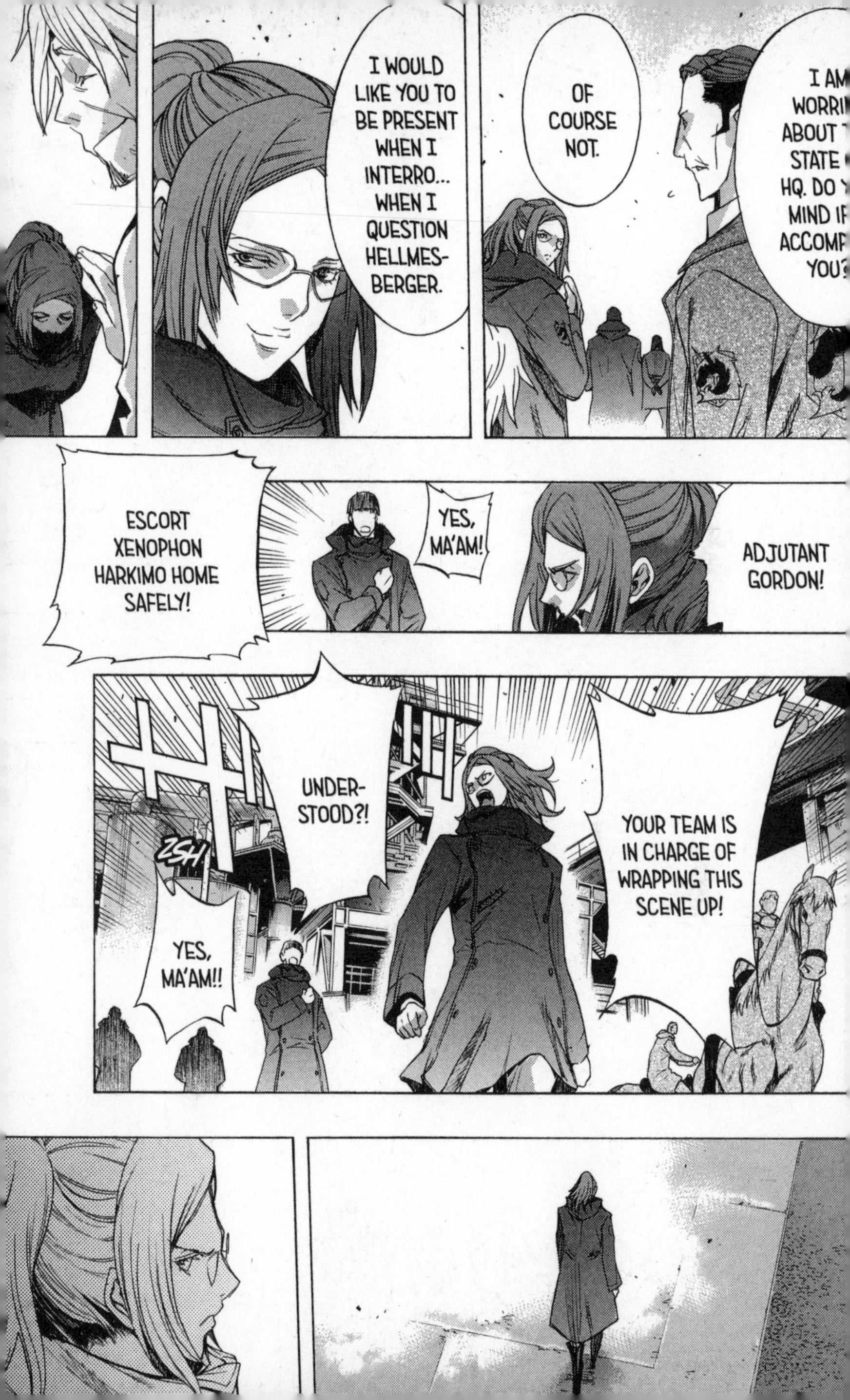
I AM WORRI ABOUT T STATE HQ. DO Y MIND IF ACCOMP YOU?
OF COURSE NOT.
I WOULD LIKE YOU TO BE PRESENT WHEN I INTERRO... WHEN I QUESTION HELLMES-BERGER.
ADJUTANT GORDON!
YES, MA'AM!
ESCORT XENOPHON HARKIMO HOME SAFELY!
YOUR TEAM IS IN CHARGE OF WRAPPING THIS SCENE UP!
UNDER-STOOD?!
ZSH
YES, MA'AM!!

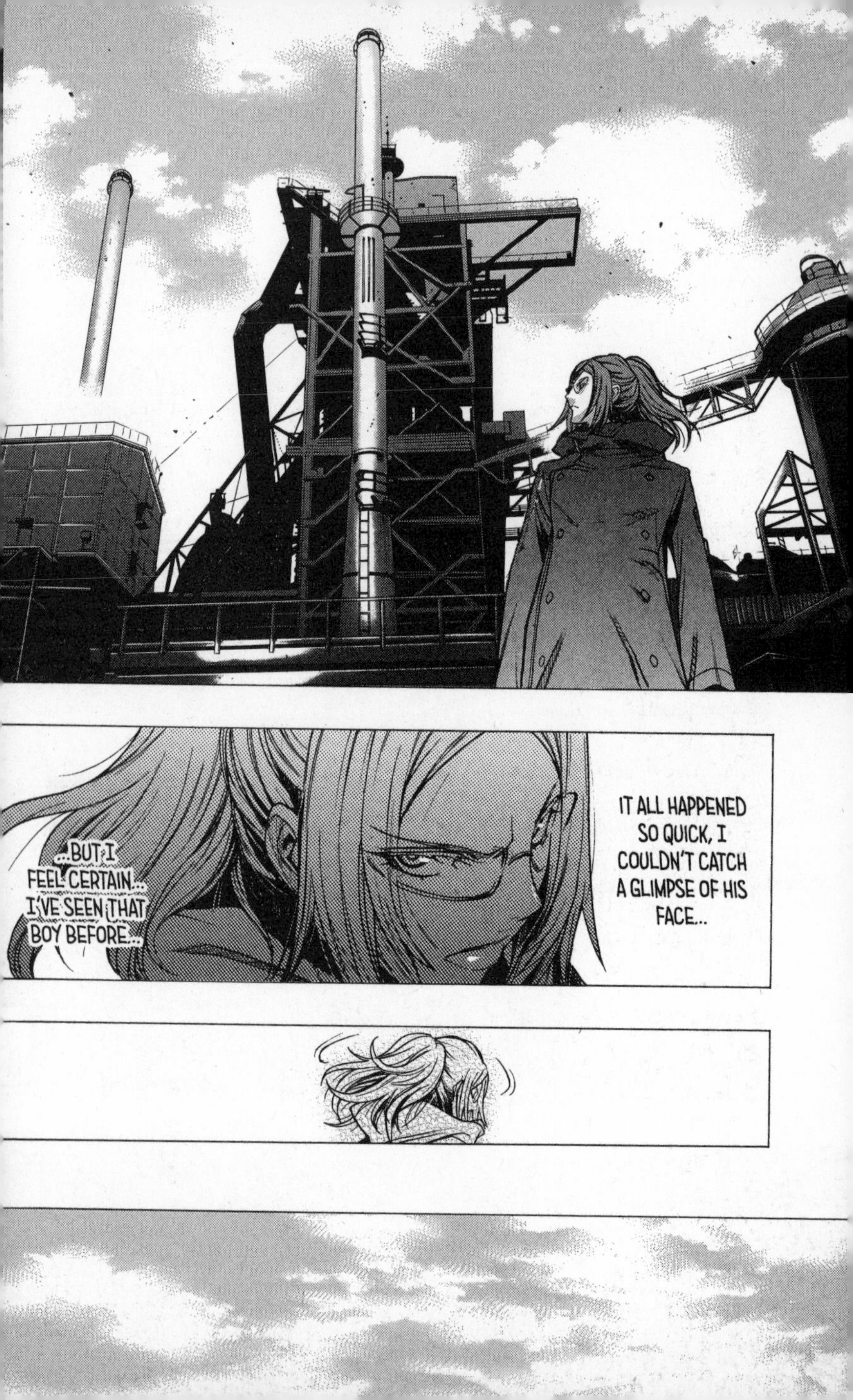
IT ALL HAPPENED SO QUICK, I COULDN'T CATCH A GLIMPSE OF HIS FACE...
...BUT I FEEL CERTAIN... I'VE SEEN THAT BOY BEFORE...

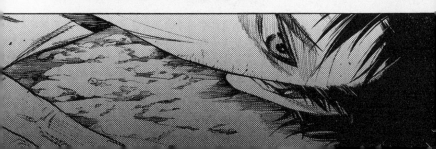

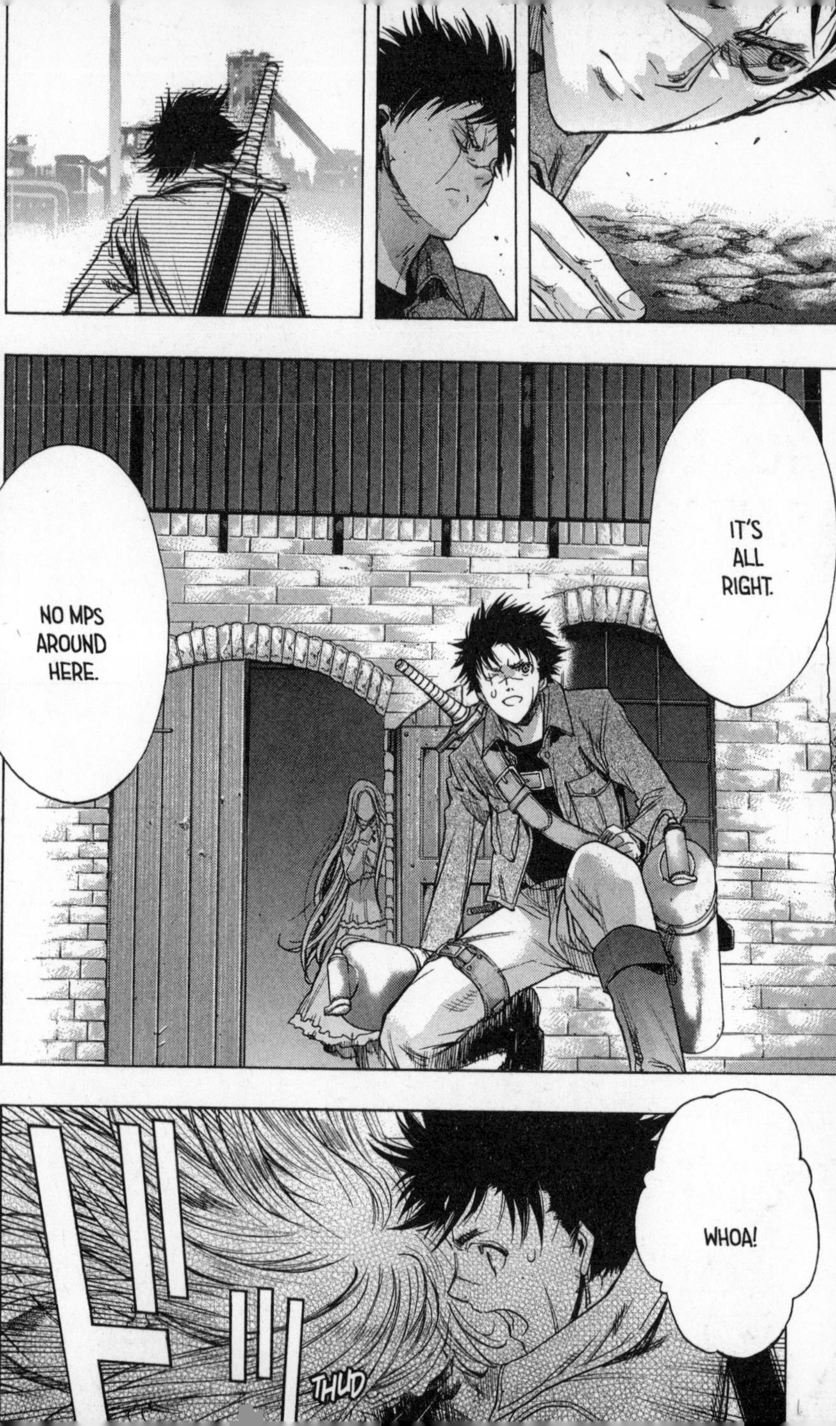
IT'S ALL RIGHT.
NO MPS AROUND HERE.
WHOA!
THUD

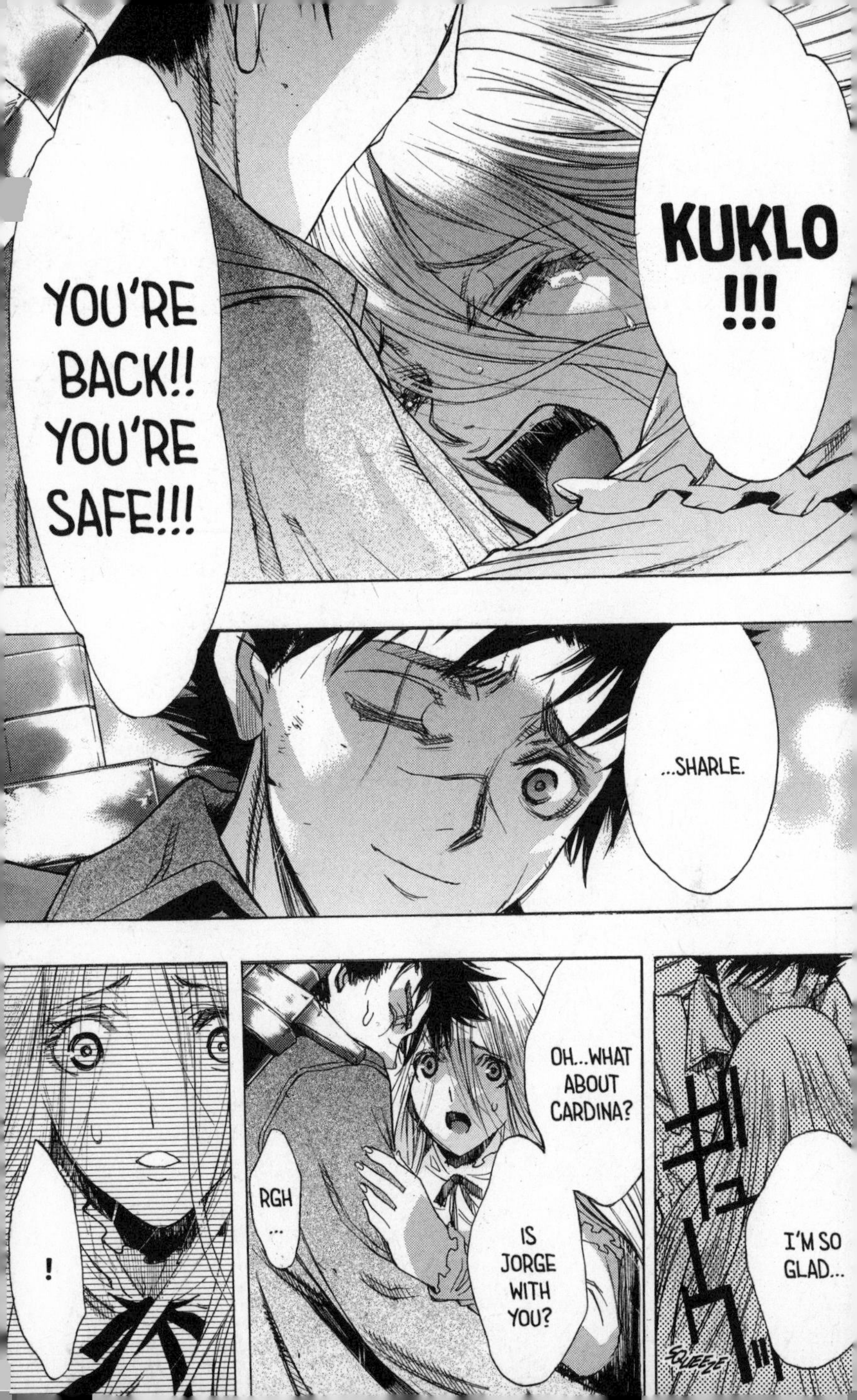
KUKLO!!!
YOU'RE BACK!! YOU'RE SAFE!!!
...SHARLE.
I'M SO GLAD...
SQUEEZE
OH...WHAT ABOUT CARDINA?
RGH...
IS JORGE WITH YOU?
!

OH...! I'M SORRY, KUKLO!

DID THAT HURT?!

THAT BANDAGE ON YOUR HAND...

HUP

ARE YOU HURT ANYWHERE ELSE?!

OH NO... THAT'S A TERRIBLE INJURY!

YEAH... IT'S A CAST...

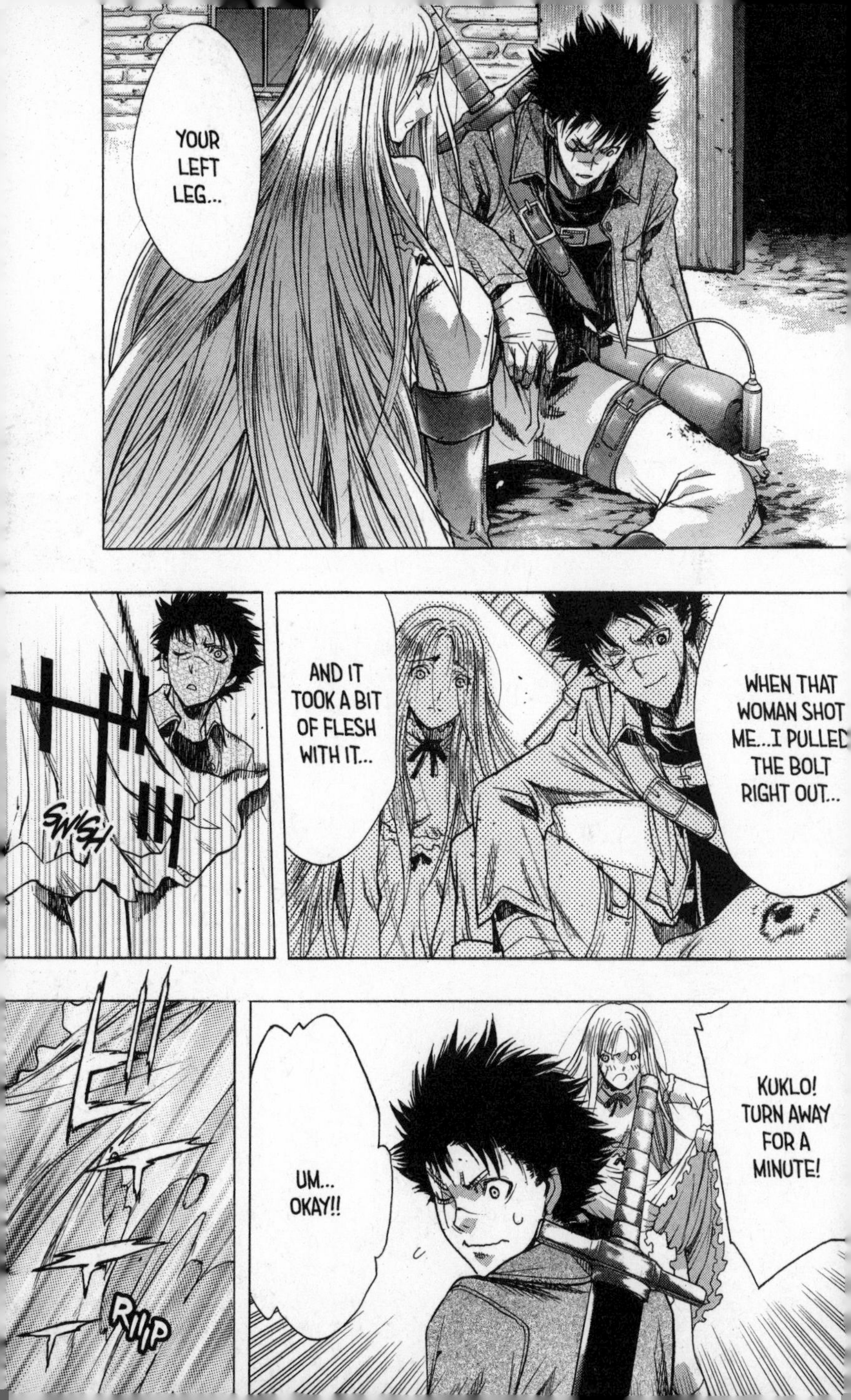
YOUR LEFT LEG...
WHEN THAT WOMAN SHOT ME...I PULLED THE BOLT RIGHT OUT...
AND IT TOOK A BIT OF FLESH WITH IT...
SWISH
KUKLO! TURN AWAY FOR A MINUTE!
UM... OKAY!!
RIIP

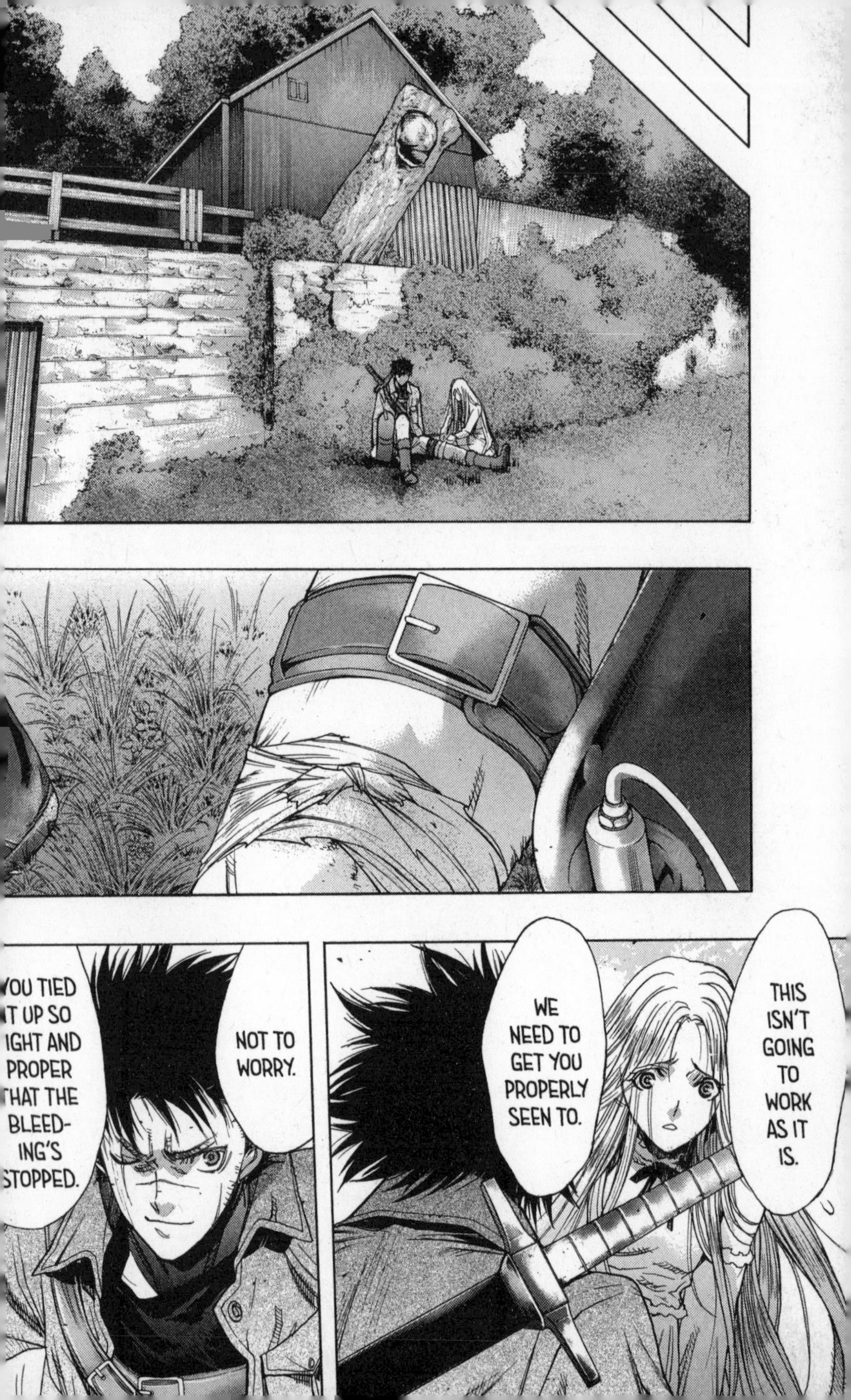
THIS ISN'T GOING TO WORK AS IT IS.
WE NEED TO GET YOU PROPERLY SEEN TO.
NOT TO WORRY.
YOU TIED T UP SO IGHT AND PROPER THAT THE BLEED-ING'S STOPPED.

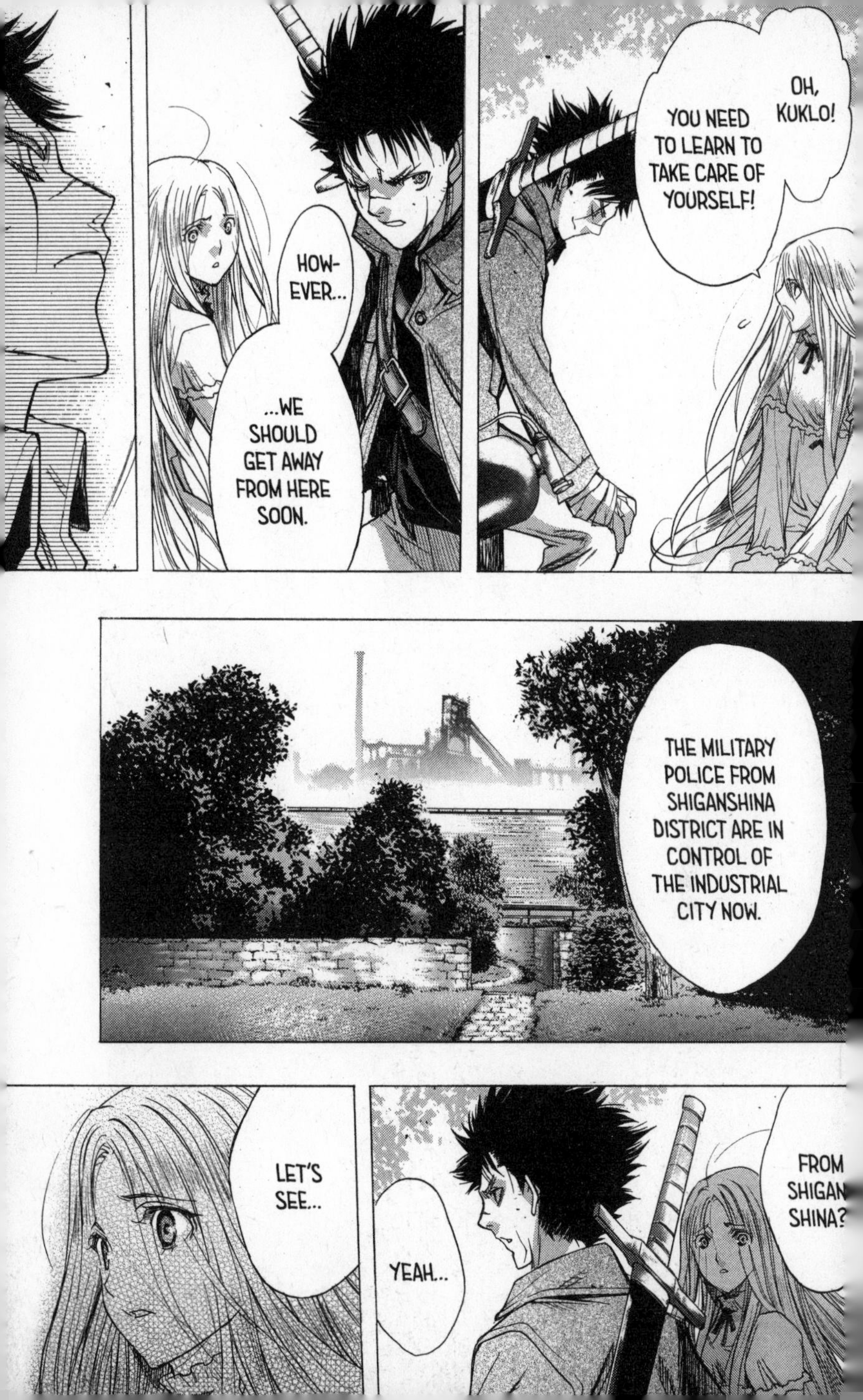
OH, KUKLO!
YOU NEED TO LEARN TO TAKE CARE OF YOURSELF!
HOW-EVER...
...WE SHOULD GET AWAY FROM HERE SOON.
THE MILITARY POLICE FROM SHIGANSHINA DISTRICT ARE IN CONTROL OF THE INDUSTRIAL CITY NOW.
FROM SHIGAN SHINA?
YEAH...
LET'S SEE...

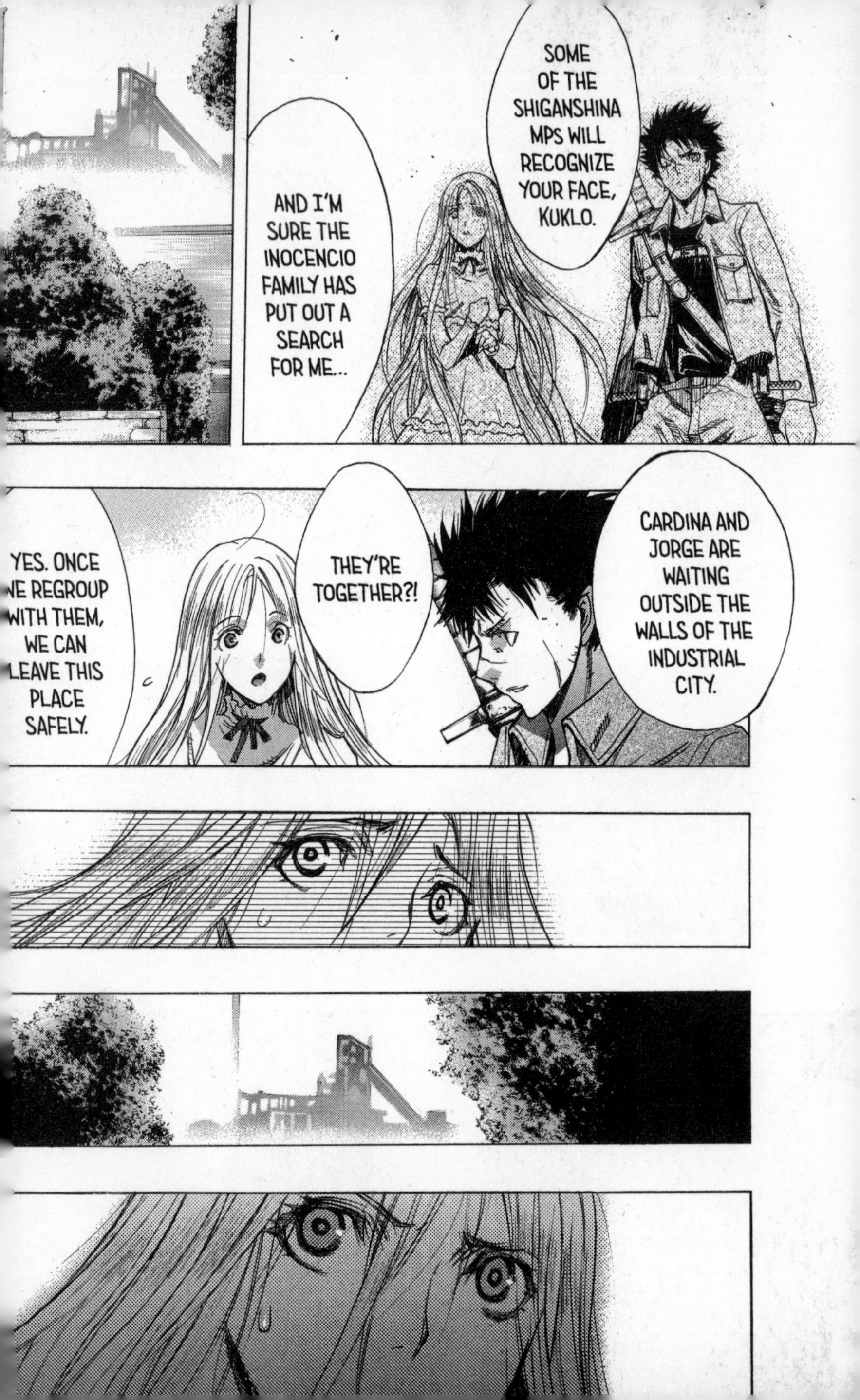
SOME OF THE SHIGANSHINA MPS WILL RECOGNIZE YOUR FACE, KUKLO.
AND I'M SURE THE INOCENCIO FAMILY HAS PUT OUT A SEARCH FOR ME...
CARDINA AND JORGE ARE WAITING OUTSIDE THE WALLS OF THE INDUSTRIAL CITY.
THEY'RE TOGETHER?!
YES. ONCE WE REGROUP WITH THEM, WE CAN LEAVE THIS PLACE SAFELY.

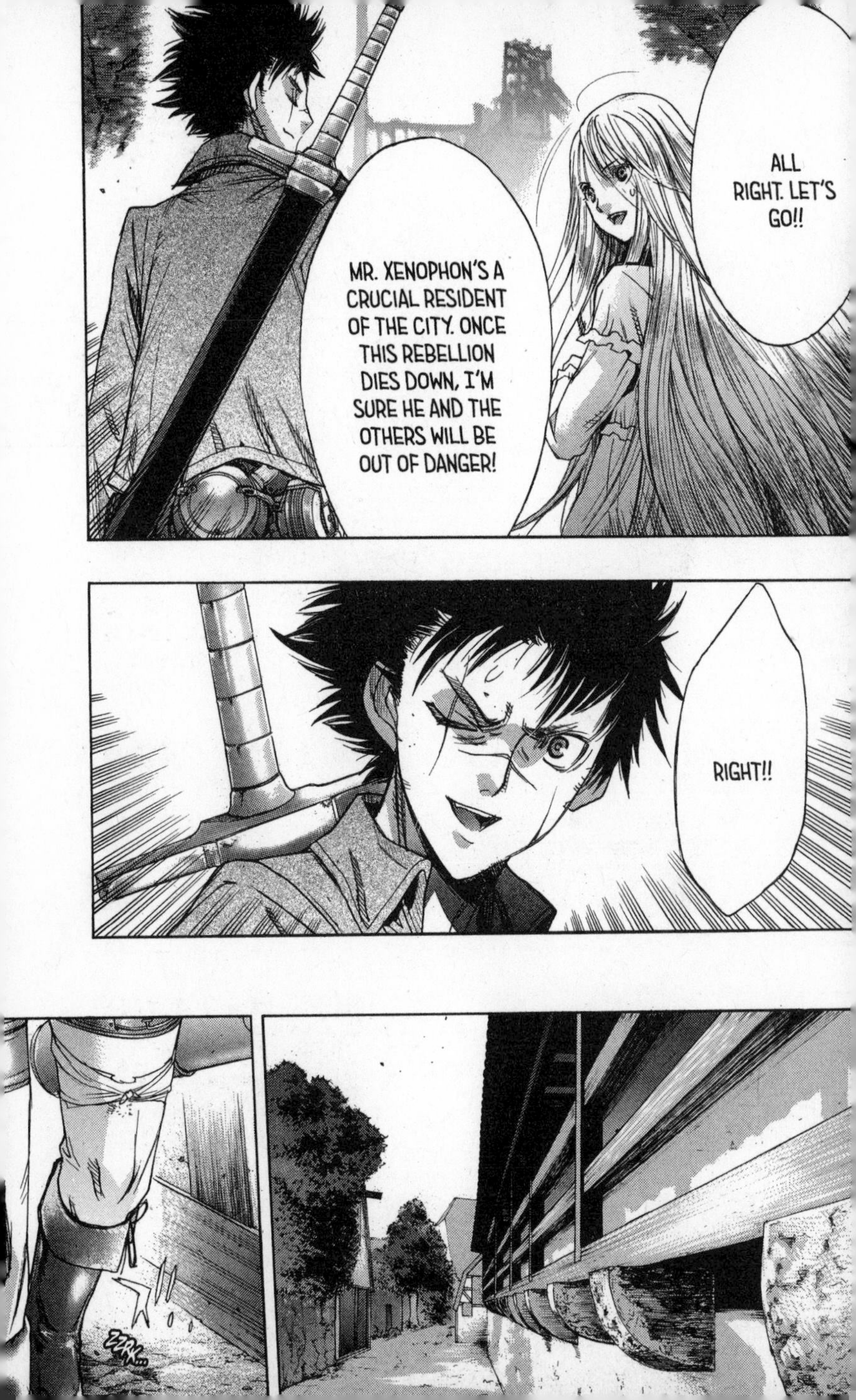
ALL RIGHT. LET'S GO!!
MR. XENOPHON'S A CRUCIAL RESIDENT OF THE CITY. ONCE THIS REBELLION DIES DOWN, I'M SURE HE AND THE OTHERS WILL BE OUT OF DANGER!
RIGHT!!
ZZRK...

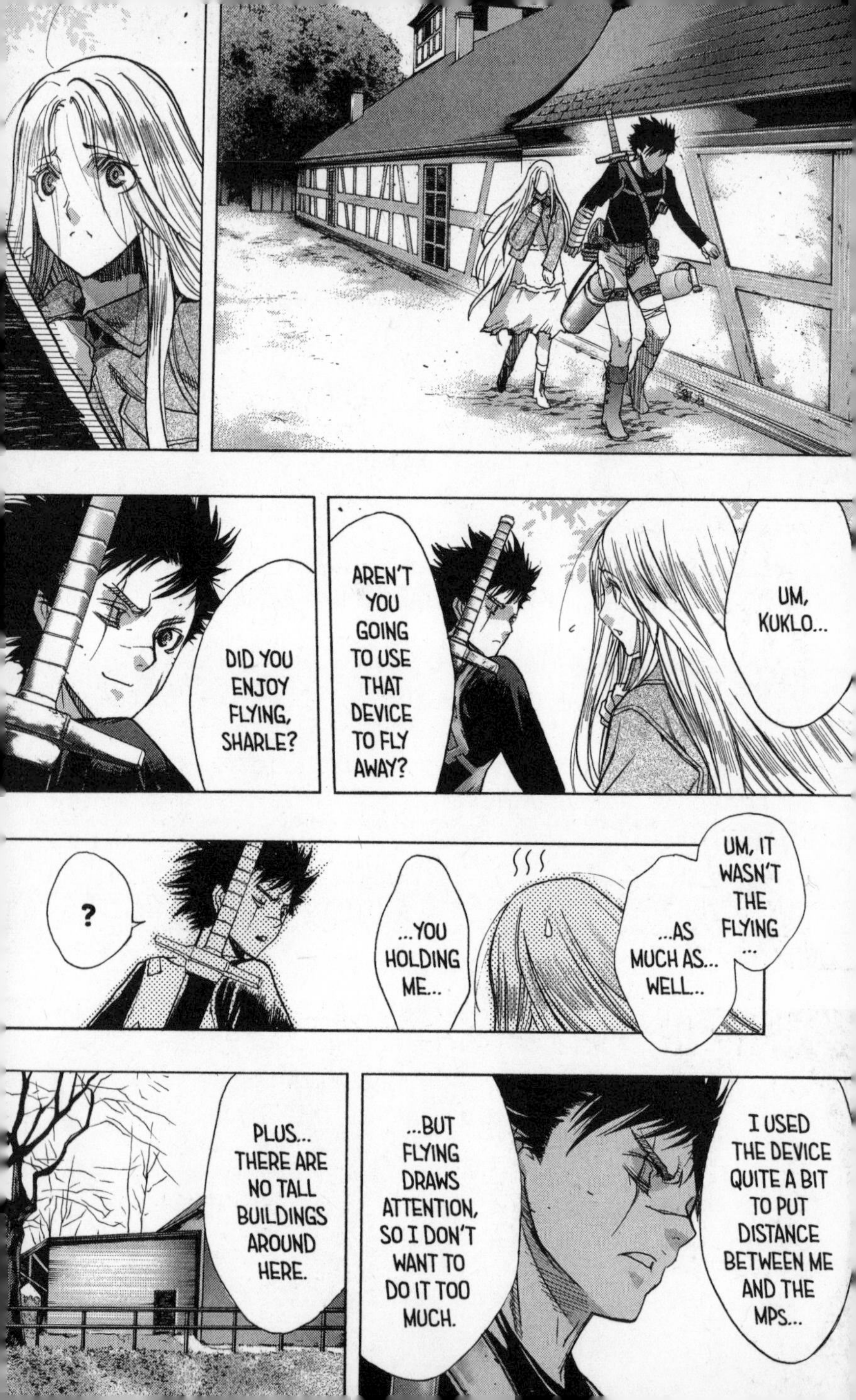
UM, KUKLO...
AREN'T YOU GOING TO USE THAT DEVICE TO FLY AWAY?
DID YOU ENJOY FLYING, SHARLE?
UM, IT WASN'T THE FLYING ...
...AS MUCH AS... WELL...
...YOU HOLDING ME...
?
I USED THE DEVICE QUITE A BIT TO PUT DISTANCE BETWEEN ME AND THE MPS...
...BUT FLYING DRAWS ATTENTION, SO I DON'T WANT TO DO IT TOO MUCH.
PLUS... THERE ARE NO TALL BUILDINGS AROUND HERE.

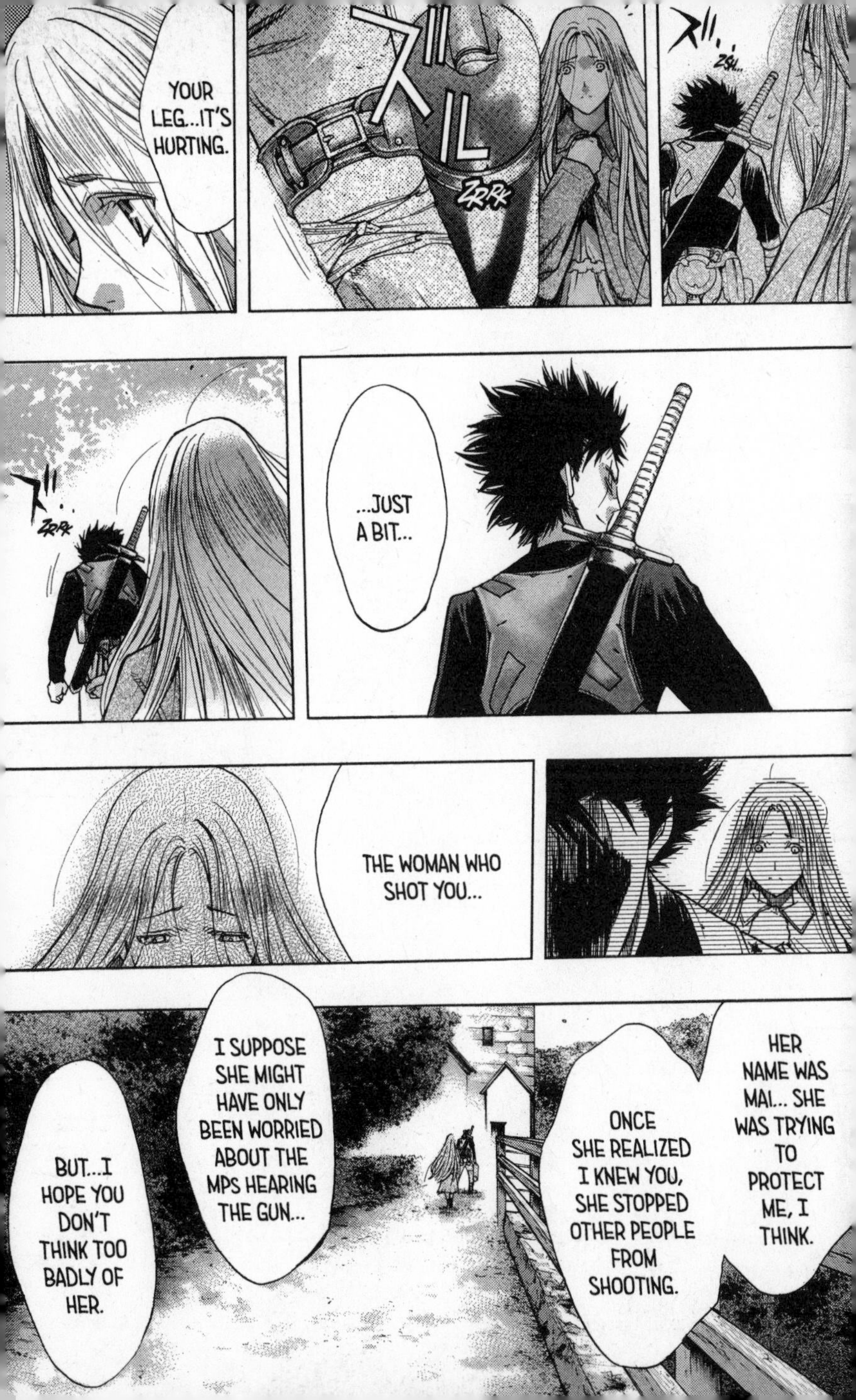
ZSH...
ZRRK
YOUR LEG...IT'S HURTING.
...JUST A BIT...
ZRRK
THE WOMAN WHO SHOT YOU...
HER NAME WAS MAI... SHE WAS TRYING TO PROTECT ME, I THINK.
ONCE SHE REALIZED I KNEW YOU, SHE STOPPED OTHER PEOPLE FROM SHOOTING.
I SUPPOSE SHE MIGHT HAVE ONLY BEEN WORRIED ABOUT THE MPS HEARING THE GUN...
BUT...I HOPE YOU DON'T THINK TOO BADLY OF HER.

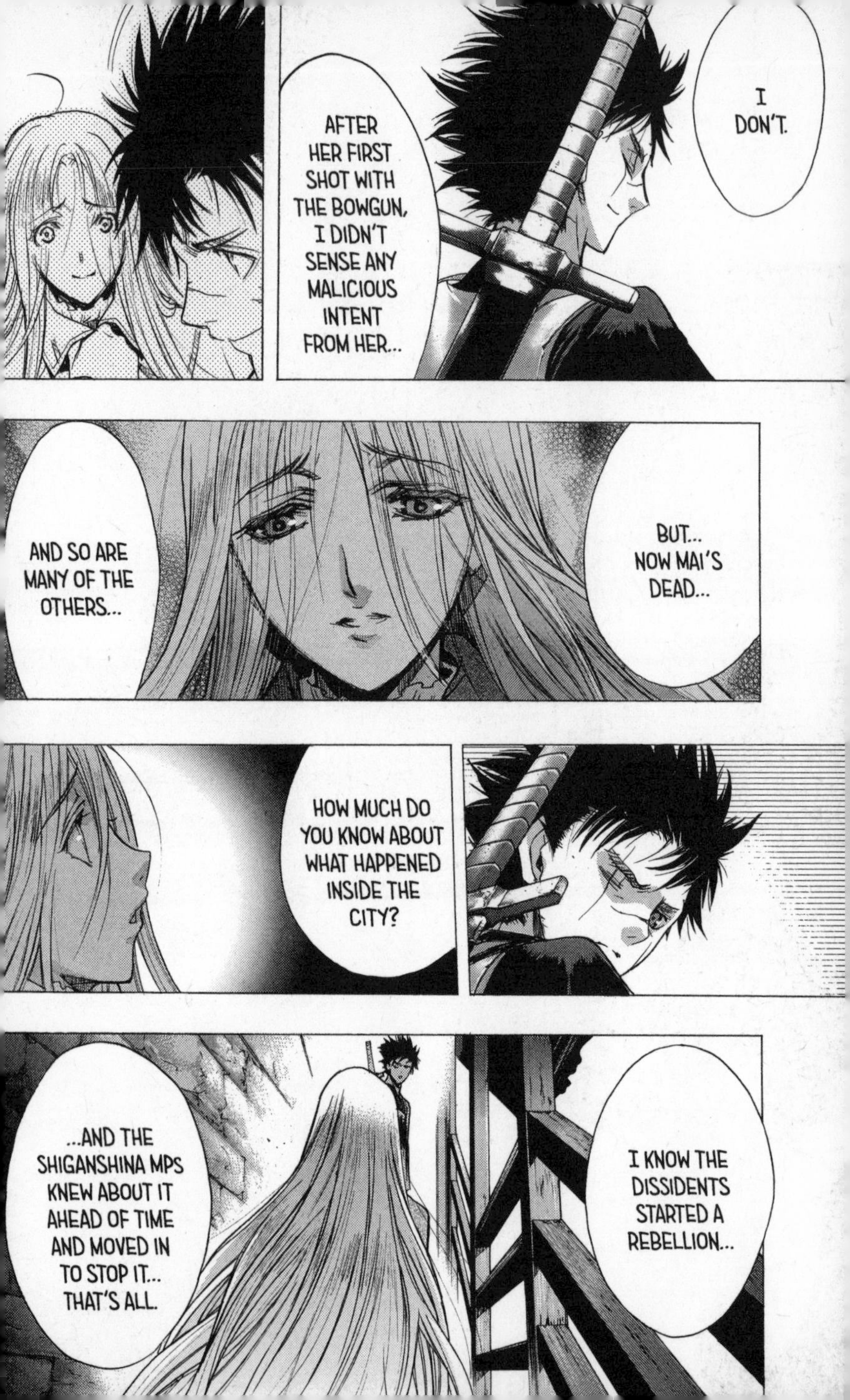
I DON'T.
AFTER HER FIRST SHOT WITH THE BOWGUN, I DIDN'T SENSE ANY MALICIOUS INTENT FROM HER...
BUT... NOW MAI'S DEAD...
AND SO ARE MANY OF THE OTHERS...
HOW MUCH DO YOU KNOW ABOUT WHAT HAPPENED INSIDE THE CITY?
I KNOW THE DISSIDENTS STARTED A REBELLION...
...AND THE SHIGANSHINA MPS KNEW ABOUT IT AHEAD OF TIME AND MOVED IN TO STOP IT... THAT'S ALL.

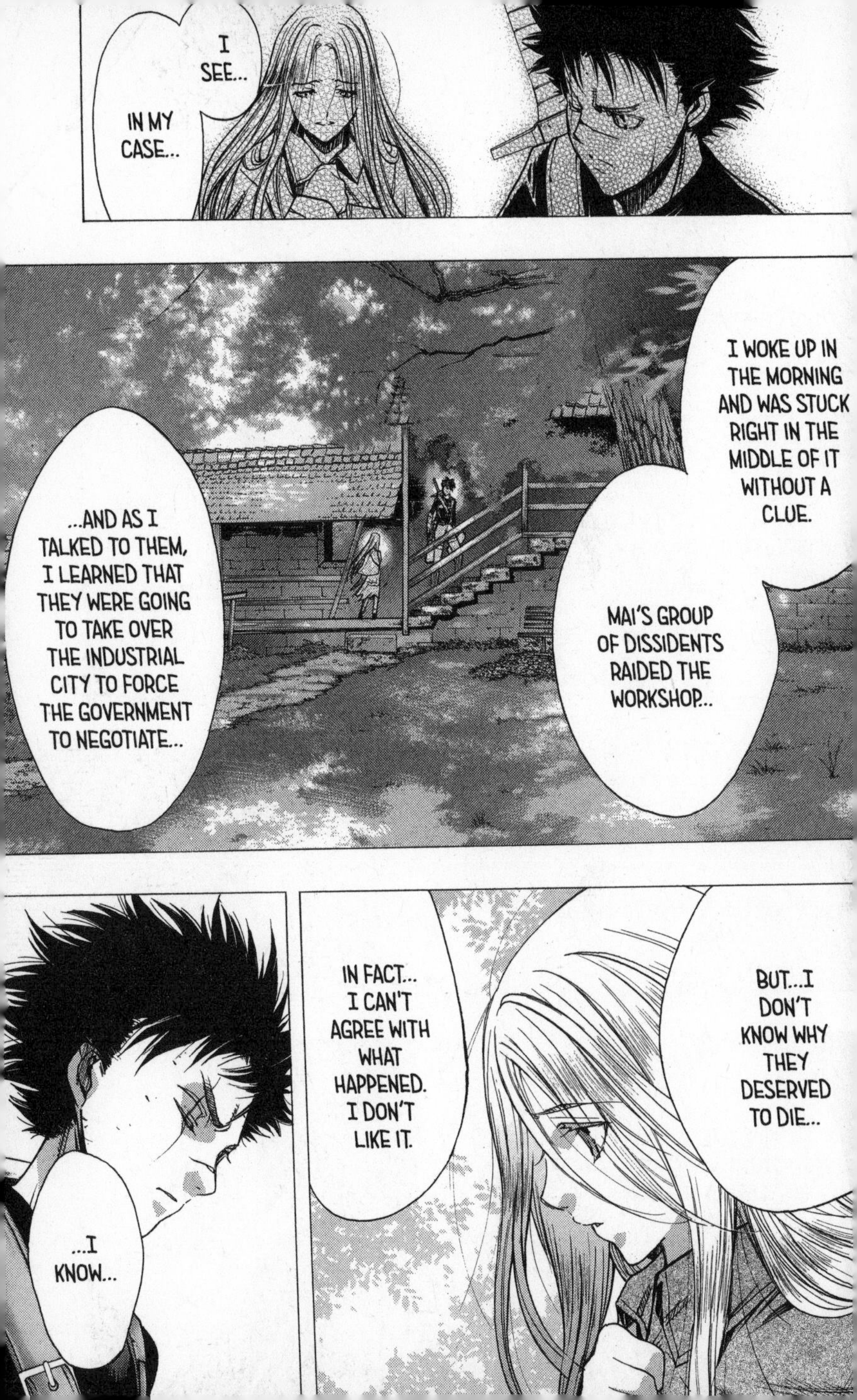
I SEE... IN MY CASE...
I WOKE UP IN THE MORNING AND WAS STUCK RIGHT IN THE MIDDLE OF IT WITHOUT A CLUE.
MAI'S GROUP OF DISSIDENTS RAIDED THE WORKSHOP...
...AND AS I TALKED TO THEM, I LEARNED THAT THEY WERE GOING TO TAKE OVER THE INDUSTRIAL CITY TO FORCE THE GOVERNMENT TO NEGOTIATE...
BUT...I DON'T KNOW WHY THEY DESERVED TO DIE...
IN FACT... I CAN'T AGREE WITH WHAT HAPPENED. I DON'T LIKE IT.
...I KNOW...

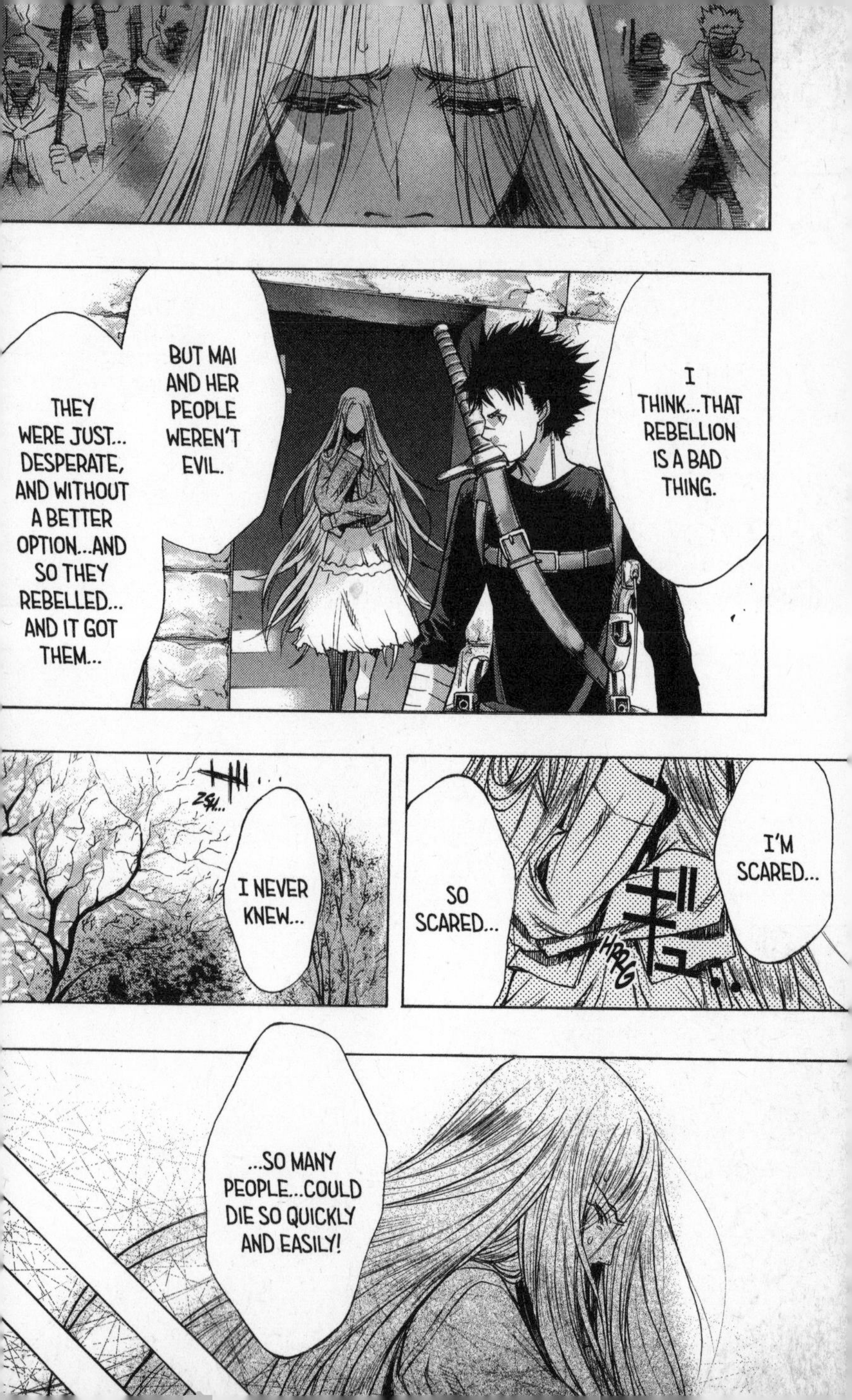
I THINK...THAT REBELLION IS A BAD THING.
BUT MAI AND HER PEOPLE WEREN'T EVIL.
THEY WERE JUST... DESPERATE, AND WITHOUT A BETTER OPTION...AND SO THEY REBELLED... AND IT GOT THEM...
I'M SCARED...
SO SCARED...
ZSH...
I NEVER KNEW...
...SO MANY PEOPLE...COULD DIE SO QUICKLY AND EASILY!

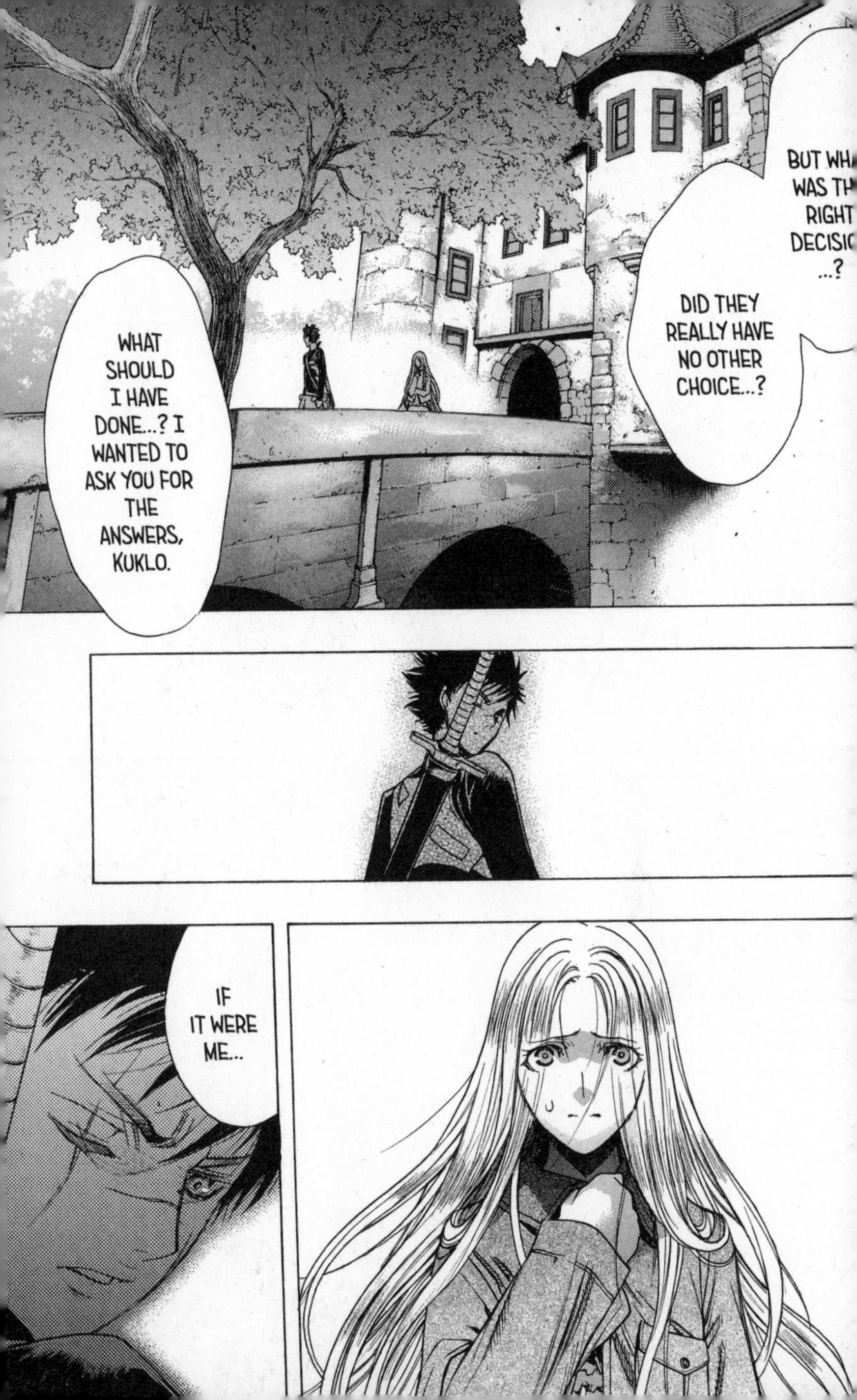
BUT WHA WAS TH RIGHT DECISI ...?
DID THEY REALLY HAVE NO OTHER CHOICE...?
WHAT SHOULD I HAVE DONE...? I WANTED TO ASK YOU FOR THE ANSWERS, KUKLO.
IF IT WERE ME...

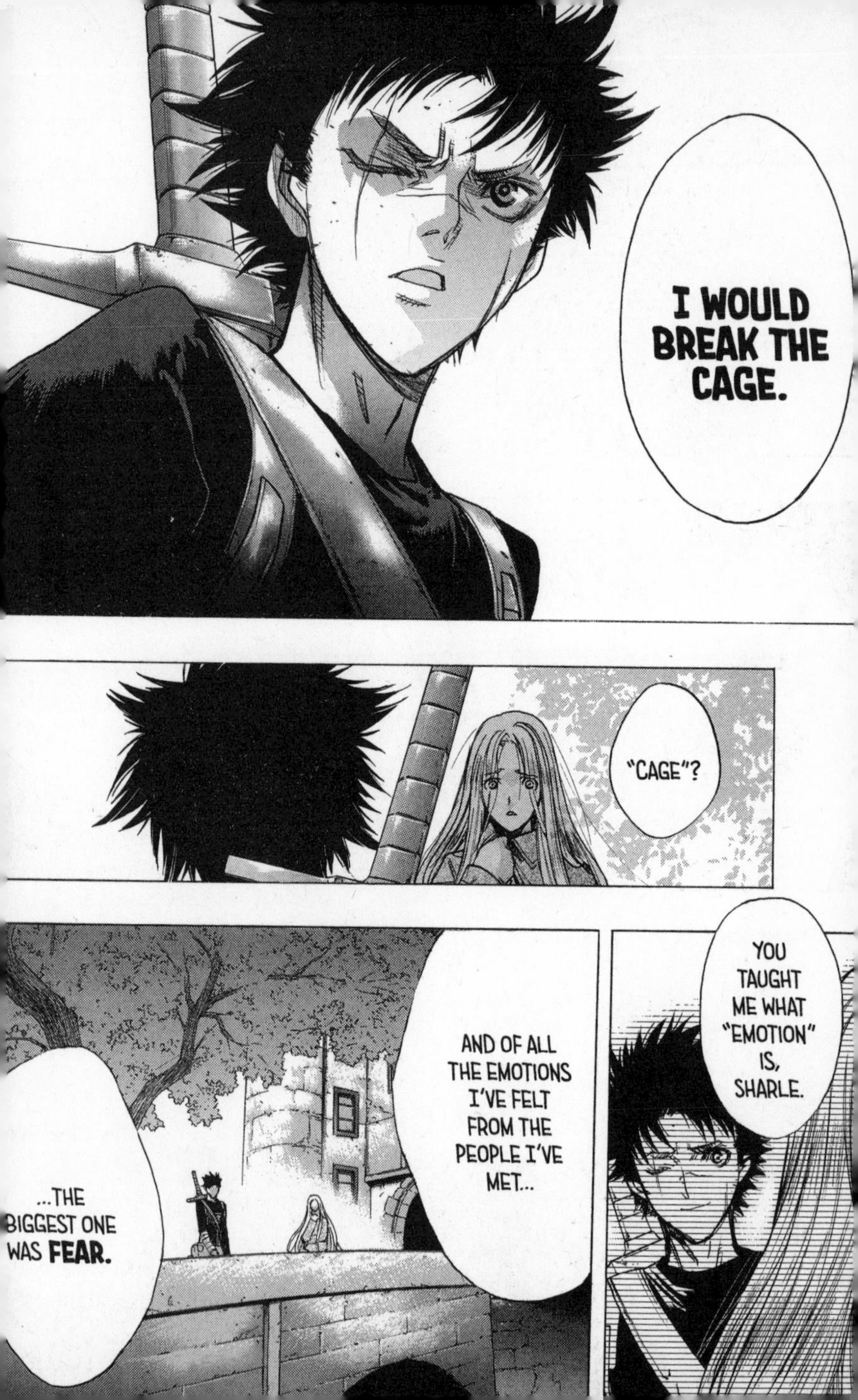
I WOULD BREAK THE CAGE.
"CAGE"?
YOU TAUGHT ME WHAT "EMOTION" IS, SHARLE.
AND OF ALL THE EMOTIONS I'VE FELT FROM THE PEOPLE I'VE MET...
...THE BIGGEST ONE WAS **FEAR.**

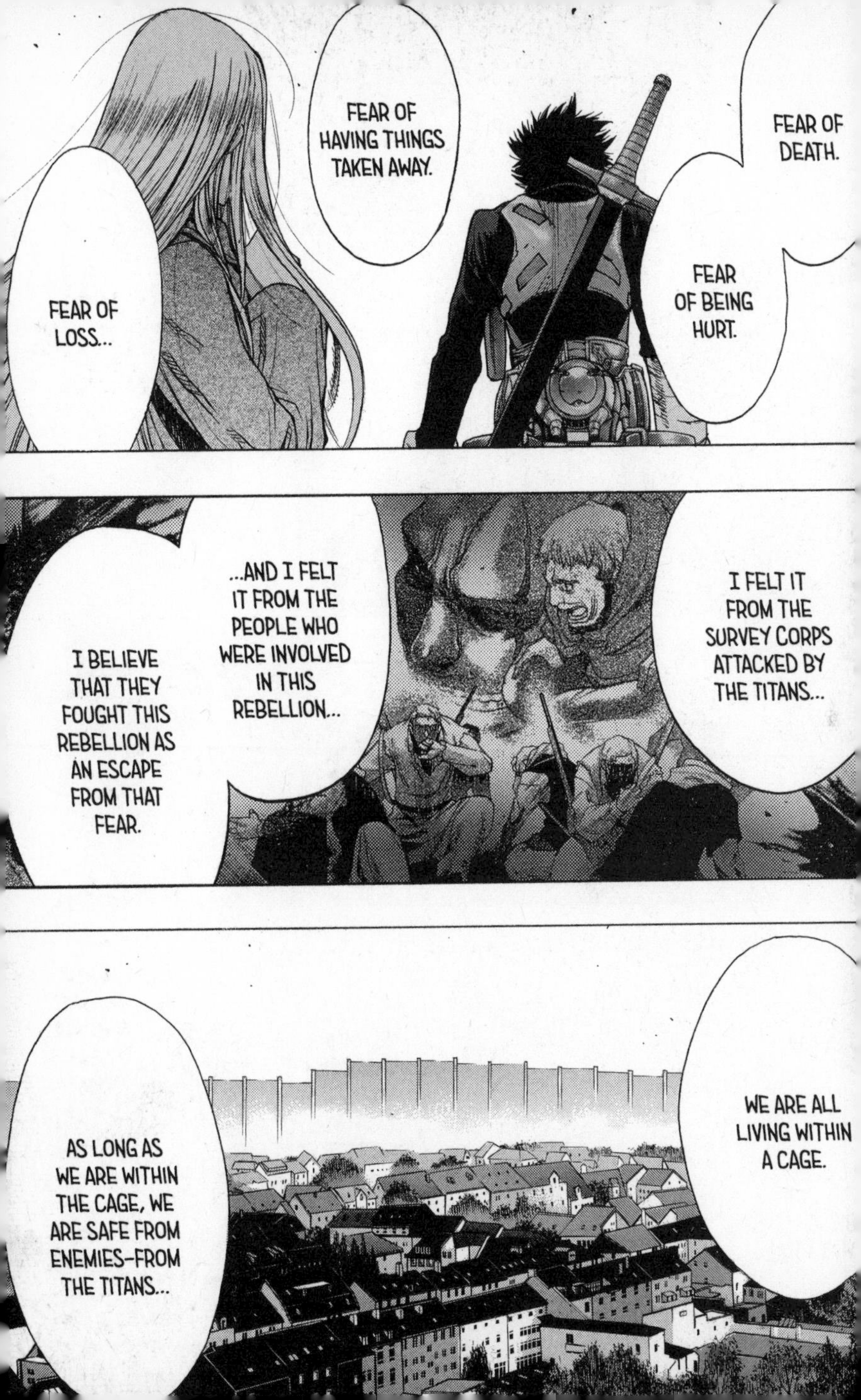
FEAR OF DEATH.
FEAR OF BEING HURT.
FEAR OF HAVING THINGS TAKEN AWAY.
FEAR OF LOSS...
I FELT IT FROM THE SURVEY CORPS ATTACKED BY THE TITANS...
...AND I FELT IT FROM THE PEOPLE WHO WERE INVOLVED IN THIS REBELLION...
I BELIEVE THAT THEY FOUGHT THIS REBELLION AS AN ESCAPE FROM THAT FEAR.
WE ARE ALL LIVING WITHIN A CAGE.
AS LONG AS WE ARE WITHIN THE CAGE, WE ARE SAFE FROM ENEMIES–FROM THE TITANS...

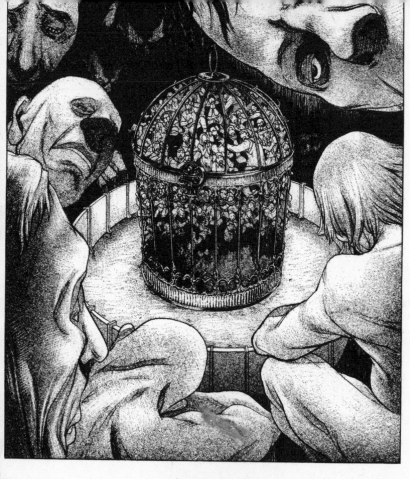

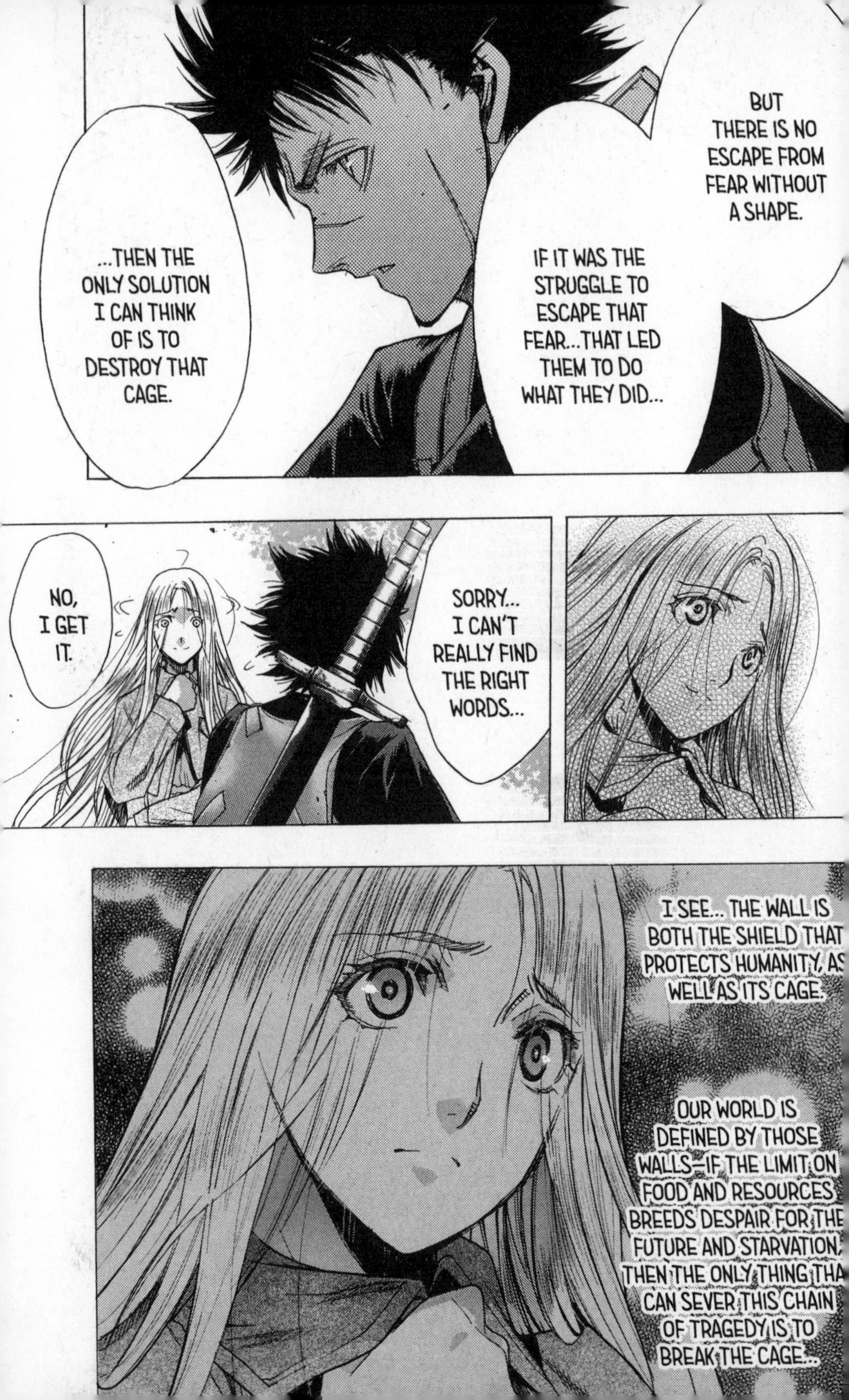
BUT THERE IS NO ESCAPE FROM FEAR WITHOUT A SHAPE.
IF IT WAS THE STRUGGLE TO ESCAPE THAT FEAR...THAT LED THEM TO DO WHAT THEY DID...
...THEN THE ONLY SOLUTION I CAN THINK OF IS TO DESTROY THAT CAGE.
SORRY... I CAN'T REALLY FIND THE RIGHT WORDS...
NO, I GET IT.
I SEE... THE WALL IS BOTH THE SHIELD THAT PROTECTS HUMANITY, AS WELL AS ITS CAGE.
OUR WORLD IS DEFINED BY THOSE WALLS—IF THE LIMIT ON FOOD AND RESOURCES BREEDS DESPAIR FOR THE FUTURE AND STARVATION, THEN THE ONLY THING THA CAN SEVER THIS CHAIN OF TRAGEDY IS TO BREAK THE CAGE...

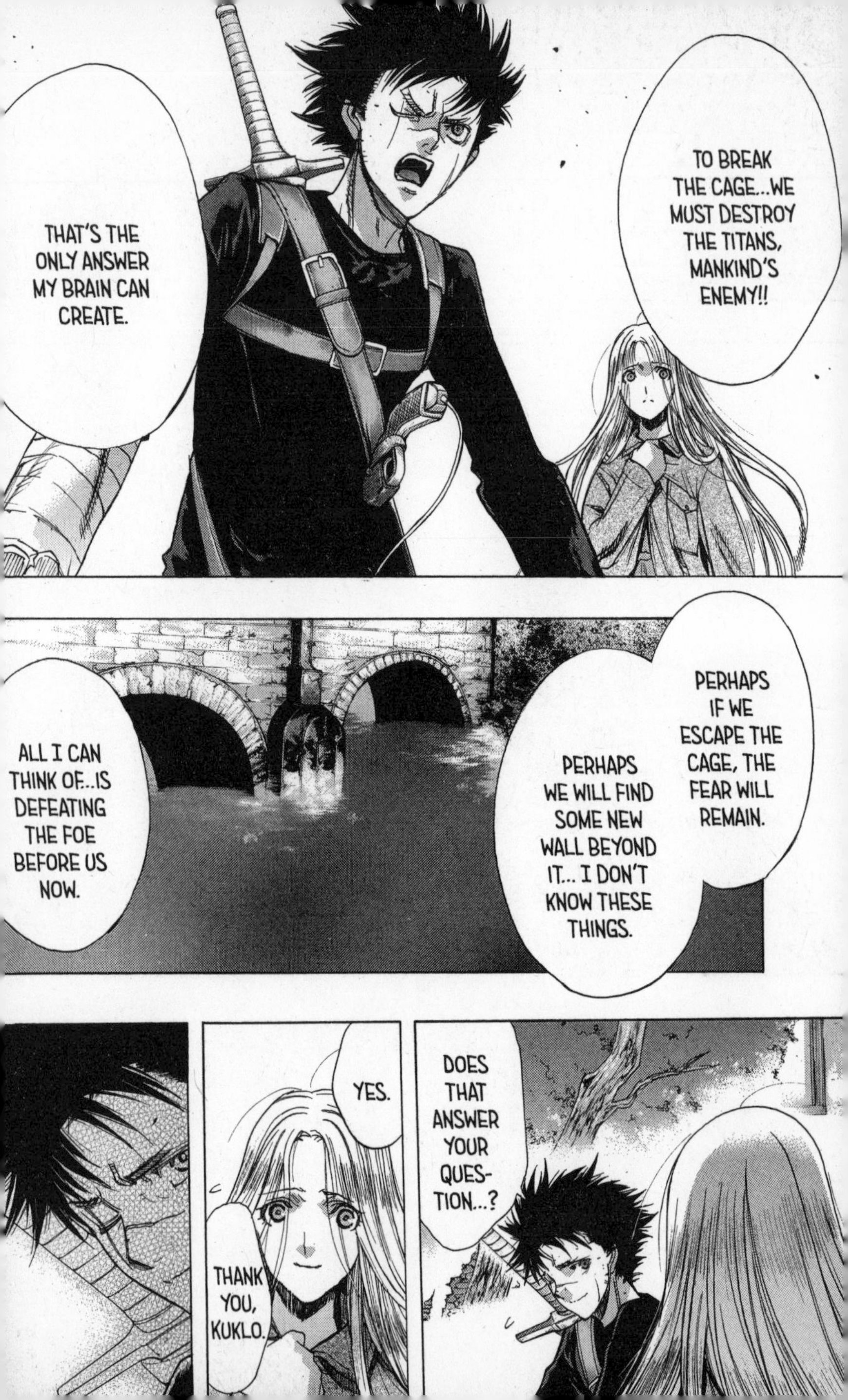
TO BREAK THE CAGE...WE MUST DESTROY THE TITANS, MANKIND'S ENEMY!!
THAT'S THE ONLY ANSWER MY BRAIN CAN CREATE.
PERHAPS IF WE ESCAPE THE CAGE, THE FEAR WILL REMAIN.
PERHAPS WE WILL FIND SOME NEW WALL BEYOND IT... I DON'T KNOW THESE THINGS.
ALL I CAN THINK OF...IS DEFEATING THE FOE BEFORE US NOW.
DOES THAT ANSWER YOUR QUES-TION...?
YES.
THANK YOU, KUKLO.

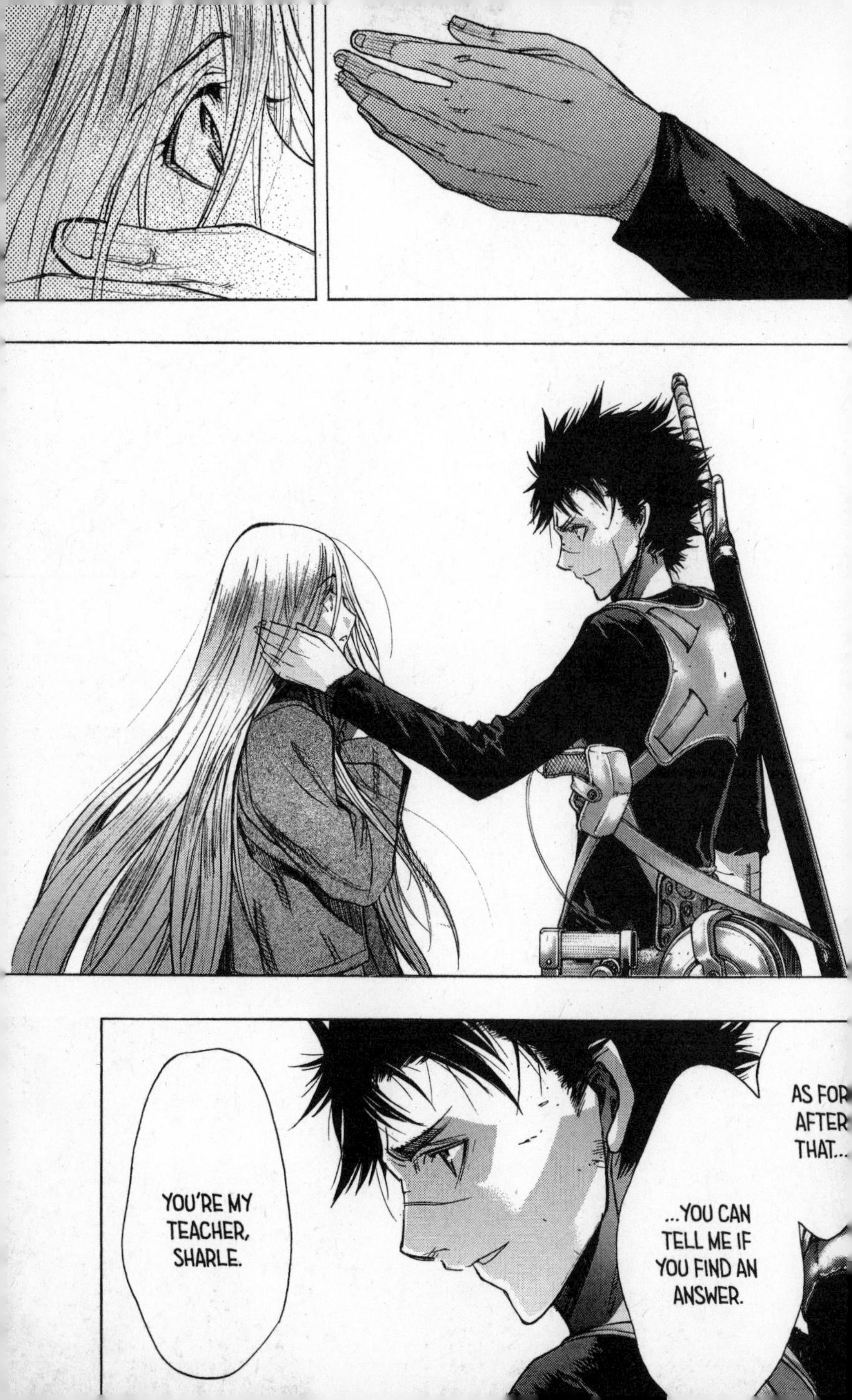
AS FOR AFTER THAT...
...YOU CAN TELL ME IF YOU FIND AN ANSWER.
YOU'RE MY TEACHER, SHARLE.

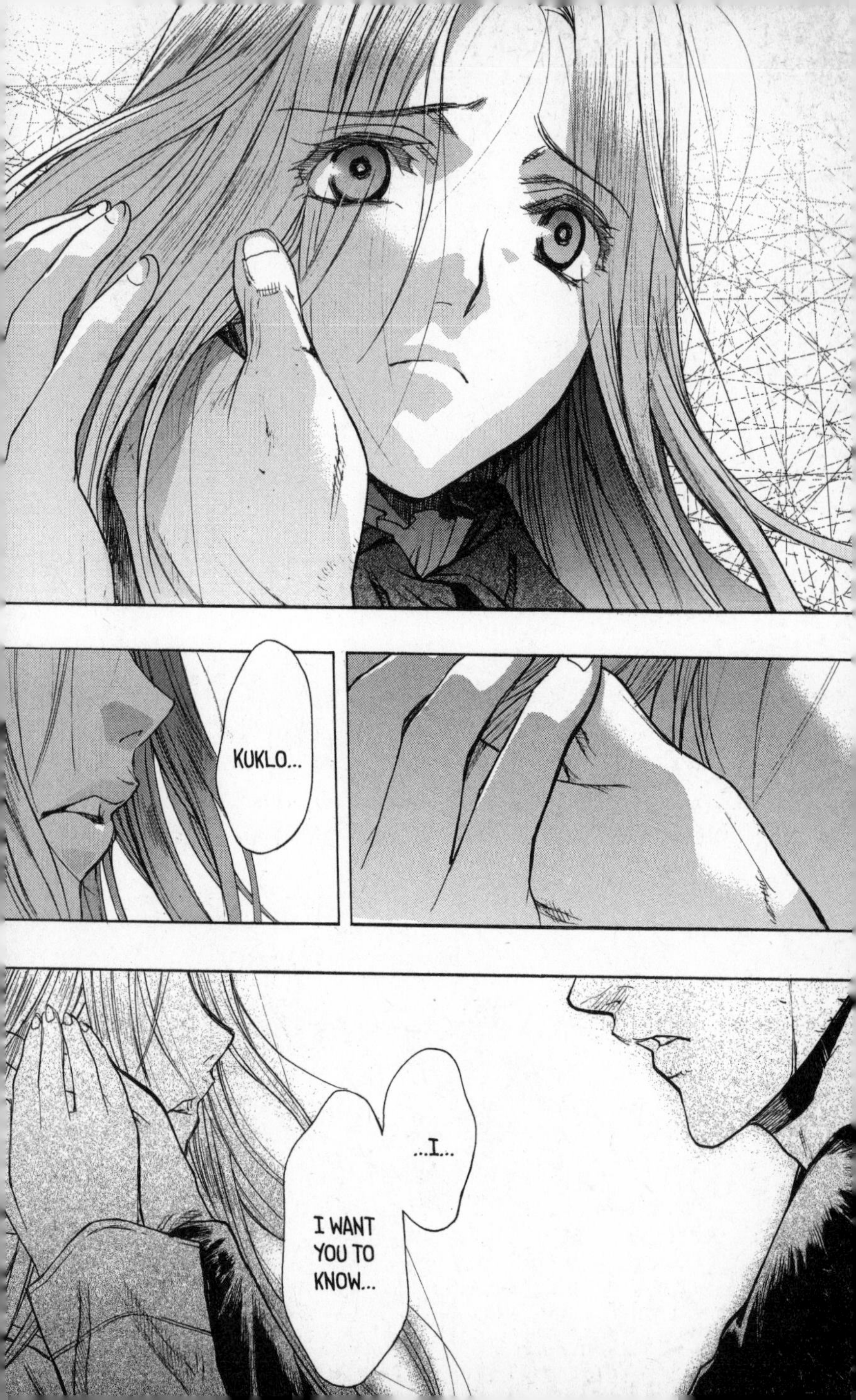
KUKLO...
...I...
I WANT YOU TO KNOW...

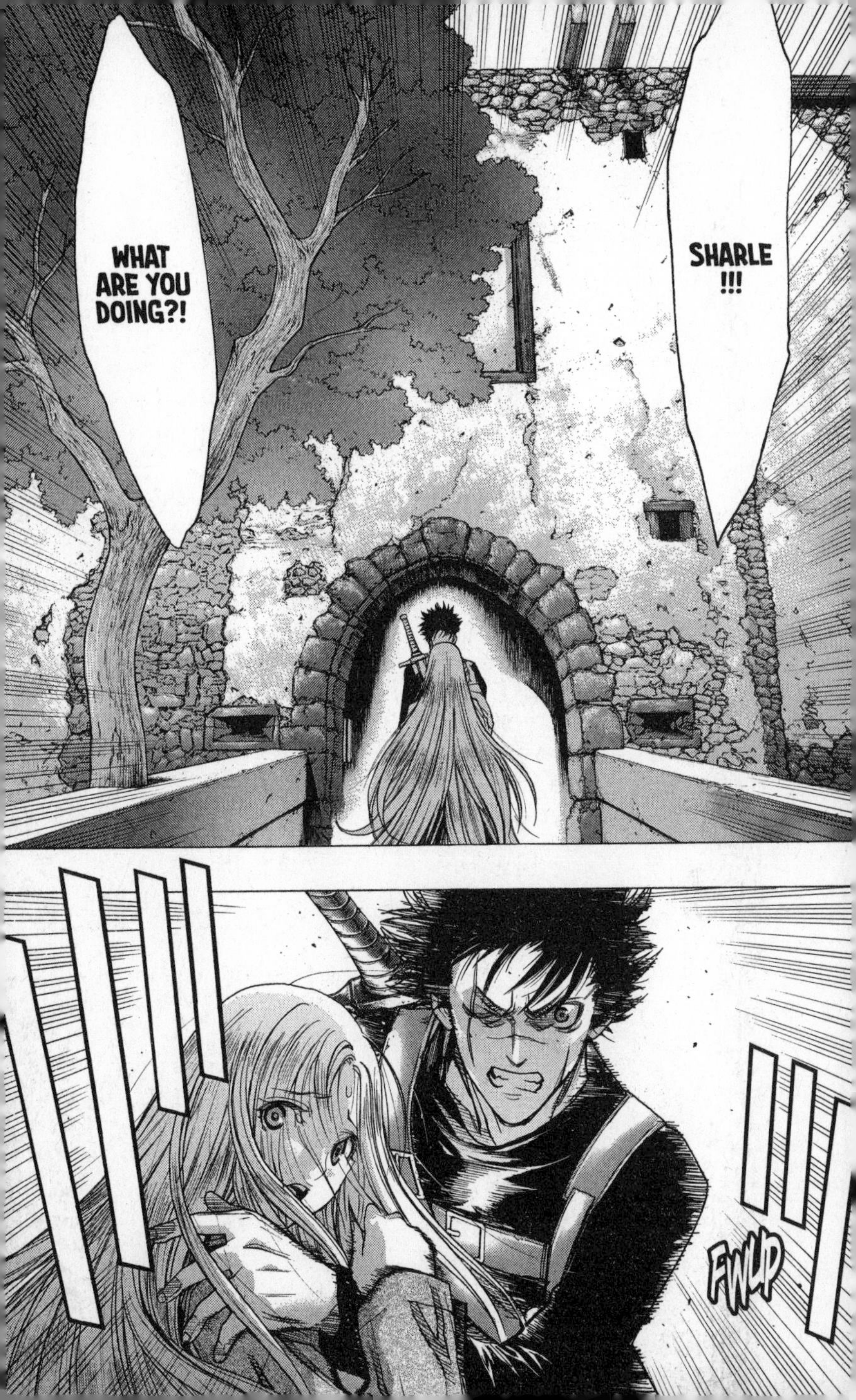
SHARLE !!!
WHAT ARE YOU DOING?!
FWUP

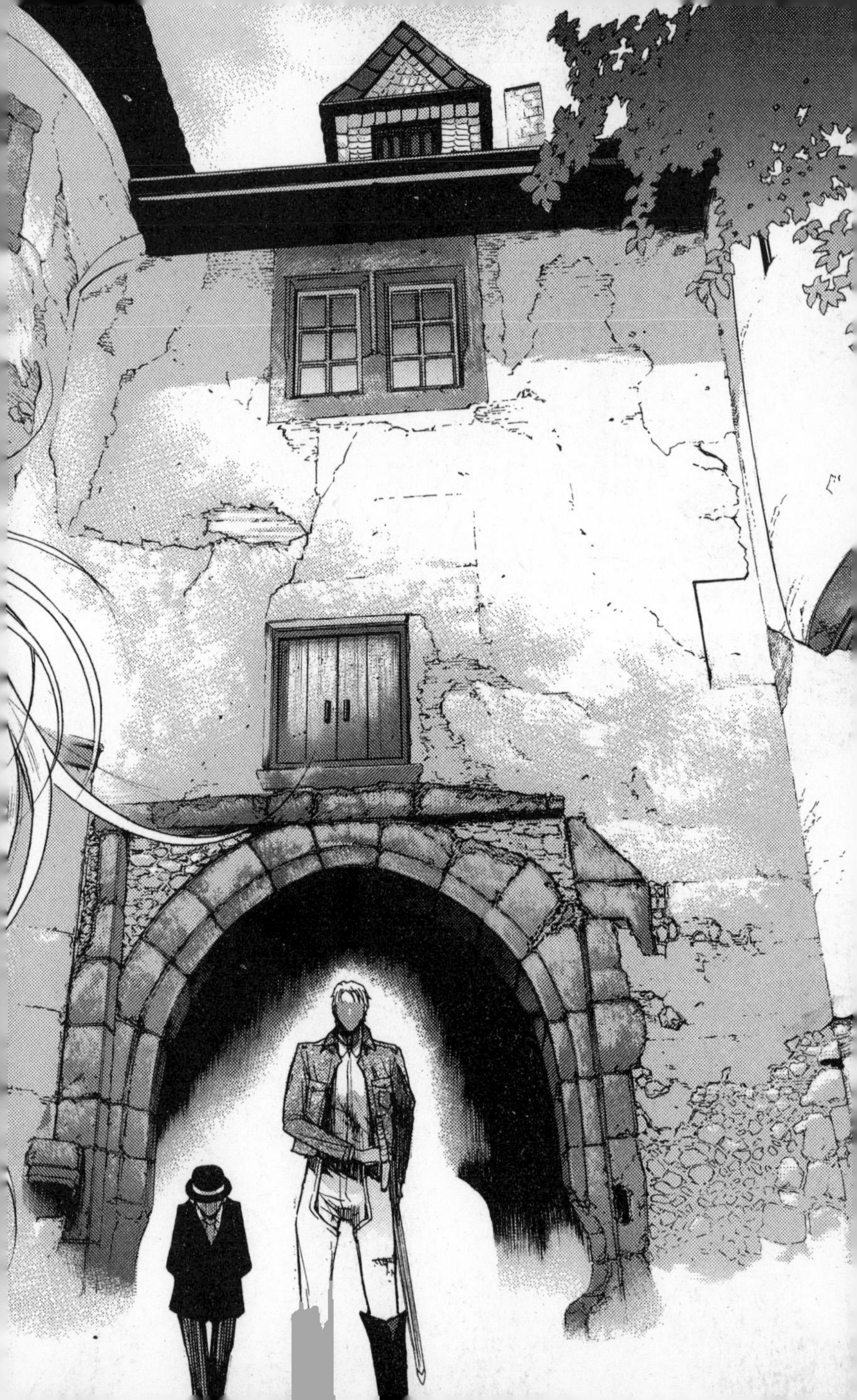

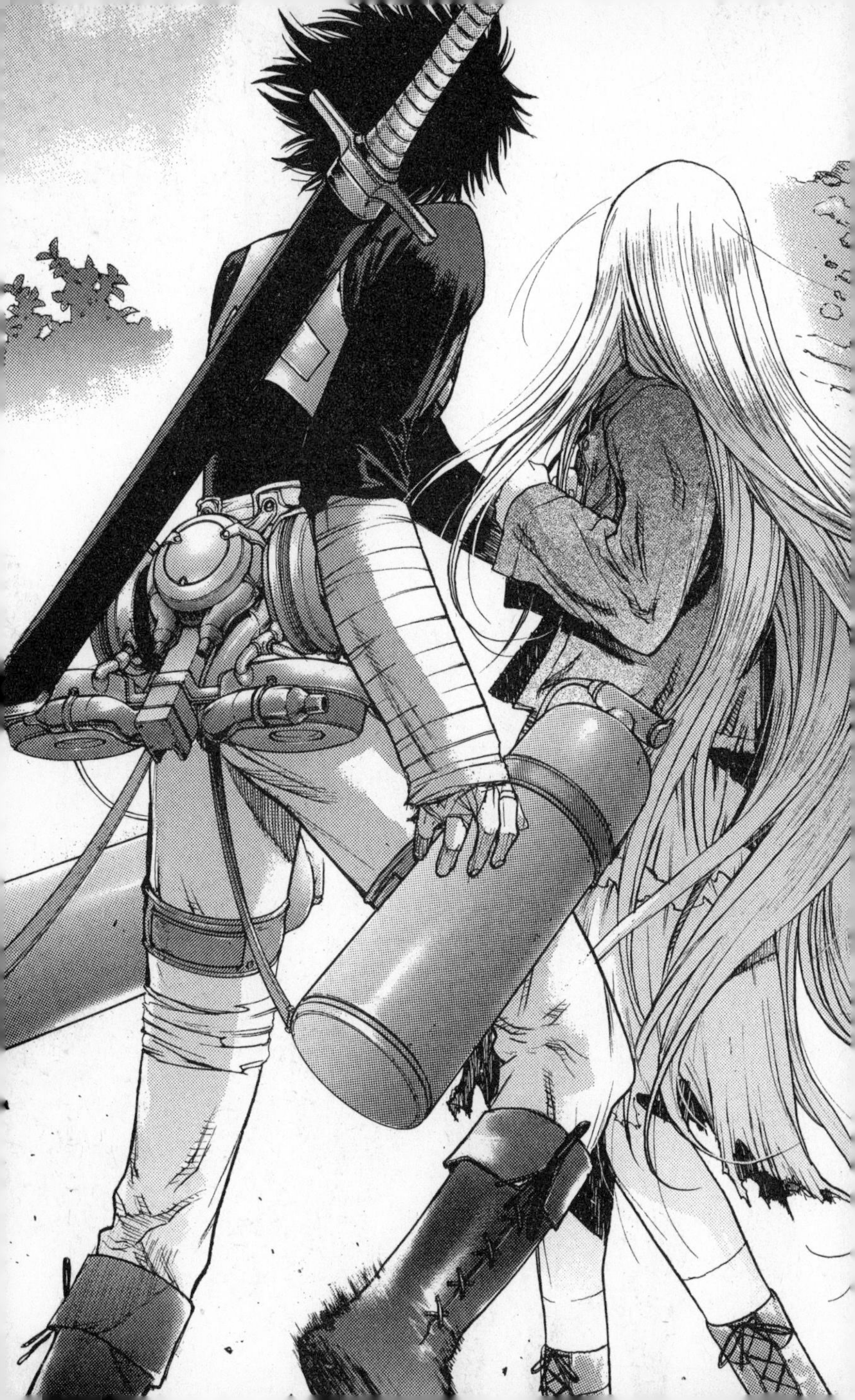

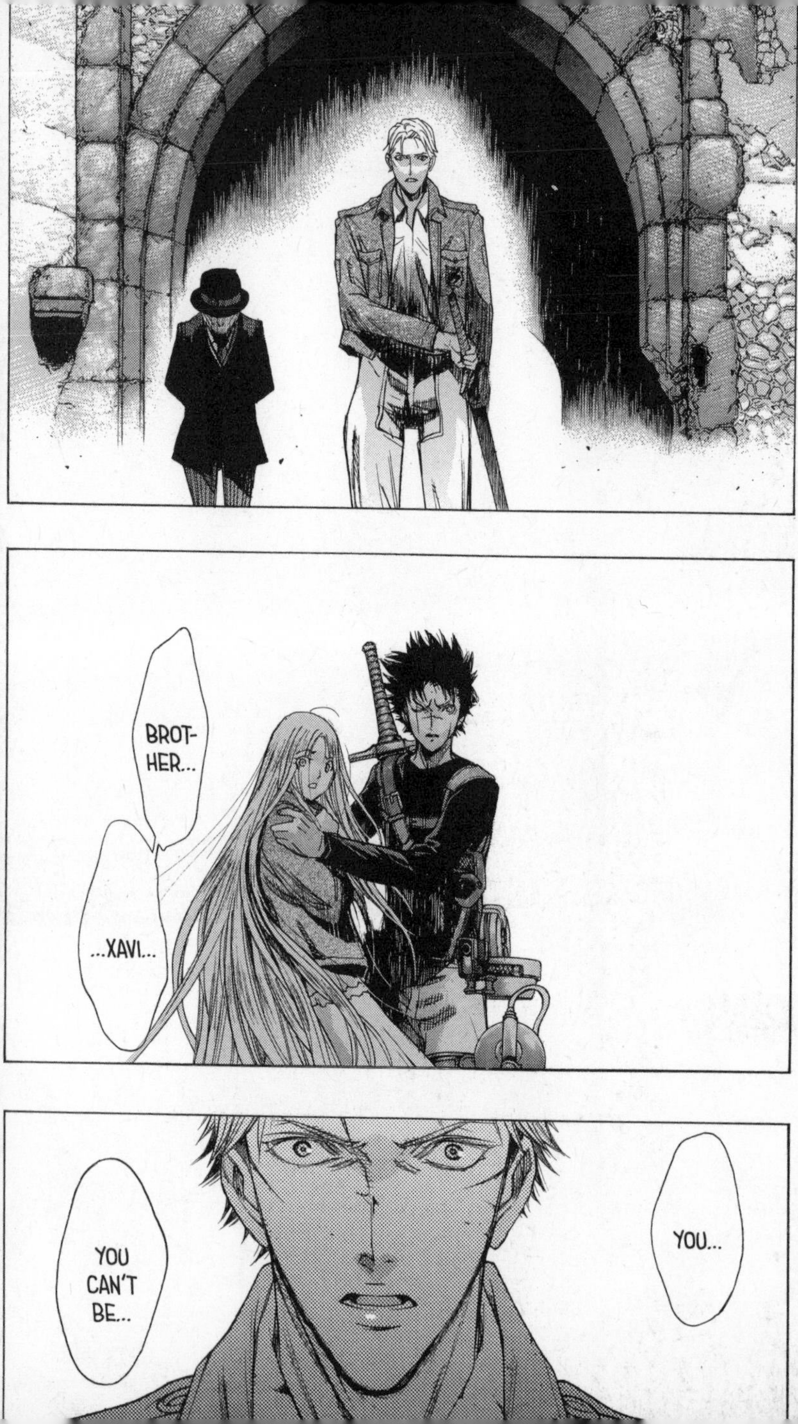
BROTHER...
...XAVI...
YOU...
YOU CAN'T BE...

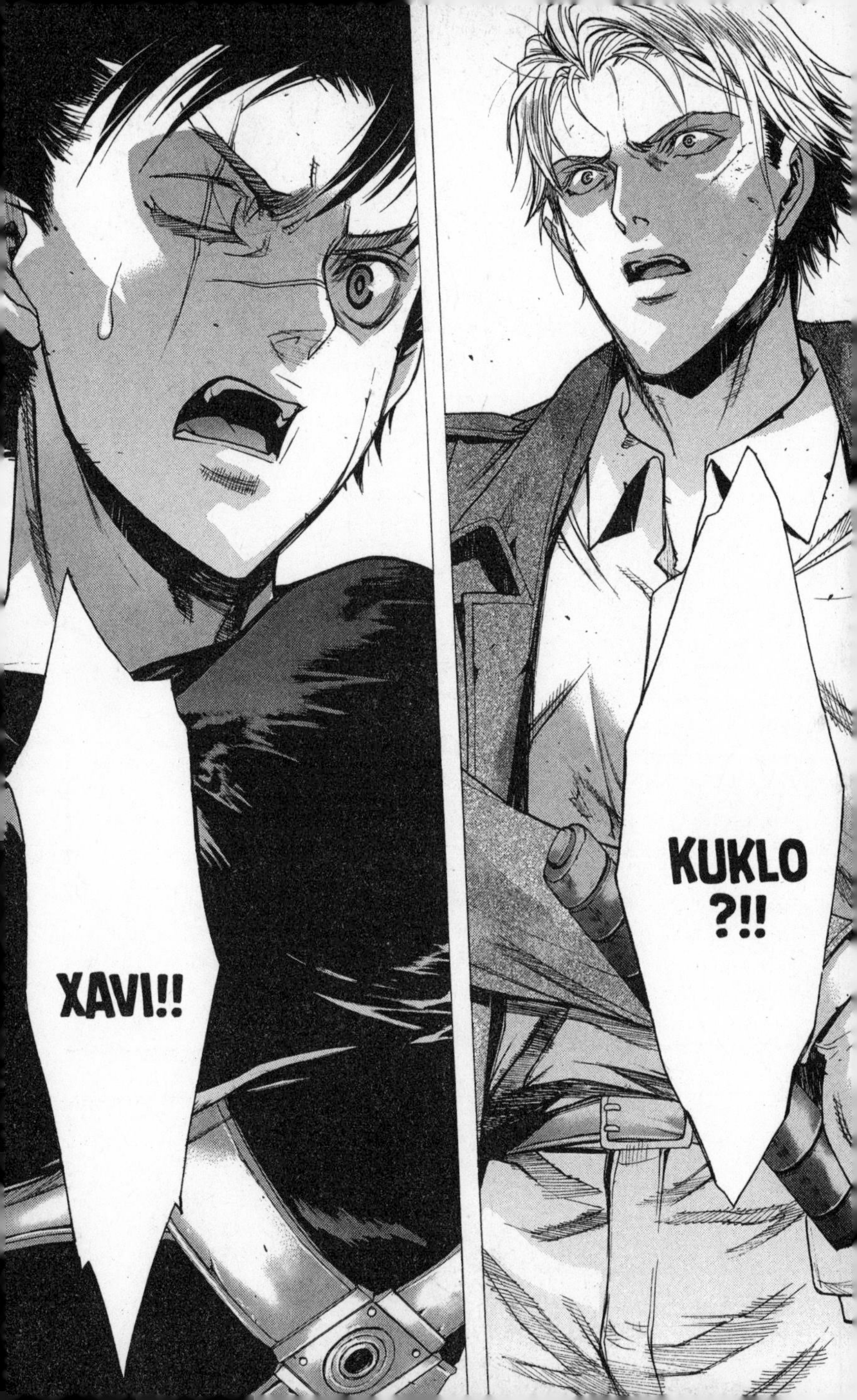
KUKLO
?!!
XAVI!!

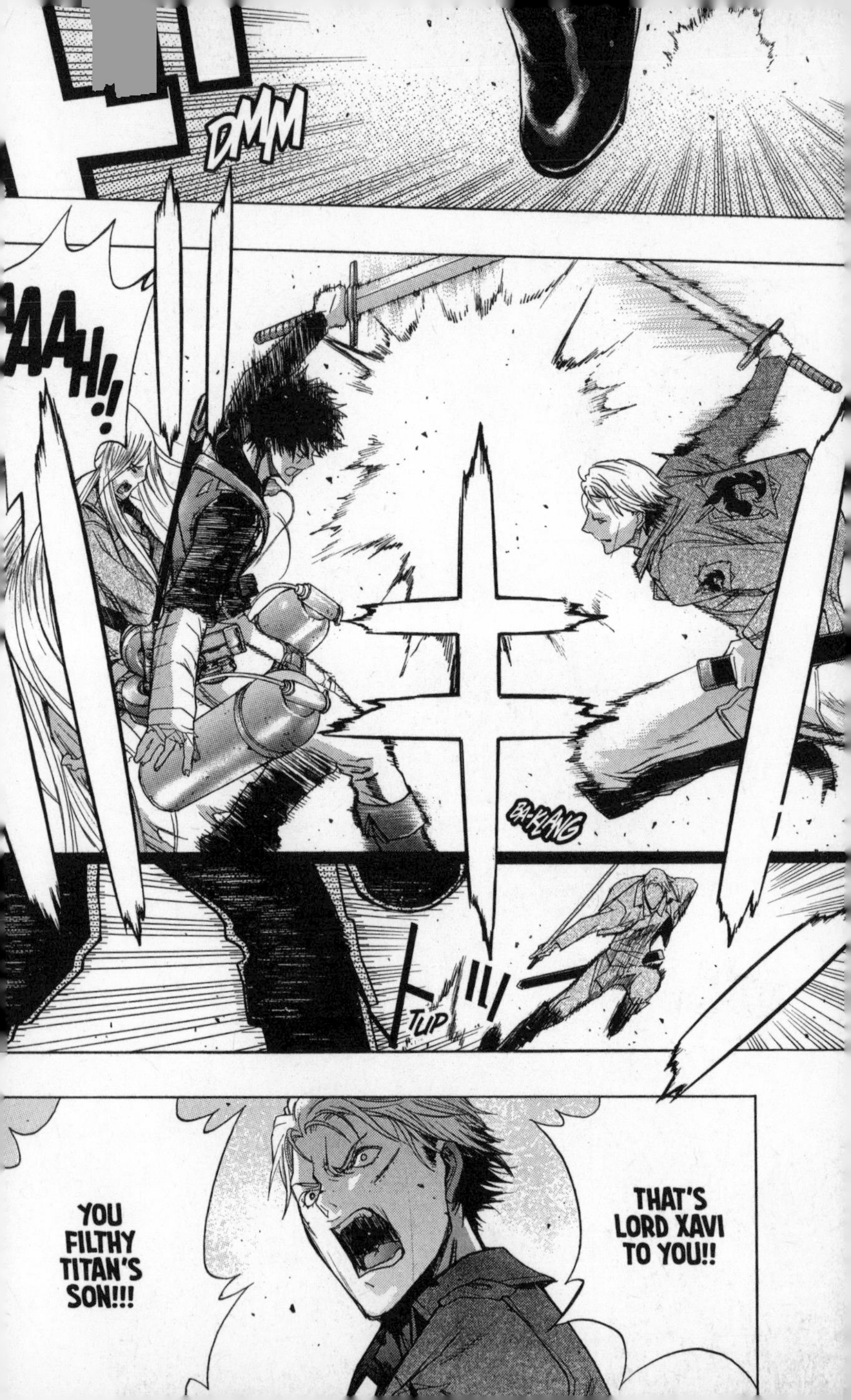
DMM
AAH!!
BA-KLANG
TUP
THAT'S LORD XAVI TO YOU!!
YOU FILTHY TITAN'S SON!!!

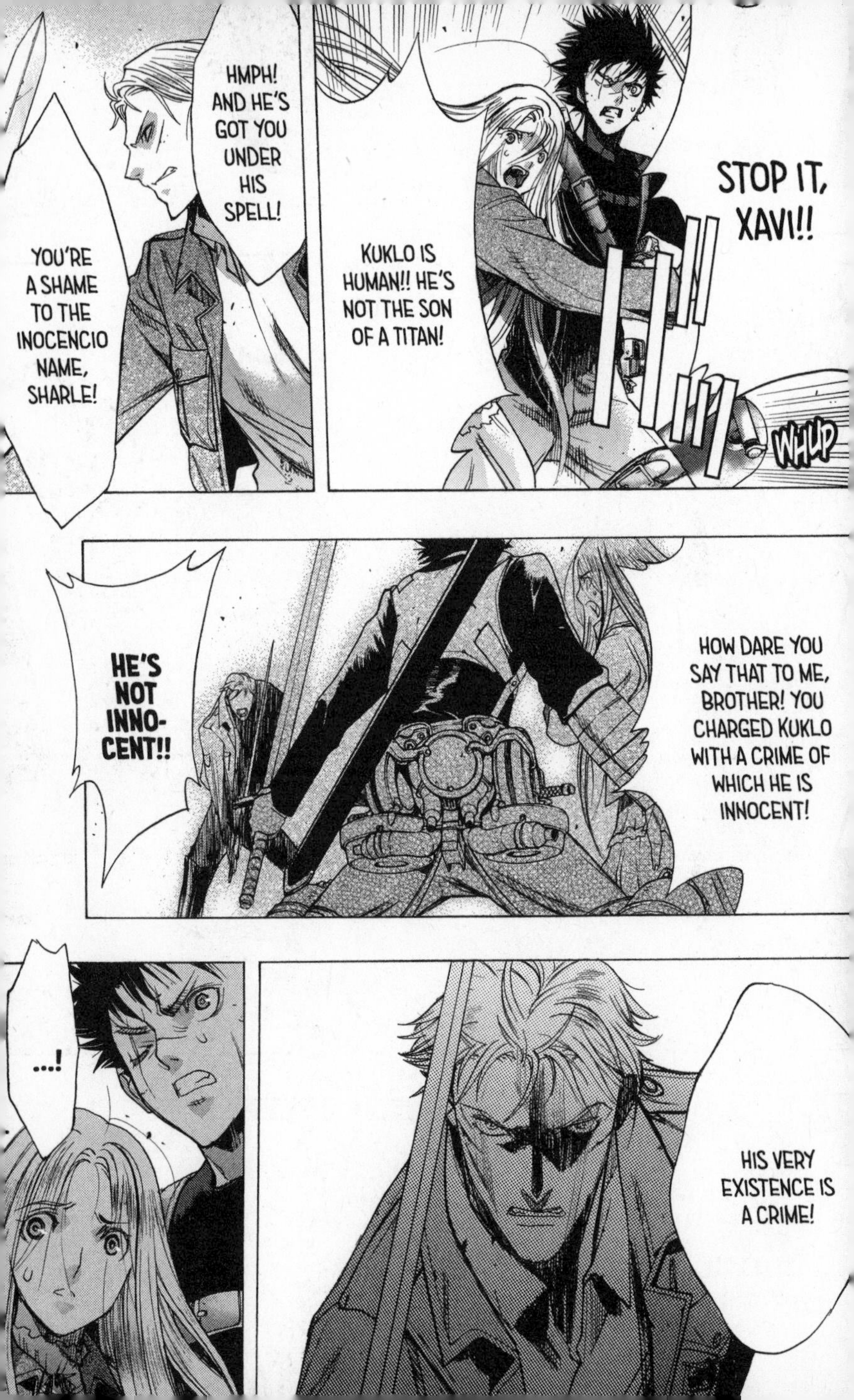
STOP IT, XAVI!!
WHUP
KUKLO IS HUMAN!! HE'S NOT THE SON OF A TITAN!
HMPH! AND HE'S GOT YOU UNDER HIS SPELL!
YOU'RE A SHAME TO THE INOCENCIO NAME, SHARLE!
HOW DARE YOU SAY THAT TO ME, BROTHER! YOU CHARGED KUKLO WITH A CRIME OF WHICH HE IS INNOCENT!
HE'S NOT INNO-CENT!!
HIS VERY EXISTENCE IS A CRIME!
...!

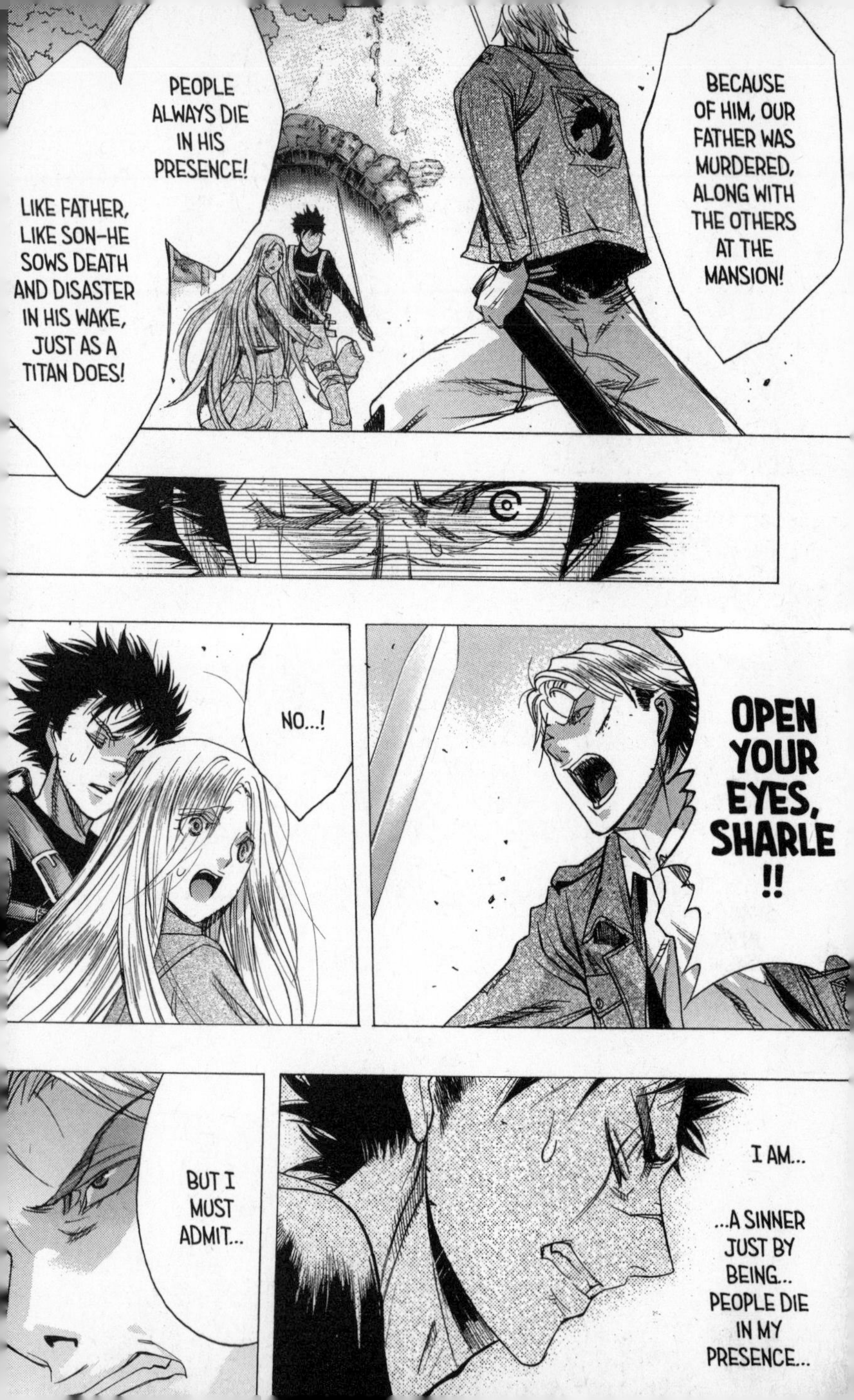
BECAUSE OF HIM, OUR FATHER WAS MURDERED, ALONG WITH THE OTHERS AT THE MANSION!
PEOPLE ALWAYS DIE IN HIS PRESENCE!
LIKE FATHER, LIKE SON—HE SOWS DEATH AND DISASTER IN HIS WAKE, JUST AS A TITAN DOES!
OPEN YOUR EYES, SHARLE !!
NO...!
I AM...
...A SINNER JUST BY BEING.. PEOPLE DIE IN MY PRESENCE...
BUT I MUST ADMIT...

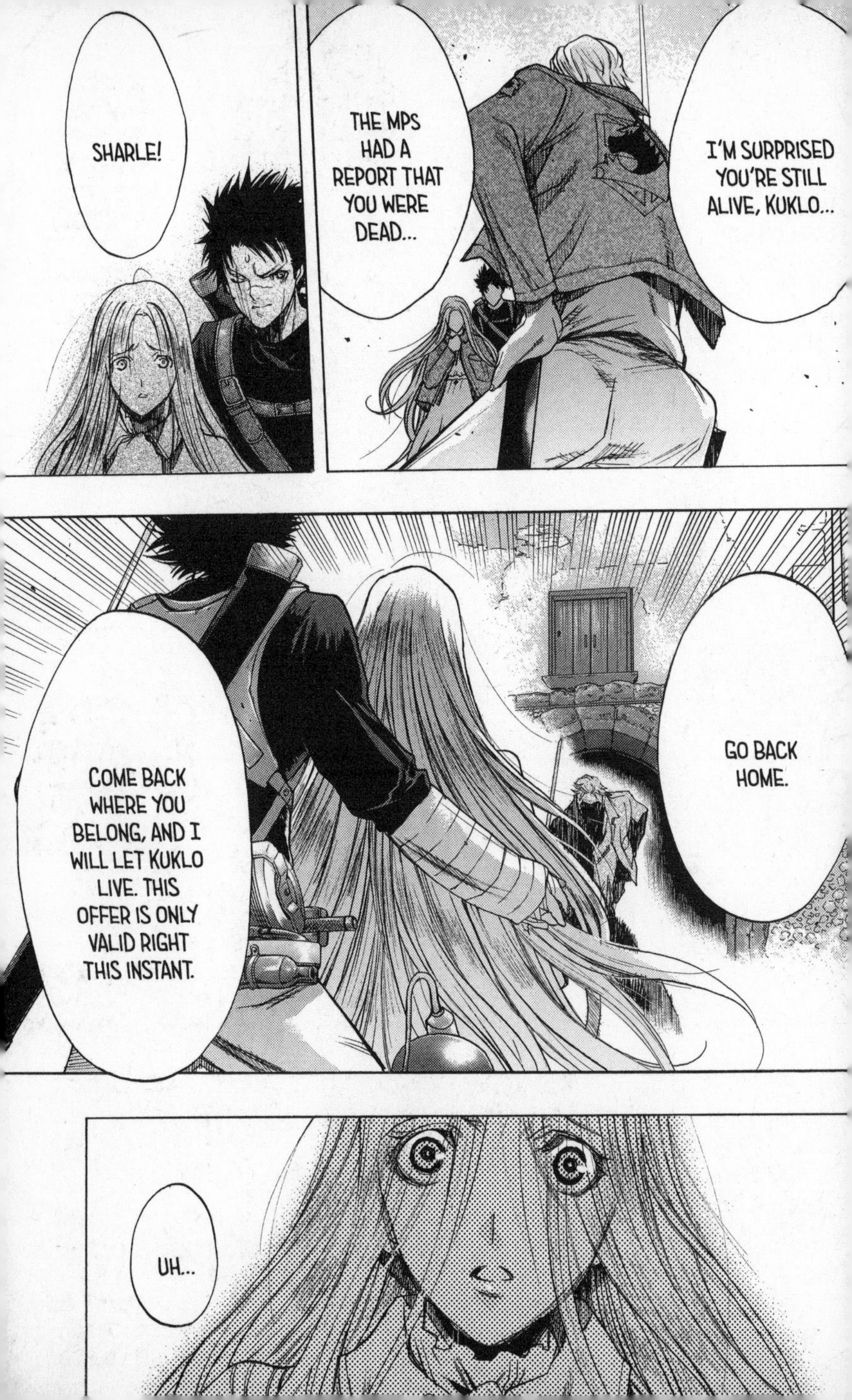
I'M SURPRISED YOU'RE STILL ALIVE, KUKLO...
THE MPS HAD A REPORT THAT YOU WERE DEAD...
SHARLE!
GO BACK HOME.
COME BACK WHERE YOU BELONG, AND I WILL LET KUKLO LIVE. THIS OFFER IS ONLY VALID RIGHT THIS INSTANT.
UH...

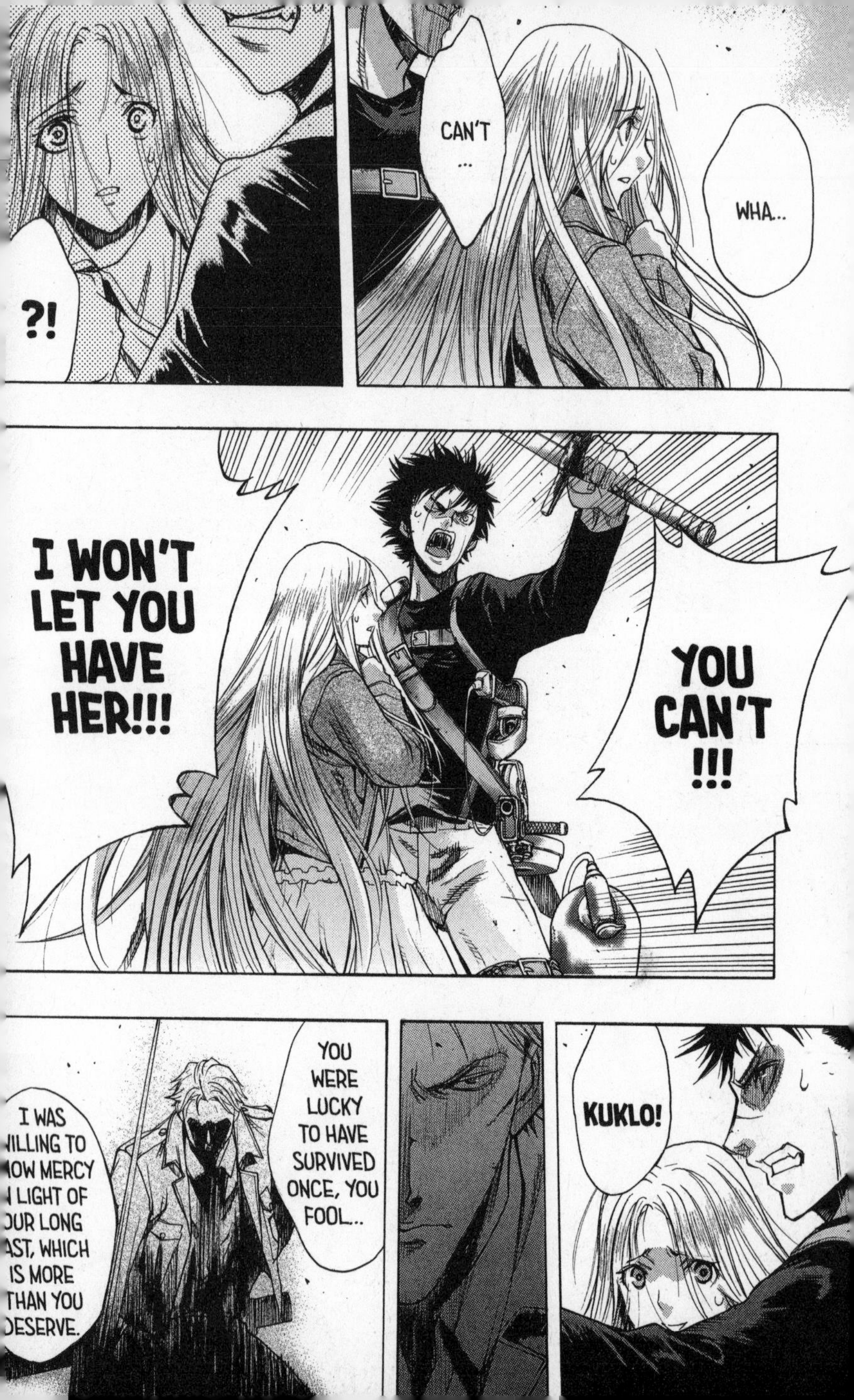
WHA..
CAN'T ...
?!
YOU CAN'T !!!
I WON'T LET YOU HAVE HER!!!
KUKLO!
YOU WERE LUCKY TO HAVE SURVIVED ONCE, YOU FOOL...
I WAS ILLING TO OW MERCY N LIGHT OF OUR LONG AST, WHICH IS MORE THAN YOU ESERVE.

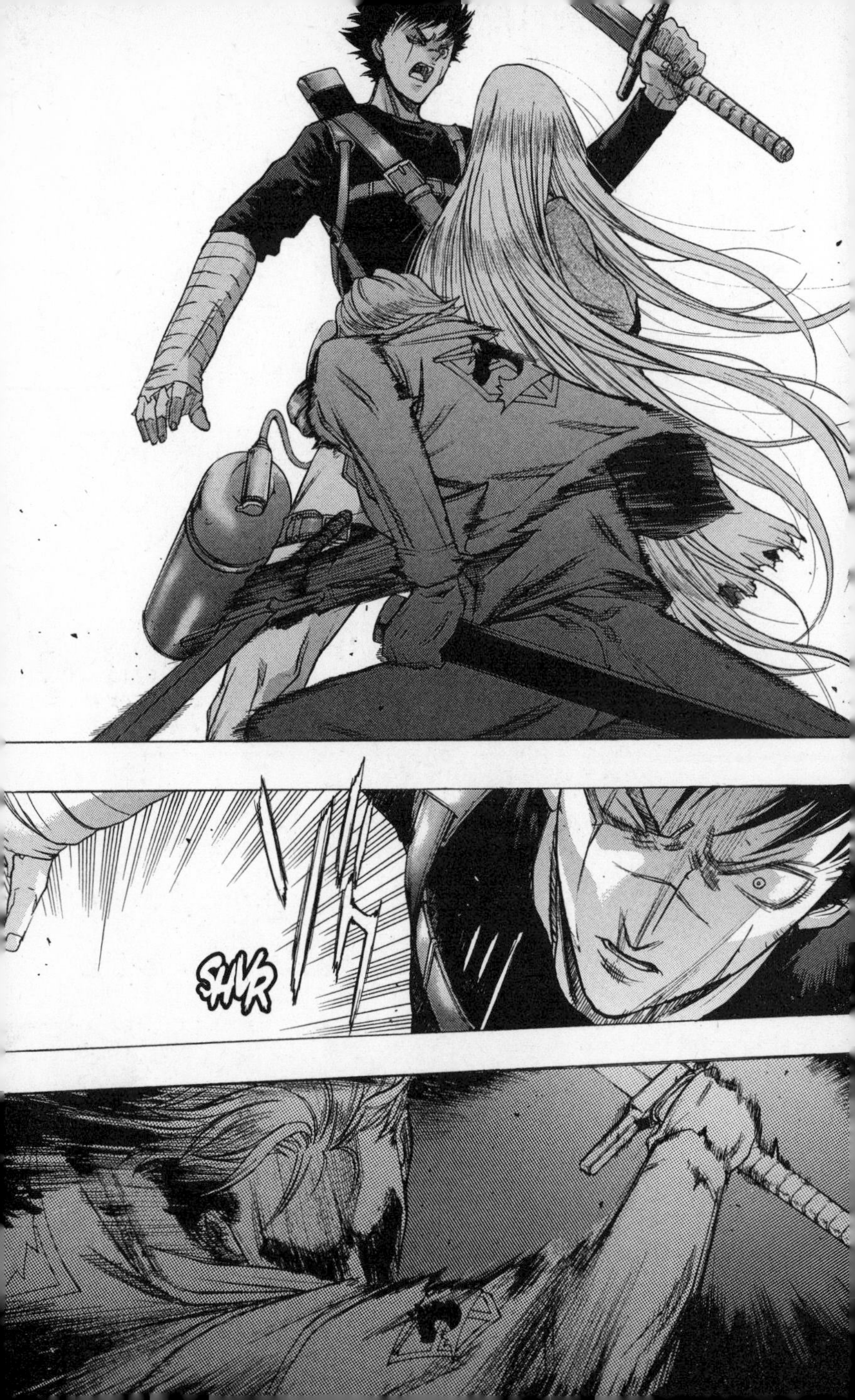
SHVR

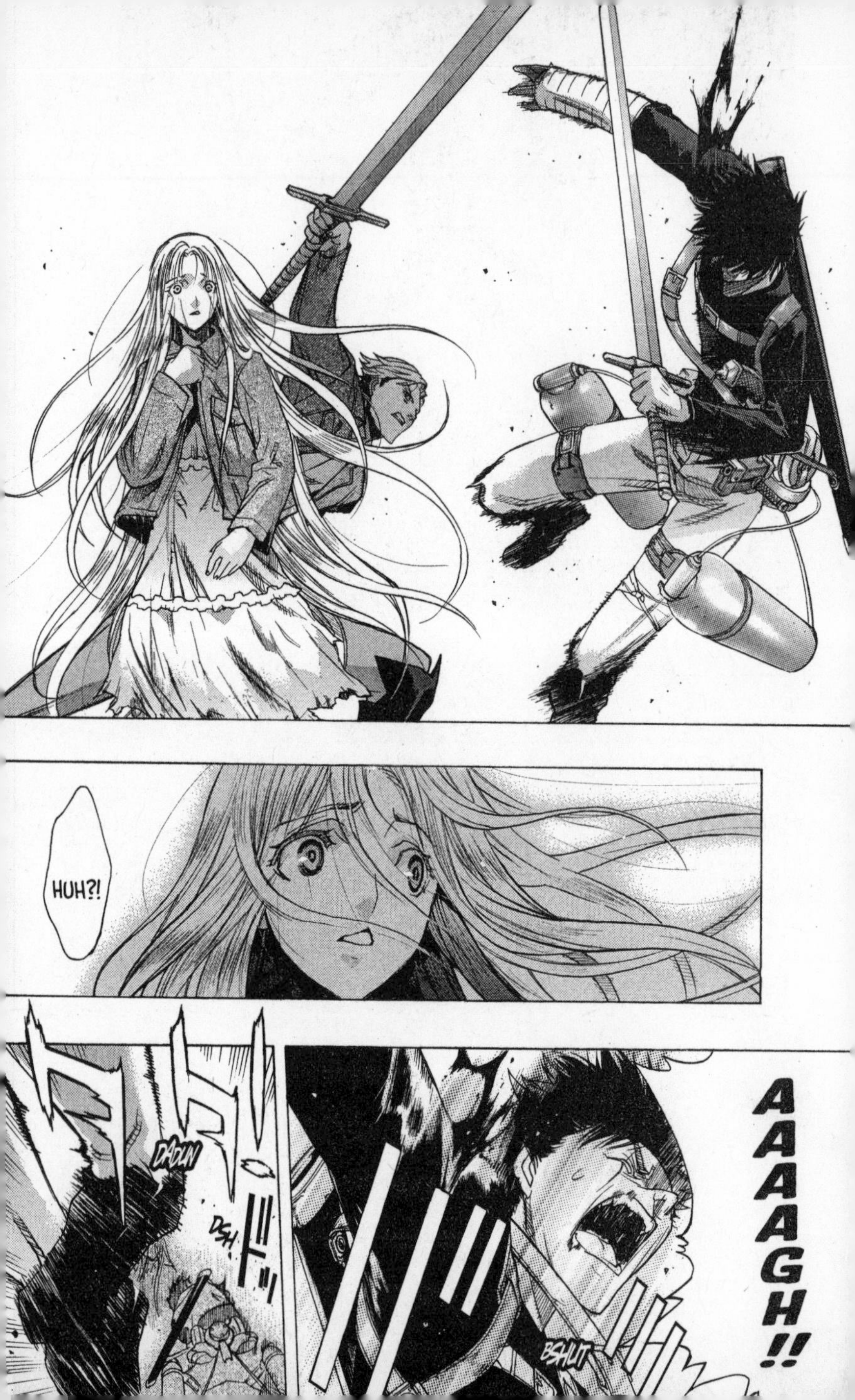
HUH?!
AAAAGH!!
DADUN
DSH!
BSHUT

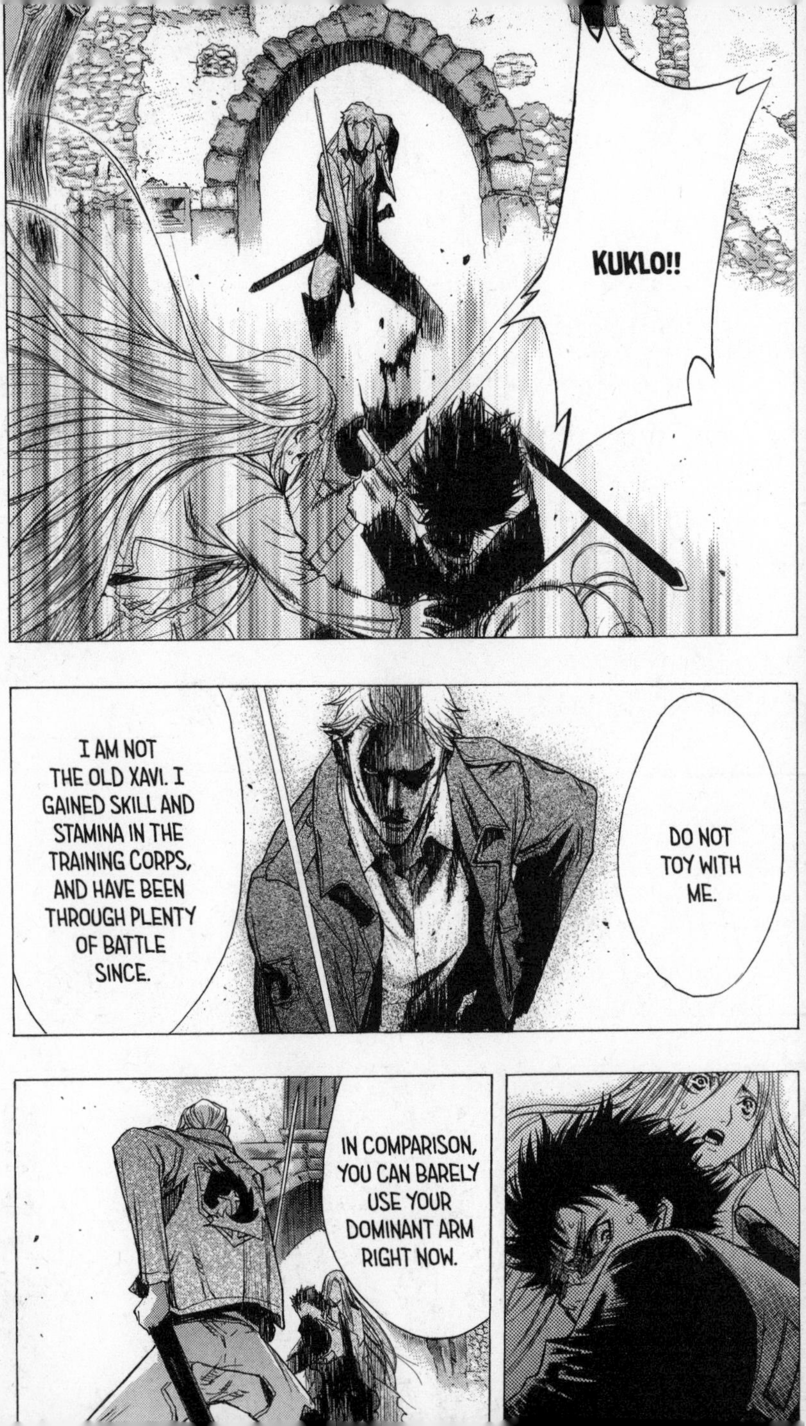
KUKLO!!
DO NOT TOY WITH ME.
I AM NOT THE OLD XAVI. I GAINED SKILL AND STAMINA IN THE TRAINING CORPS, AND HAVE BEEN THROUGH PLENTY OF BATTLE SINCE.
IN COMPARISON, YOU CAN BARELY USE YOUR DOMINANT ARM RIGHT NOW.

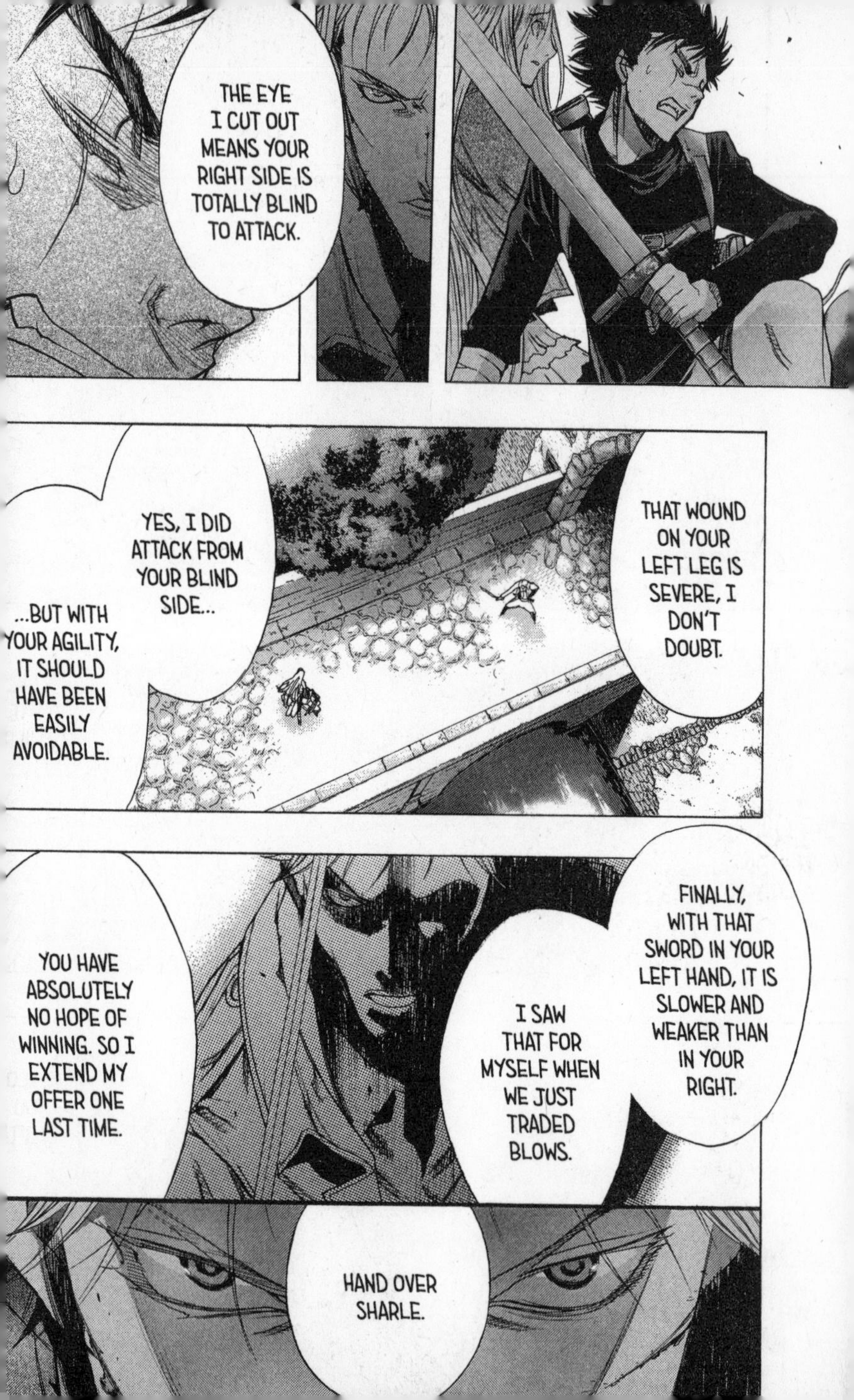
THE EYE I CUT OUT MEANS YOUR RIGHT SIDE IS TOTALLY BLIND TO ATTACK.
THAT WOUND ON YOUR LEFT LEG IS SEVERE, I DON'T DOUBT.
YES, I DID ATTACK FROM YOUR BLIND SIDE...
...BUT WITH YOUR AGILITY, IT SHOULD HAVE BEEN EASILY AVOIDABLE.
FINALLY, WITH THAT SWORD IN YOUR LEFT HAND, IT IS SLOWER AND WEAKER THAN IN YOUR RIGHT.
I SAW THAT FOR MYSELF WHEN WE JUST TRADED BLOWS.
YOU HAVE ABSOLUTELY NO HOPE OF WINNING. SO I EXTEND MY OFFER ONE LAST TIME.
HAND OVER SHARLE.

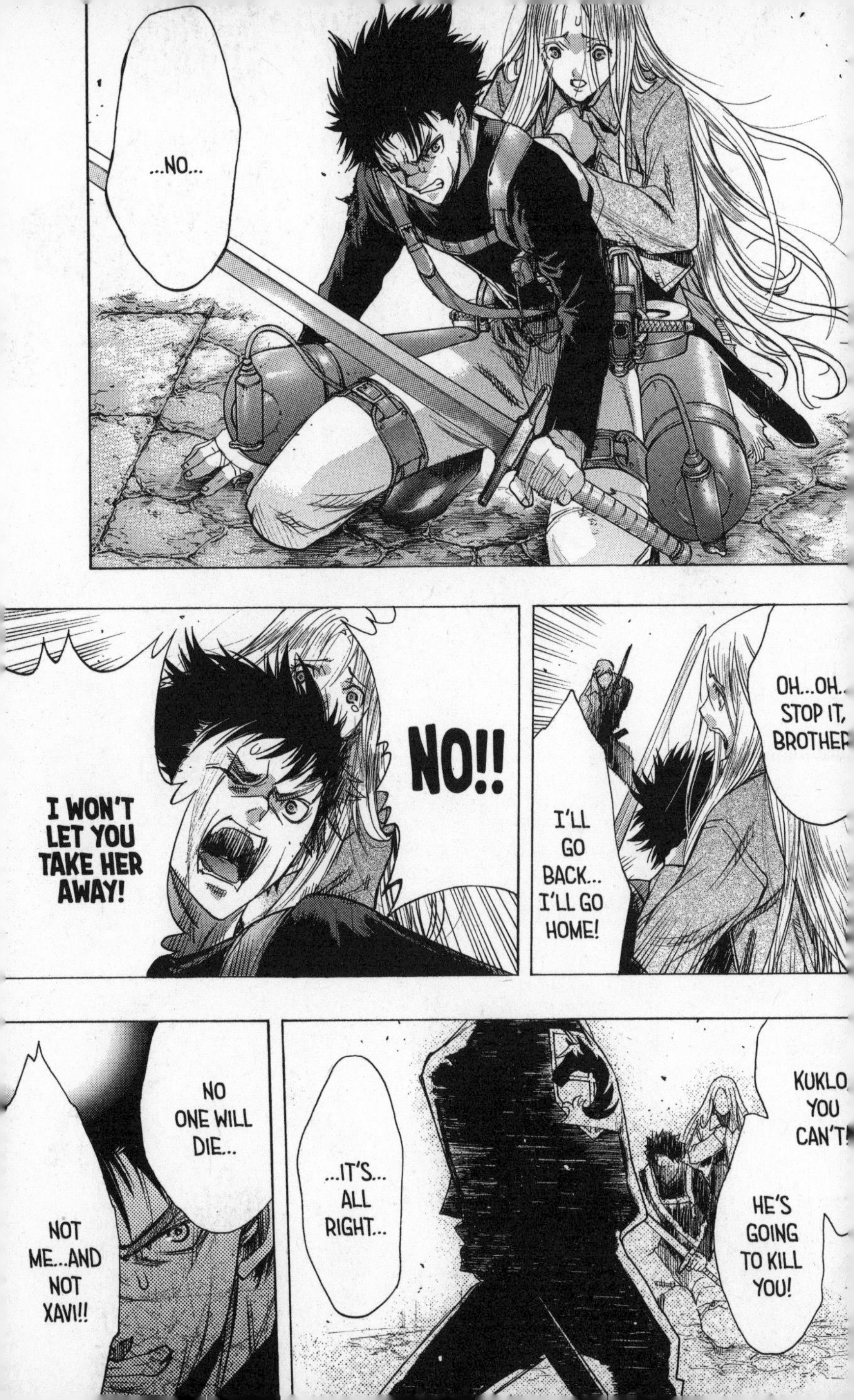
...NO...
OH...OH... STOP IT, BROTHER
I'LL GO BACK... I'LL GO HOME!
NO!!
I WON'T LET YOU TAKE HER AWAY!
KUKLO YOU CAN'T!
HE'S GOING TO KILL YOU!
...IT'S... ALL RIGHT...
NO ONE WILL DIE...
NOT ME...AND NOT XAVI!!

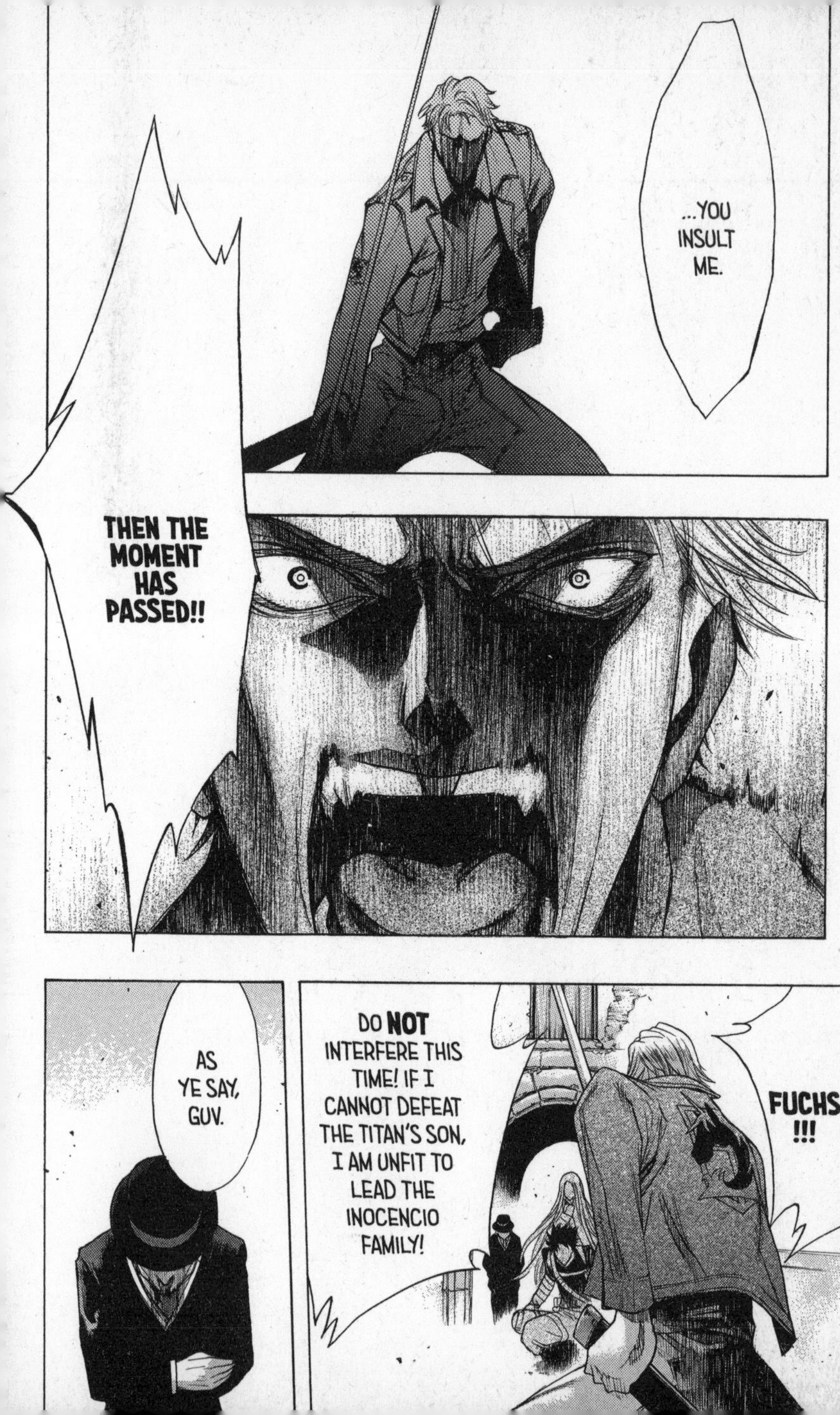
...YOU INSULT ME.
THEN THE MOMENT HAS PASSED!!
FUCHS!!!
DO NOT INTERFERE THIS TIME! IF I CANNOT DEFEAT THE TITAN'S SON, I AM UNFIT TO LEAD THE INOCENCIO FAMILY!
AS YE SAY, GUV.

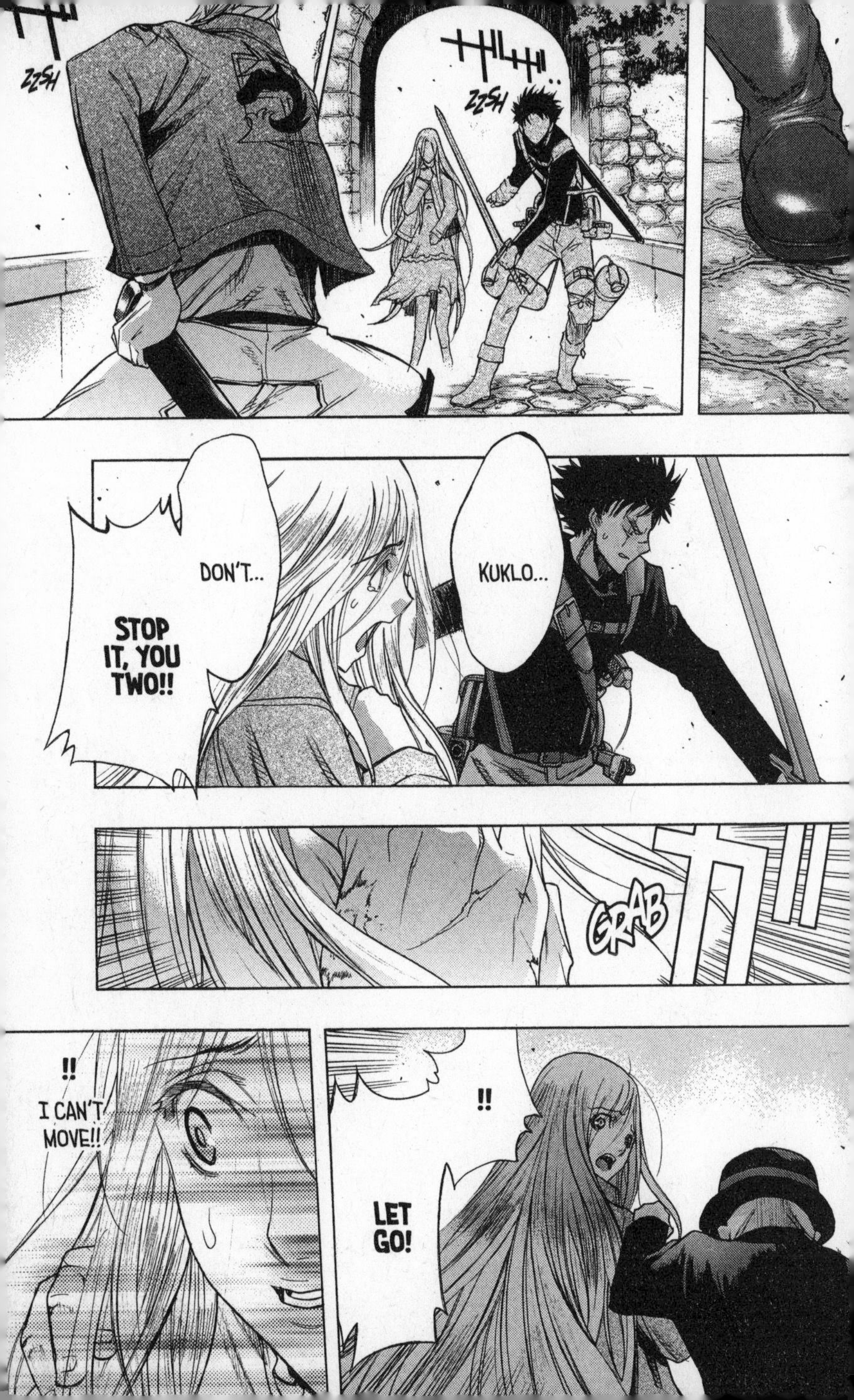
ZZSH
ZZSH
KUKLO...
DON'T...
STOP IT, YOU TWO!!
GRAB
!!
LET GO!
!!
I CAN'T MOVE!!

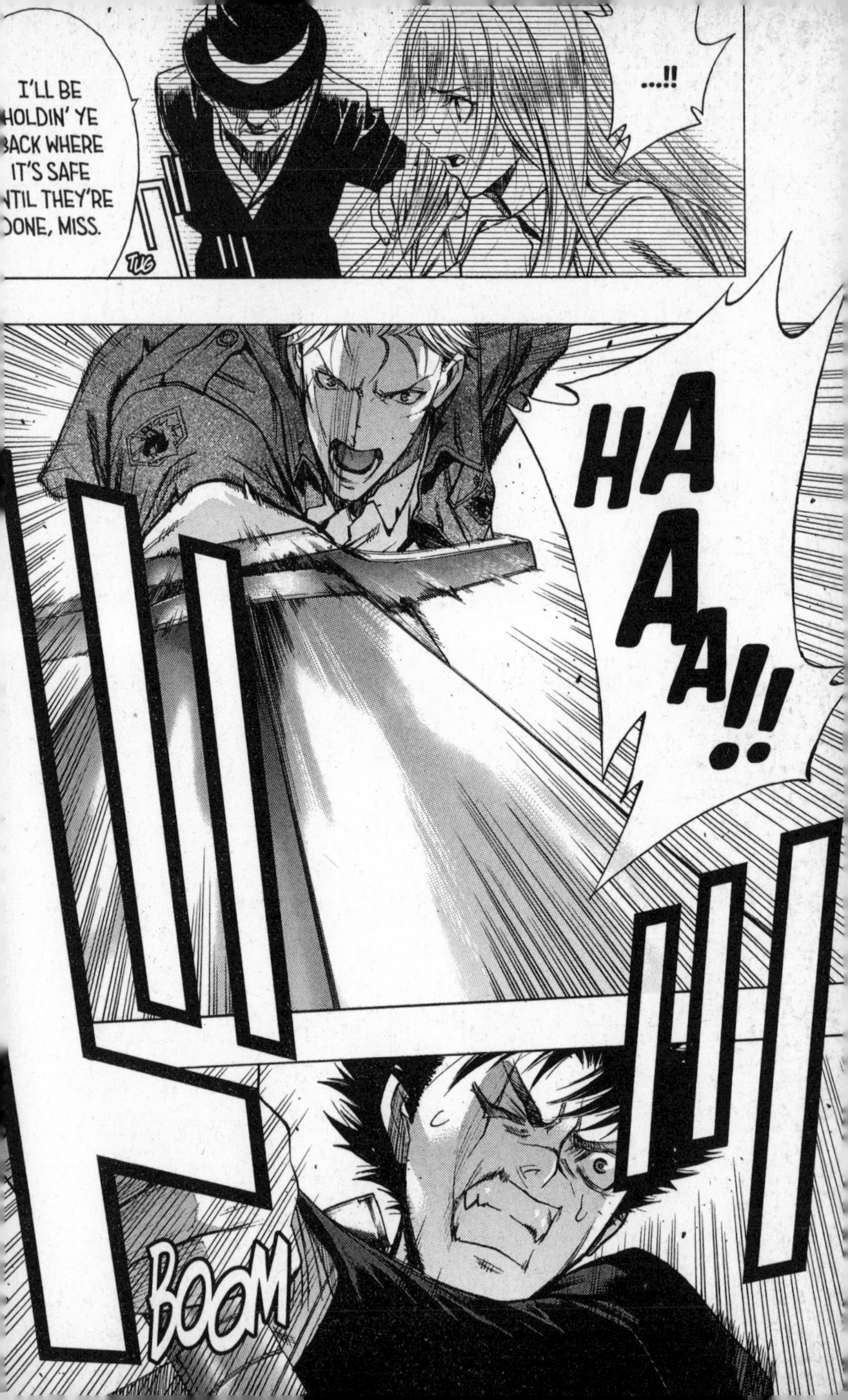
...!!
I'LL BE HOLDIN' YE BACK WHERE IT'S SAFE NTIL THEY'RE DONE, MISS.
TUG
HAAAA!!
BOOM

Chapter 31: Blades of Karma · End

ATTACK on TITAN

BEFORE THE FALL

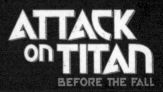

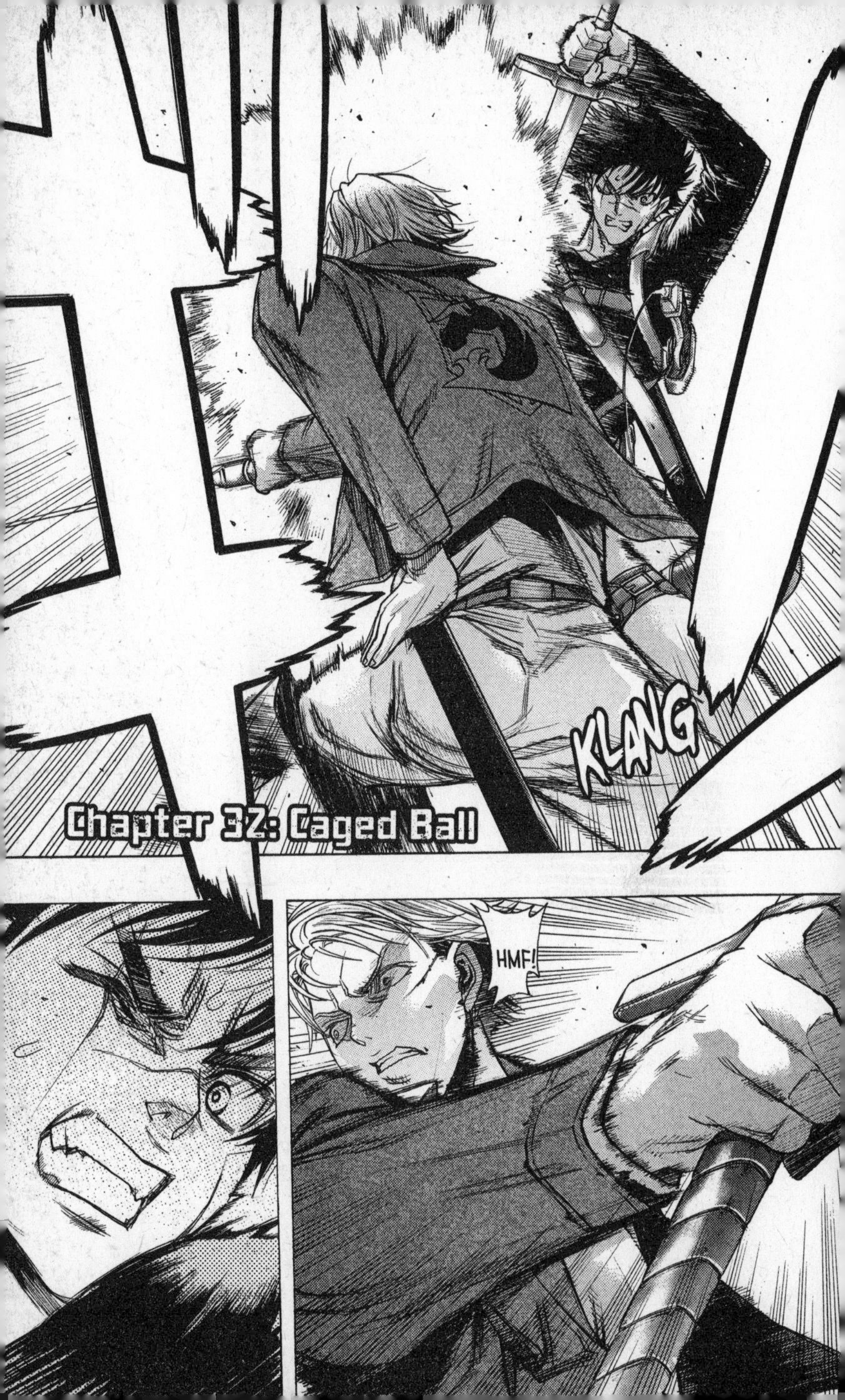
KLANG
Chapter 32: Caged Ball
HMF!

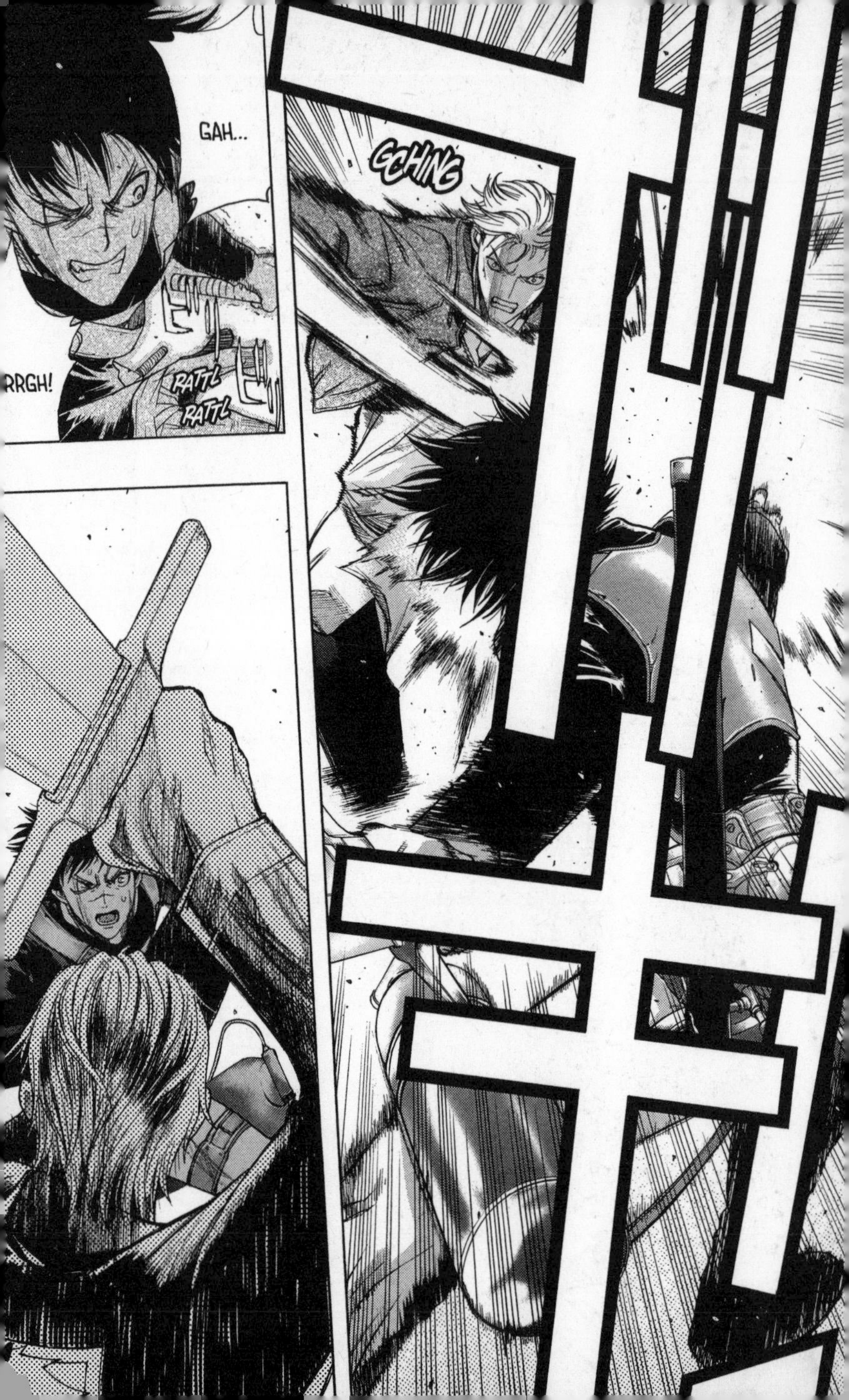
GCHING
GAH...
RATTL
RATTL
RRGH!

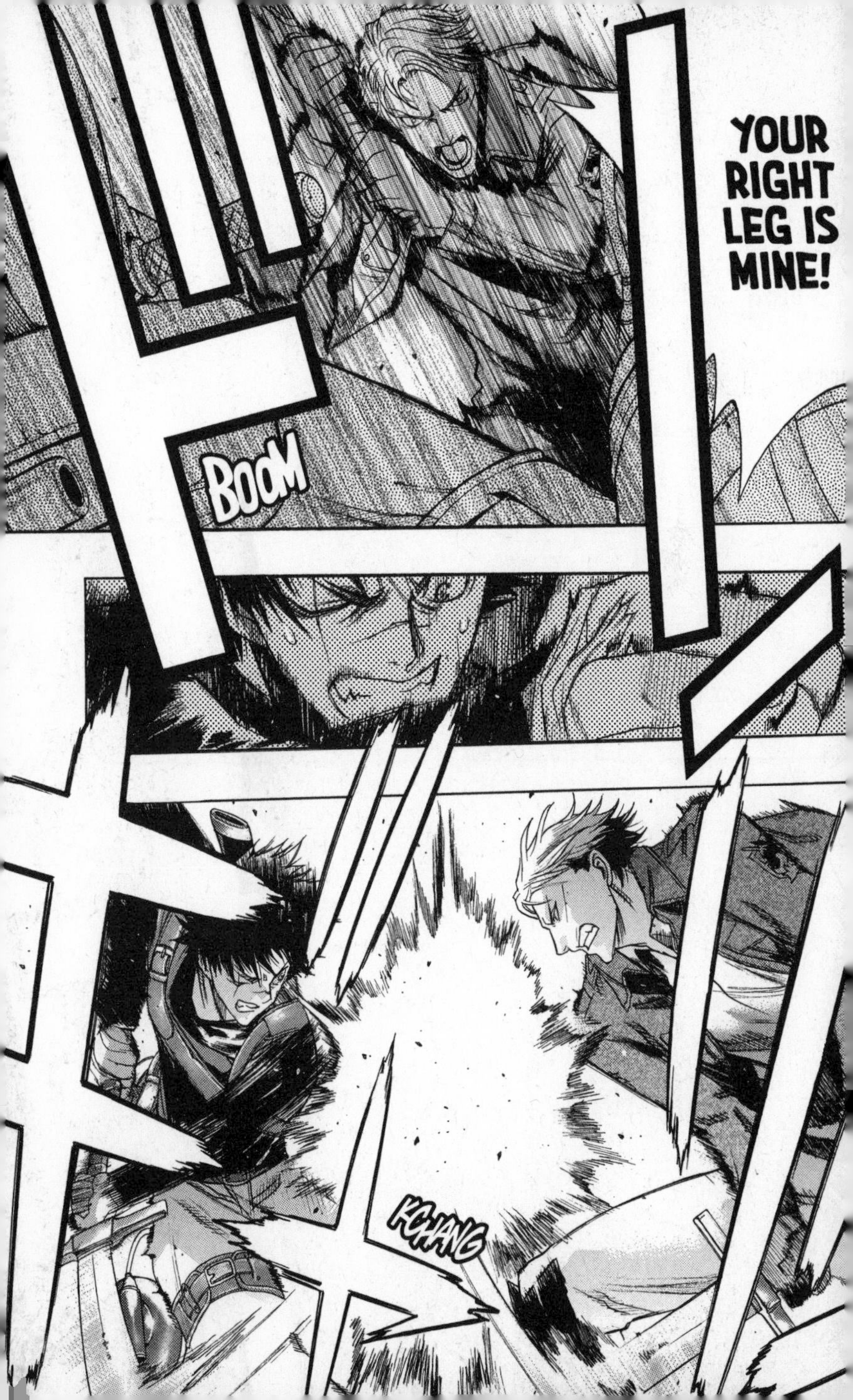
YOUR RIGHT LEG IS MINE!
BOOM
KCHANG

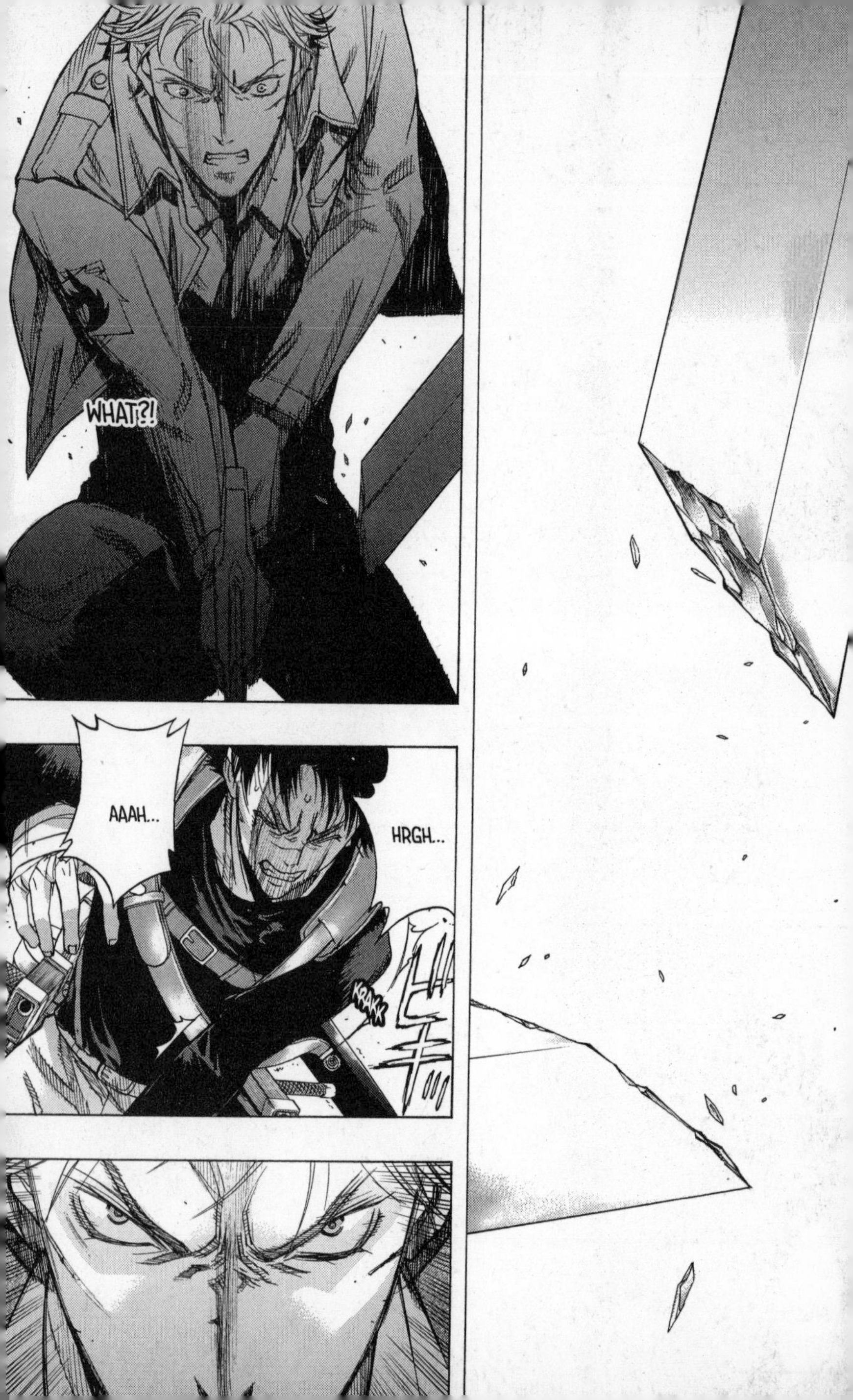
WHAT?!
HRGH...
AAAH...
KRAKK

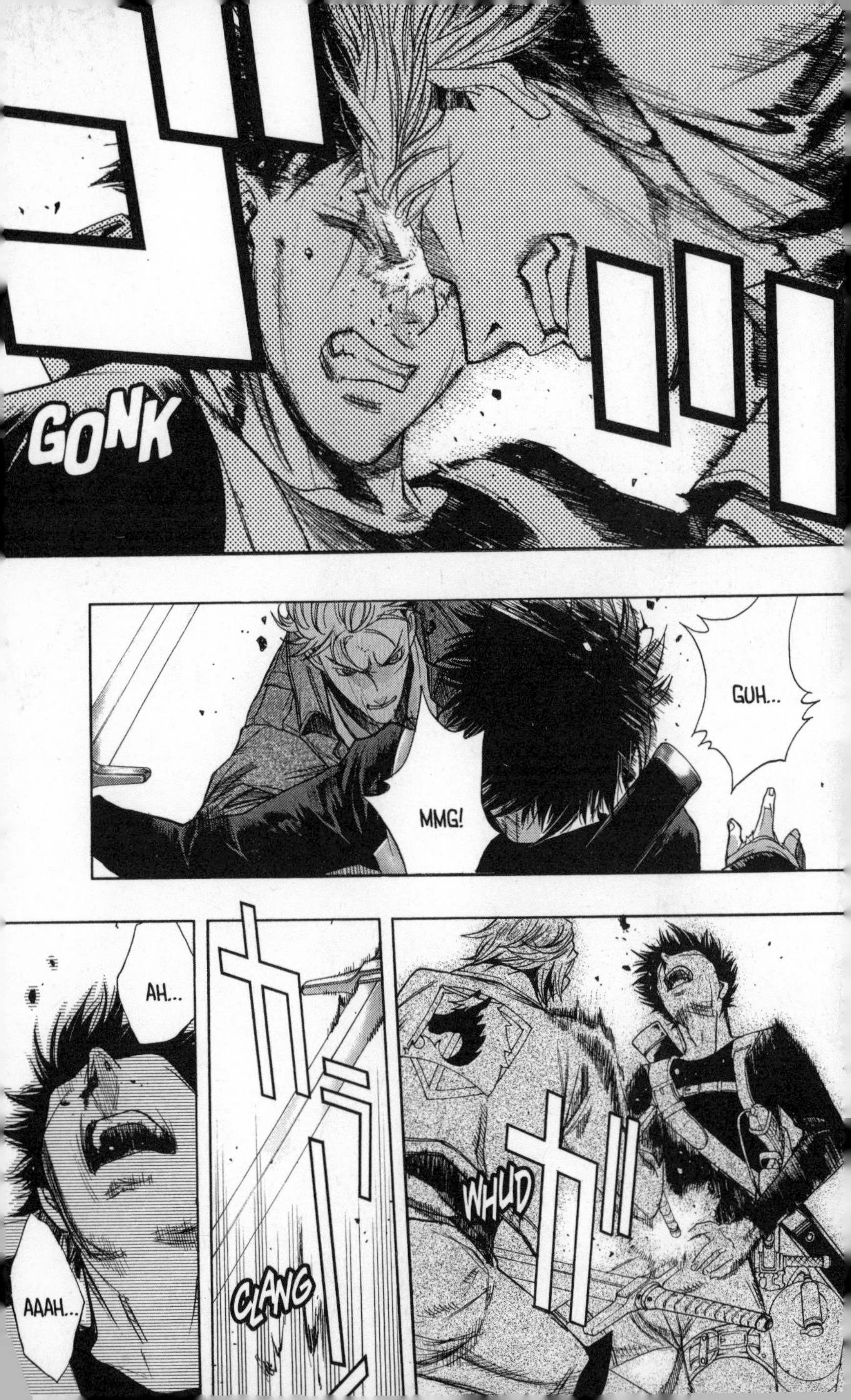
GONK
GUH...
MMG!
WHUD
CLANG
AH...
AAAH...

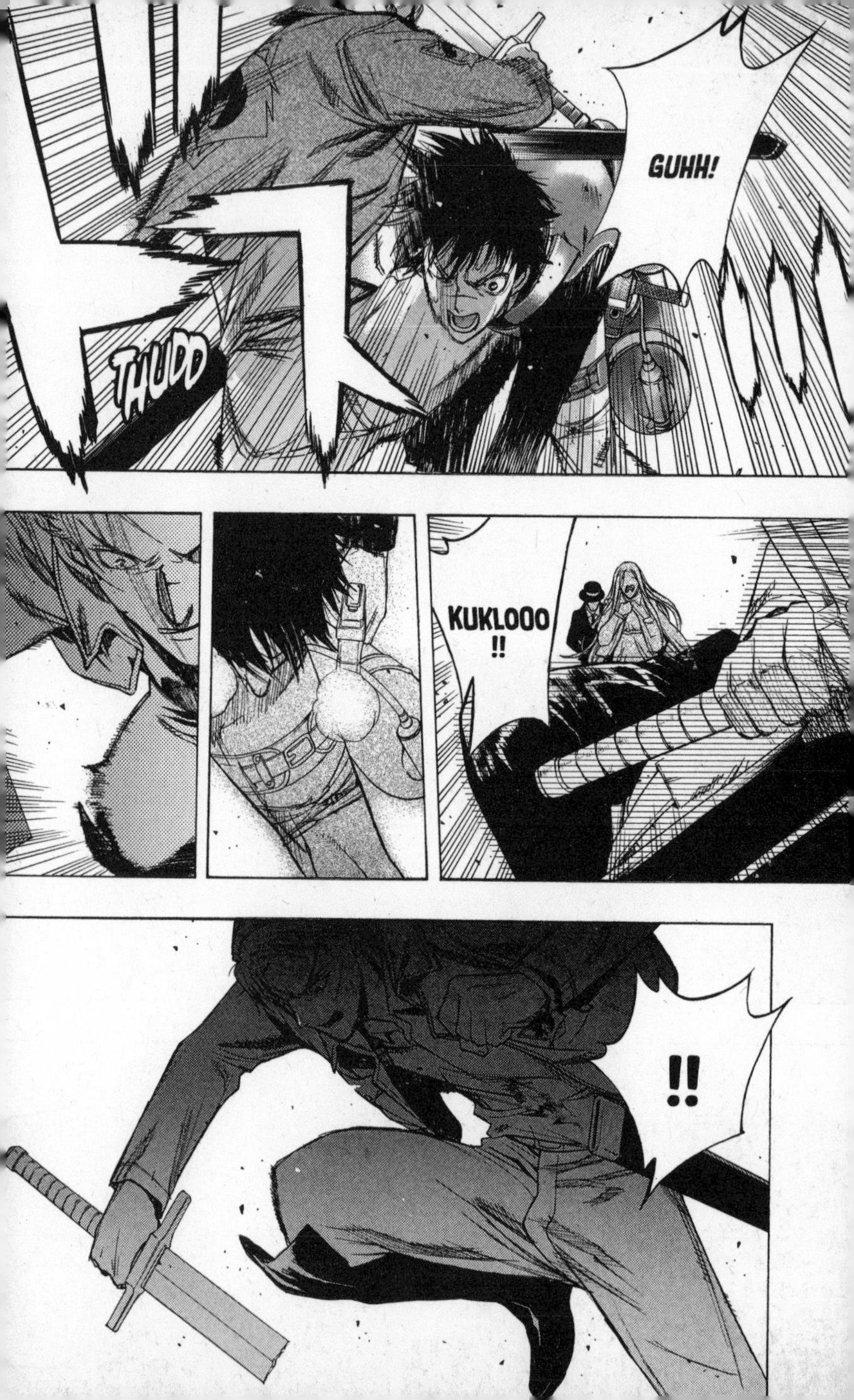
GUHH!
THUDD
KUKLOOO !!
!!

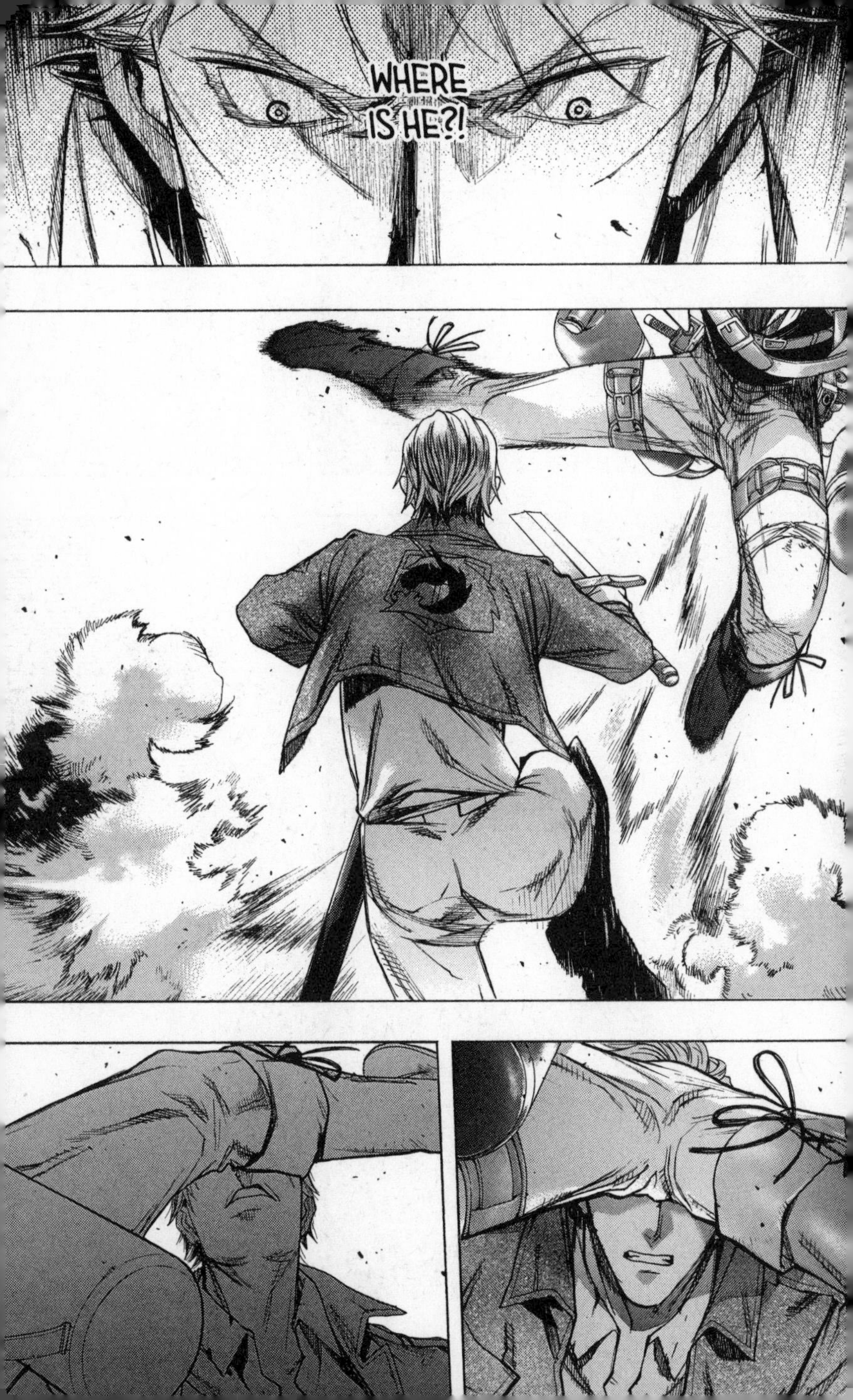
WHERE IS HE?!

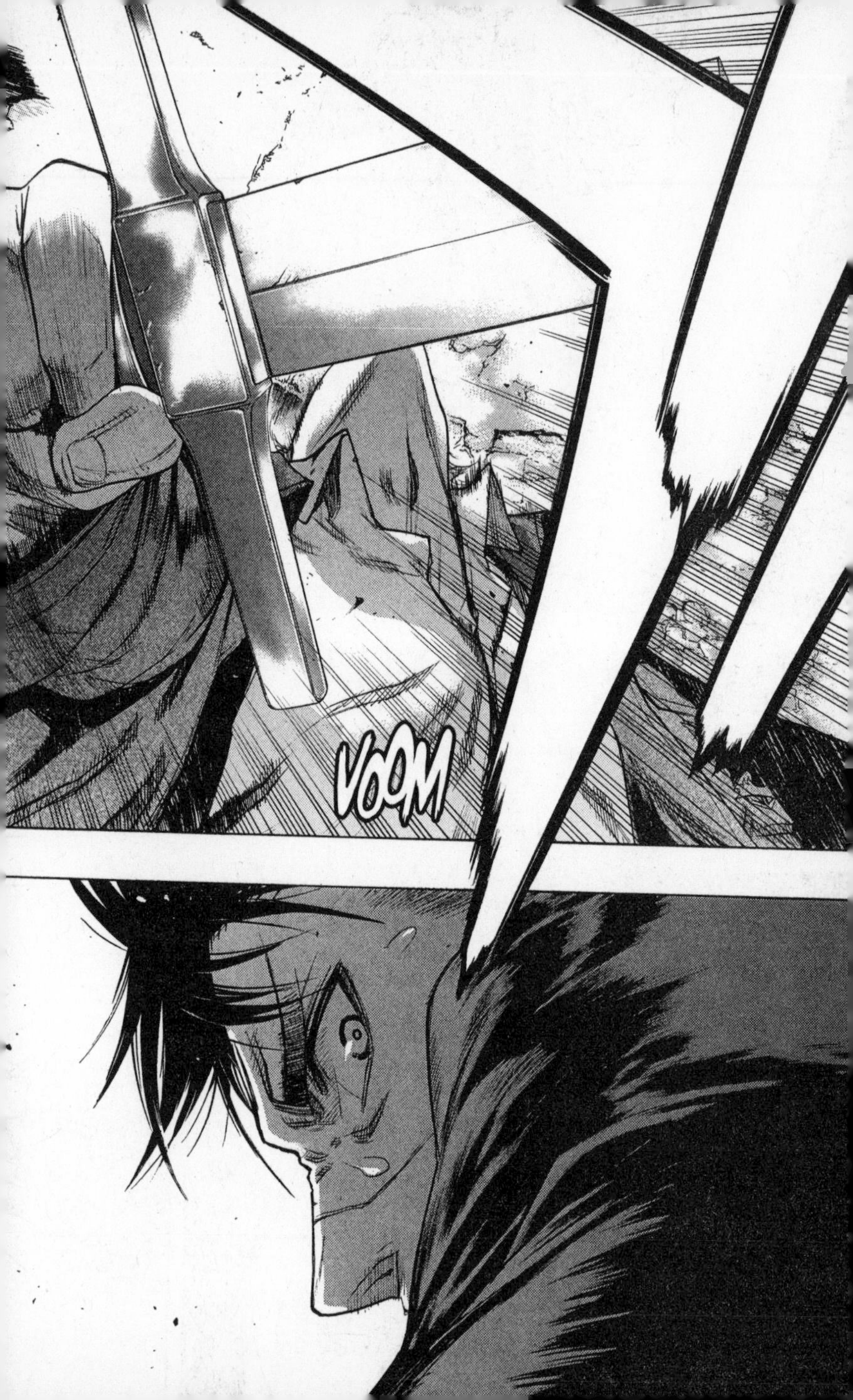
VOOM

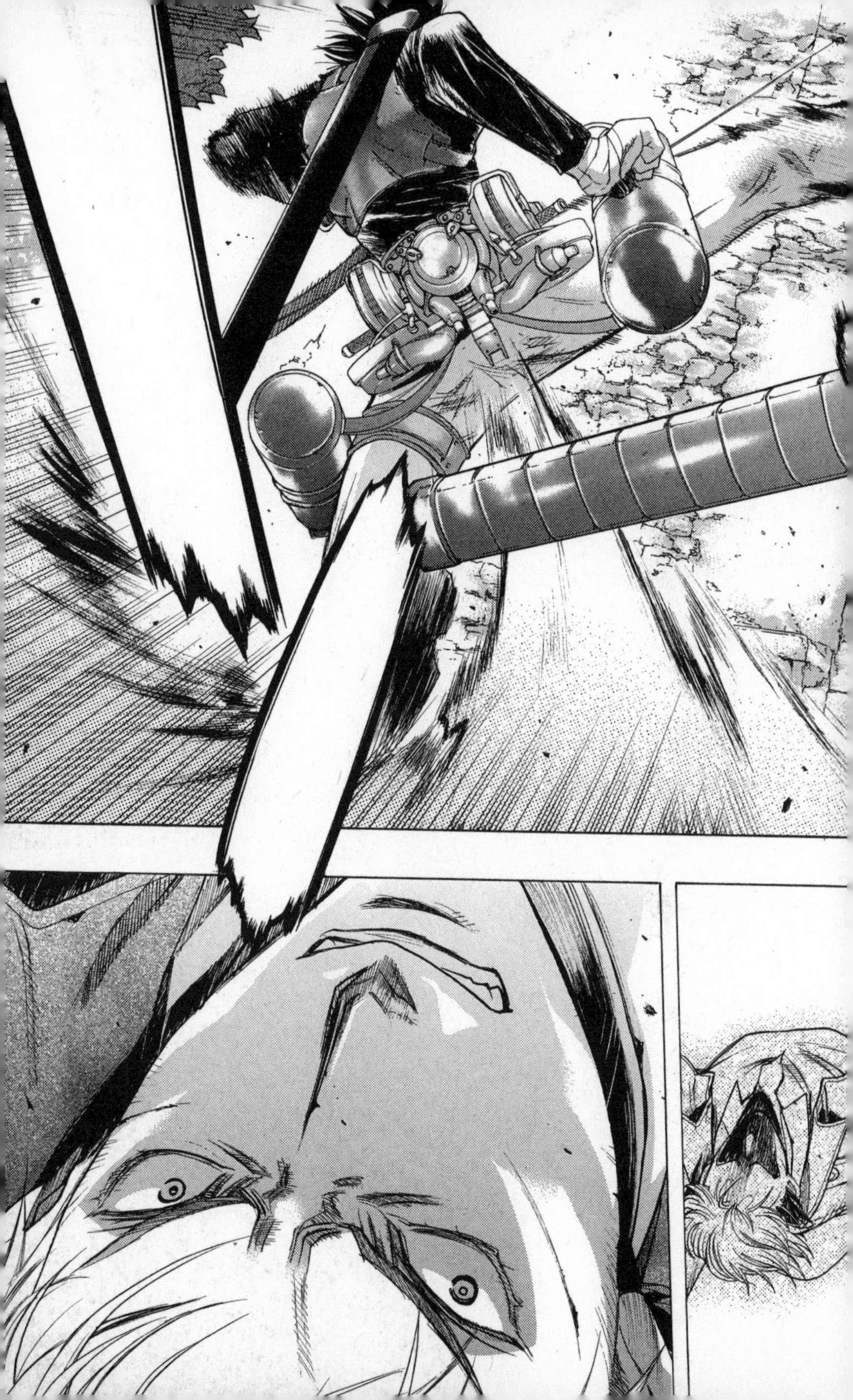

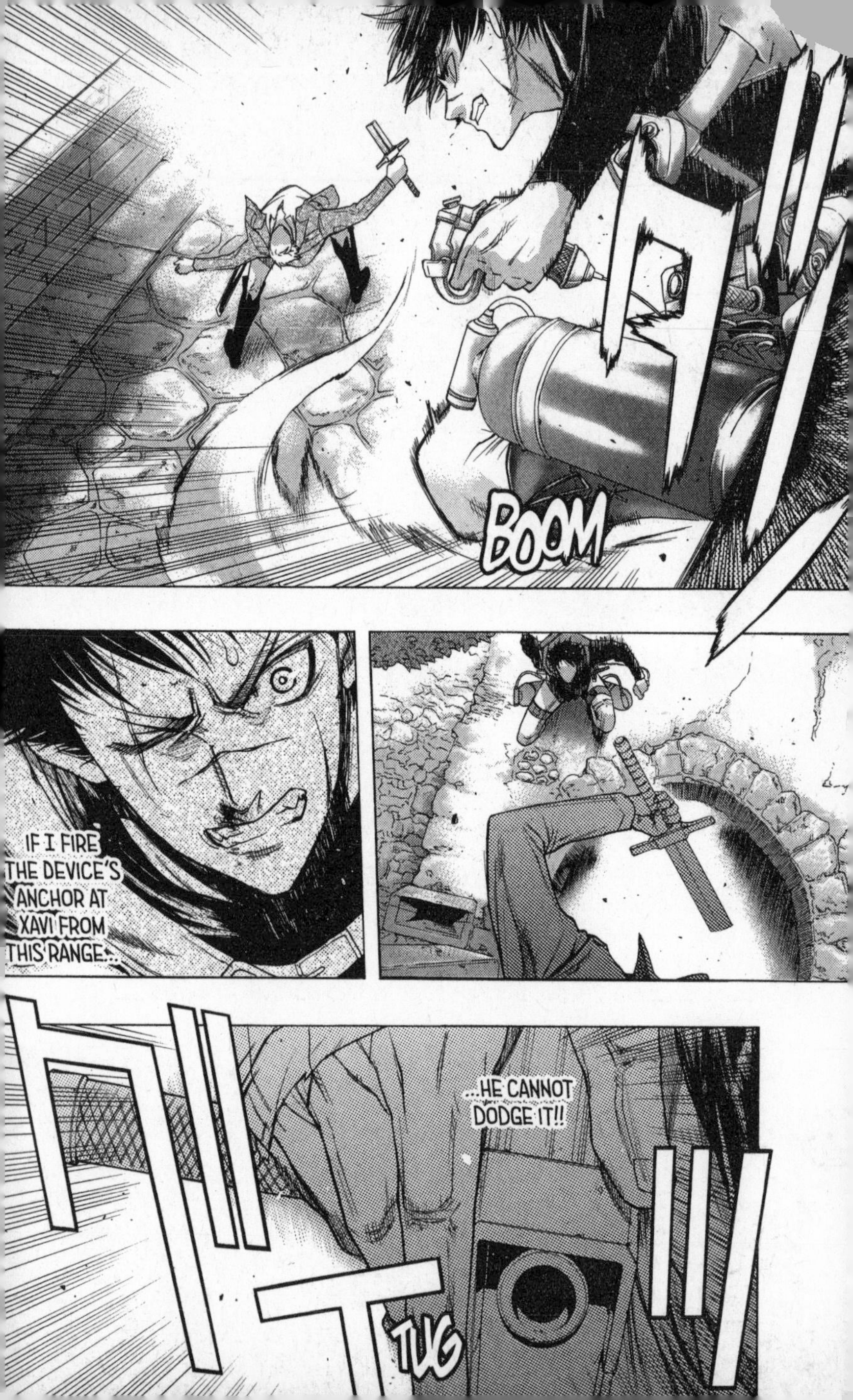
BOOM
IF I FIRE THE DEVICE'S ANCHOR AT XAVI FROM THIS RANGE...
...HE CANNOT DODGE IT!!
TUG

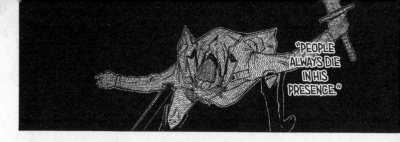

"PEOPLE ALWAYS DIE IN HIS PRESENCE."

"HE SOWS DEATH AND DISASTER IN HIS WAKE."

KRK

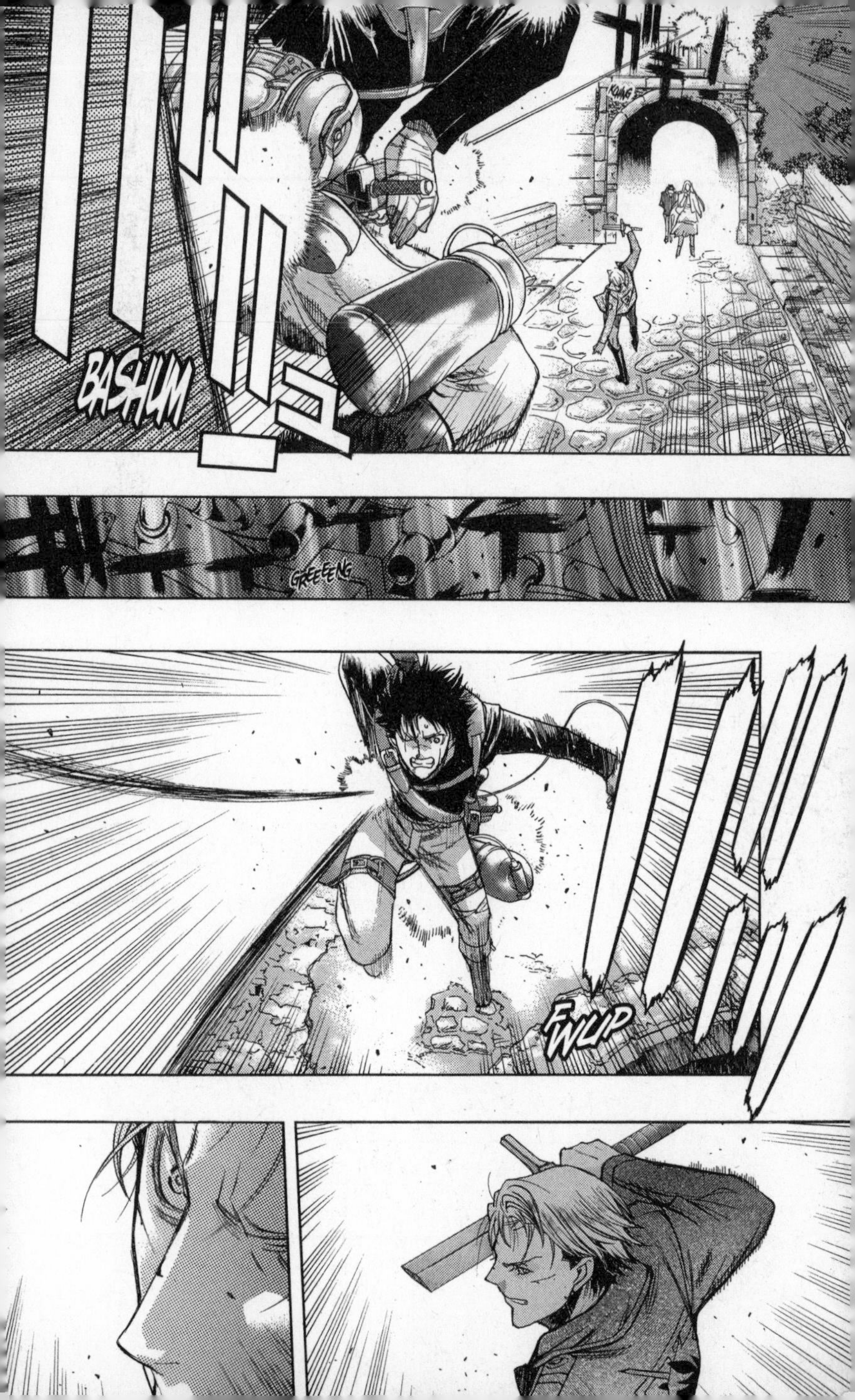
KOANG
BASHUM
GREEEENG
FWUP

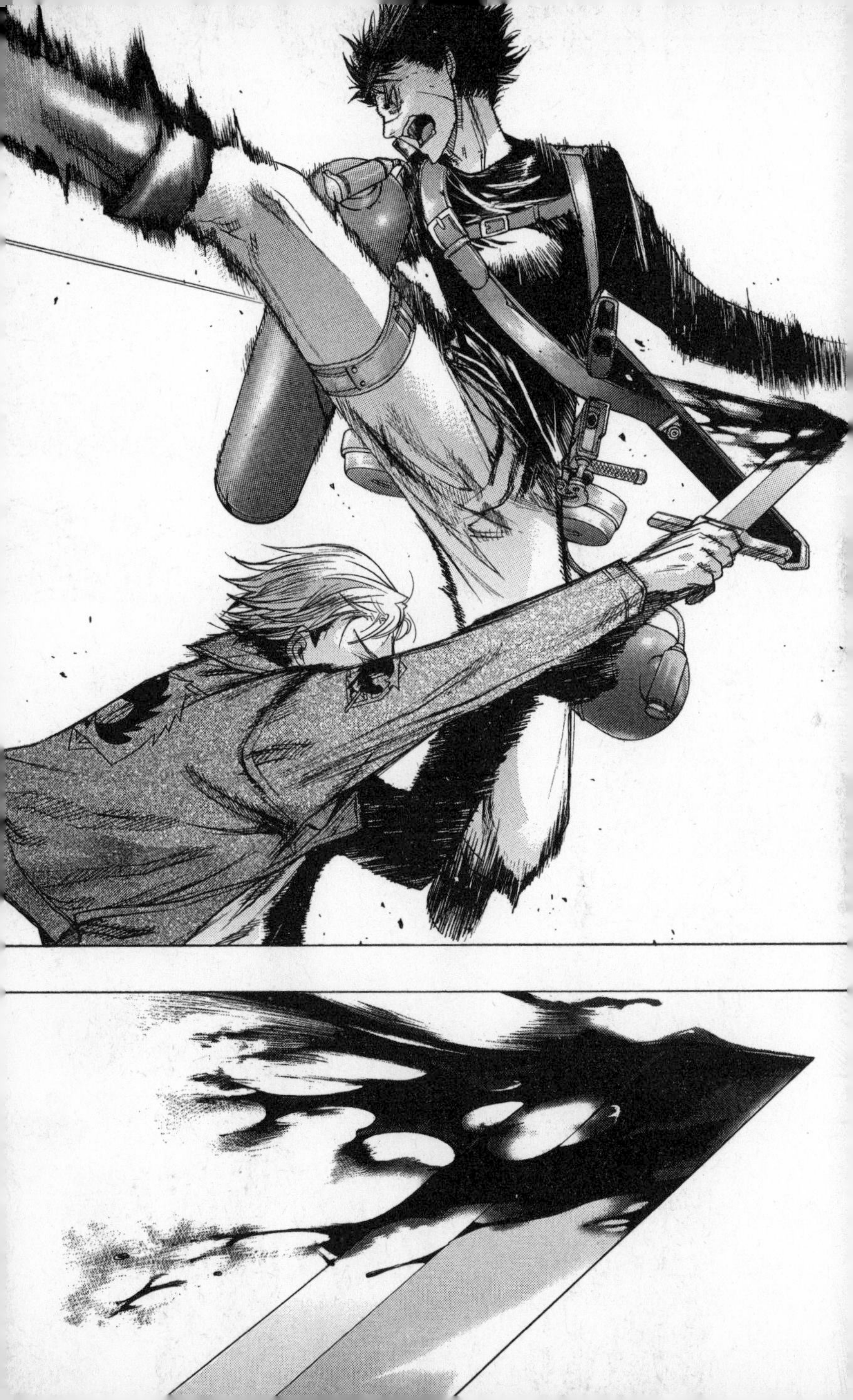

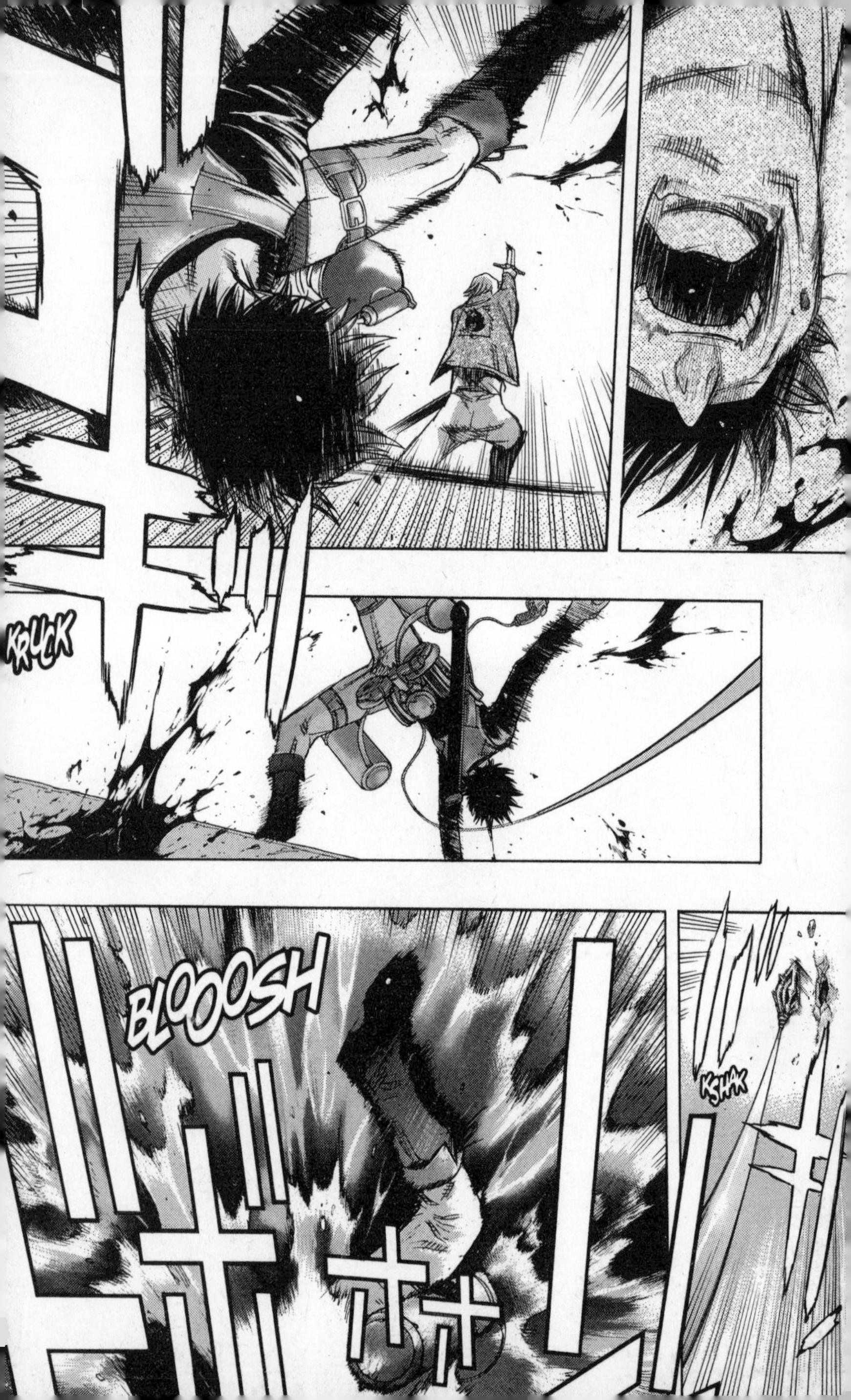
KRUCK
KSHAK
BLOOOSH

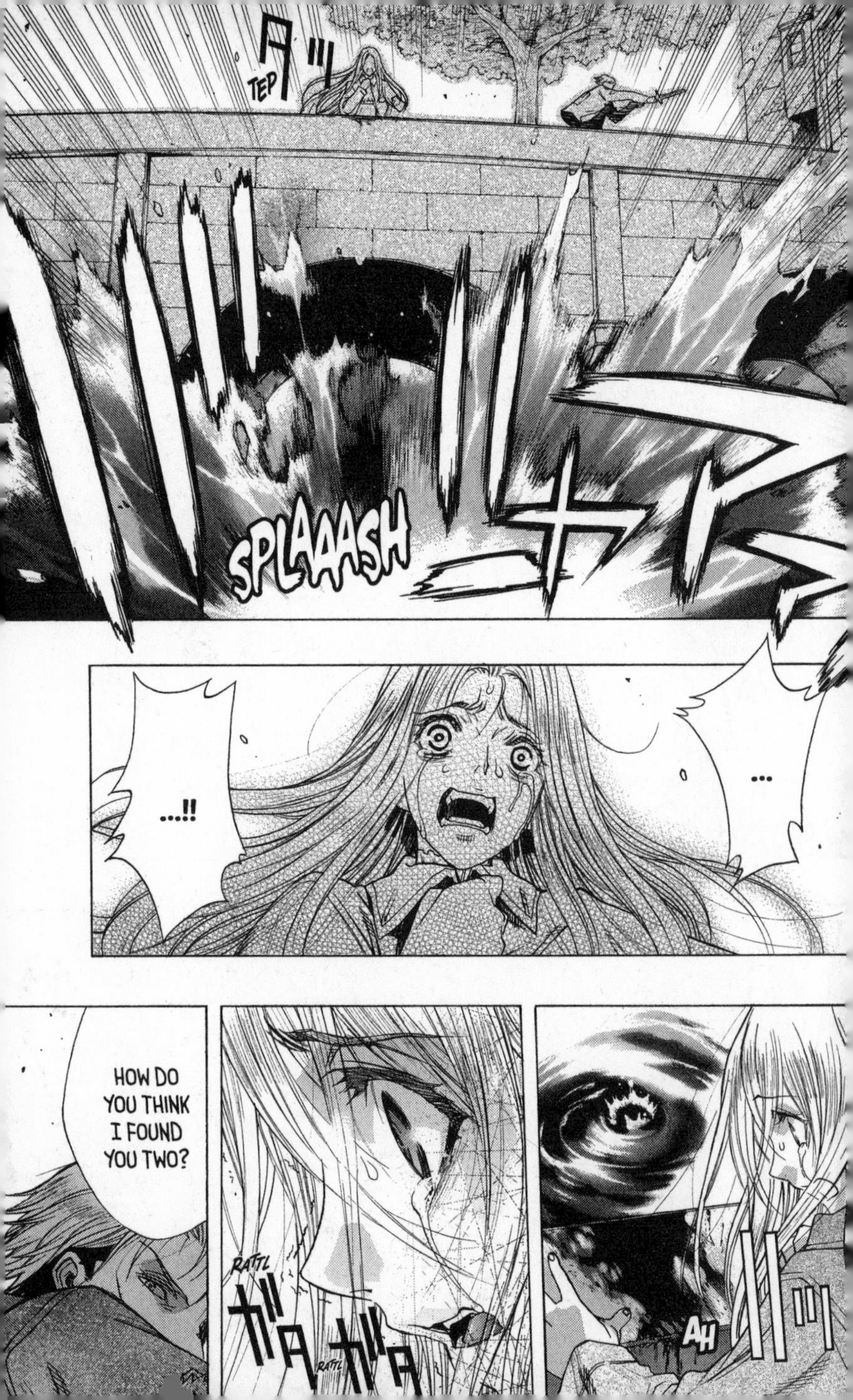
TEP
SPLAAASH
...
...!!
AH
RATTL
RATTL
HOW DO YOU THINK I FOUND YOU TWO?

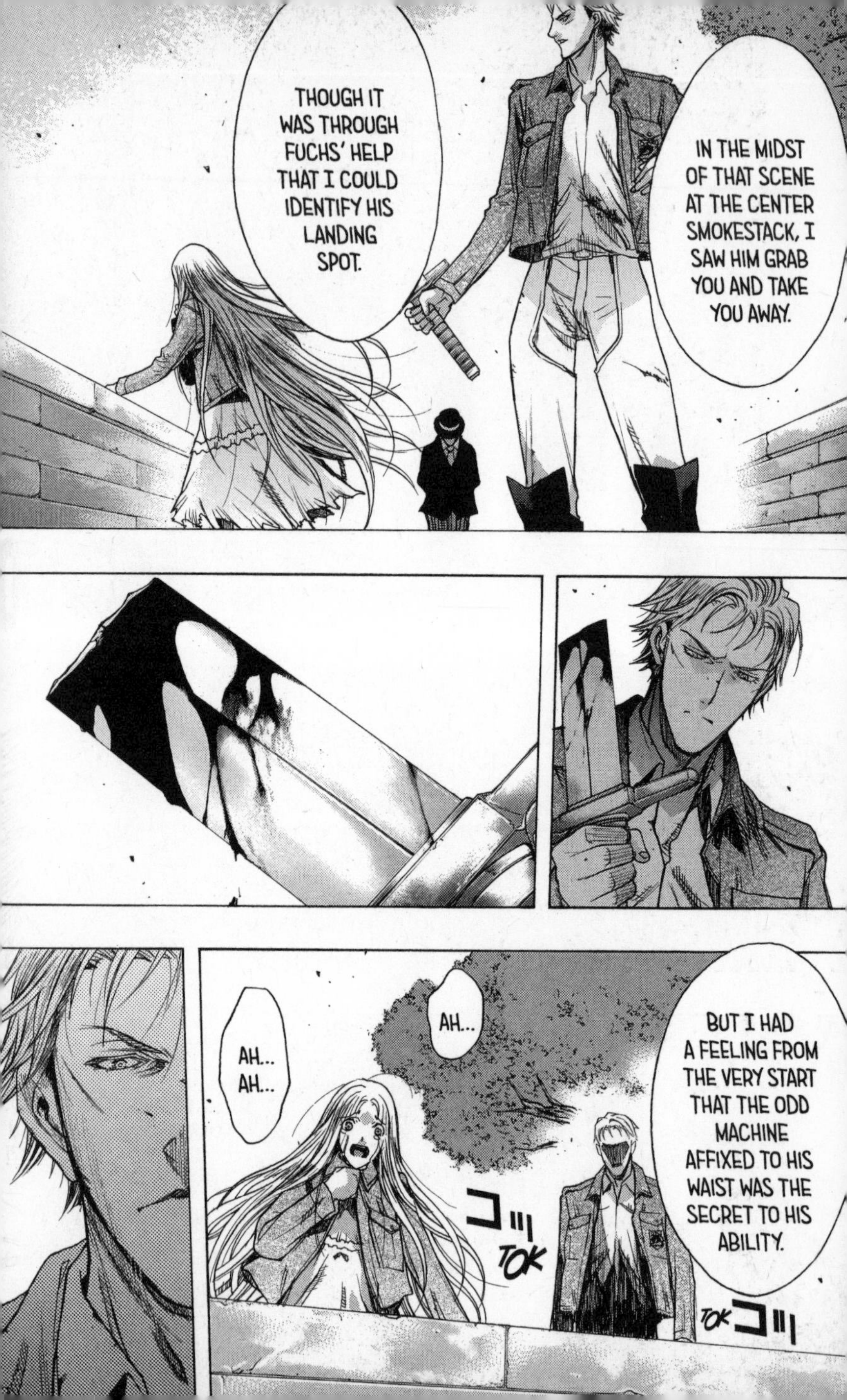
IN THE MIDST OF THAT SCENE AT THE CENTER SMOKESTACK, I SAW HIM GRAB YOU AND TAKE YOU AWAY.
THOUGH IT WAS THROUGH FUCHS' HELP THAT I COULD IDENTIFY HIS LANDING SPOT.
BUT I HAD A FEELING FROM THE VERY START THAT THE ODD MACHINE AFFIXED TO HIS WAIST WAS THE SECRET TO HIS ABILITY.
AH...
AH... AH...
TOK
TOK

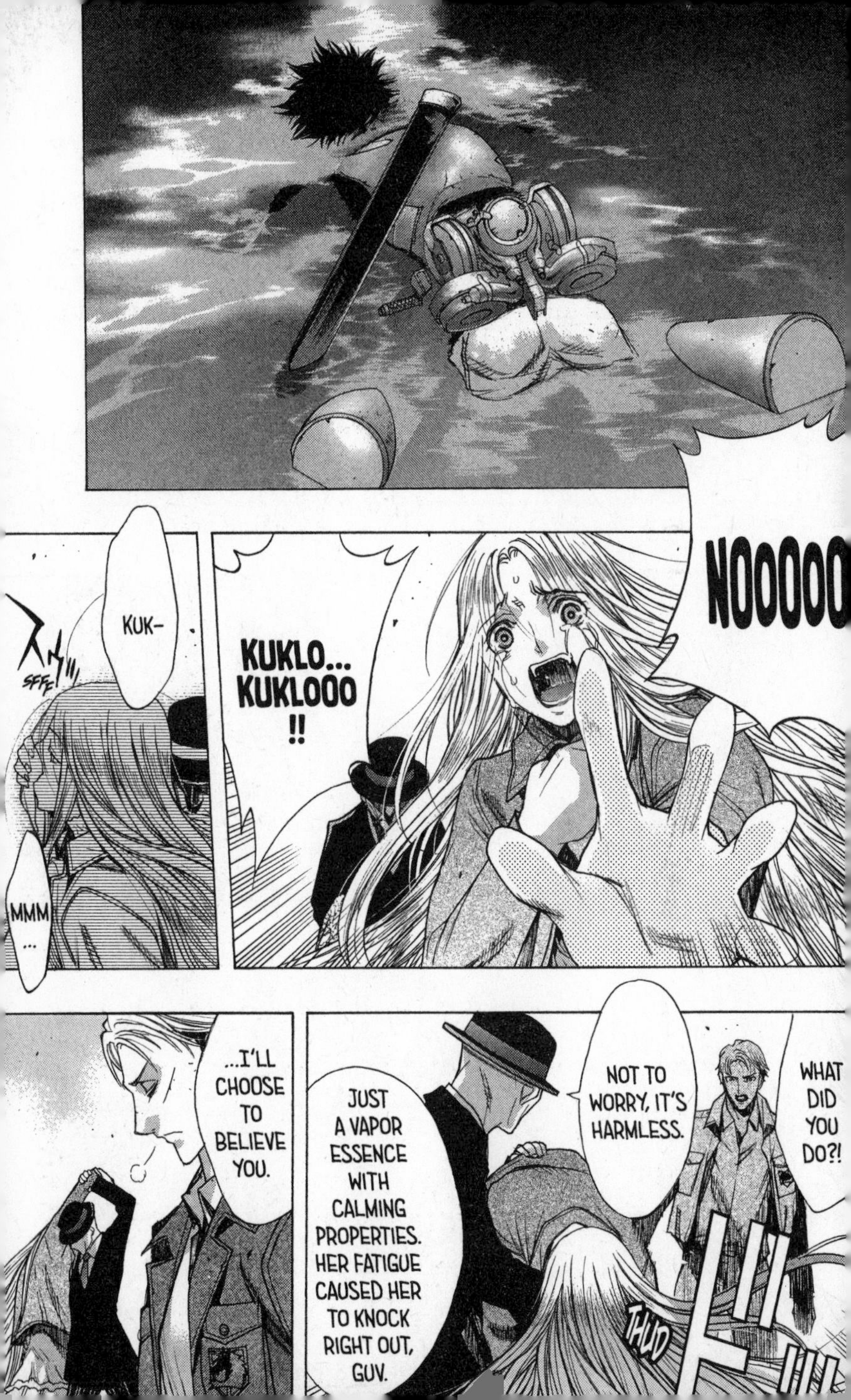
NOOOOO
KUKLO... KUKLOOO!!
KUK-
SFFF
MMM...
WHAT DID YOU DO?!
NOT TO WORRY, IT'S HARMLESS.
JUST A VAPOR ESSENCE WITH CALMING PROPERTIES. HER FATIGUE CAUSED HER TO KNOCK RIGHT OUT, GUV.
THUD
...I'LL CHOOSE TO BELIEVE YOU.

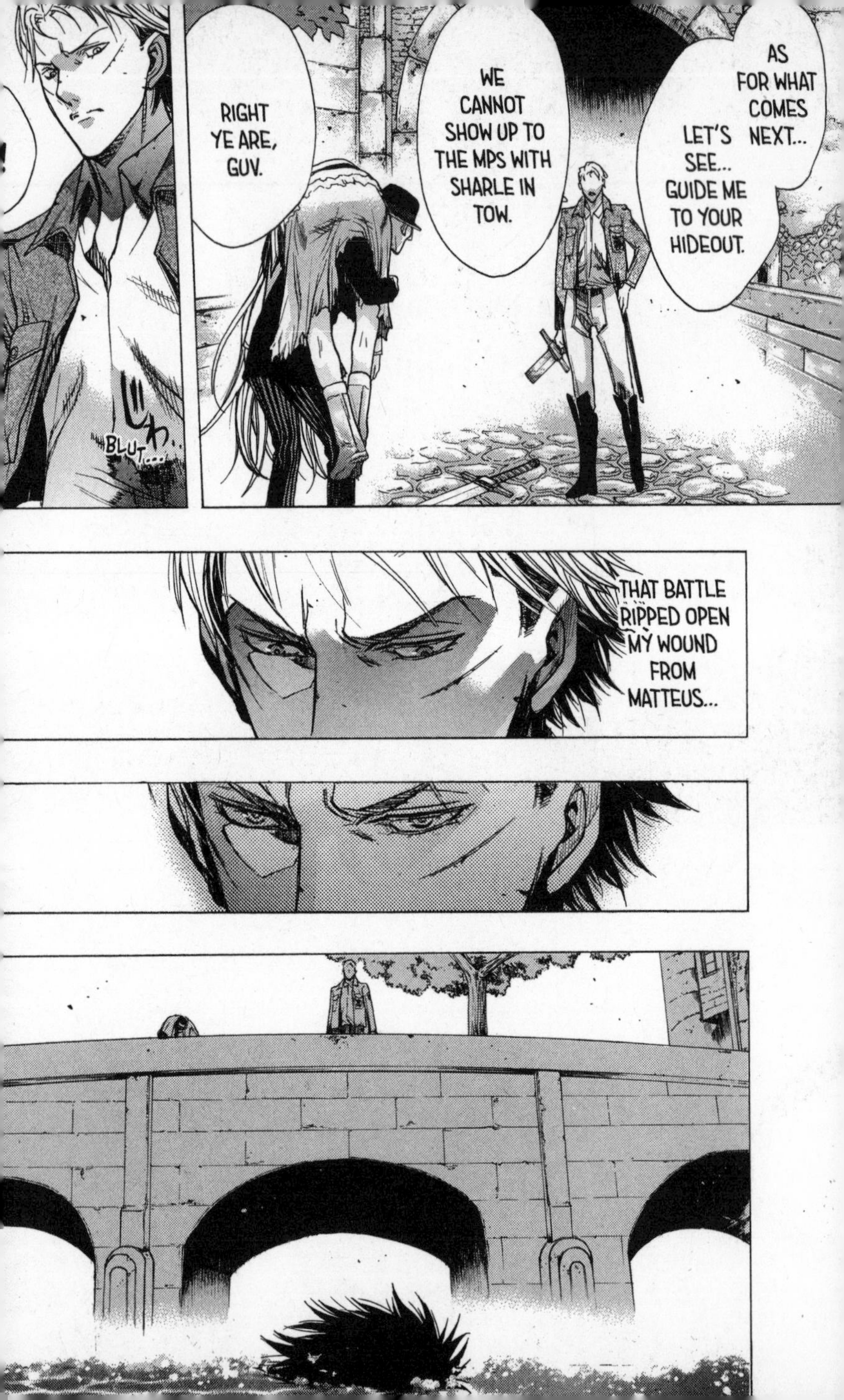
AS FOR WHAT COMES NEXT...
LET'S SEE... GUIDE ME TO YOUR HIDEOUT.
WE CANNOT SHOW UP TO THE MPS WITH SHARLE IN TOW.
RIGHT YE ARE, GUV.
じわ…
BLUT...
THAT BATTLE RIPPED OPEN MY WOUND FROM MATTEUS...

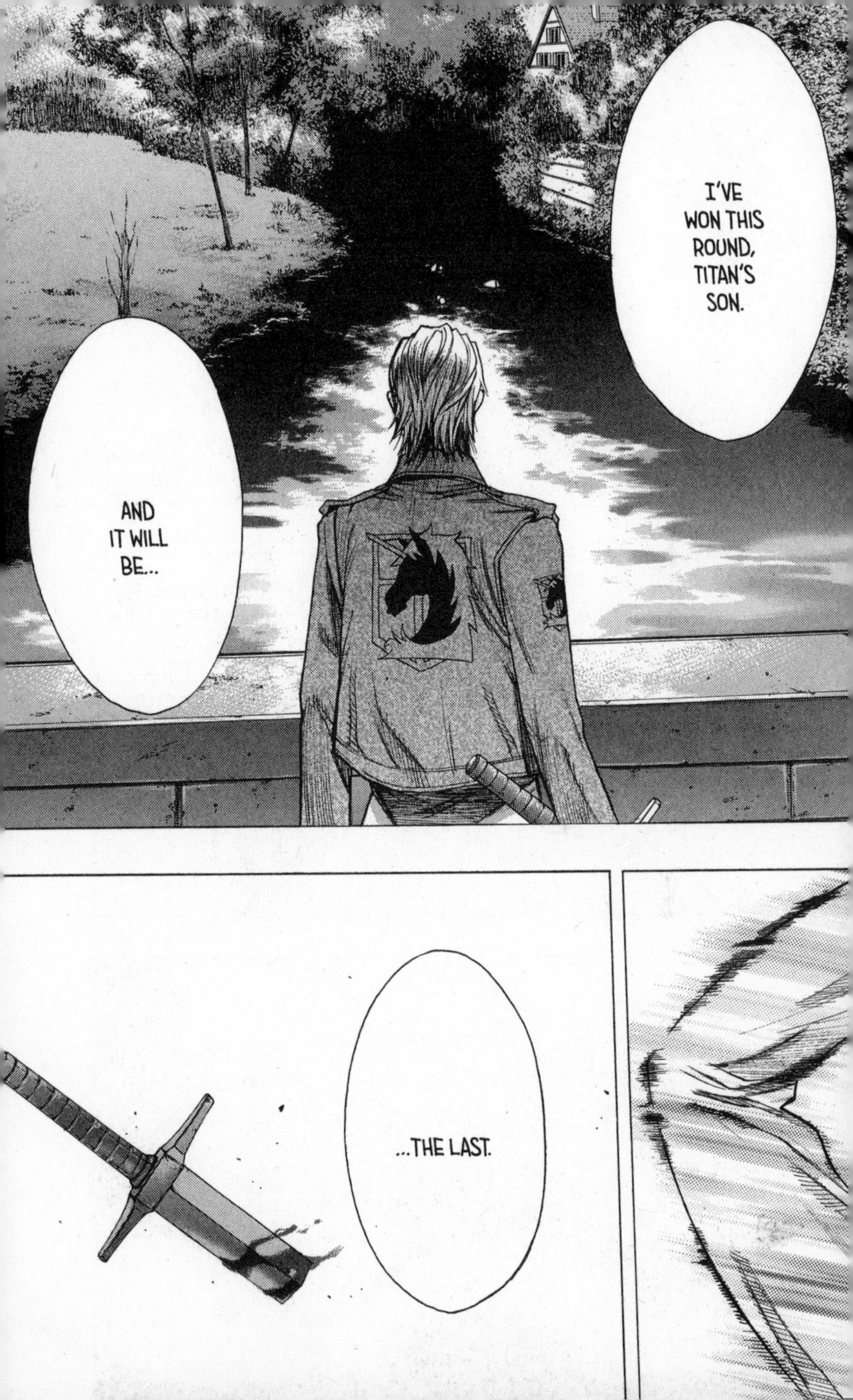
I'VE WON THIS ROUND, TITAN'S SON.
AND IT WILL BE...
...THE LAST.

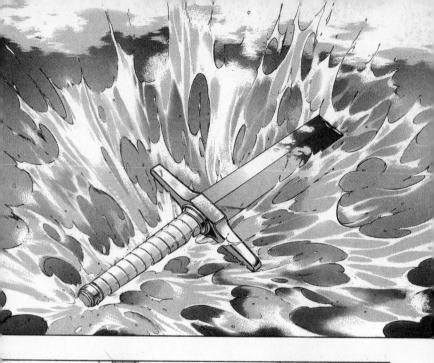

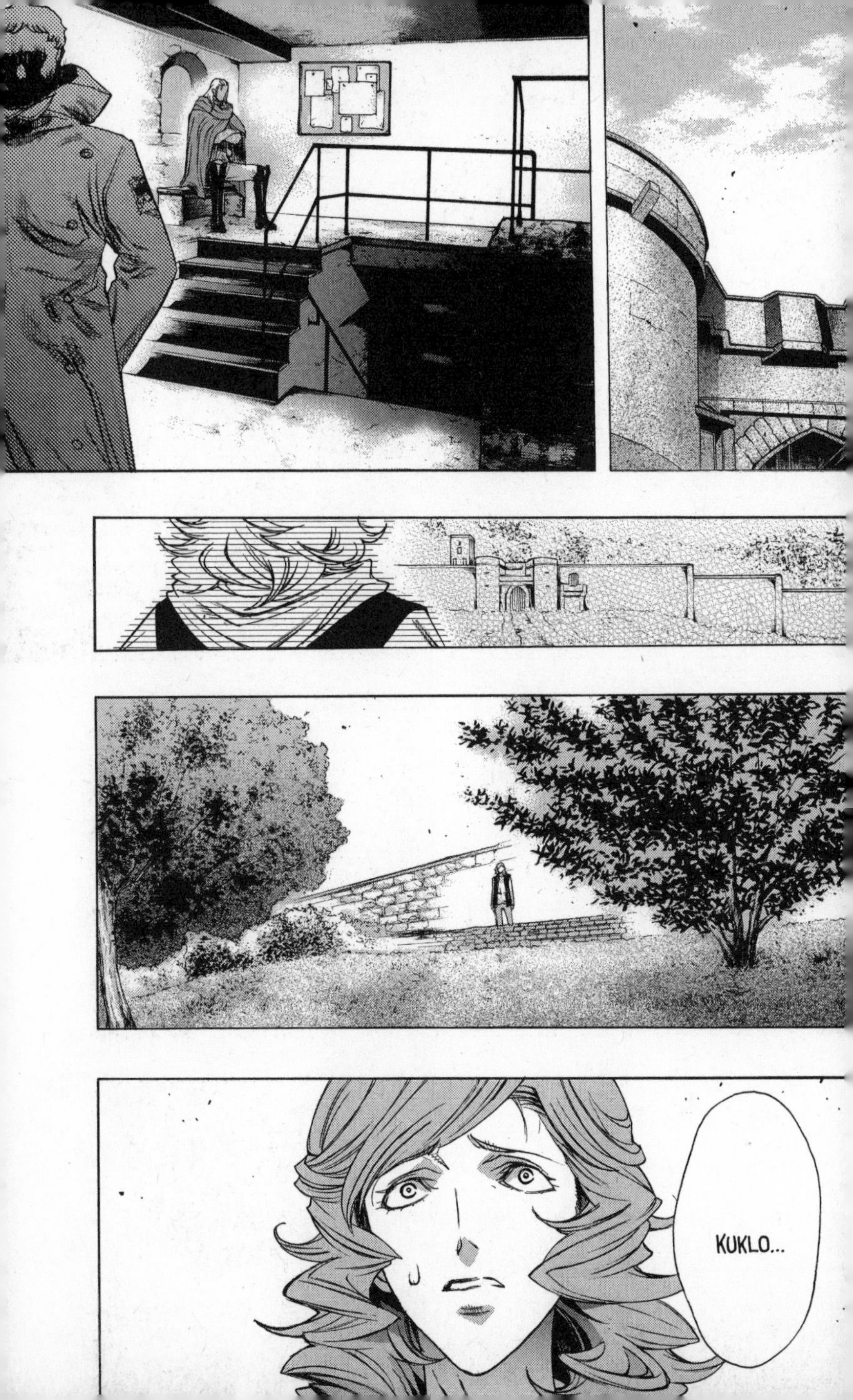
KUKLO...

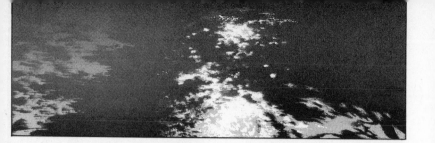

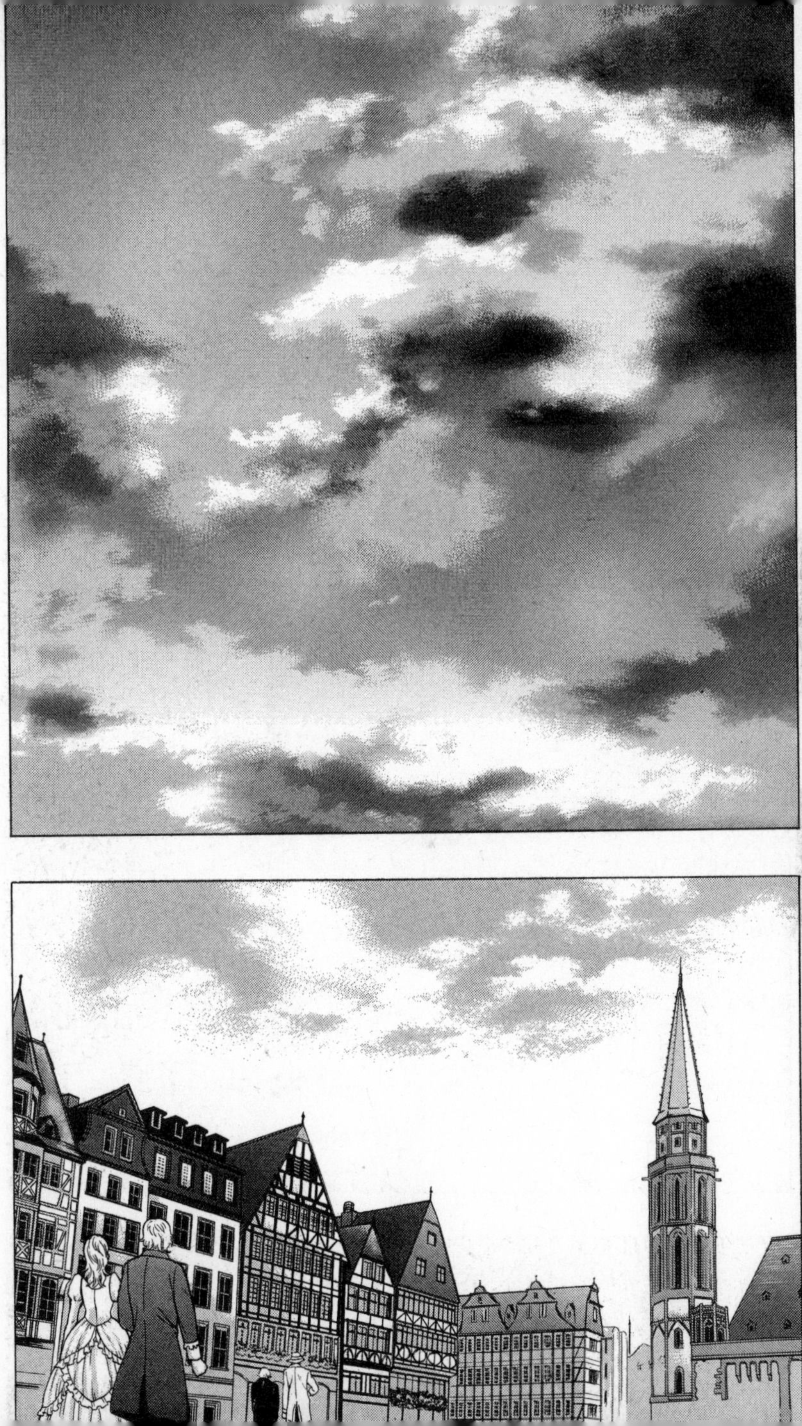

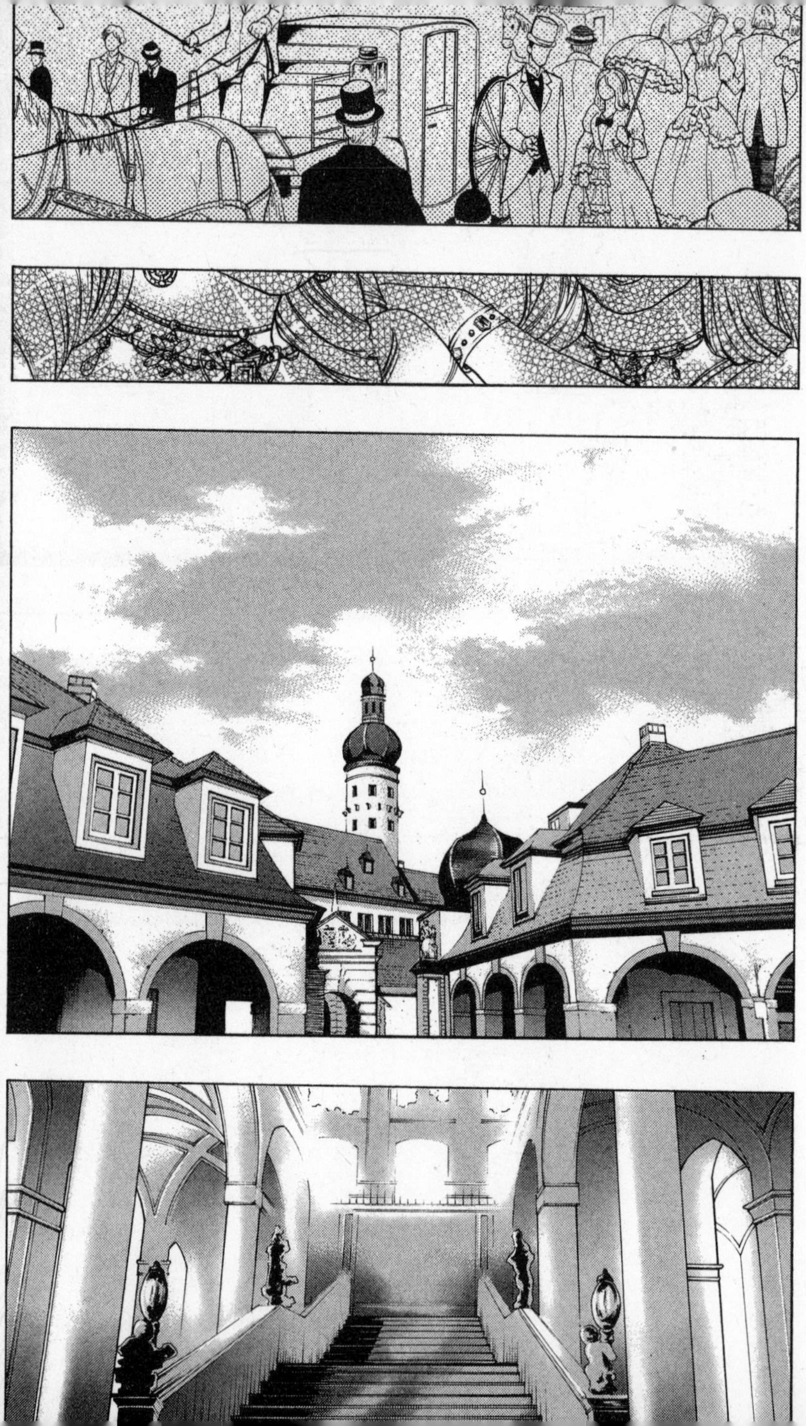

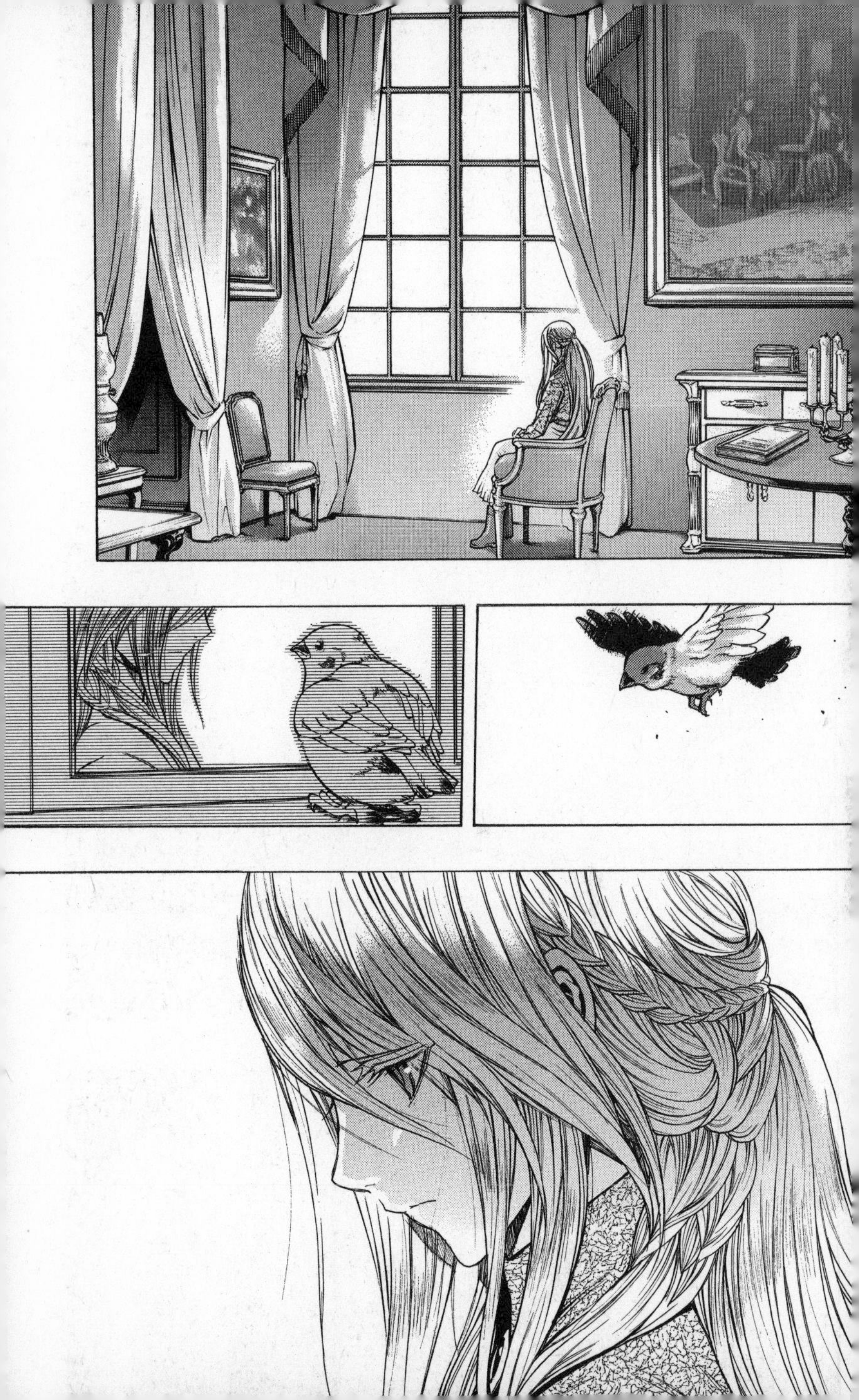

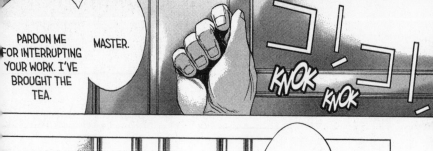

PARDON ME FOR INTERRUPTING YOUR WORK. I'VE BROUGHT THE TEA.

MASTER.

KNOK KNOK

VERY GOOD. YOU MAY ENTER.

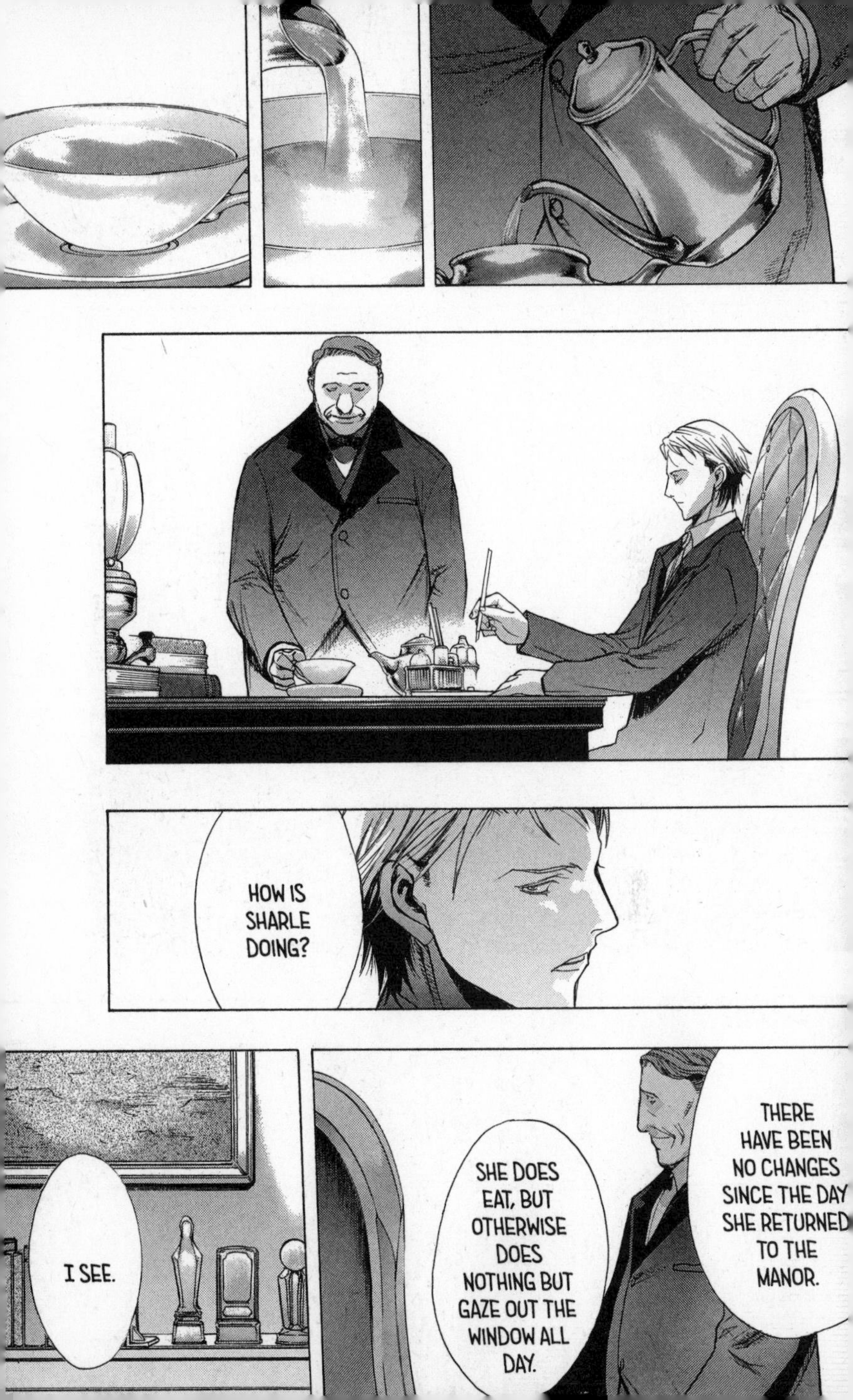
HOW IS SHARLE DOING?
THERE HAVE BEEN NO CHANGES SINCE THE DAY SHE RETURNED TO THE MANOR.
SHE DOES EAT, BUT OTHERWISE DOES NOTHING BUT GAZE OUT THE WINDOW ALL DAY.
I SEE.

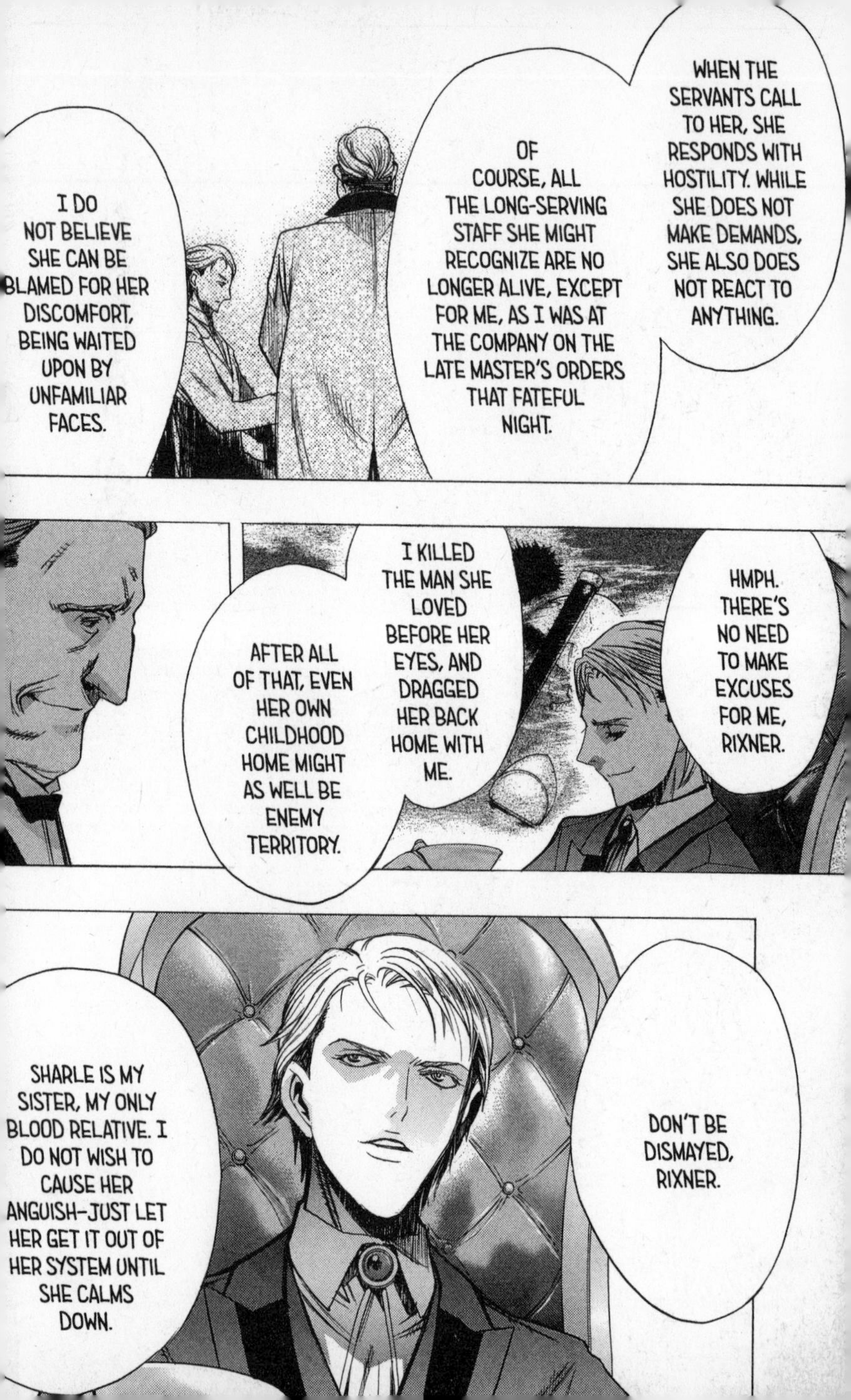
WHEN THE SERVANTS CALL TO HER, SHE RESPONDS WITH HOSTILITY. WHILE SHE DOES NOT MAKE DEMANDS, SHE ALSO DOES NOT REACT TO ANYTHING.
OF COURSE, ALL THE LONG-SERVING STAFF SHE MIGHT RECOGNIZE ARE NO LONGER ALIVE, EXCEPT FOR ME, AS I WAS AT THE COMPANY ON THE LATE MASTER'S ORDERS THAT FATEFUL NIGHT.
I DO NOT BELIEVE SHE CAN BE BLAMED FOR HER DISCOMFORT, BEING WAITED UPON BY UNFAMILIAR FACES.
HMPH. THERE'S NO NEED TO MAKE EXCUSES FOR ME, RIXNER.
I KILLED THE MAN SHE LOVED BEFORE HER EYES, AND DRAGGED HER BACK HOME WITH ME.
AFTER ALL OF THAT, EVEN HER OWN CHILDHOOD HOME MIGHT AS WELL BE ENEMY TERRITORY.
DON'T BE DISMAYED, RIXNER.
SHARLE IS MY SISTER, MY ONLY BLOOD RELATIVE. I DO NOT WISH TO CAUSE HER ANGUISH–JUST LET HER GET IT OUT OF HER SYSTEM UNTIL SHE CALMS DOWN.

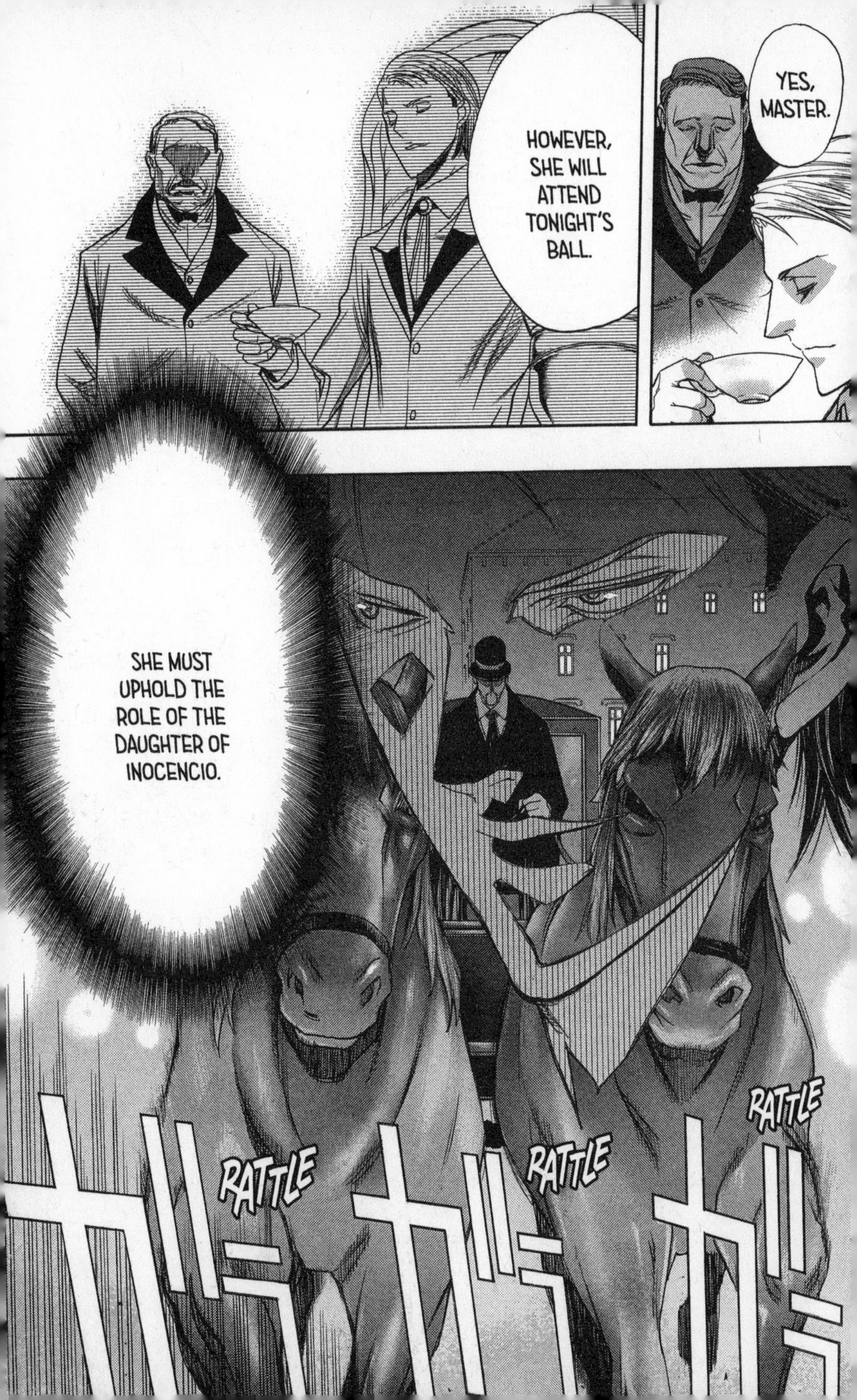
YES, MASTER.
HOWEVER, SHE WILL ATTEND TONIGHT'S BALL.
SHE MUST UPHOLD THE ROLE OF THE DAUGHTER OF INOCENCIO.
RATTLE
RATTLE
RATTLE

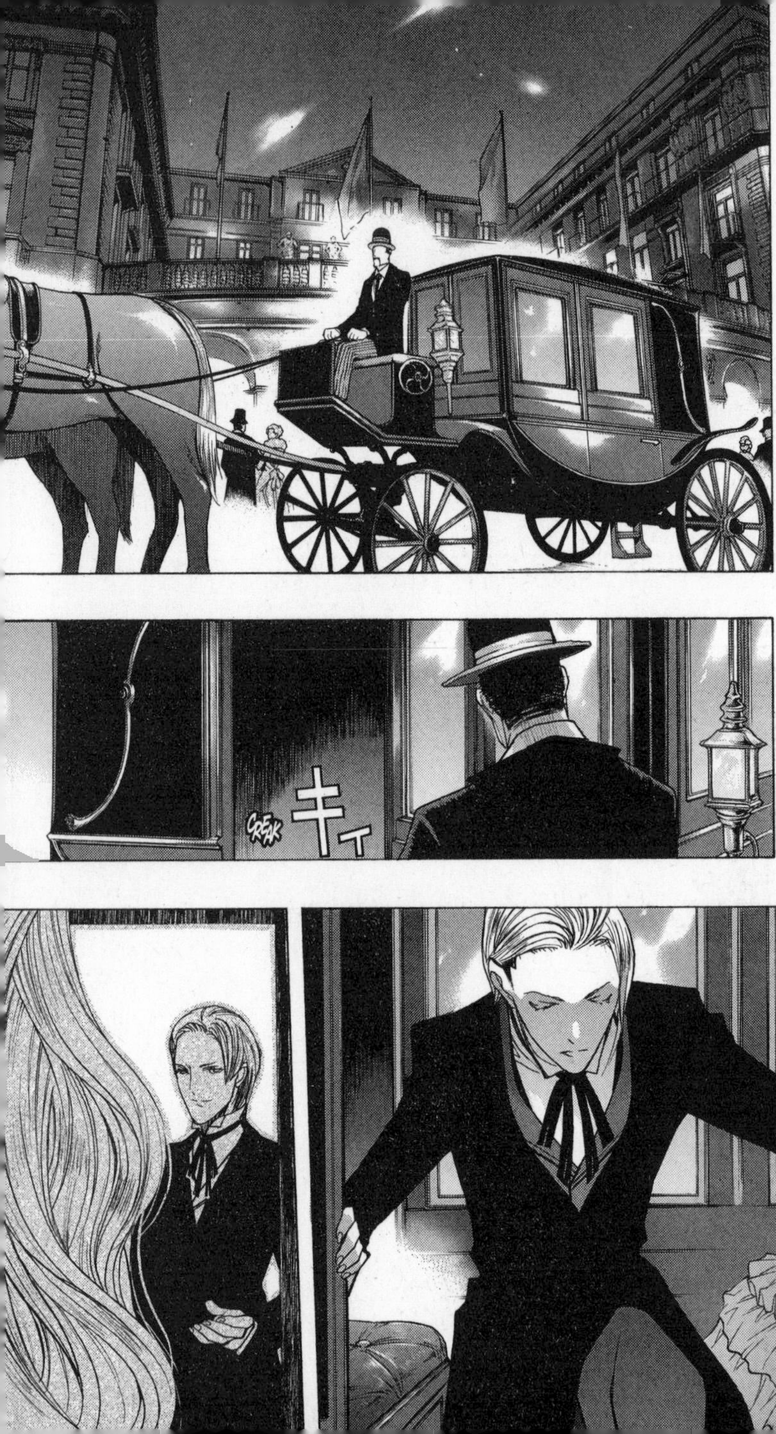
キィ
CREAK

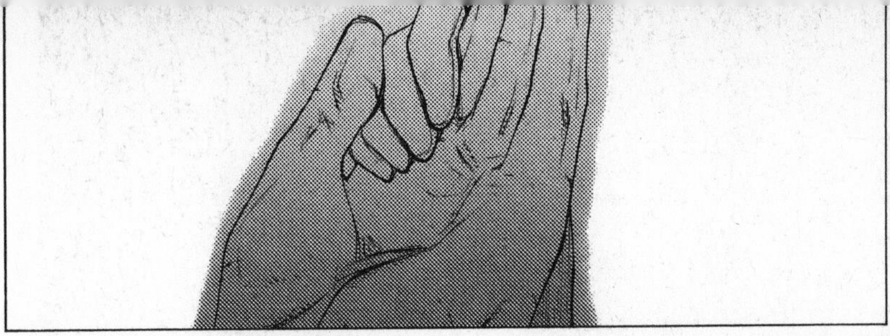
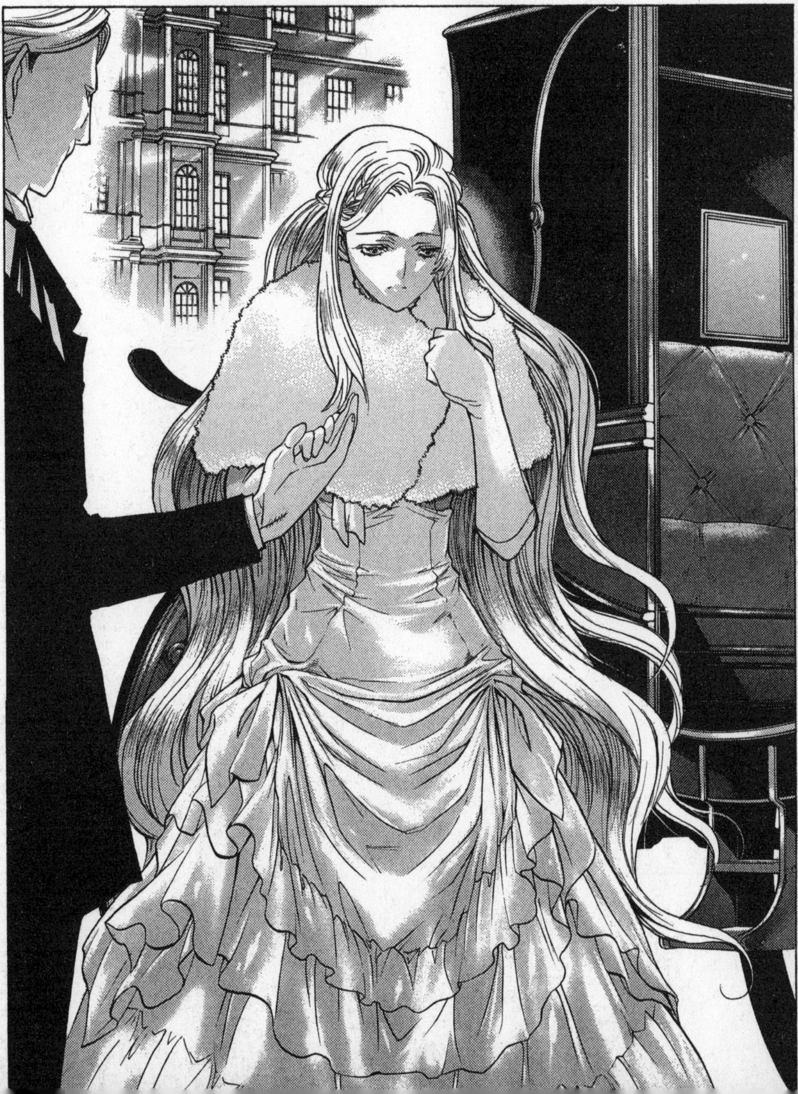

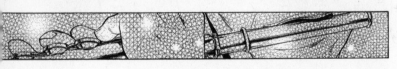

I MUST SAY, I'M ASTONISHED.

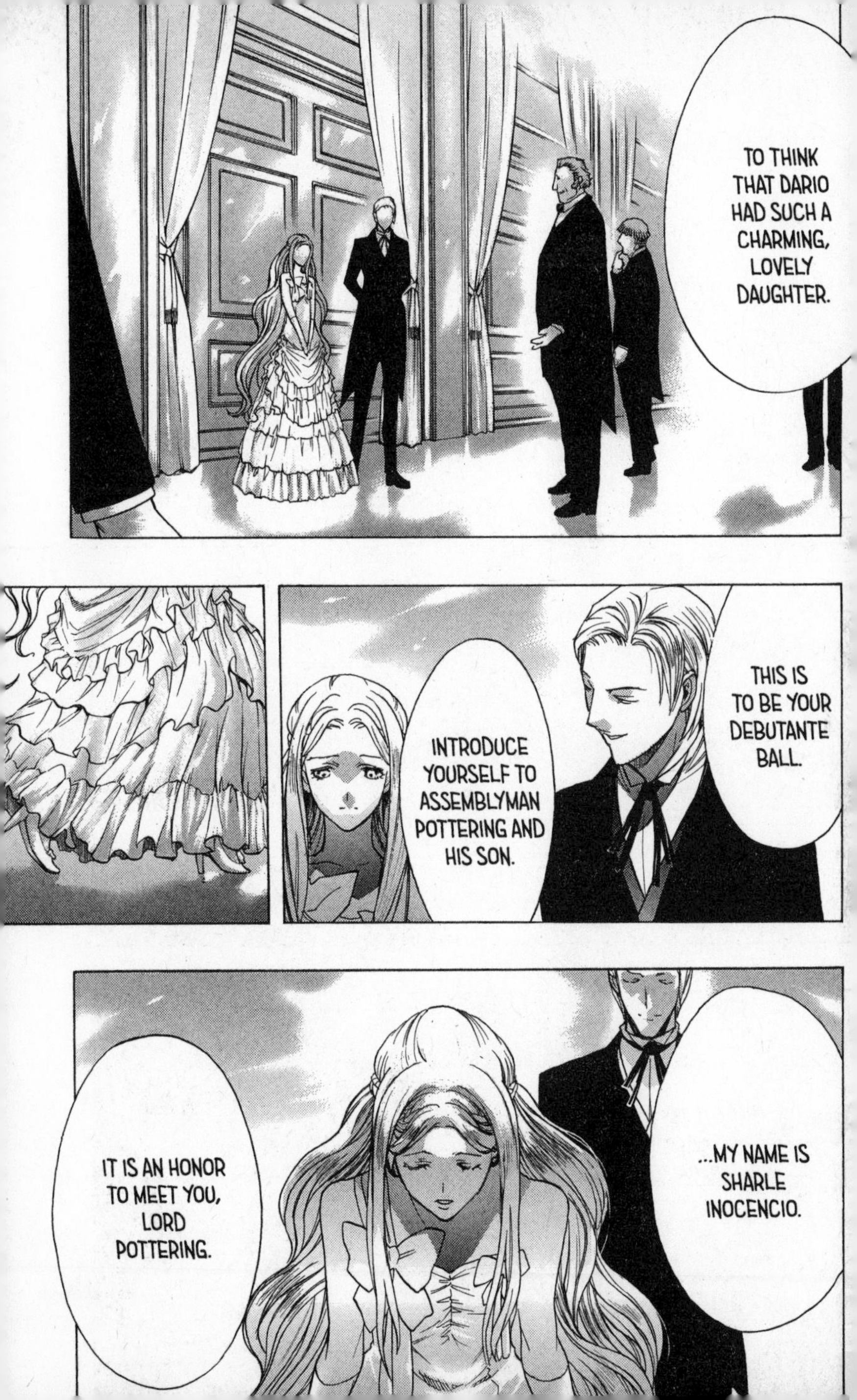

TO THINK THAT DARIO HAD SUCH A CHARMING, LOVELY DAUGHTER.
THIS IS TO BE YOUR DEBUTANTE BALL.
INTRODUCE YOURSELF TO ASSEMBLYMAN POTTERING AND HIS SON.
...MY NAME IS SHARLE INOCENCIO.
IT IS AN HONOR TO MEET YOU, LORD POTTERING.

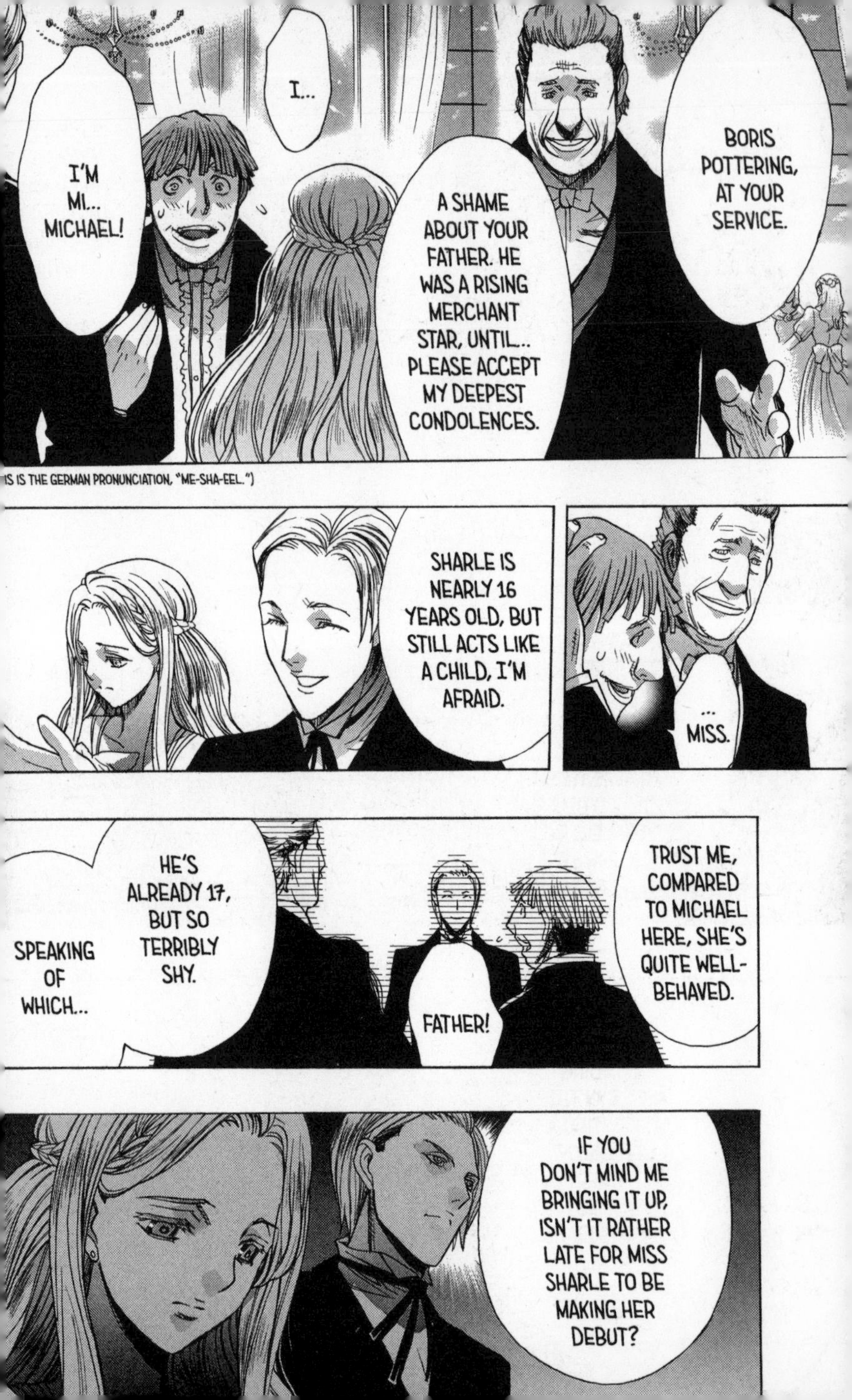
BORIS POTTERING, AT YOUR SERVICE.
A SHAME ABOUT YOUR FATHER. HE WAS A RISING MERCHANT STAR, UNTIL... PLEASE ACCEPT MY DEEPEST CONDOLENCES.
I...
I'M MI... MICHAEL!
IS IS THE GERMAN PRONUNCIATION, "ME-SHA-EEL.")
... MISS.
SHARLE IS NEARLY 16 YEARS OLD, BUT STILL ACTS LIKE A CHILD, I'M AFRAID.
TRUST ME, COMPARED TO MICHAEL HERE, SHE'S QUITE WELL-BEHAVED.
FATHER!
HE'S ALREADY 17, BUT SO TERRIBLY SHY.
SPEAKING OF WHICH...
IF YOU DON'T MIND ME BRINGING IT UP, ISN'T IT RATHER LATE FOR MISS SHARLE TO BE MAKING HER DEBUT?

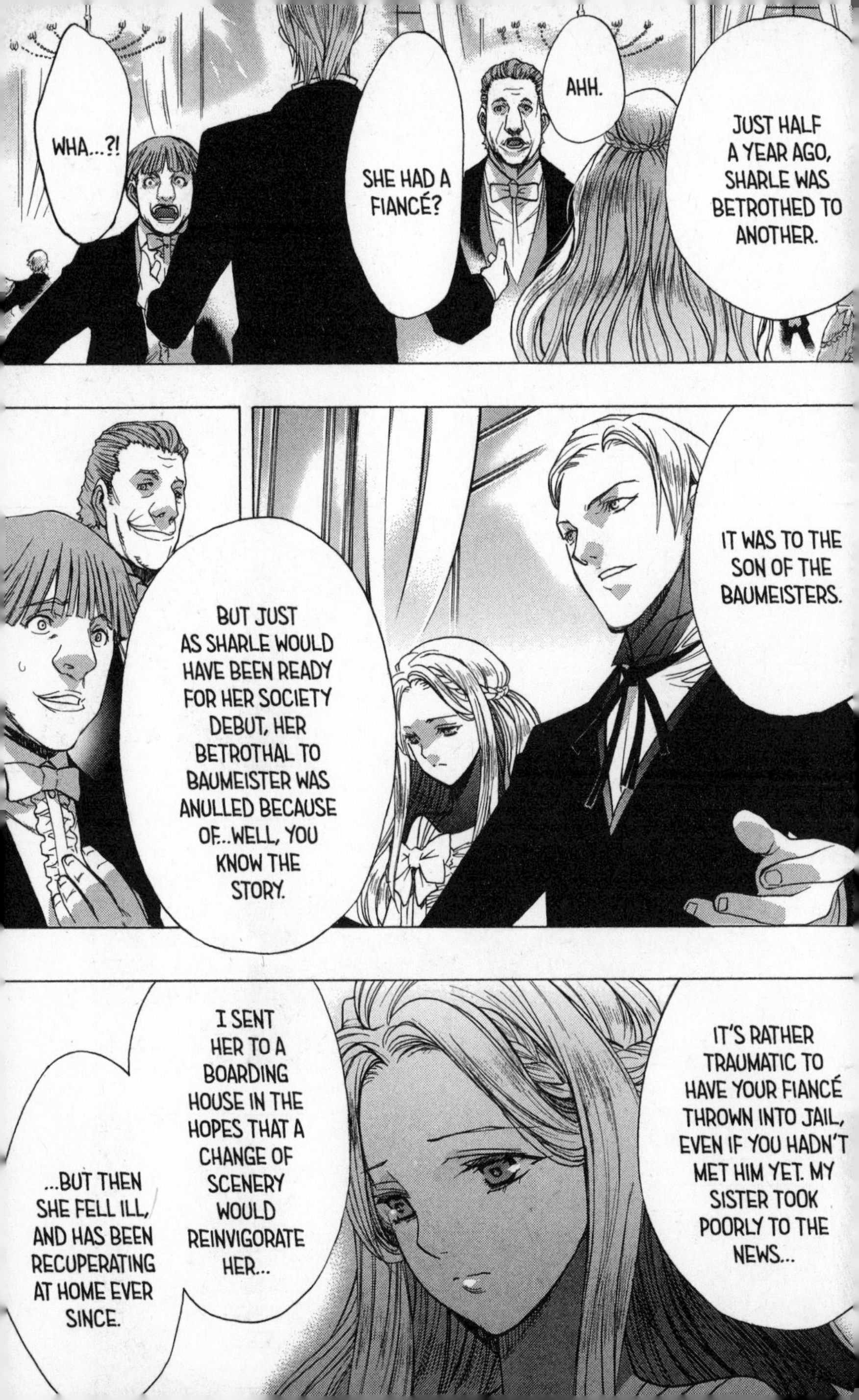
JUST HALF A YEAR AGO, SHARLE WAS BETROTHED TO ANOTHER.
AHH.
SHE HAD A FIANCÉ?
WHA...?!
IT WAS TO THE SON OF THE BAUMEISTERS.
BUT JUST AS SHARLE WOULD HAVE BEEN READY FOR HER SOCIETY DEBUT, HER BETROTHAL TO BAUMEISTER WAS ANULLED BECAUSE OF...WELL, YOU KNOW THE STORY.
IT'S RATHER TRAUMATIC TO HAVE YOUR FIANCÉ THROWN INTO JAIL, EVEN IF YOU HADN'T MET HIM YET. MY SISTER TOOK POORLY TO THE NEWS...
I SENT HER TO A BOARDING HOUSE IN THE HOPES THAT A CHANGE OF SCENERY WOULD REINVIGORATE HER...
...BUT THEN SHE FELL ILL, AND HAS BEEN RECUPERATING AT HOME EVER SINCE.

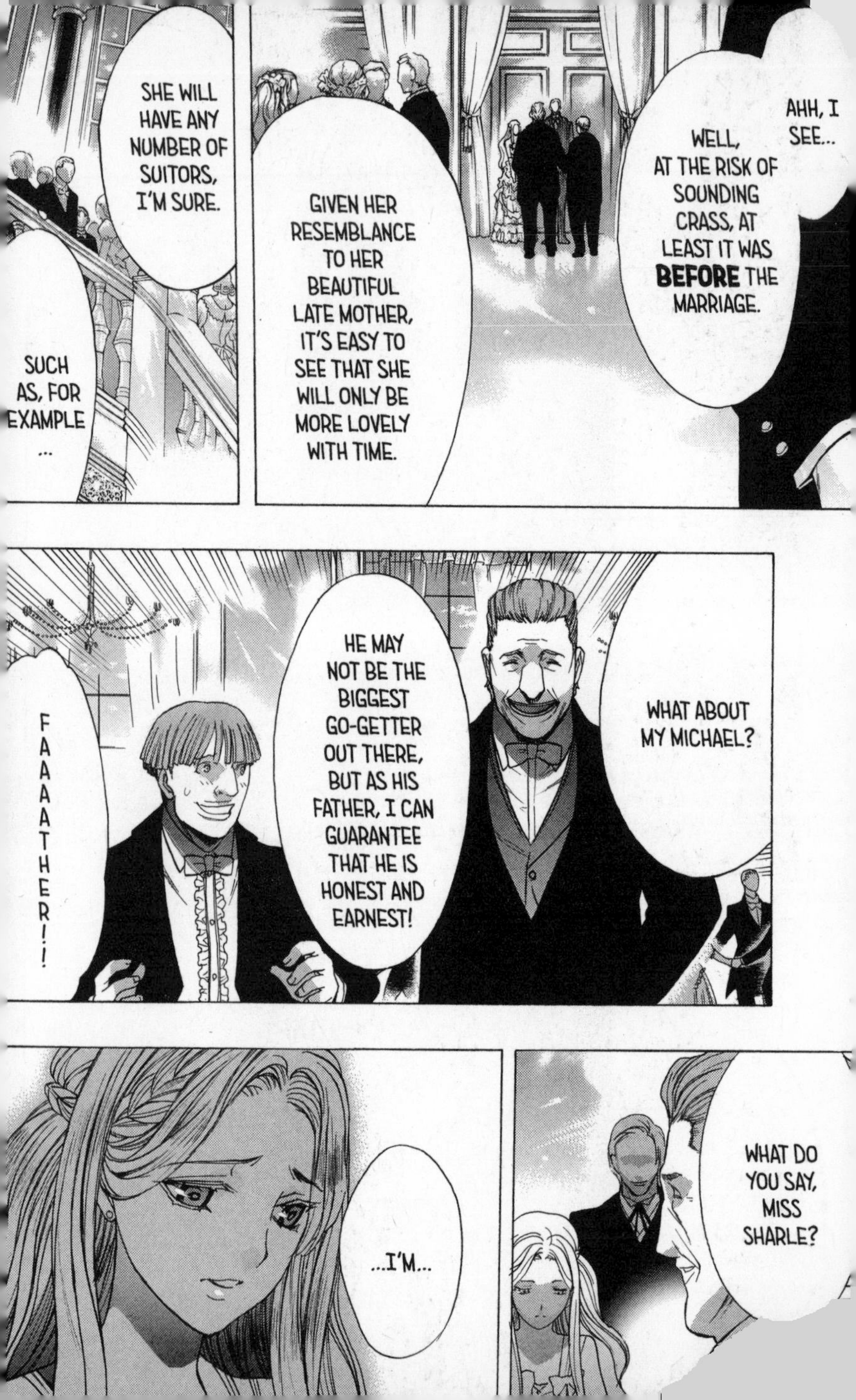
AHH, I SEE...
WELL, AT THE RISK OF SOUNDING CRASS, AT LEAST IT WAS **BEFORE** THE MARRIAGE.
GIVEN HER RESEMBLANCE TO HER BEAUTIFUL LATE MOTHER, IT'S EASY TO SEE THAT SHE WILL ONLY BE MORE LOVELY WITH TIME.
SHE WILL HAVE ANY NUMBER OF SUITORS, I'M SURE.
SUCH AS, FOR EXAMPLE ...
WHAT ABOUT MY MICHAEL?
HE MAY NOT BE THE BIGGEST GO-GETTER OUT THERE, BUT AS HIS FATHER, I CAN GUARANTEE THAT HE IS HONEST AND EARNEST!
FAAAATHER!!
WHAT DO YOU SAY, MISS SHARLE?
...I'M...

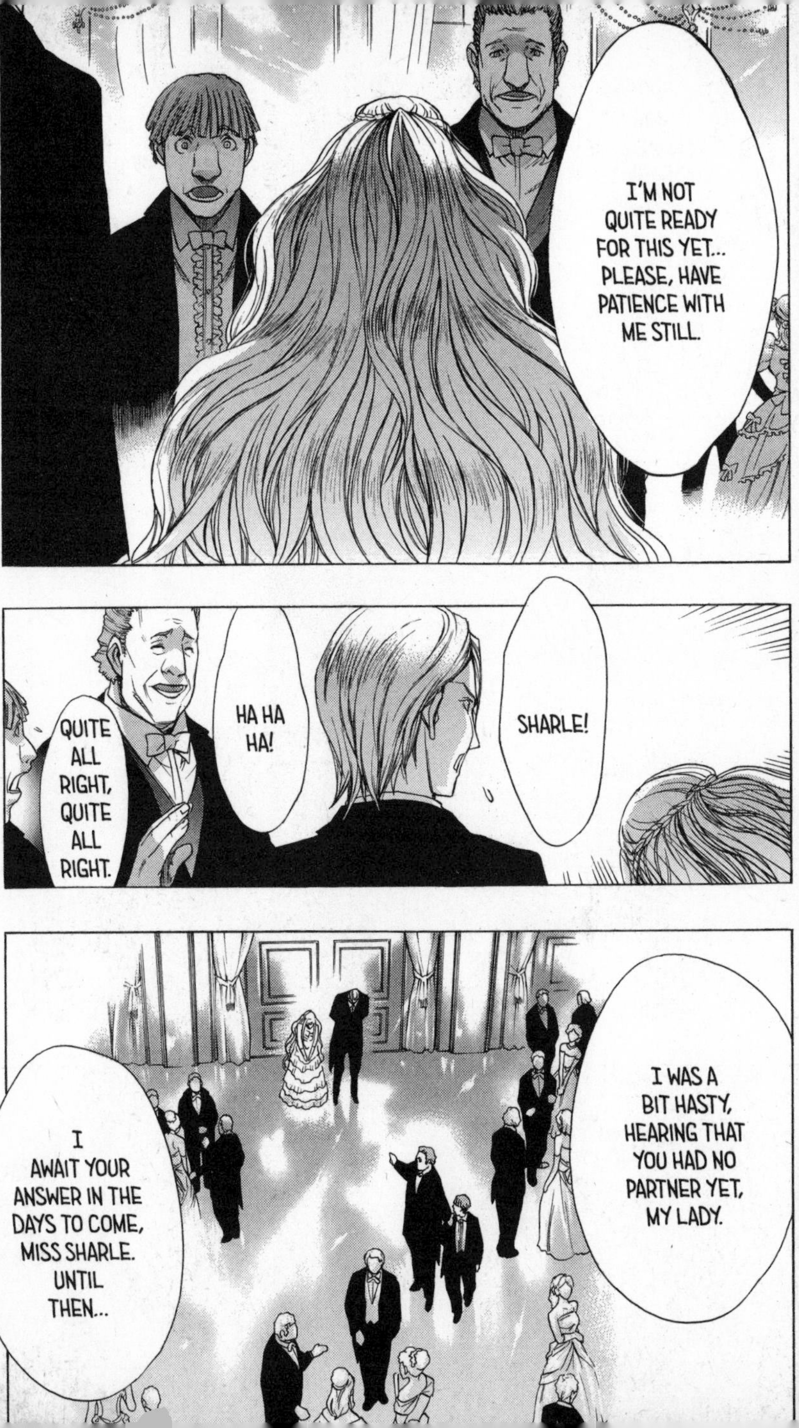
I'M NOT QUITE READY FOR THIS YET... PLEASE, HAVE PATIENCE WITH ME STILL.
SHARLE!
HA HA HA!
QUITE ALL RIGHT, QUITE ALL RIGHT.
I WAS A BIT HASTY, HEARING THAT YOU HAD NO PARTNER YET, MY LADY.
I AWAIT YOUR ANSWER IN THE DAYS TO COME, MISS SHARLE. UNTIL THEN...

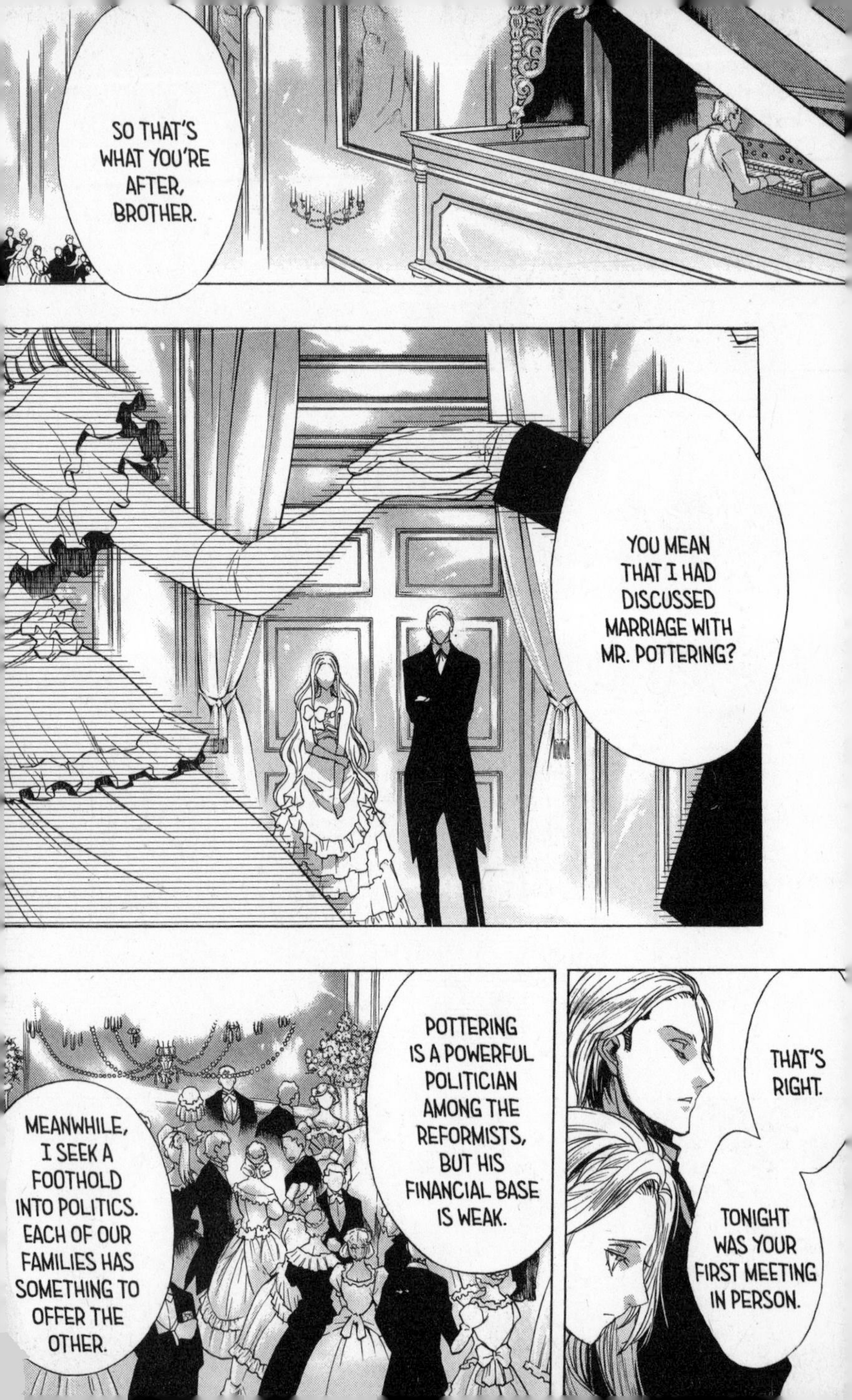
SO THAT'S WHAT YOU'RE AFTER, BROTHER.
YOU MEAN THAT I HAD DISCUSSED MARRIAGE WITH MR. POTTERING?
THAT'S RIGHT.
TONIGHT WAS YOUR FIRST MEETING IN PERSON.
POTTERING IS A POWERFUL POLITICIAN AMONG THE REFORMISTS, BUT HIS FINANCIAL BASE IS WEAK.
MEANWHILE, I SEEK A FOOTHOLD INTO POLITICS. EACH OF OUR FAMILIES HAS SOMETHING TO OFFER THE OTHER.

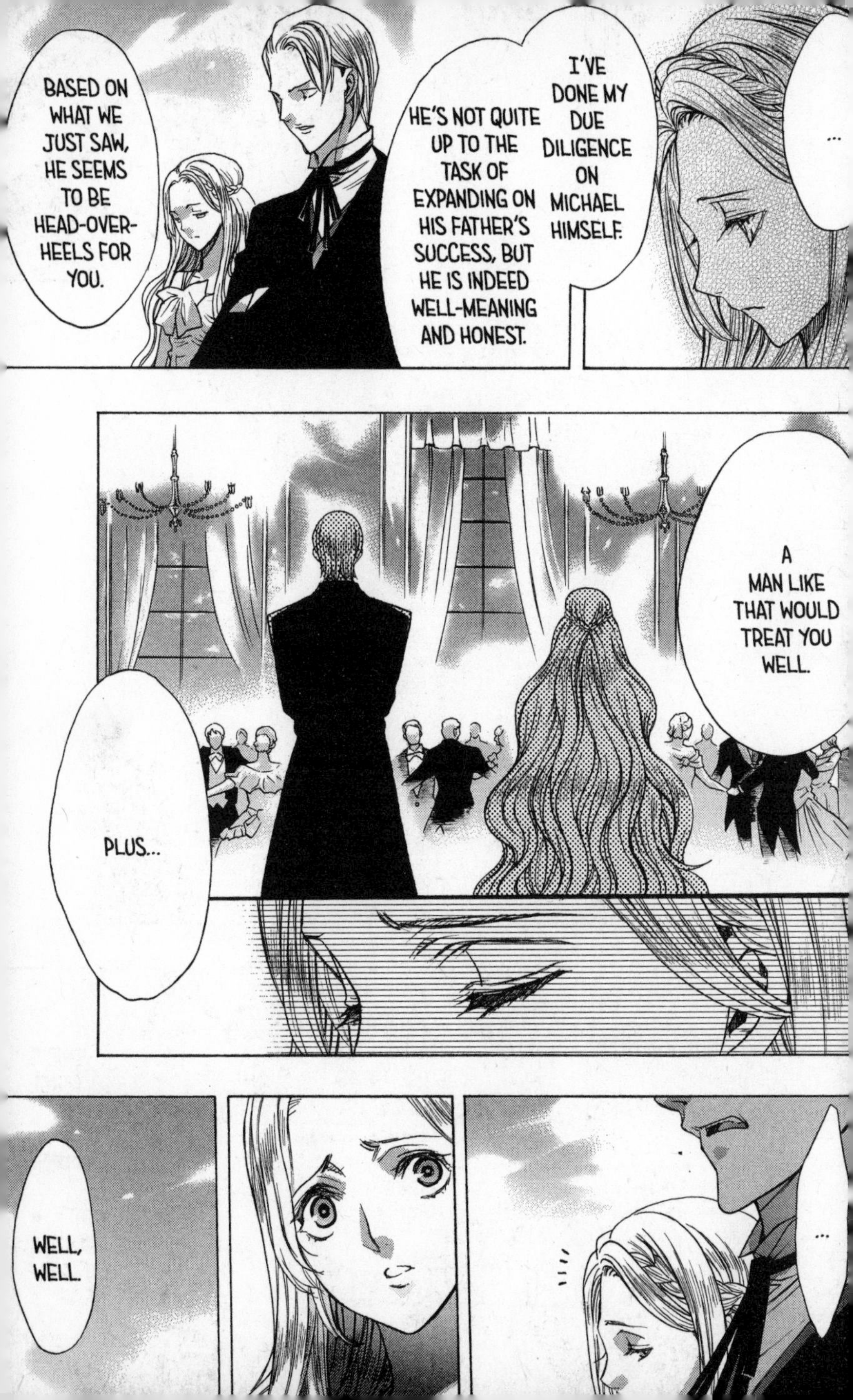
...
I'VE DONE MY DUE DILIGENCE ON MICHAEL HIMSELF.
HE'S NOT QUITE UP TO THE TASK OF EXPANDING ON HIS FATHER'S SUCCESS, BUT HE IS INDEED WELL-MEANING AND HONEST.
BASED ON WHAT WE JUST SAW, HE SEEMS TO BE HEAD-OVER-HEELS FOR YOU.
A MAN LIKE THAT WOULD TREAT YOU WELL.
PLUS...
...
WELL, WELL.

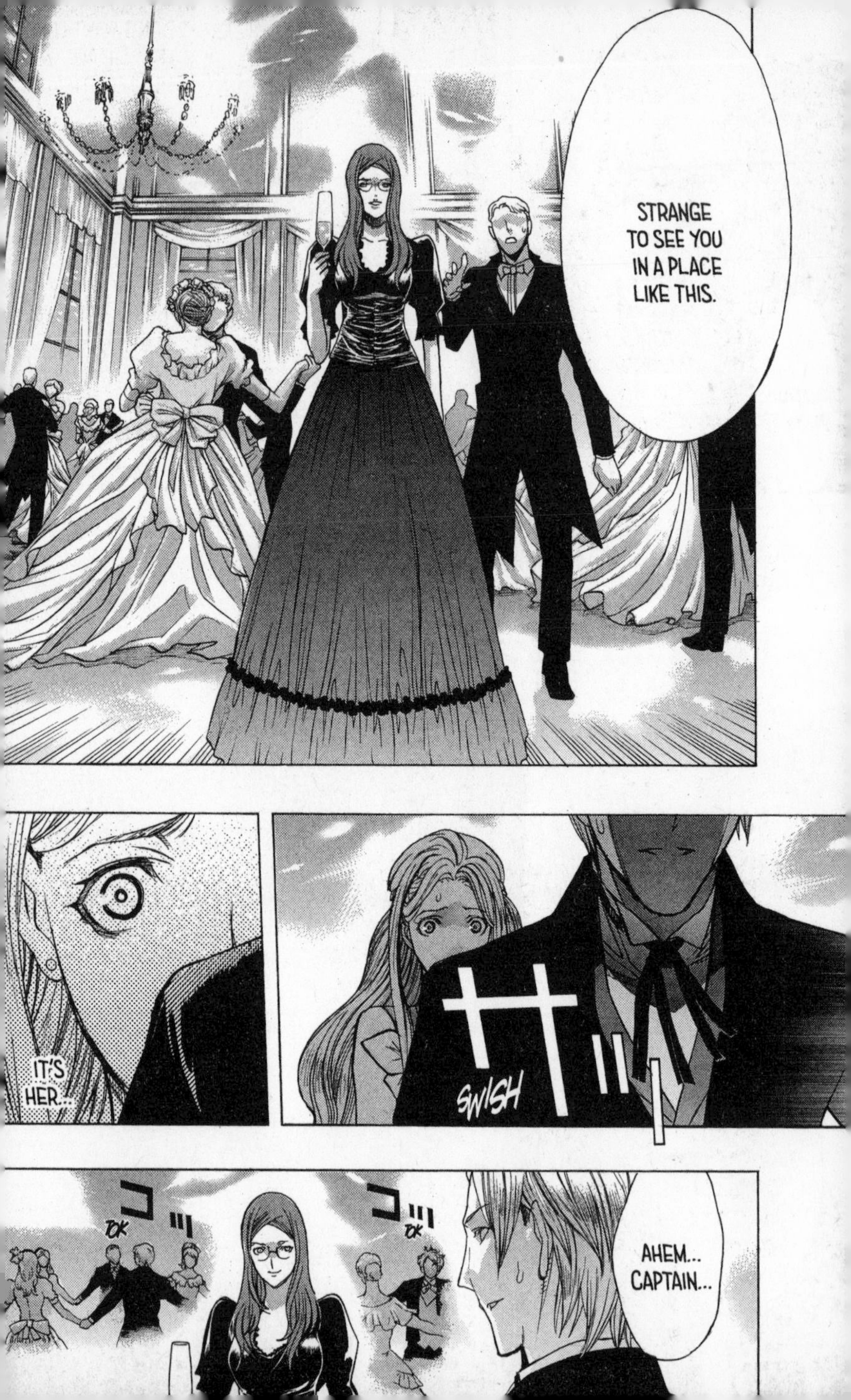
STRANGE TO SEE YOU IN A PLACE LIKE THIS.
SWISH
IT'S HER...
AHEM... CAPTAIN...
TOK
TOK

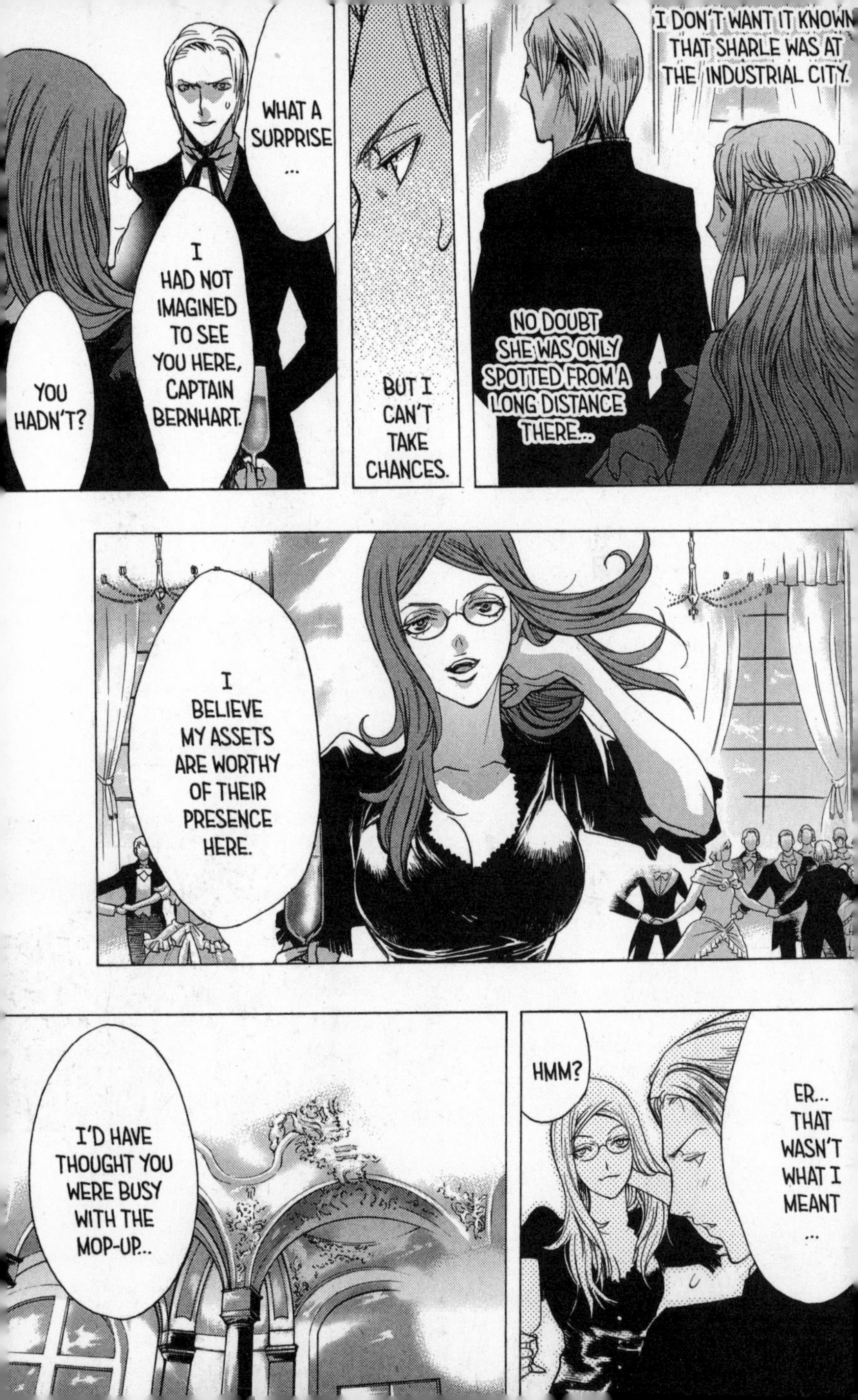
I DON'T WANT IT KNOWN THAT SHARLE WAS AT THE INDUSTRIAL CITY.
NO DOUBT SHE WAS ONLY SPOTTED FROM A LONG DISTANCE THERE...
BUT I CAN'T TAKE CHANCES.
WHAT A SURPRISE ...
I HAD NOT IMAGINED TO SEE YOU HERE, CAPTAIN BERNHART.
YOU HADN'T?
I BELIEVE MY ASSETS ARE WORTHY OF THEIR PRESENCE HERE.
HMM?
ER... THAT WASN'T WHAT I MEANT ...
I'D HAVE THOUGHT YOU WERE BUSY WITH THE MOP-UP...

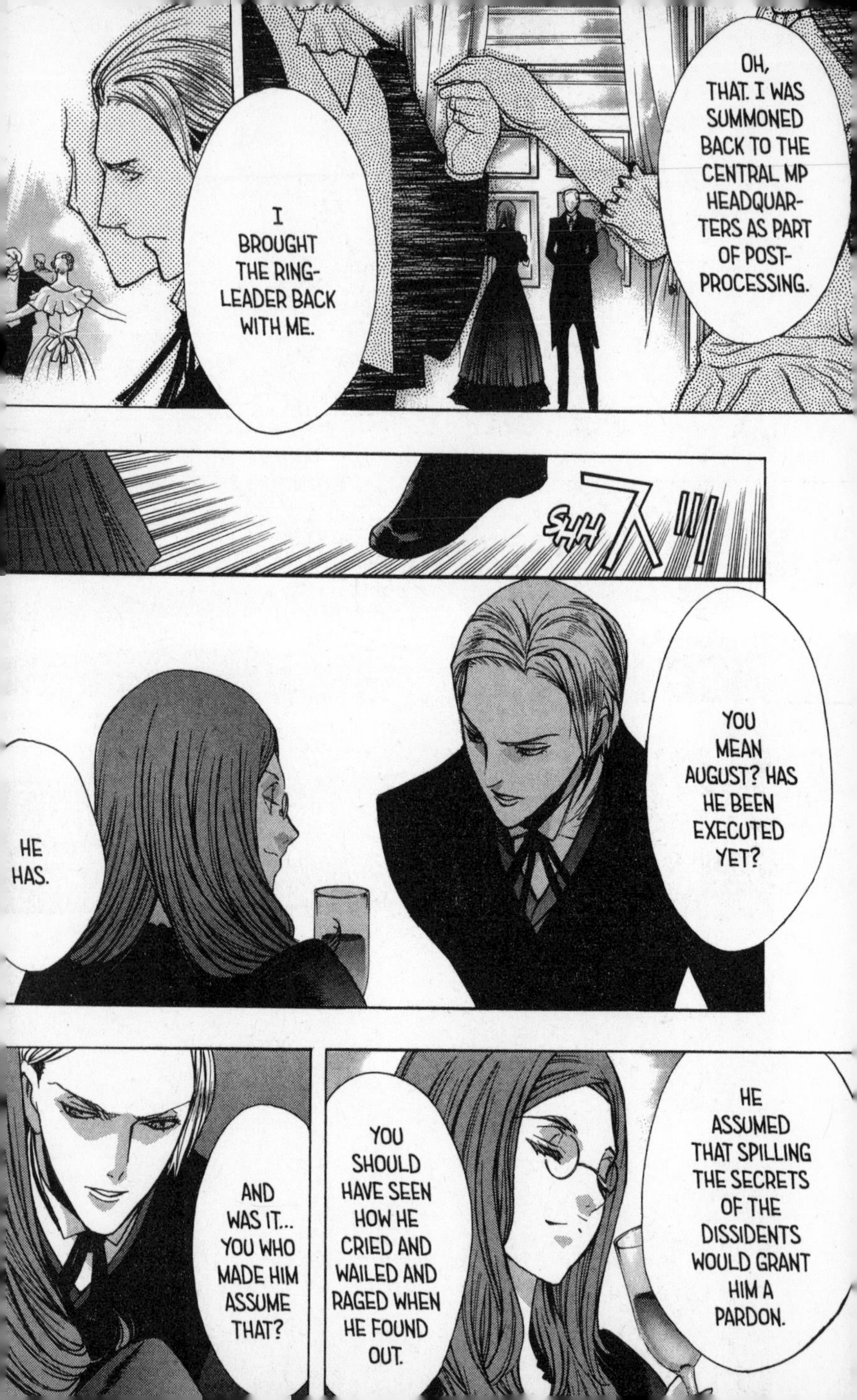
OH, THAT. I WAS SUMMONED BACK TO THE CENTRAL MP HEADQUARTERS AS PART OF POST-PROCESSING.
I BROUGHT THE RING-LEADER BACK WITH ME.
SHH
YOU MEAN AUGUST? HAS HE BEEN EXECUTED YET?
HE HAS.
HE ASSUMED THAT SPILLING THE SECRETS OF THE DISSIDENTS WOULD GRANT HIM A PARDON.
YOU SHOULD HAVE SEEN HOW HE CRIED AND WAILED AND RAGED WHEN HE FOUND OUT.
AND WAS IT... YOU WHO MADE HIM ASSUME THAT?

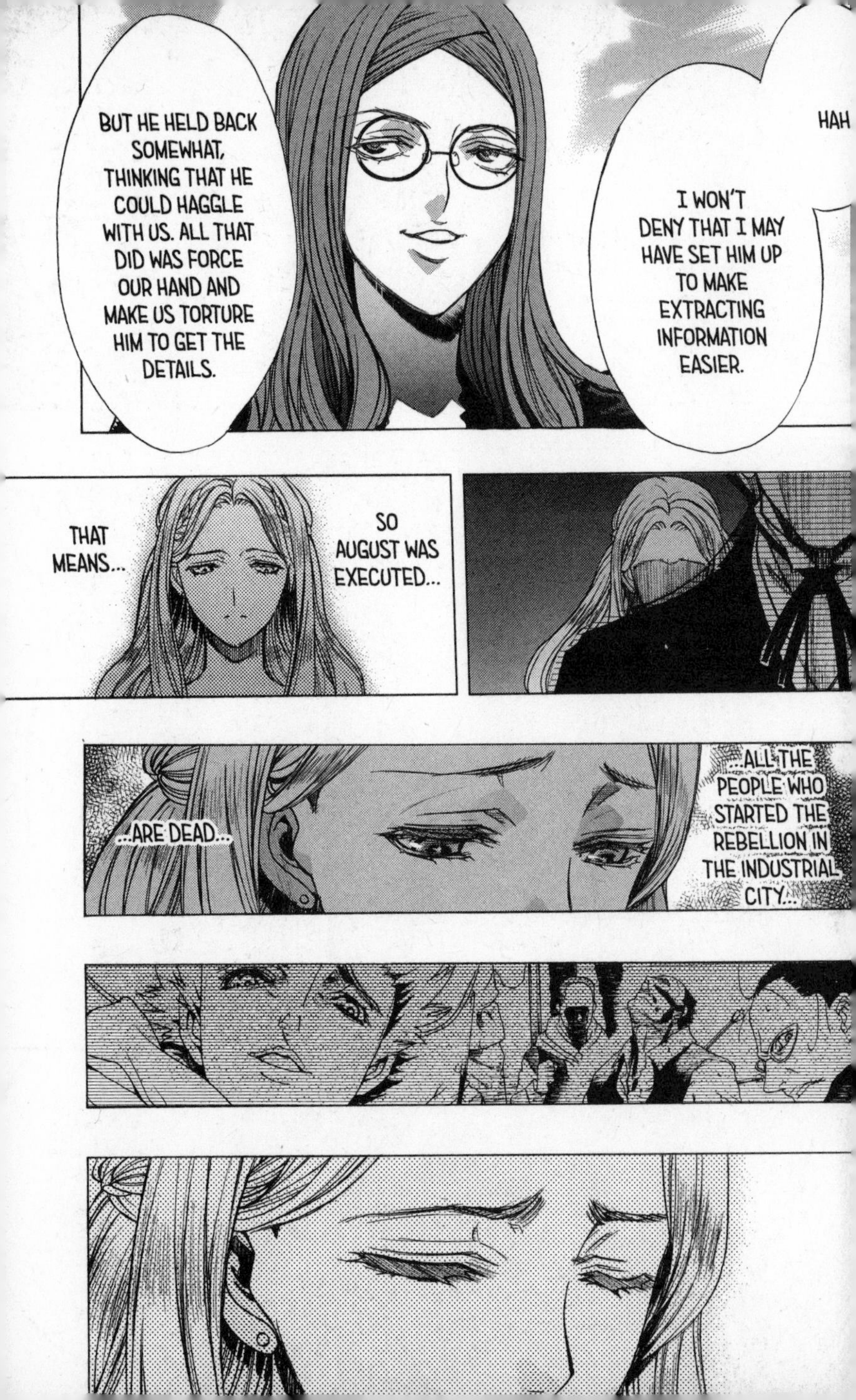
HAH
I WON'T DENY THAT I MAY HAVE SET HIM UP TO MAKE EXTRACTING INFORMATION EASIER.
BUT HE HELD BACK SOMEWHAT, THINKING THAT HE COULD HAGGLE WITH US. ALL THAT DID WAS FORCE OUR HAND AND MAKE US TORTURE HIM TO GET THE DETAILS.
SO AUGUST WAS EXECUTED...
THAT MEANS...
...ALL THE PEOPLE WHO STARTED THE REBELLION IN THE INDUSTRIAL CITY...
...ARE DEAD...

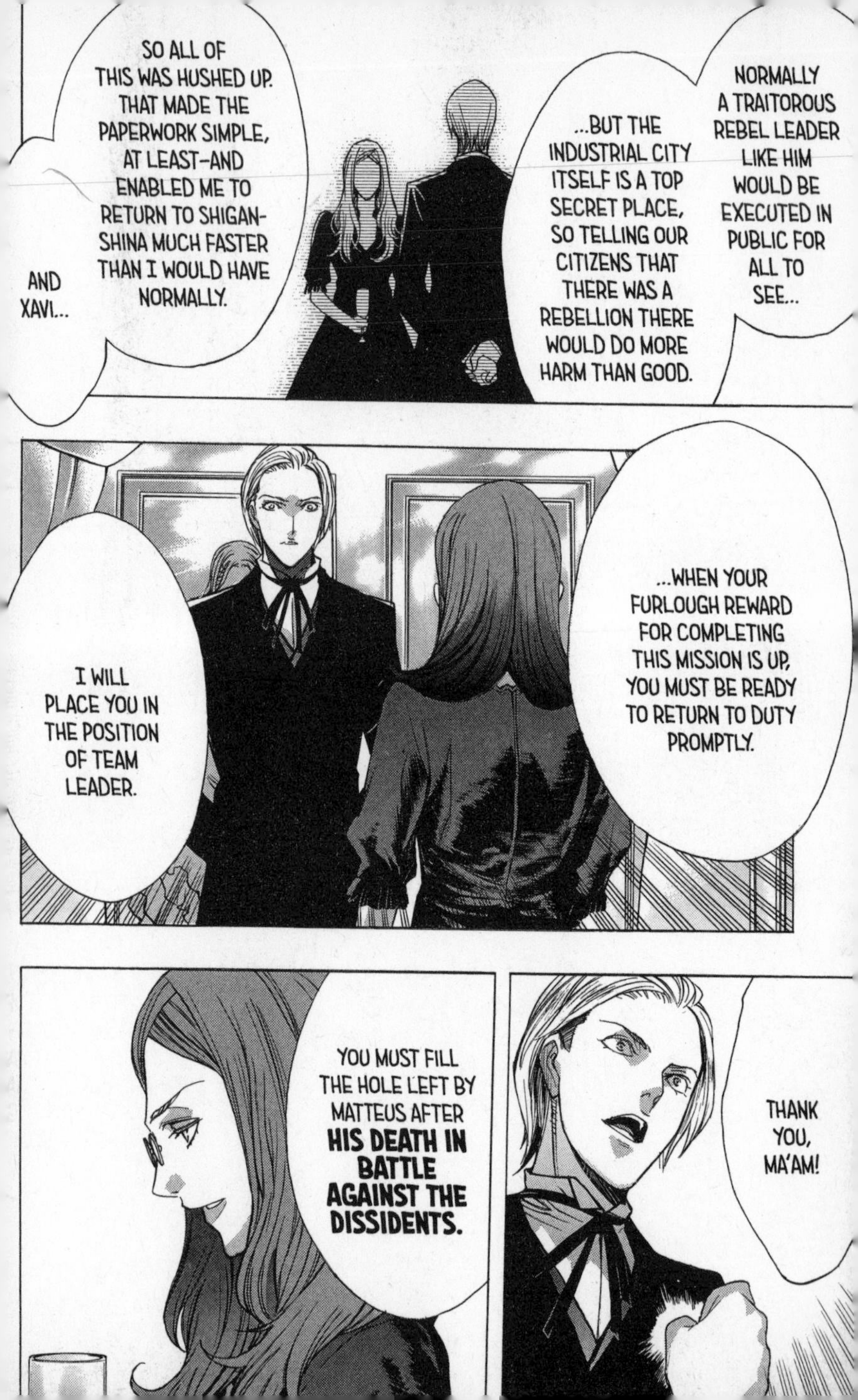

NORMALLY A TRAITOROUS REBEL LEADER LIKE HIM WOULD BE EXECUTED IN PUBLIC FOR ALL TO SEE...
...BUT THE INDUSTRIAL CITY ITSELF IS A TOP SECRET PLACE, SO TELLING OUR CITIZENS THAT THERE WAS A REBELLION THERE WOULD DO MORE HARM THAN GOOD.
SO ALL OF THIS WAS HUSHED UP. THAT MADE THE PAPERWORK SIMPLE, AT LEAST—AND ENABLED ME TO RETURN TO SHIGAN-SHINA MUCH FASTER THAN I WOULD HAVE NORMALLY.
AND XAVI...
...WHEN YOUR FURLOUGH REWARD FOR COMPLETING THIS MISSION IS UP, YOU MUST BE READY TO RETURN TO DUTY PROMPTLY.
I WILL PLACE YOU IN THE POSITION OF TEAM LEADER.
THANK YOU, MA'AM!
YOU MUST FILL THE HOLE LEFT BY MATTEUS AFTER **HIS DEATH IN BATTLE AGAINST THE DISSIDENTS.**

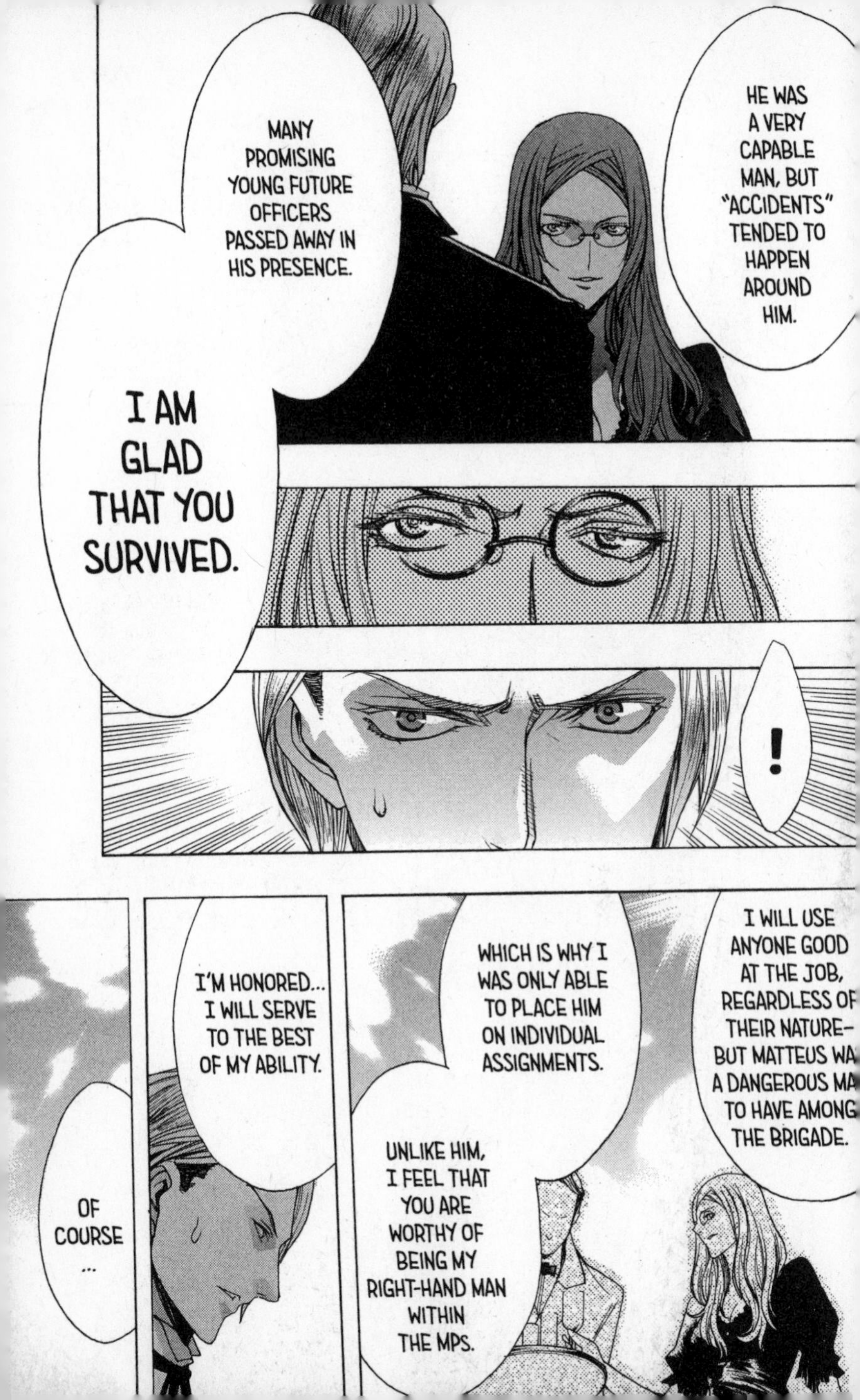
HE WAS A VERY CAPABLE MAN, BUT "ACCIDENTS" TENDED TO HAPPEN AROUND HIM.
MANY PROMISING YOUNG FUTURE OFFICERS PASSED AWAY IN HIS PRESENCE.
I AM GLAD THAT YOU SURVIVED.
!
I WILL USE ANYONE GOOD AT THE JOB, REGARDLESS OF THEIR NATURE— BUT MATTEUS WA A DANGEROUS MA TO HAVE AMONG THE BRIGADE.
WHICH IS WHY I WAS ONLY ABLE TO PLACE HIM ON INDIVIDUAL ASSIGNMENTS.
UNLIKE HIM, I FEEL THAT YOU ARE WORTHY OF BEING MY RIGHT-HAND MAN WITHIN THE MPS.
I'M HONORED... I WILL SERVE TO THE BEST OF MY ABILITY.
OF COURSE ...

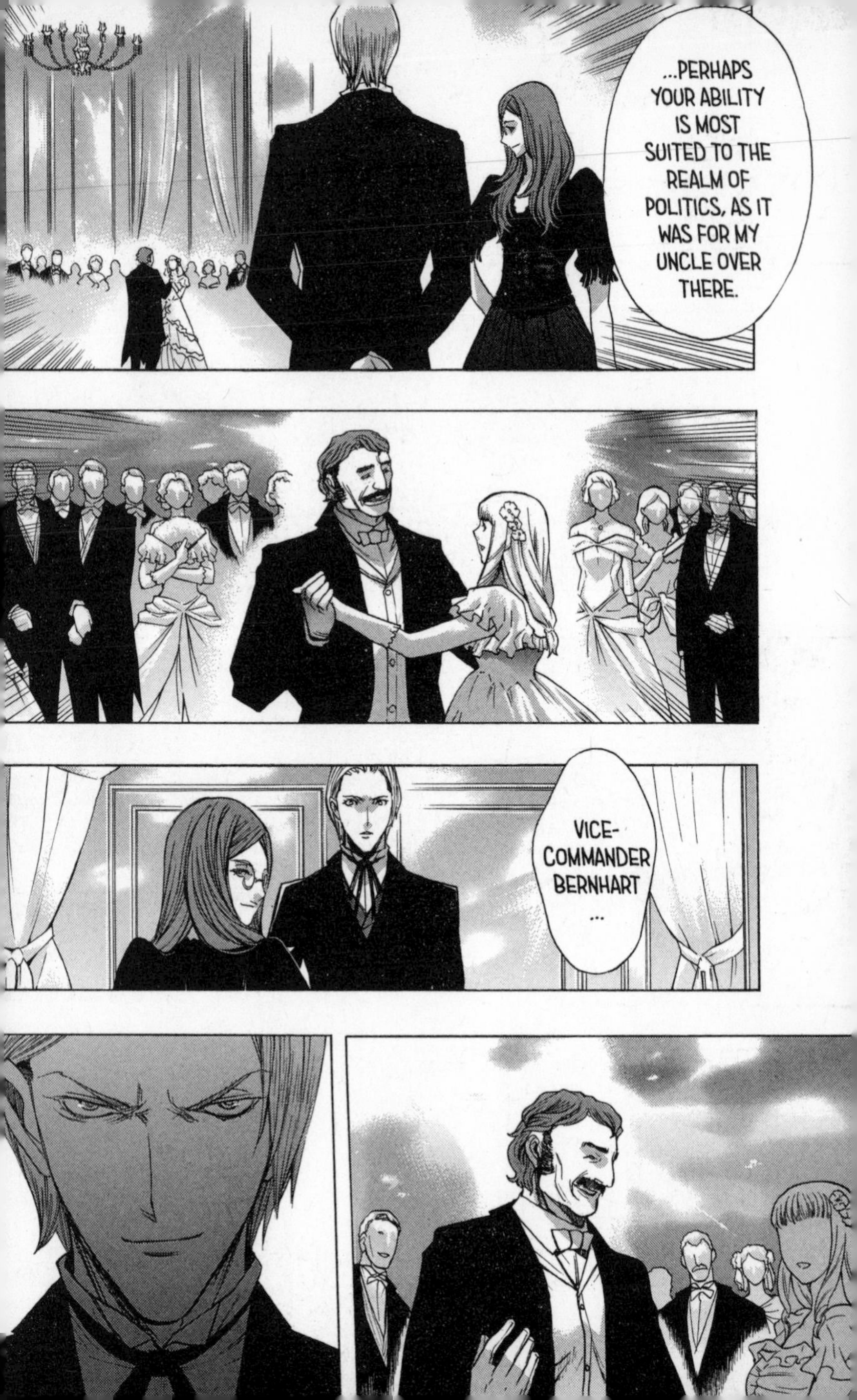
...PERHAPS YOUR ABILITY IS MOST SUITED TO THE REALM OF POLITICS, AS IT WAS FOR MY UNCLE OVER THERE.
VICE-COMMANDER BERNHART ...

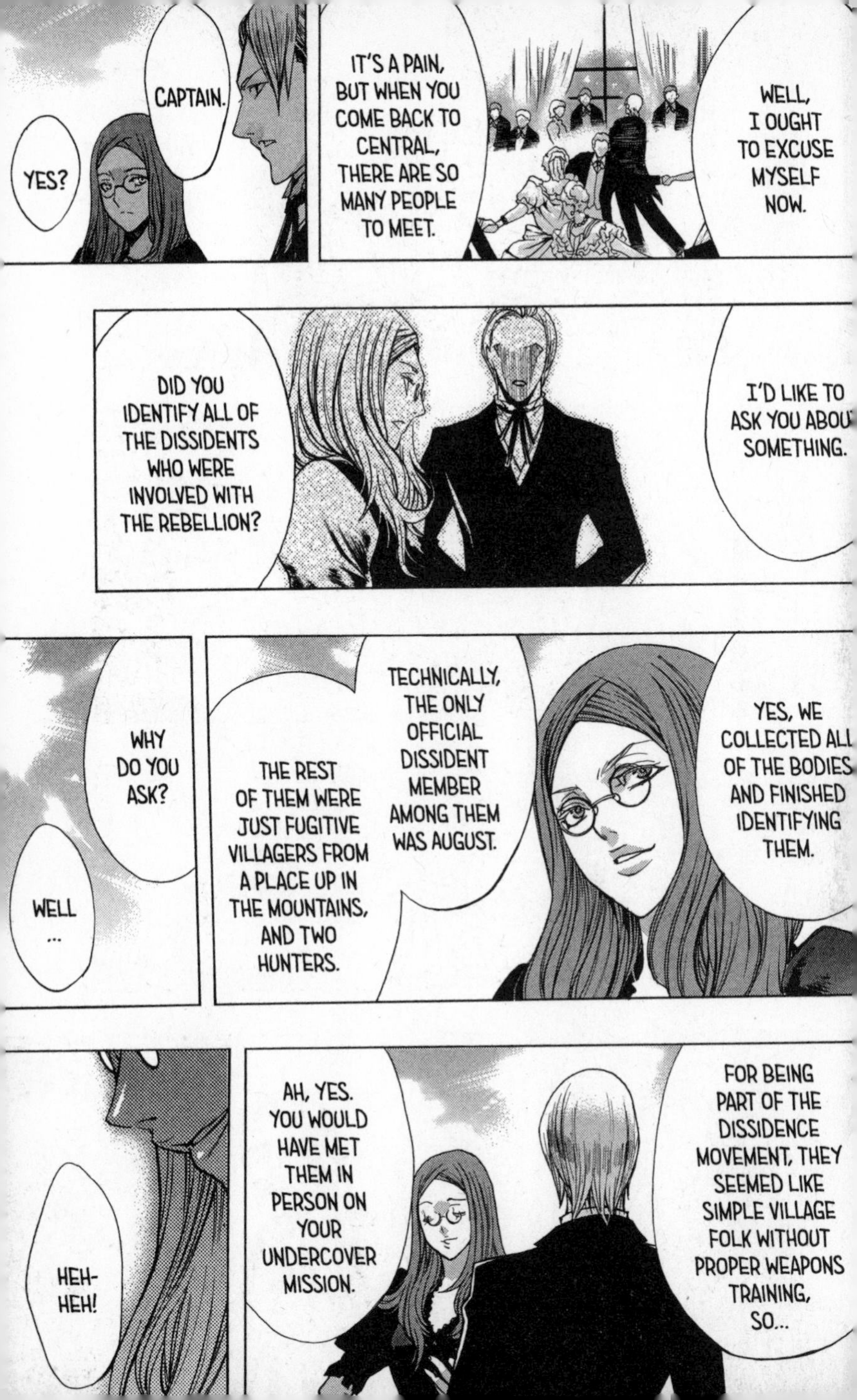
WELL, I OUGHT TO EXCUSE MYSELF NOW.
IT'S A PAIN, BUT WHEN YOU COME BACK TO CENTRAL, THERE ARE SO MANY PEOPLE TO MEET.
CAPTAIN.
YES?
I'D LIKE TO ASK YOU ABOUT SOMETHING.
DID YOU IDENTIFY ALL OF THE DISSIDENTS WHO WERE INVOLVED WITH THE REBELLION?
YES, WE COLLECTED ALL OF THE BODIES AND FINISHED IDENTIFYING THEM.
TECHNICALLY, THE ONLY OFFICIAL DISSIDENT MEMBER AMONG THEM WAS AUGUST.
THE REST OF THEM WERE JUST FUGITIVE VILLAGERS FROM A PLACE UP IN THE MOUNTAINS, AND TWO HUNTERS.
WHY DO YOU ASK?
WELL ...
FOR BEING PART OF THE DISSIDENCE MOVEMENT, THEY SEEMED LIKE SIMPLE VILLAGE FOLK WITHOUT PROPER WEAPONS TRAINING, SO...
AH, YES. YOU WOULD HAVE MET THEM IN PERSON ON YOUR UNDERCOVER MISSION.
HEH-HEH!

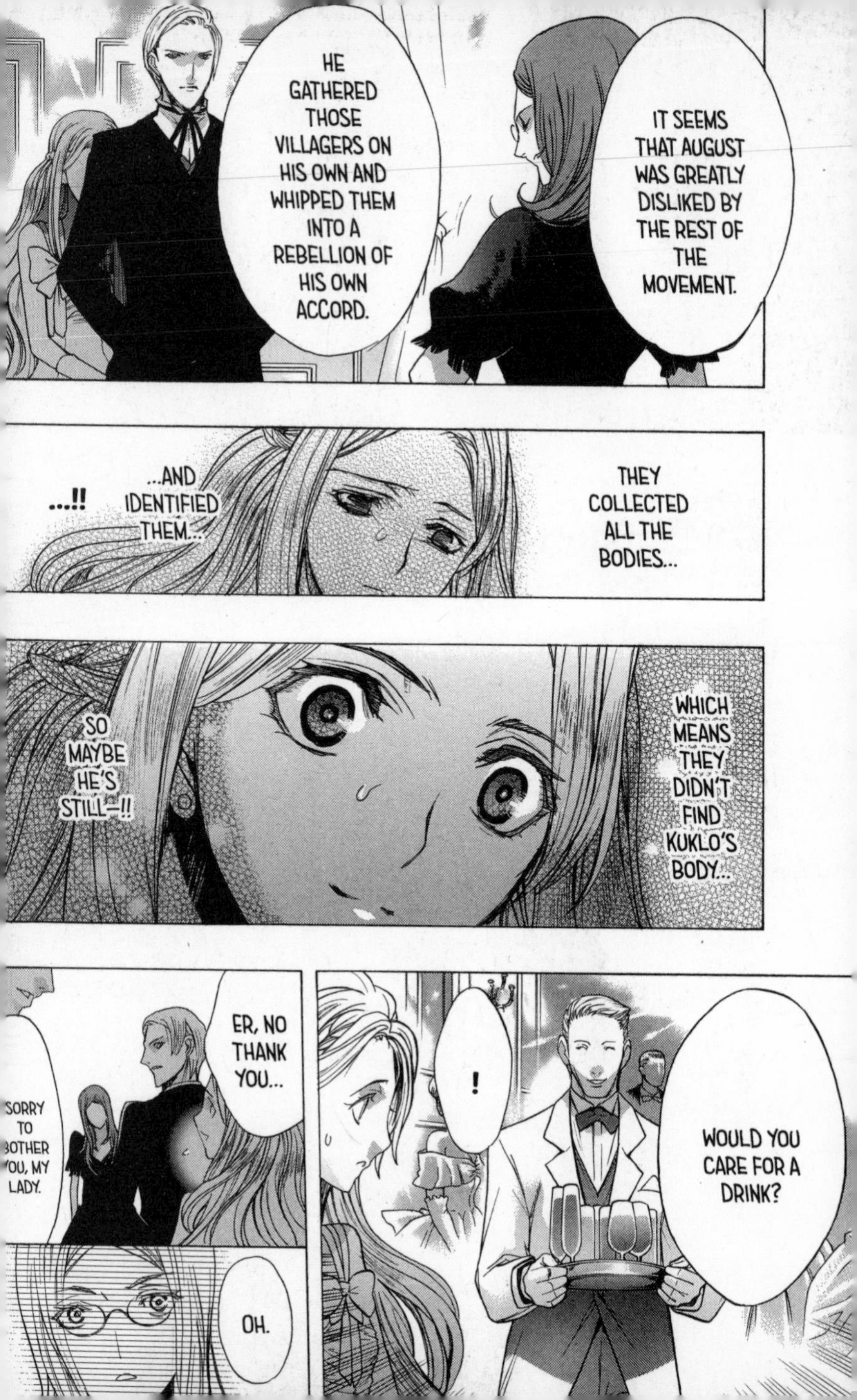
IT SEEMS THAT AUGUST WAS GREATLY DISLIKED BY THE REST OF THE MOVEMENT.
HE GATHERED THOSE VILLAGERS ON HIS OWN AND WHIPPED THEM INTO A REBELLION OF HIS OWN ACCORD.
THEY COLLECTED ALL THE BODIES...
...AND IDENTIFIED THEM...
...!!
WHICH MEANS THEY DIDN'T FIND KUKLO'S BODY...
SO MAYBE HE'S STILL—!!
WOULD YOU CARE FOR A DRINK?
!
ER, NO THANK YOU...
SORRY TO BOTHER YOU, MY LADY.
OH.

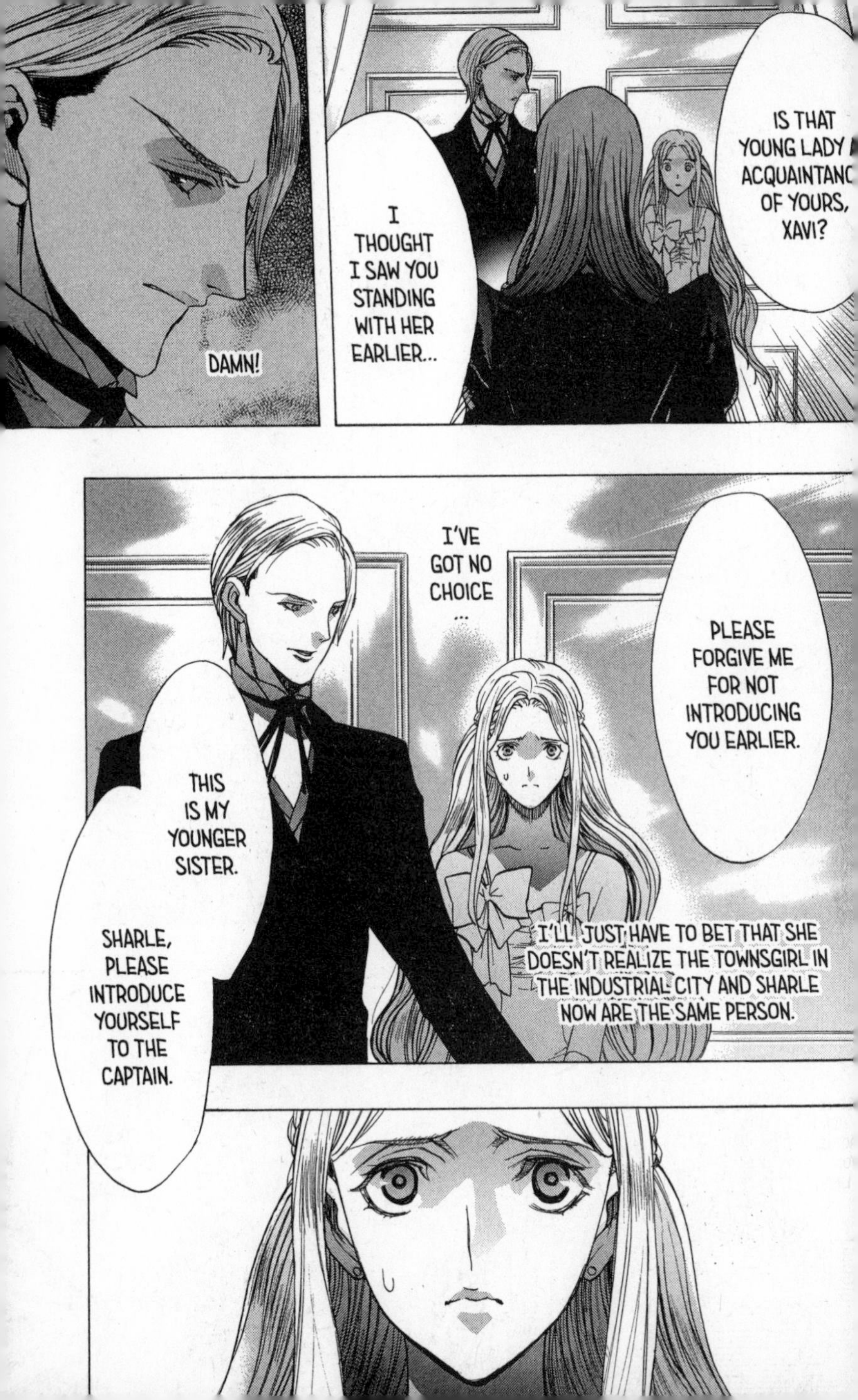
IS THAT YOUNG LADY ACQUAINTANC OF YOURS, XAVI?
I THOUGHT I SAW YOU STANDING WITH HER EARLIER...
DAMN!
PLEASE FORGIVE ME FOR NOT INTRODUCING YOU EARLIER.
I'VE GOT NO CHOICE ...
THIS IS MY YOUNGER SISTER.
I'LL JUST HAVE TO BET THAT SHE DOESN'T REALIZE THE TOWNSGIRL IN THE INDUSTRIAL CITY AND SHARLE NOW ARE THE SAME PERSON.
SHARLE, PLEASE INTRODUCE YOURSELF TO THE CAPTION.

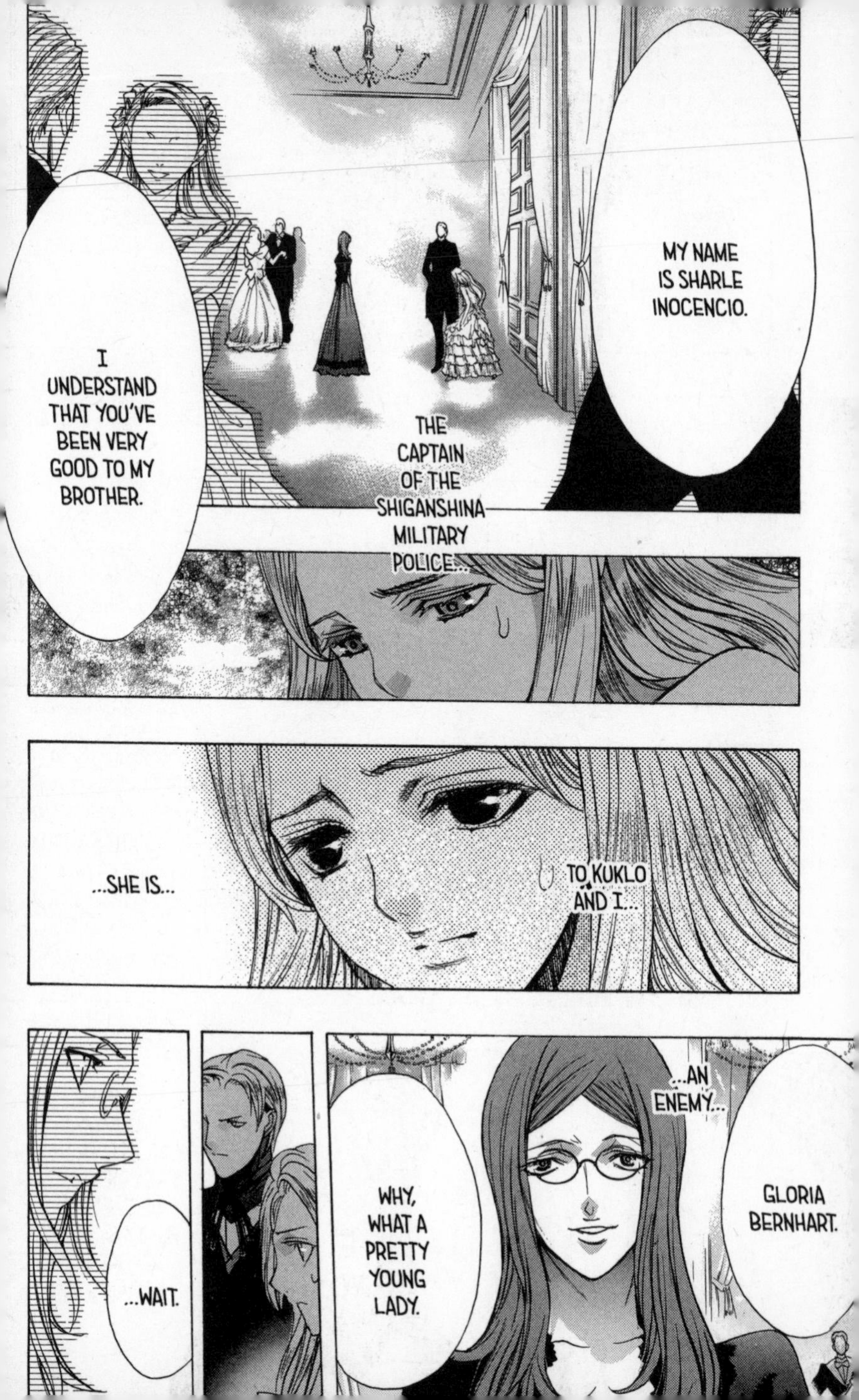
MY NAME IS SHARLE INOCENCIO.
I UNDERSTAND THAT YOU'VE BEEN VERY GOOD TO MY BROTHER.
THE CAPTAIN OF THE SHIGANSHINA MILITARY POLICE...
TO KUKLO AND I...
...SHE IS...
GLORIA BERNHART.
...AN ENEMY...
WHY, WHAT A PRETTY YOUNG LADY.
...WAIT.

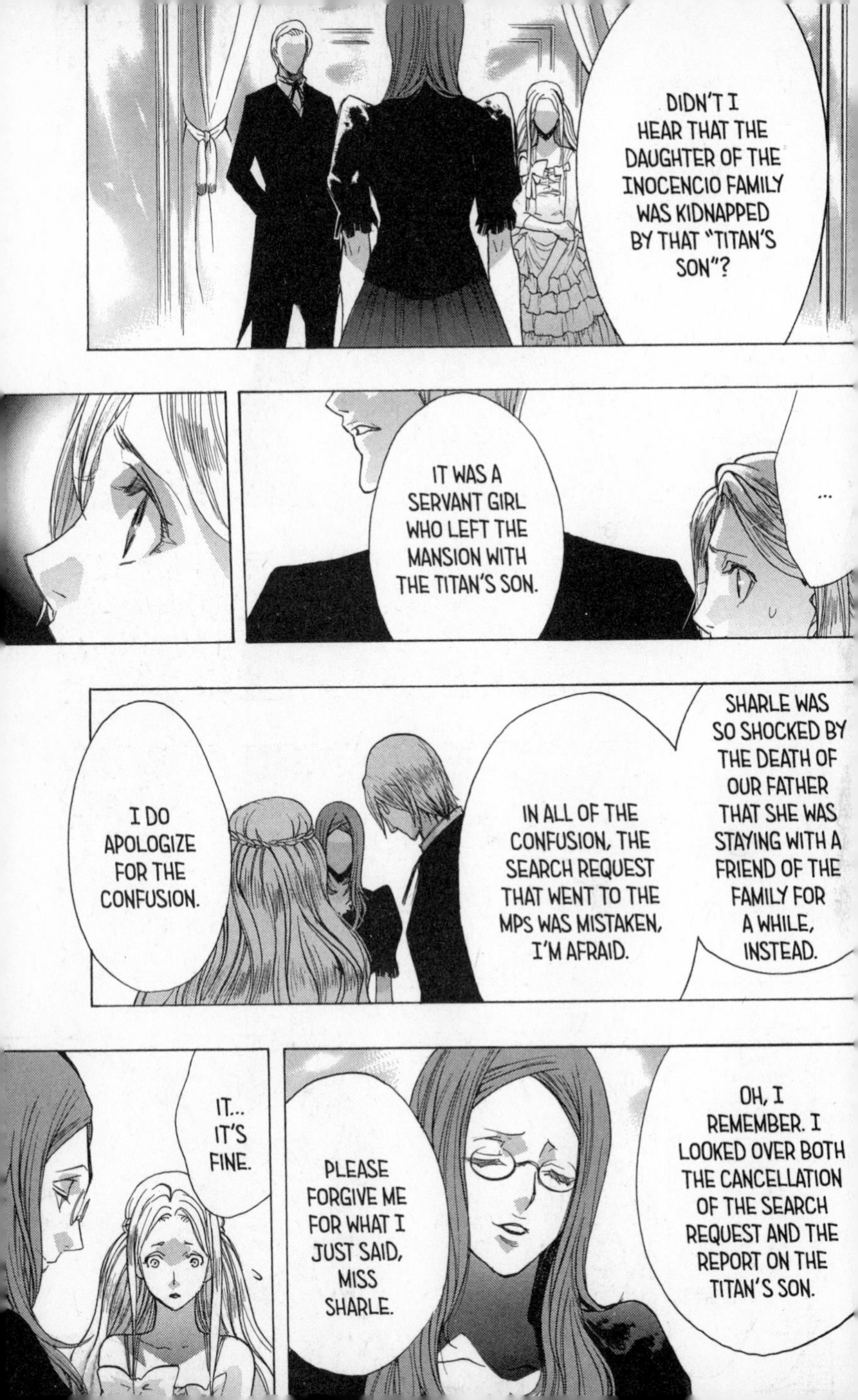
DIDN'T I HEAR THAT THE DAUGHTER OF THE INOCENCIO FAMILY WAS KIDNAPPED BY THAT "TITAN'S SON"?
...
IT WAS A SERVANT GIRL WHO LEFT THE MANSION WITH THE TITAN'S SON.
SHARLE WAS SO SHOCKED BY THE DEATH OF OUR FATHER THAT SHE WAS STAYING WITH A FRIEND OF THE FAMILY FOR A WHILE, INSTEAD.
IN ALL OF THE CONFUSION, THE SEARCH REQUEST THAT WENT TO THE MPS WAS MISTAKEN, I'M AFRAID.
I DO APOLOGIZE FOR THE CONFUSION.
OH, I REMEMBER. I LOOKED OVER BOTH THE CANCELLATION OF THE SEARCH REQUEST AND THE REPORT ON THE TITAN'S SON.
PLEASE FORGIVE ME FOR WHAT I JUST SAID, MISS SHARLE.
IT... IT'S FINE.

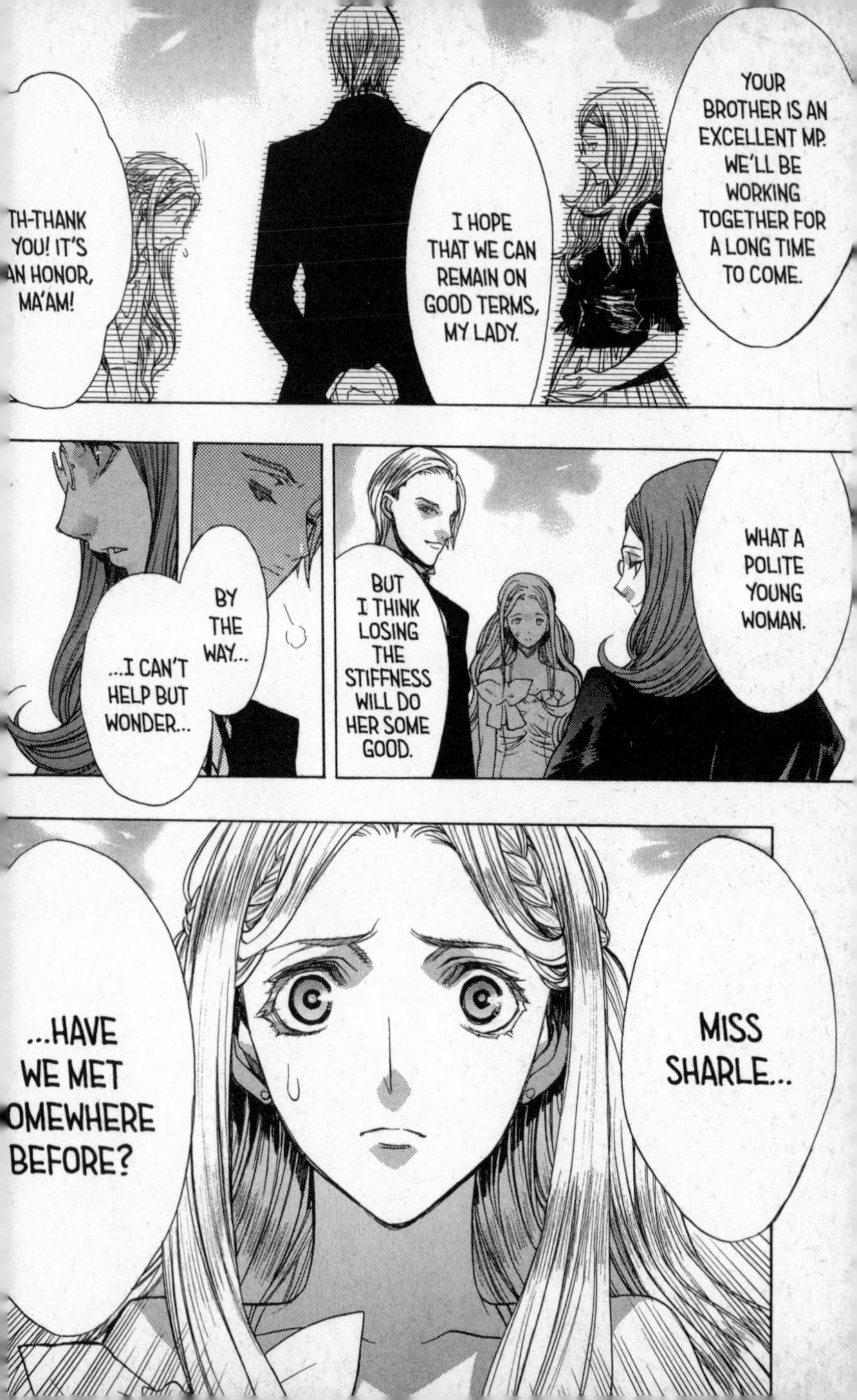
YOUR BROTHER IS AN EXCELLENT MP. WE'LL BE WORKING TOGETHER FOR A LONG TIME TO COME.
I HOPE THAT WE CAN REMAIN ON GOOD TERMS, MY LADY.
TH-THANK YOU! IT'S AN HONOR, MA'AM!
WHAT A POLITE YOUNG WOMAN.
BUT I THINK LOSING THE STIFFNESS WILL DO HER SOME GOOD.
BY THE WAY...
...I CAN'T HELP BUT WONDER...
MISS SHARLE...
...HAVE WE MET OMEWHERE BEFORE?

ATTACK ON TITAN
BEFORE THE FALL

TO BE CONTINUED

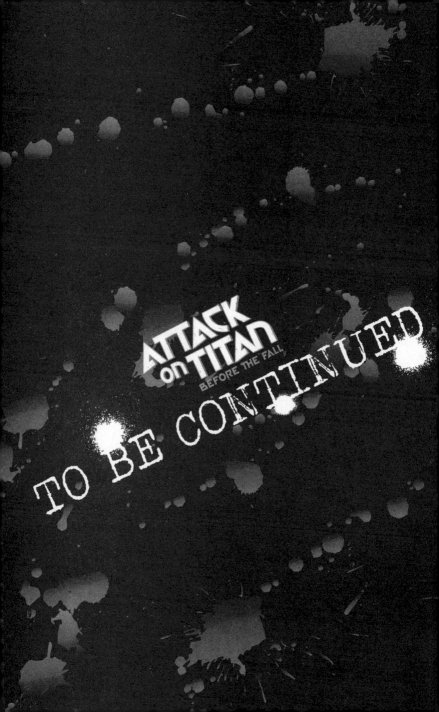

BUDDING AMBITION

A glimpse at Xavi and Sharle just before Dario brought Kuklo into the Inocencio mansion.

Originally published: Bessatsu Shonen Magazine, May 2016 issue

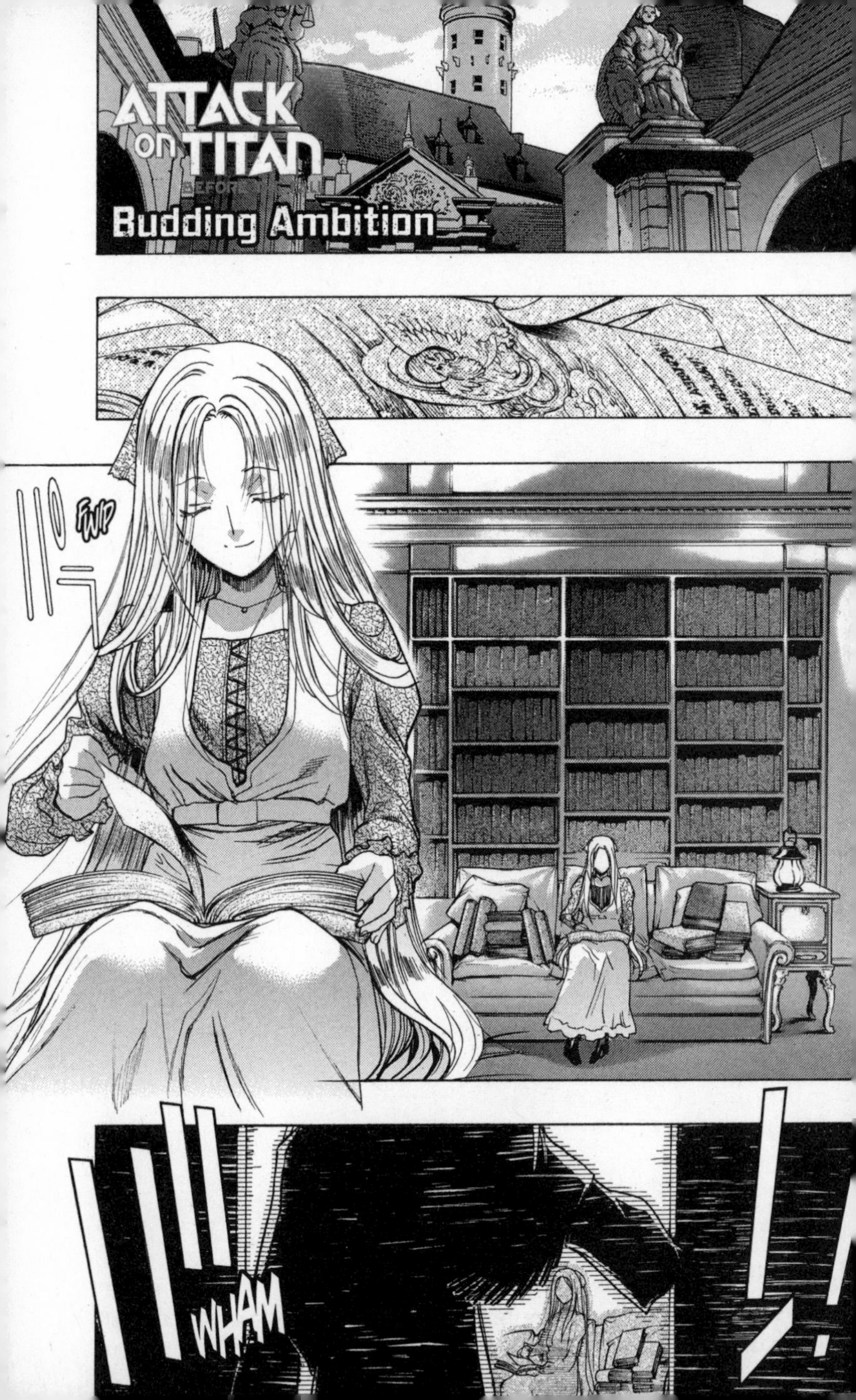
ATTACK on TITAN
Budding Ambition
FWIP
WHAM

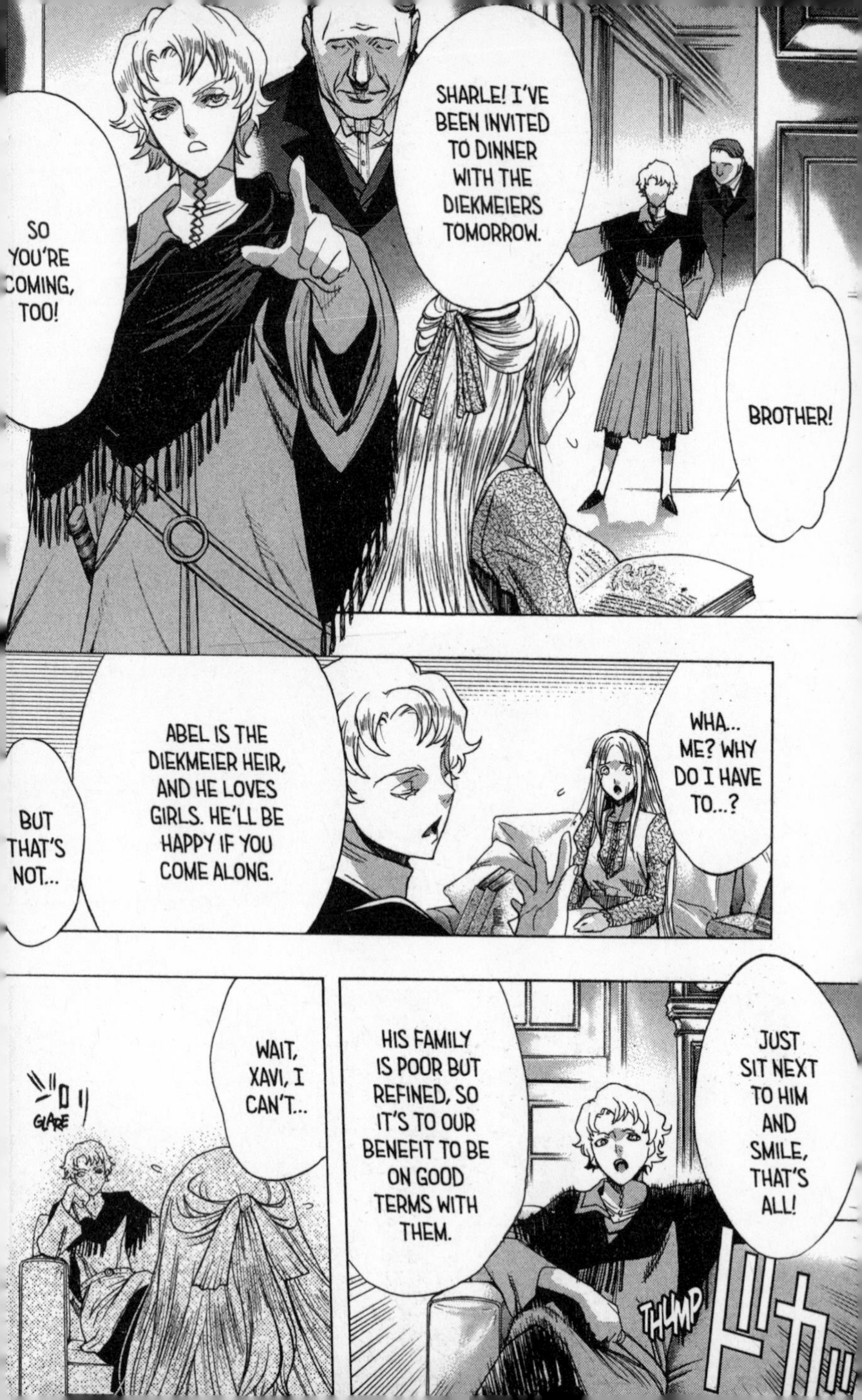
BROTHER!
SHARLE! I'VE BEEN INVITED TO DINNER WITH THE DIEKMEIERS TOMORROW.
SO YOU'RE COMING, TOO!
WHA.. ME? WHY DO I HAVE TO...?
ABEL IS THE DIEKMEIER HEIR, AND HE LOVES GIRLS. HE'LL BE HAPPY IF YOU COME ALONG.
BUT THAT'S NOT...
JUST SIT NEXT TO HIM AND SMILE, THAT'S ALL!
THUMP
HIS FAMILY IS POOR BUT REFINED, SO IT'S TO OUR BENEFIT TO BE ON GOOD TERMS WITH THEM.
WAIT, XAVI, I CAN'T...
GLARE

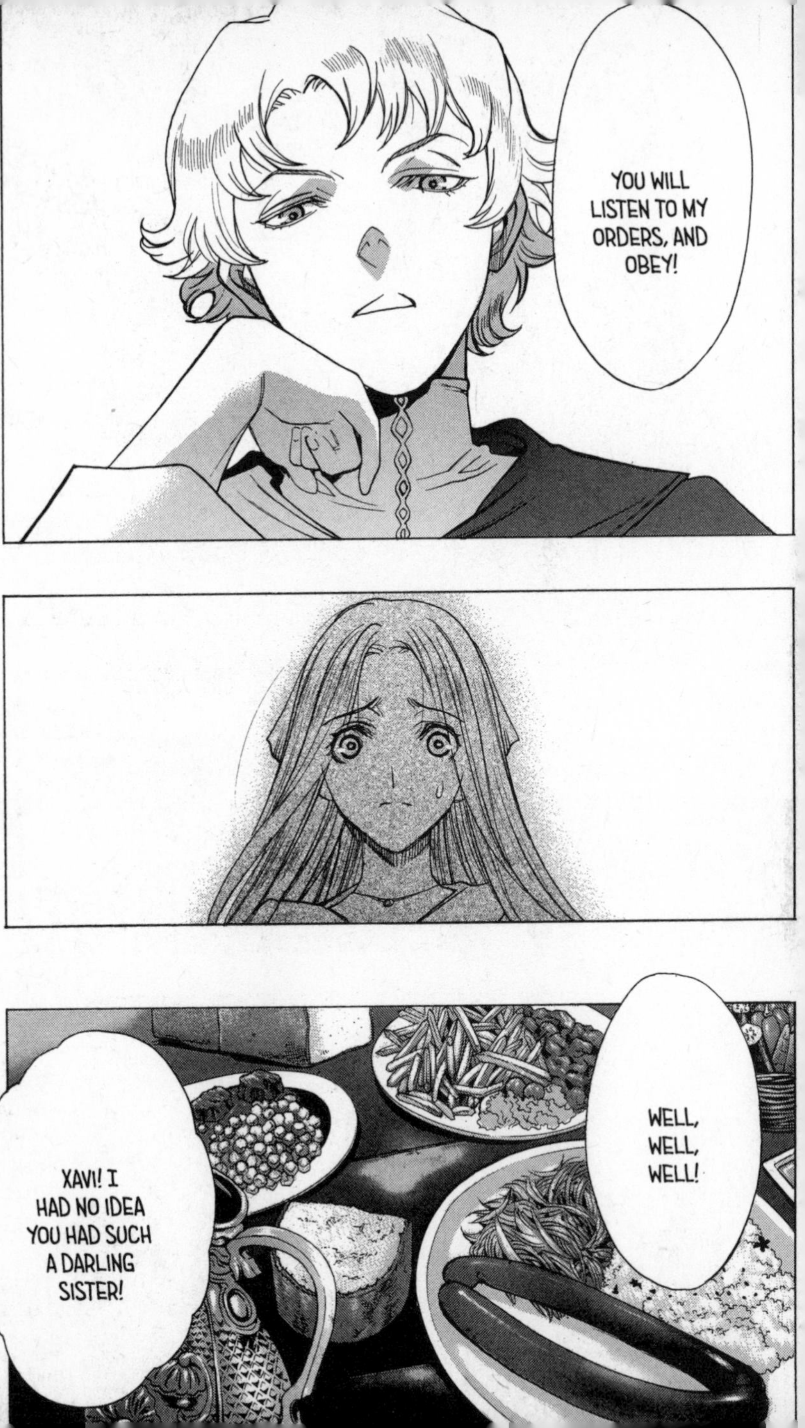
YOU WILL LISTEN TO MY ORDERS, AND OBEY!
WELL, WELL, WELL!
XAVI! I HAD NO IDEA YOU HAD SUCH A DARLING SISTER!

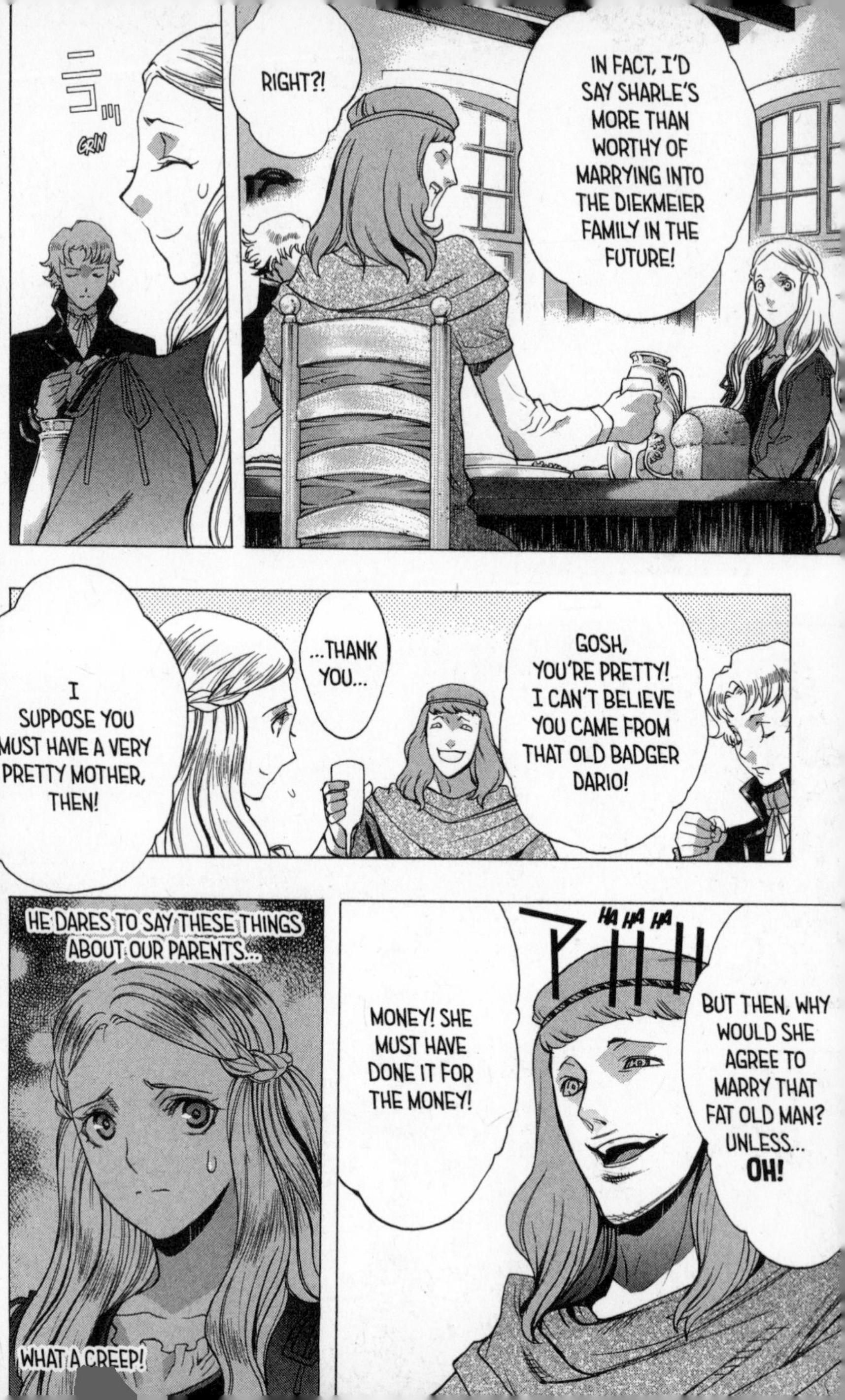
IN FACT, I'D SAY SHARLE'S MORE THAN WORTHY OF MARRYING INTO THE DIEKMEIER FAMILY IN THE FUTURE!
RIGHT?!
GRIN
GOSH, YOU'RE PRETTY! I CAN'T BELIEVE YOU CAME FROM THAT OLD BADGER DARIO!
...THANK YOU...
I SUPPOSE YOU MUST HAVE A VERY PRETTY MOTHER, THEN!
HA HA HA
BUT THEN, WHY WOULD SHE AGREE TO MARRY THAT FAT OLD MAN? UNLESS... **OH!**
MONEY! SHE MUST HAVE DONE IT FOR THE MONEY!
HE DARES TO SAY THESE THINGS ABOUT OUR PARENTS...
WHAT A CREEP!

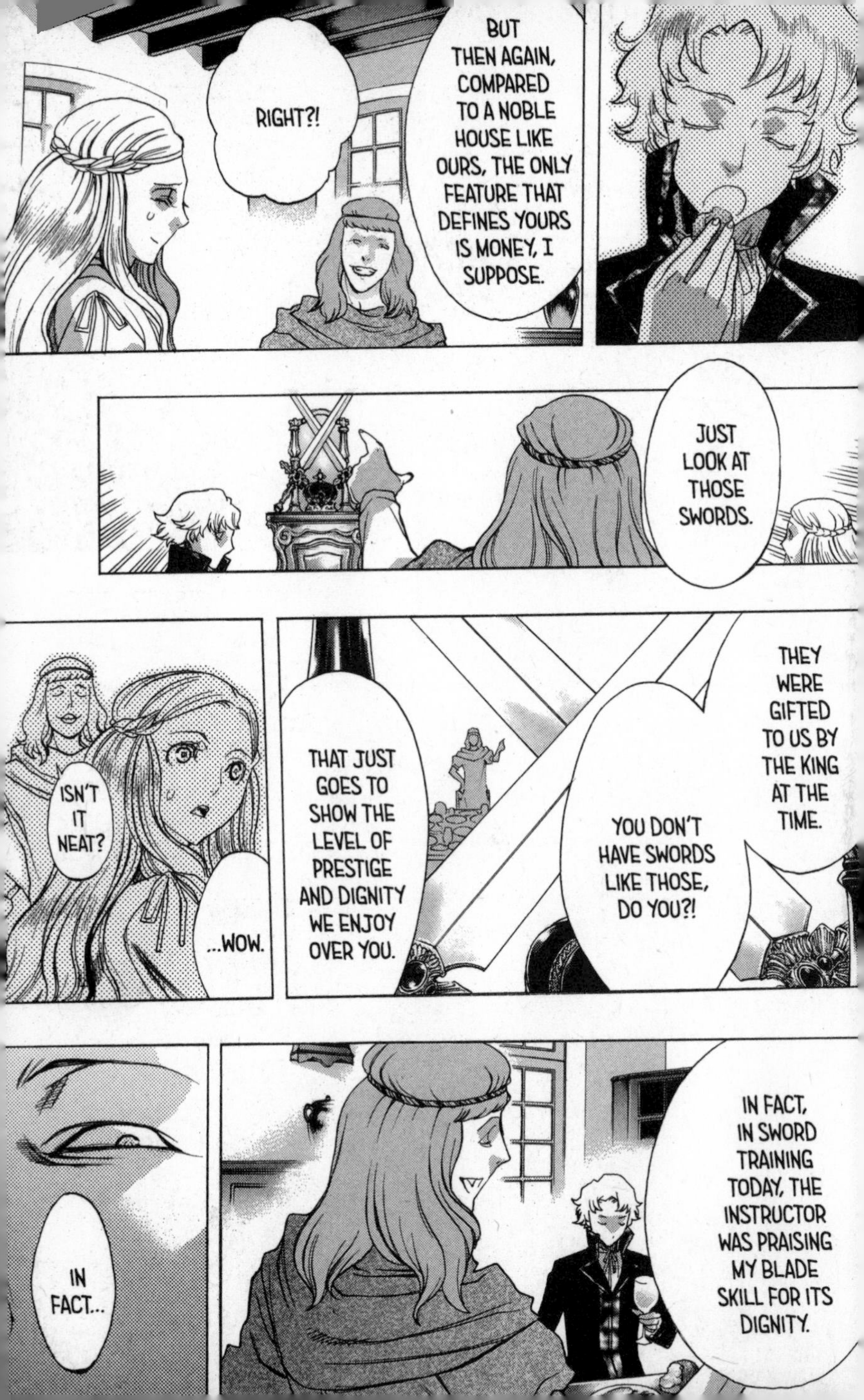
BUT THEN AGAIN, COMPARED TO A NOBLE HOUSE LIKE OURS, THE ONLY FEATURE THAT DEFINES YOURS IS MONEY, I SUPPOSE.
RIGHT?!
JUST LOOK AT THOSE SWORDS.
THEY WERE GIFTED TO US BY THE KING AT THE TIME.
YOU DON'T HAVE SWORDS LIKE THOSE, DO YOU?!
THAT JUST GOES TO SHOW THE LEVEL OF PRESTIGE AND DIGNITY WE ENJOY OVER YOU.
ISN'T IT NEAT?
...WOW.
IN FACT, IN SWORD TRAINING TODAY, THE INSTRUCTOR WAS PRAISING MY BLADE SKILL FOR ITS DIGNITY.
IN FACT...

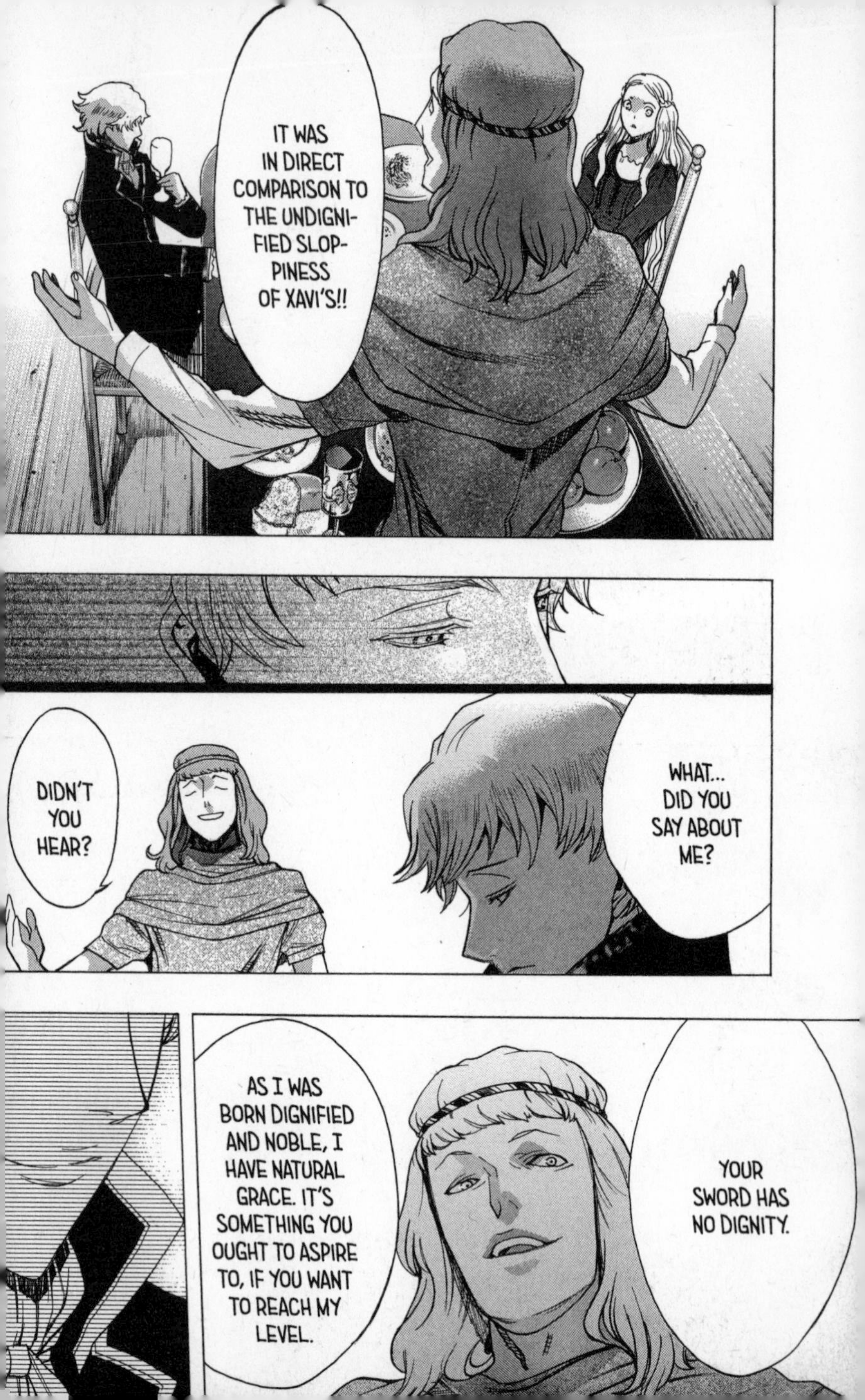
IT WAS IN DIRECT COMPARISON TO THE UNDIGNIFIED SLOPPINESS OF XAVI'S!!
WHAT... DID YOU SAY ABOUT ME?
DIDN'T YOU HEAR?
YOUR SWORD HAS NO DIGNITY.
AS I WAS BORN DIGNIFIED AND NOBLE, I HAVE NATURAL GRACE. IT'S SOMETHING YOU OUGHT TO ASPIRE TO, IF YOU WANT TO REACH MY LEVEL.

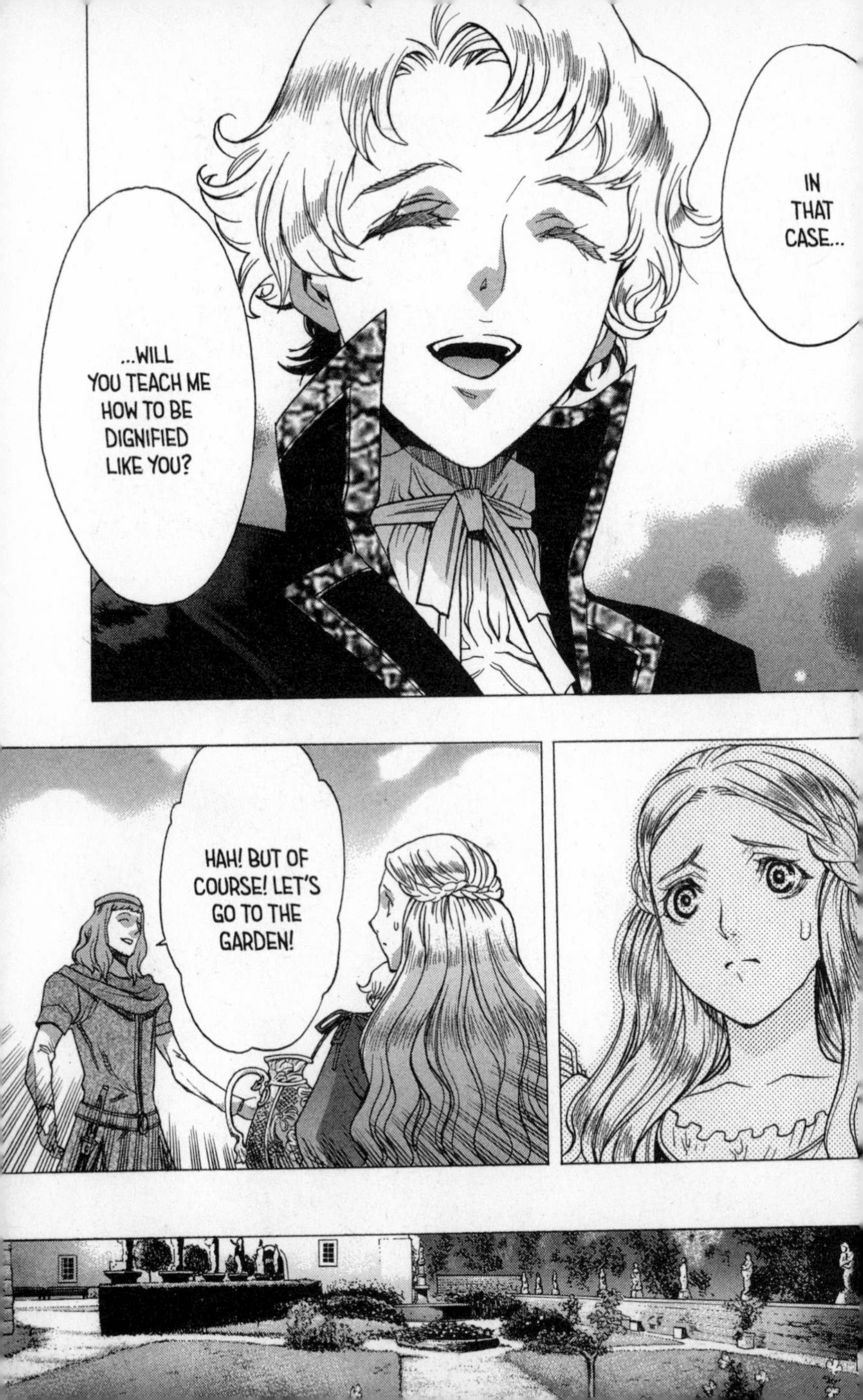
IN THAT CASE...
...WILL YOU TEACH ME HOW TO BE DIGNIFIED LIKE YOU?
HAH! BUT OF COURSE! LET'S GO TO THE GARDEN!

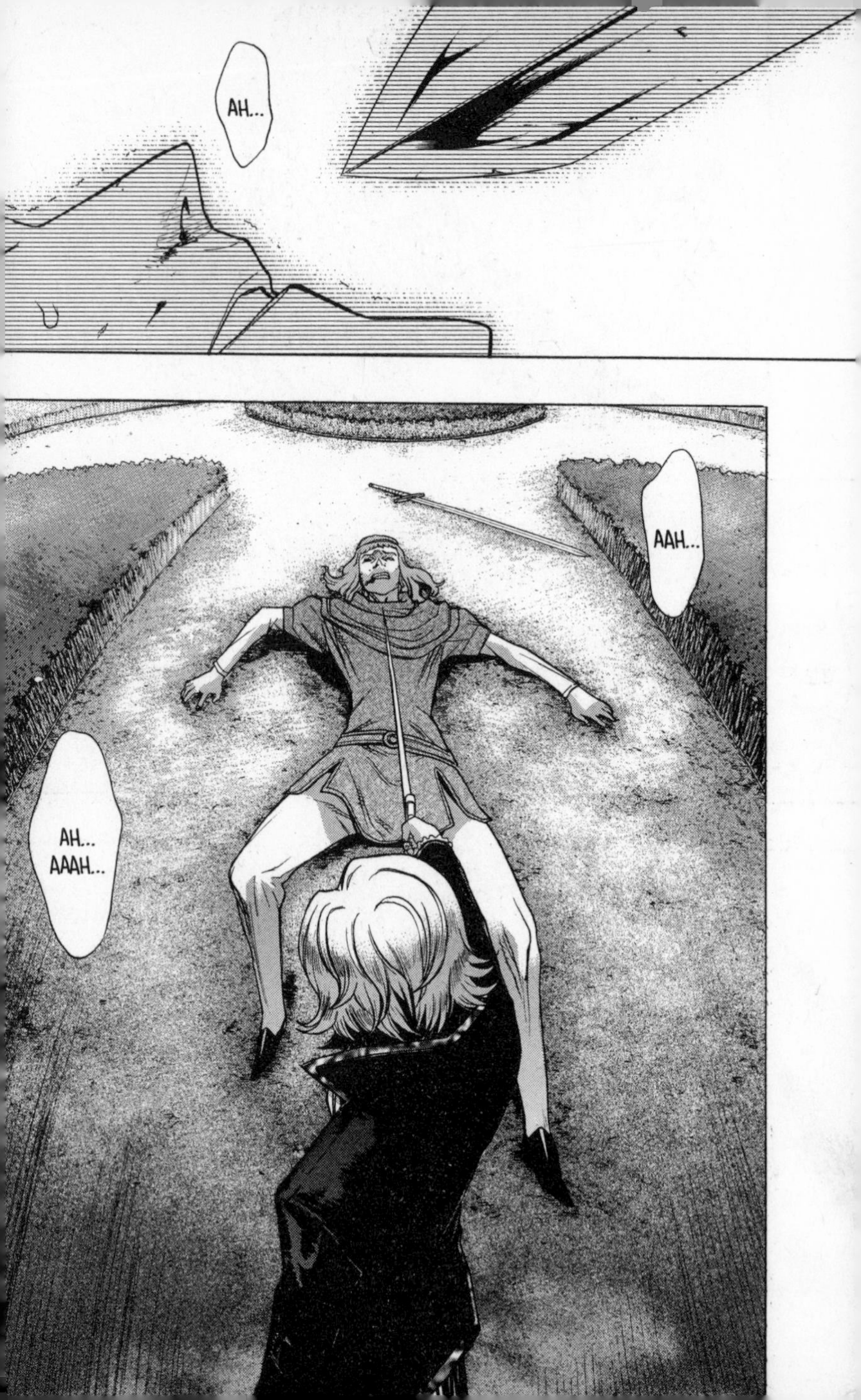
AH...
AAH...
AH... AAAH...

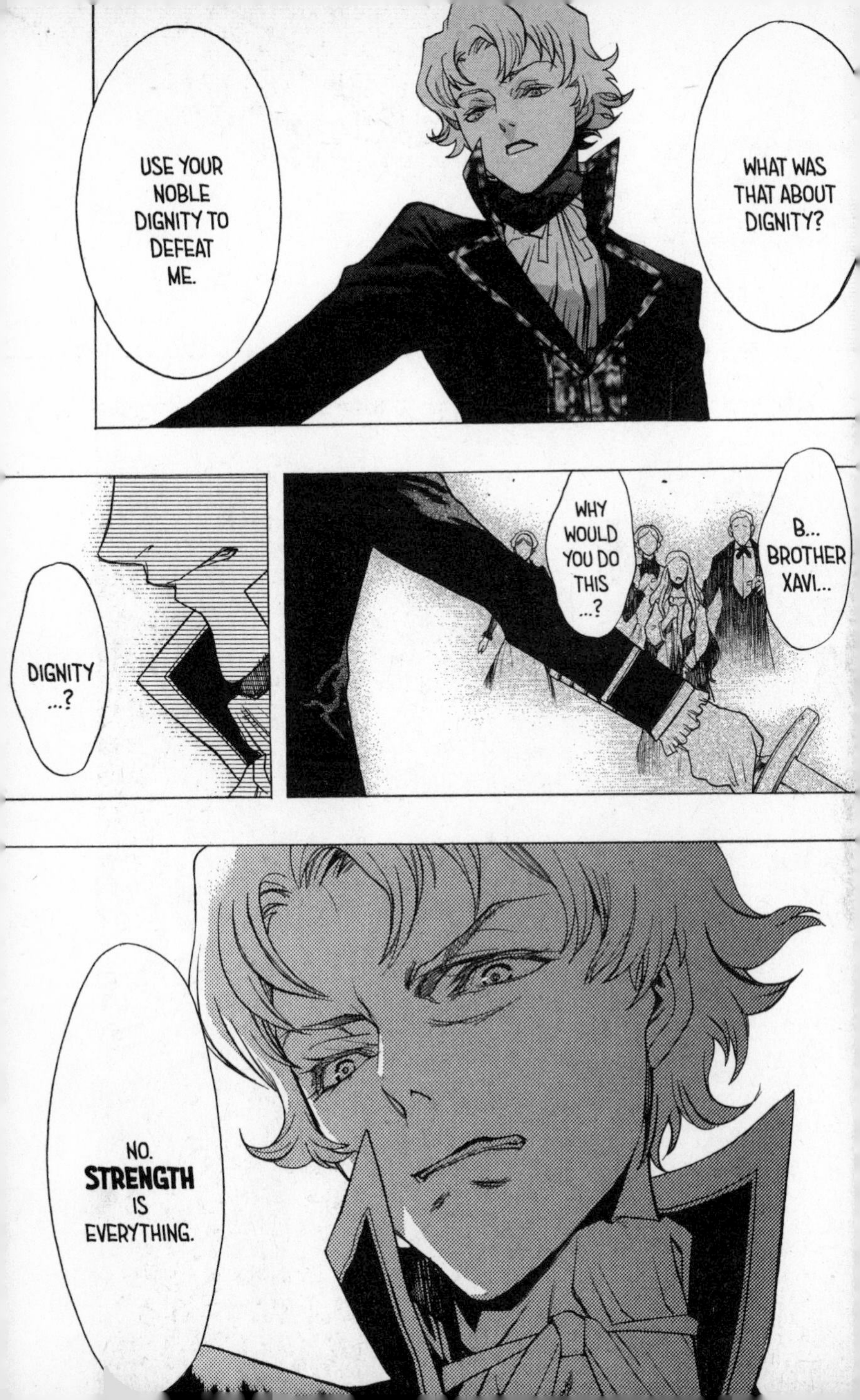
WHAT WAS THAT ABOUT DIGNITY?
USE YOUR NOBLE DIGNITY TO DEFEAT ME.
B... BROTHER XAVI...
WHY WOULD YOU DO THIS ...?
DIGNITY ...?
NO. **STRENGTH** IS EVERYTHING.

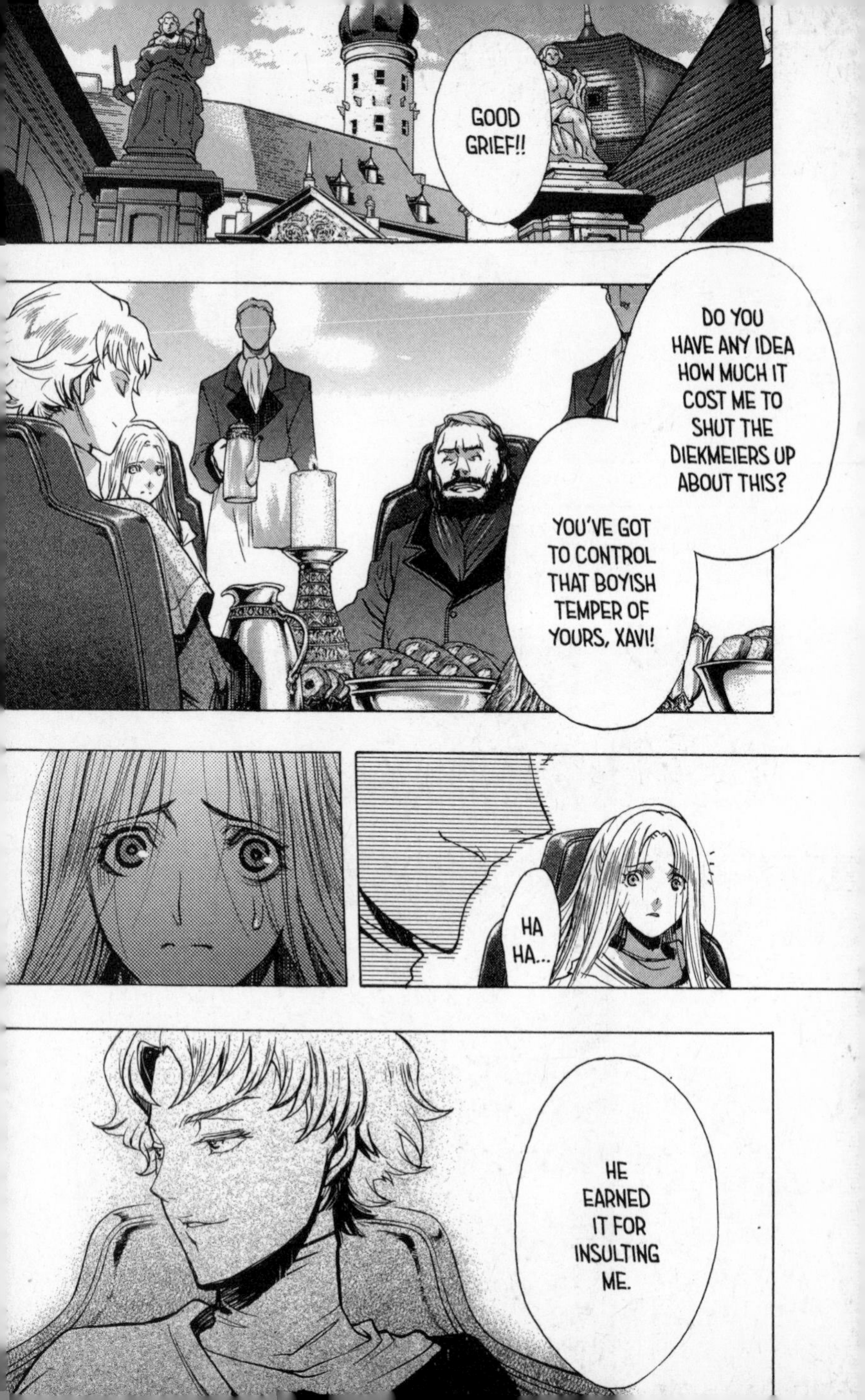
GOOD GRIEF!!
DO YOU HAVE ANY IDEA HOW MUCH IT COST ME TO SHUT THE DIEKMEIERS UP ABOUT THIS?
YOU'VE GOT TO CONTROL THAT BOYISH TEMPER OF YOURS, XAVI!
HA HA...
HE EARNED IT FOR INSULTING ME.

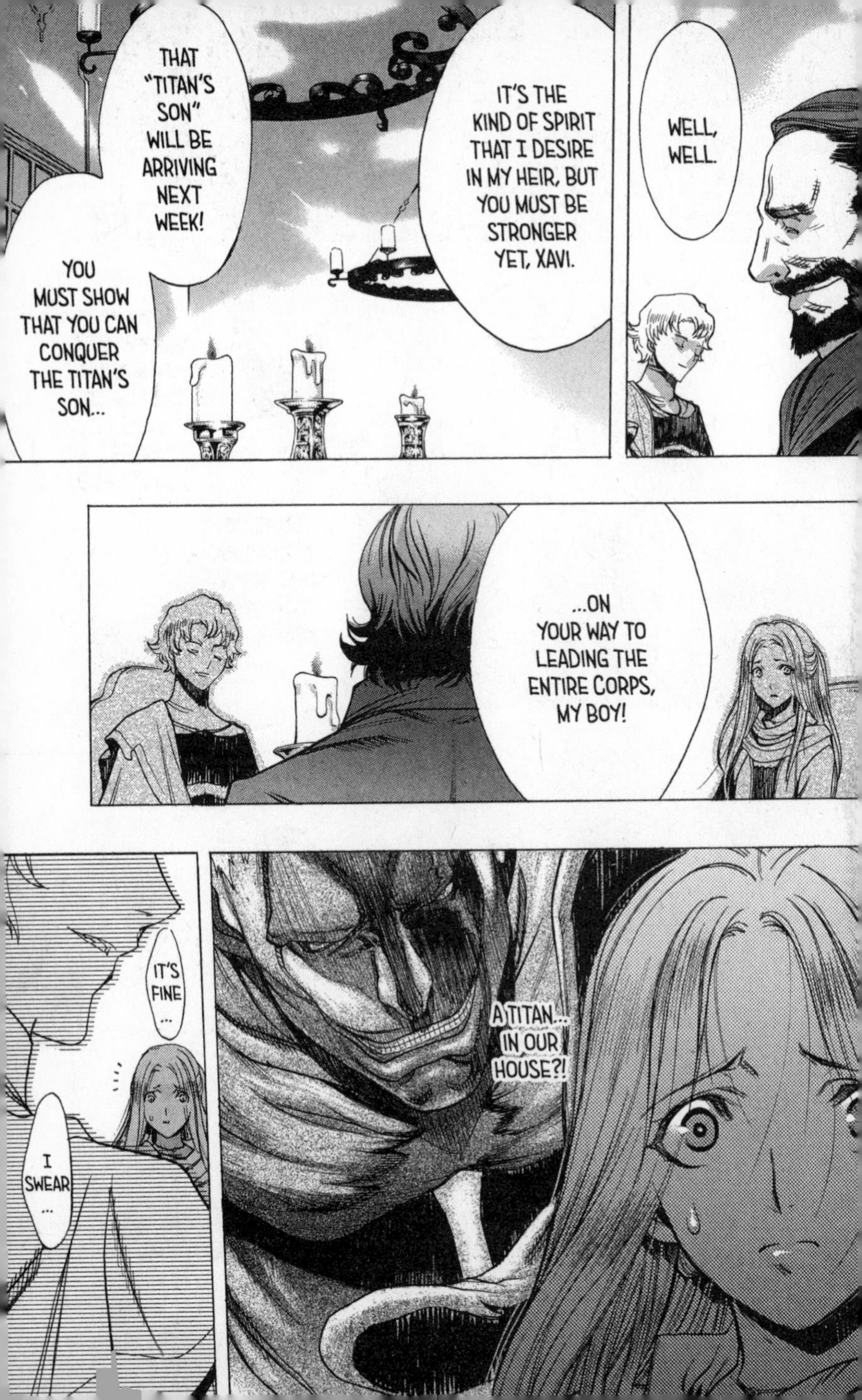
WELL, WELL.
IT'S THE KIND OF SPIRIT THAT I DESIRE IN MY HEIR, BUT YOU MUST BE STRONGER YET, XAVI.
THAT "TITAN'S SON" WILL BE ARRIVING NEXT WEEK!
YOU MUST SHOW THAT YOU CAN CONQUER THE TITAN'S SON...
...ON YOUR WAY TO LEADING THE ENTIRE CORPS, MY BOY!
A TITAN... IN OUR HOUSE?!
IT'S FINE...
I SWEAR...

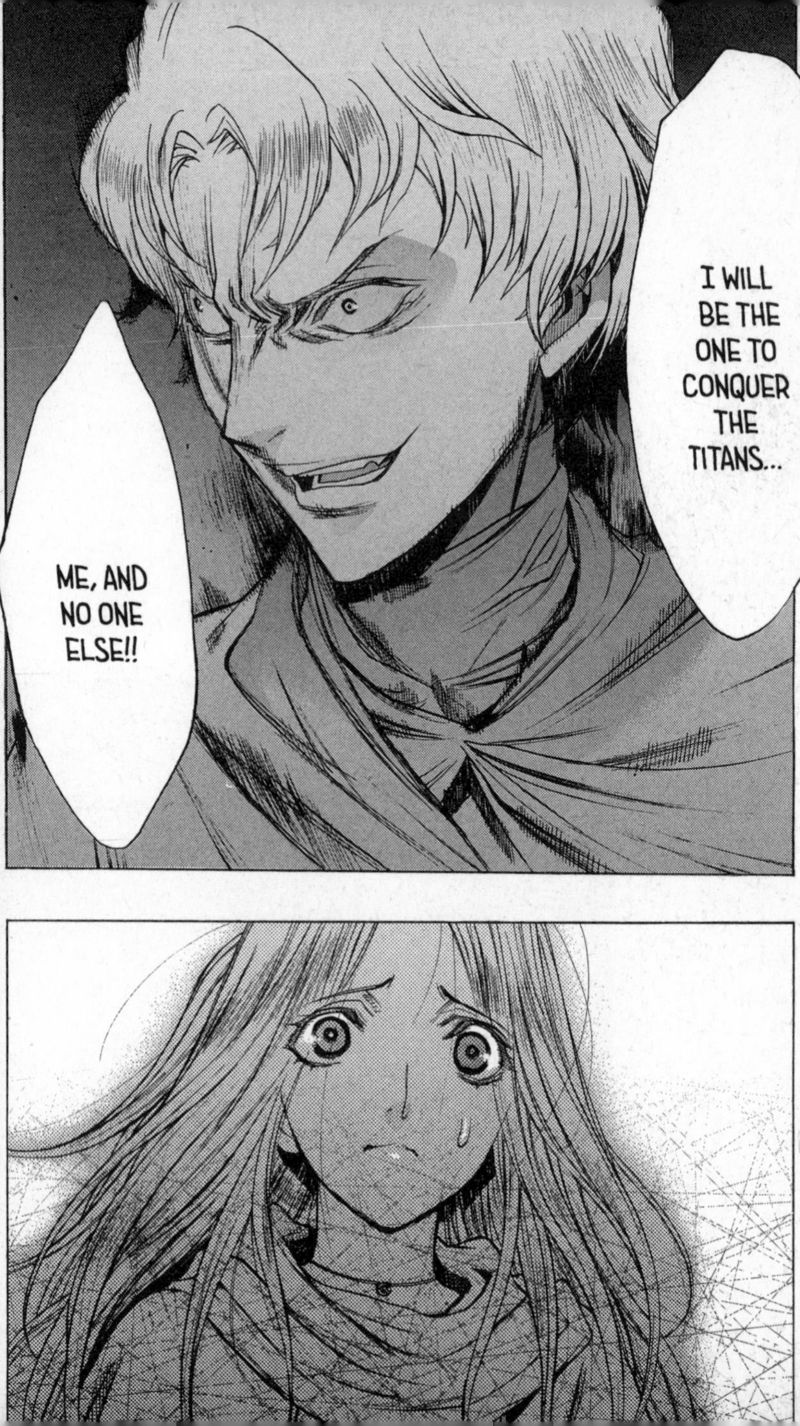
I WILL BE THE ONE TO CONQUER THE TITANS...
ME, AND NO ONE ELSE!!

Budding Ambition · End

DON'T MISS THE MOST ACCLAIMED ACTION MANGA OF 2013!

"Gripping doesn't begin to describe Vinland Saga. 5 stars."
—ICv2

"Deeply engrossing... If you have any interest at all in Vikings, the Medieval period, or pirates, this is not a series you want to miss."
—Anime News Network

"The art is gorgeous, a combination of beautiful cartooning and realistic backgrounds. Yukimura is also a master of pacing, both in frenetic battle scenes and charged emotional moments."
—Faith Erin Hicks, *Friends With Boys*

"For those who love Berserk, you'll love this too... Worth the long wait."
—A Case Suitable for Treatment

"It will be impossible to stop watching this story unfold."
—Japan Media Arts Awards jury

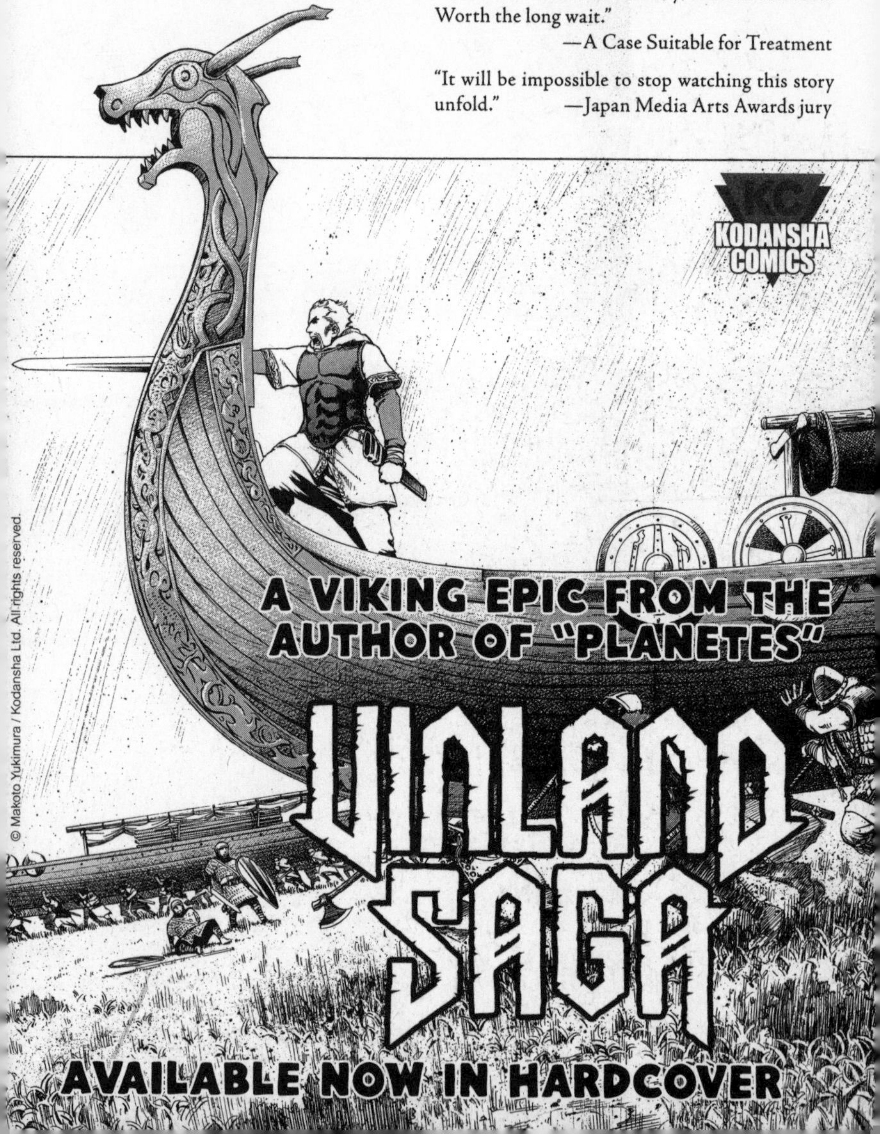

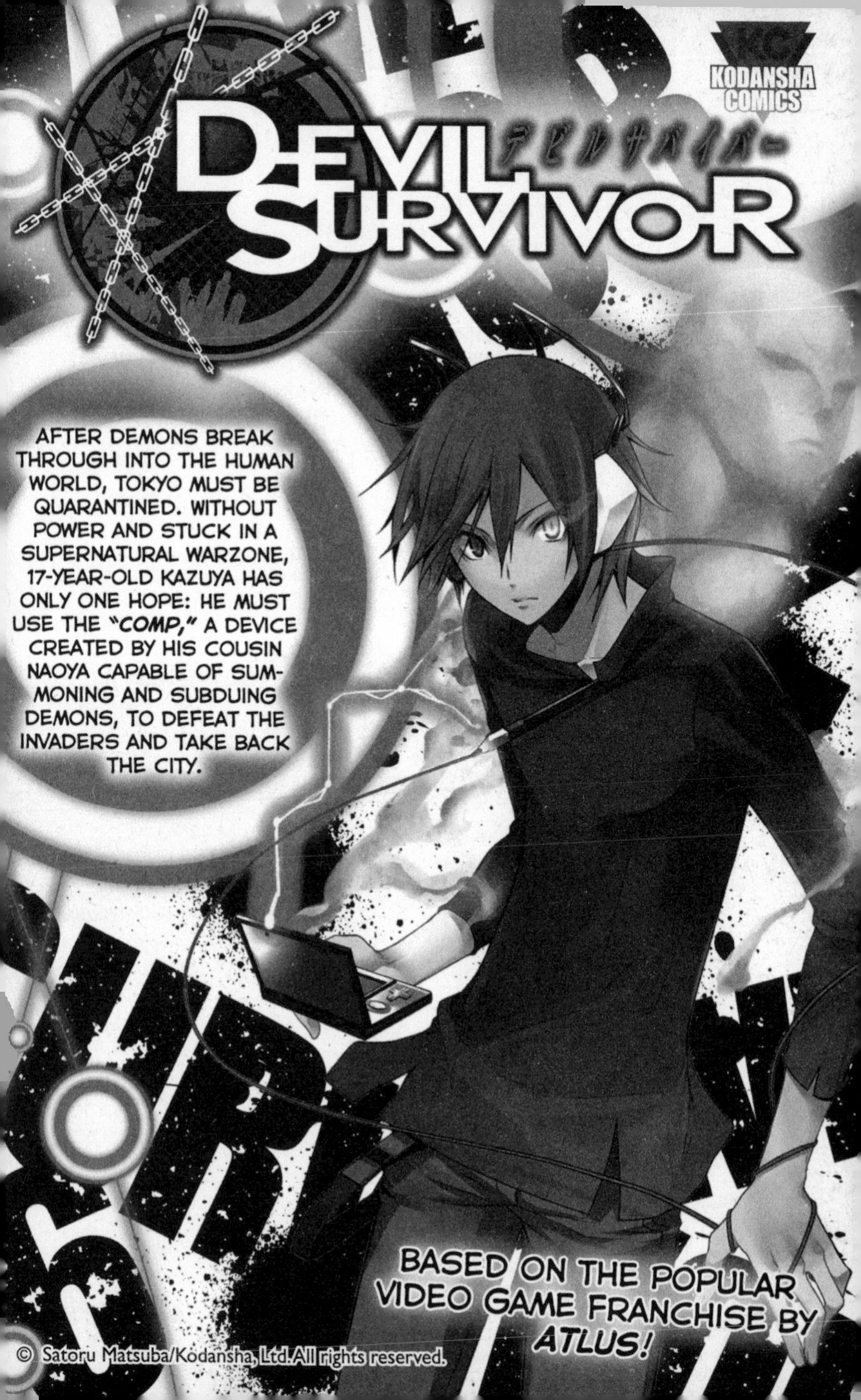
KC
KODANSHA COMICS
DEVIL SURVIVOR
AFTER DEMONS BREAK THROUGH INTO THE HUMAN WORLD, TOKYO MUST BE QUARANTINED. WITHOUT POWER AND STUCK IN A SUPERNATURAL WARZONE, 17-YEAR-OLD KAZUYA HAS ONLY ONE HOPE: HE MUST USE THE *"COMP,"* A DEVICE CREATED BY HIS COUSIN NAOYA CAPABLE OF SUMMONING AND SUBDUING DEMONS, TO DEFEAT THE INVADERS AND TAKE BACK THE CITY.
BASED ON THE POPULAR VIDEO GAME FRANCHISE BY *ATLUS!*
© Satoru Matsuba/Kodansha, Ltd. All rights reserved.

INUYASHIKI

A superhero like none you've ever seen, from the creator of "Gantz"!

Ichiro Inuyashiki is down on his luck. He looks much older than his 58 years, his children despise him, and his wife thinks he's a useless coward. So when he's diagnosed with stomach cancer and given three months to live, it seems the only one who'll miss him is his dog.

Then a blinding light fills the sky, and the old man is killed... only to wake up later in a body he almost recognizes as his own. Can it be that Ichiro Inuyashiki is no longer human?

Comes in extra-large editions with color pages!

KODANSHA COMICS

a Silent Voice

"The word heartwarming was made for manga like this." –Manga Book-shelf

"A harsh and biting social commentary… delivers in its depth of character and emotional strength." -Comics Bulletin

"A very powerful story about being different and the consequences of childhood bullying… Read it." –Anime News Network

Shoya is a bully. When Shoko, a girl who can't hear, enters his elementary school class, she becomes their favorite target, and Shoya and his friends goad each other into devising new tortures for her. But the children's cruelty goes too far. Shoko is forced to leave the school, and Shoya ends up shouldering all the blame. Six years later, the two meet again. Can Shoya make up for his past mistakes, or is it too late?

Available now in print and digitally!

FINALLY, A LOWER-COST OMNIBUS EDITION OF FAIRY TAIL! CONTAINS VOLUMES 1-5. ONLY $39.99!

- NEARLY 1,000 PAGES!
- EXTRA LARGE 7"×10.5" TRIM SIZE!
- HIGH-QUALITY PAPER!

Fairy Tail takes place in a world filled with magic. 17-year-old Lucy is a wizard-in-training who wants to join a magic guild so that she can become a full-fledged wizard. She dreams of joining the most famous guild, known as Fairy Tail. One day she meets Natsu, a boy raised by a dragon which vanished when he was young. Natsu has devoted his life to finding his dragon father. When Natsu helps Lucy out of a tricky situation, she discovers that he is a member of Fairy Tail, and our heroes' adventure together begins.

FAIRY TAIL

MASTER'S EDITION

SWAPPED WITH A KISS?!

Class troublemaker Ryu Yamada is already having a bad day when he stumbles down a staircase along with star student Urara Shiraishi. When he wakes up, he realizes they have switched bodies—and that Ryu has the power to trade places with anyone just by kissing them! Ryu and Urara take full advantage of the situation to improve their lives, but with such an oddly amazing power, just how long will they be able to keep their secret under wraps?

Available now in print and digitally!

A Kodansha Comics Trade Paperback Original
Attack on Titan: Before the Fall volume 9 copyright © 2016 Hajime Isayama/
Ryo Suzukaze/Satoshi Shiki
English translation copyright © 2016 Hajime Isayama/Ryo Suzukaze/Satoshi Shiki

Published in the United States by Kodansha Comics, an imprint of
Kodansha USA Publishing, LLC, New York.

Publication rights for this English edition arranged through
Kodansha Ltd, Tokyo.

First published in Japan in 2016 by Kodansha Ltd., Tokyo
as *Shingeki no kyojin Before the fall*, volume 9.

ISBN 978-1-63236-320-6

Character designs by Thores Shibamoto
Original cover design by Takashi Shimoyama (Red Rooster)

Printed in the United States of America.

www.kodanshacomics.com

9 8 7 6 5 4 3 2 1
Translation: Stephen Paul
Lettering: Steve Wands
Editing: Lauren Scanlan
Kodansha Comics edition cover design by Phil Balsman

STOP!

You are going the *wrong way!*

Manga is a *completely* different type of reading experience.

To start at the *BEGINNING,* go to the *END!*

That's right! Authentic manga is read the traditional Japanese way—from right to left, exactly the opposite of how American books are read. It's easy to follow: just go to the other end of the book, and read each page—and each panel—from the right side to the left side, starting at the top right. Now you're experiencing manga as it was meant to be.